Major League Rebels

PRAISE FOR *MAJOR LEAGUE REBELS*

"*Major League Rebels* is as radical and important a baseball book as I've read in a long time. It restores a history that the minders of baseball would soon have us forget: battles over not only race, gender, and sexuality but also over worker rights and the uses of baseball as a tool for U.S. empire."—Dave Zirin, host of *Edge of Sports*

"There's a long pedigree of professional athletes who have fought for player rights and worker rights for all Americans. *Major League Rebels* compellingly tells the story of these heroes from the 1870s to the 2020s and how their struggles have helped shape U.S. culture and politics."—Andrew Zimbalist, economist, Smith College, and author of *Baseball and Billions*

"*Major League Rebels* offers a timely look at two underappreciated sides of baseball history—attempts to organize ballplayers as employees and the roles that the business of baseball plays in the world order."—Bill Nowlin, author of *Working a "Perfect Game": Conversations with Umpires*

"*Major League Rebels* is as rare, fair, and fascinating as an unassisted triple play. In this crisp and compelling narrative, Elias and Dreier profile an impressive roster of often unfamiliar players who pursued justice."—Joseph L. Price, director of the Institute for Baseball Studies, Whittier College, and author of *Perfect Pitch: The National Anthem for the National Pastime*

"*Major League Rebels* is major league American history. It's a must-read for anyone who loves baseball and the quest for worker and social justice."—Harold Meyerson, editor-at-large, *American Prospect*, and columnist, *Los Angeles Times*

"Get ready to sink your teeth into shocking stories of baseball heroes of a different stripe who withstood blacklists, violence, and other forms of intimidation by owners to create a better life and working conditions for players."—Jon Leonoudakis, baseball documentarian/filmmaker and historian

"The baseball rebels portrayed by Elias and Dreier range from the renowned Roberto Clemente to the more obscure James 'Orator' O'Rourke as they battle for workers' rights and social justice while challenging corporate monopoly and colonialism. *Major League Rebels* provides an essential corrective to the assumption that the national pastime is a bastion of conservatism."—Ron Briley, author of *The Politics of Baseball*

"*Major League Rebels* is about the rebels who have pushed the national pastime forward in terms of social, economic, and political consciousness. Elias and Dreier bring them all together in one uniquely constructed history."—Richard Crepeau, author of *Baseball: America's Diamond Mind*

Major League Rebels

Baseball Battles over Workers' Rights and American Empire

ROBERT ELIAS AND PETER DREIER

ROWMAN & LITTLEFIELD
Lanham • Boulder • New York • London

Published by Rowman & Littlefield
An imprint of The Rowman & Littlefield Publishing Group, Inc.
4501 Forbes Boulevard, Suite 200, Lanham, Maryland 20706
www.rowman.com

86-90 Paul Street, London EC2A 4NE, United Kingdom

British Library Cataloguing in Publication Information Available

Library of Congress Cataloging-in-Publication Data

Names: Elias, Robert, 1950– author. | Dreier, Peter, 1948– author.
Title: Major league rebels : baseball battles over workers' rights and American empire / Robert Elias and Peter Dreier.
Description: Lanham : Rowman & Littlefield, [2022] | Includes index. | Summary: "This book tells the fascinating stories of the baseball rebels who were influenced by, and in turn influenced, America's political and social protest movements throughout history-including battles over labor, anti-trust, corporate power, immigration, and America's wars and military interventions worldwide"—Provided by publisher.
Identifiers: LCCN 2021034089 (print) | LCCN 2021034090 (ebook) | ISBN 9781538158883 (cloth : acid-free paper) | ISBN 9781538158890 (ePub)
Subjects: LCSH: Baseball—Political aspects—United States. | Baseball—Social aspects—United States. | Discrimination in sports—United States. | Racism in sports—United States. | Social change—United States—History—20th century. | Social justice—United States—History—20th century.
Classification: LCC GV863.A1 E45 2022 (print) | LCC GV863.A1 (ebook) | DDC 796.3570973—dc23
LC record available at https://lccn.loc.gov/2021034089
LC ebook record available at https://lccn.loc.gov/2021034090

To Terry Cannon, Jim Bouton, Curt Flood, and Marvin Miller.
May their memories be an inspiration.

Contents

Foreword by Bill Lee

They call me the "Spaceman." I'm a throwback in baseball who embraces the virtues of playing for the love of the game. A decade ago, I coauthored a book, *Baseball Eccentrics*. I'm one of those eccentrics, and coauthor Jim Prime and I discussed many more. Baseball is an eccentric game if you let it be. It offers infinite possibilities for the bizarre. As we wrote, "anyone who doesn't fit into the tight stereotype of who belongs in the Major Leagues [belongs in this book]." They're the people who "make the game interesting and colorful by giving it a human face." They might be "malcontents, characters, cranks, rebels, fruitcakes, nut jobs, wingnuts, whackos, space cadets, head cases, nonconformists, goofs, free thinkers, book readers, geography majors, and left-handed Californians."

But what you're about to read goes beyond eccentric. The rebels featured here stood out, but for different reasons. They may have been eccentric too, but they also directly challenged the status quo, both on and off the field, often taking risks and making sacrifices to do so. The authors, Robert Elias and Peter Dreier, claim I'm one of those rebels. I came from a pretty conservative background growing up but something happened to me once I got to college at USC. I began seeing the world differently. I had a strong baseball pedigree since my dad played semipro ball and my grandfather was a standout infielder in the Pacific Coast League. Most important, my aunt, Annabelle Lee, was a star pitcher in the Women's Semi-Pro Hardball League and the

All-American Girls Professional Baseball League. She's the one who taught me how to pitch.

I discovered early on, however, that baseball isn't just a sport but also an "arena for the human imagination"—in the words of the Baseball Reliquary and its Shrine of the Eternals (of which I'm a proud member). And when one unleashes one's imagination and looks around, it's hard not to respond. I couldn't sit idly by watching injustice both inside and outside the game. I've been a kind of Bernie Sanders for baseball in many ways.

This book couldn't be more timely. We are experiencing a backward crawl to when athletes and workers of many backgrounds were treated badly because of their economic status or the color of their skin or the culture that produced them. Always, it seems, not only prejudice but also business and political priorities impede real progress. Today, a third of major league baseball (MLB) players are Latino, but is that because they're swooped up cheaply, without agents, from the Caribbean? Seventy years after Jackie Robinson broke the color barrier, only 7 percent of major leaguers are Black. In MLB, players are making as much as $35 million a year while minor leaguers earn only $7,500–$12,000 a year, and MLB has contracted more than forty minor league teams. These are the kinds of issues addressed in this book and the rebels who have confronted them.

In this book, you'll experience an alternative history of baseball going back to its earliest days and ending with ballplayers today still fighting the good fight. As they say, we must learn from history otherwise we'll only repeat the mistakes of our forefathers. But we need to know who our forefathers (and mothers) were so that we can stand on their shoulders rather than keep reinventing the wheel.

Of all these historic rebels, I probably identify most with "Fido," aka Mark Baldwin. He was a hard-throwing right-hander (although I am not) from Homestead, Pennsylvania. He fought the owners for players rights during the season and he fought Frick and Carnegie during the Homestead Strike in the off season, even being charged with arming workers against the Pinkerton thugs. My grandfather, Francis Lee, was pushed out of Chicago after the Pullman Strike. His oldest son, William Francis Lee, went to California and produced William Francis Lee Jr., who then produced me, William Francis Lee, III. I don't have any photos of Francis but I imagine him as the baseball character Billy Phalen in William Kennedy's Pulitzer Prize–winning novel,

Ironweed. And I suspect my nickname "Spaceman" was first penned in a newspaper column by H. L. Mencken. Somehow, from Baldwin I think I "inherited the wind." They say there are six degrees of separation from Kevin Bacon. From me too.

In this book, you'll revisit the battles against the Spaldings, the commissioners (Landis on forward), the robber baron owners, and the modern corporations that often run our teams. You'll read about resistance to labor exploitation and American colonialism and empire. As a player representative, I played a role in at least one of those battles. I was Marvin Miller's "left-hand" man in the fight against the reserve clause. Joe Torre and I worked with Marvin as well as Curt Flood and Dick Moss to start the process toward free agency. They did most of the work, and finally the Hall of Fame has erased the injustice of excluding Miller from its ranks.

For me, the greatness of this book is that it forces me to question my preexisting beliefs. It'll do the same for you too. I think I'm on the right side of history, working for the greatest good, for the country and also for baseball. It's where we all should be. The sport faces many challenges. Increasingly, for example, new ballplayers are specialists, and as R. Buckminster Fuller warned in *Operation Spaceship Earth*, overspecialization breeds extinction. While Fuller was talking about saving the planet, I'm the Spaceman dedicated to saving the game. As true baseball fans, it's our job to rescue the sport, to return it to its true roots when it represented something great about America. To help accomplish that, you need to read this book. You can't understand the history of baseball unless you know its hidden history: the positive contributions made by baseball rebels who stood up and protested to preserve the game and make it more just and equal and worthy of its label, the "National Pastime."

—Bill "Spaceman" Lee, Craftsbury, Vermont

Acknowledgments

Robert Elias: After long years devoted to other academic pursuits, I've returned more recently to my childhood obsession: baseball. It's been a pleasure exploring it not merely as a player and fan but also as a serious scholarly endeavor via my recent baseball books. For this book, I thank Michael Bloch, George Gmelch, Howard Nemerovski, Brian Weiner, Bill Hoynes, and Miles Theeman for their supportive friendship. My thanks also go to my research assistants, Clowie Ang and Kirsten Saldana at the University of San Francisco, and June Gleed at McGill University. I appreciate the inspiration and insights provided by fellow baseball writers George Gmelch, Ron Briley, Dave Zirin, Jon Leonoudakis, Bill Lee, Mitchell Nathanson, Rob Fitts, the late Peter Bjarkman, Jean Ardell, Lawrence Baldassaro, and my fellow members of the Society for American Baseball Research. I'm indebted to the helpful staff at the Giamatti Research Center of the Baseball Hall of Fame; the Negro Leagues Baseball Museum; the Gleeson Library of the University of San Francisco; the San Francisco Public Library; and the Mill Valley Public Library. Grants from the University of San Francisco Faculty Development Fund provided valuable financial assistance. Many thanks to Dan Gordon for his helpful editorial work. I'm also thankful for Rowman & Littlefield editor Christen Karniski for her patience and belief in this project and for her assistant Erinn Slanina for her administrative support. Most of all, I'm grateful for the support and love of my family: "Baseball" Jack, Madeleine, Andre, Smalley, and my wife, Jennifer.

Peter Dreier: This book combines my two passions, baseball and politics. But it wouldn't have been written without the support and friendship of many people. I hope this book reflects the spirit of Terry Cannon, the founder of the Baseball Reliquary, to whom the book is dedicated. The reliquary is an organization of baseball fans (or fanatics) who love the game but not the business of baseball and who admire the sport's mavericks and iconoclasts. I'm particularly grateful to Kelly Candaele, with whom I have shared many baseball adventures and written many articles on various aspects of the sport. Over the course of many years I have appreciated the encouragement and help of Alan Barra, Peter Bjarkman, Clifford Blau, Jim Bouton, Jim Buzinski, Mary Cannon, Bill Carle, Merritt Clifton, Warren Corbett, Rory Costello, Dave Davis, Neil deMause, Dan Gordon, Steve Greenhouse, Bill Hickman, Neil Lanctot, Jon Leonoudakis, Bob Locker, Lee Lowenfish, John McReynolds, Marvin Miller, Ivan Nahem, Bill Nowlin, Jennifer Piscopo, Jacob Promrenke, Steve Rosenthal, Rob Ruck, William Simons, Christian Trudeau, Bob Tufts, and Dave Zirin. I met some of these folks through my membership in the Society for American Baseball Research, a serious group of baseball fanatics with a wealth of knowledge and a willingness to share it through their research, writing, and correspondence. Jim Gates and Cassidy Lent at the Baseball Hall of Fame Giamatti Research Center have been very helpful. For research assistance, I want to thank Occidental College students Andrea Mateo and Chiaki Ma. For instilling in me the love of baseball, grateful thanks to the late Ted Dreier (my father), Bernie Dreier (my uncle), and Joe Black (my former baseball coach). For their patience and tolerance as well as their love of baseball, I thank my wife, Terry Meng, and our daughters, Amelia and Sarah.

Introduction

In 2003, to expand the war on terror, President George W. Bush launched a preemptive attack on Iraq based on false claims that Saddam Hussein was responsible for the 9/11 terrorist attacks and was harboring weapons of mass destruction. In response, Major League Baseball commissioner Bud Selig mandated the singing of "God Bless America" during the seventh inning stretch of every MLB game. Toronto Blue Jays first baseman, Carlos Delgado, objected, claiming the song was being used to justify U.S. military intervention. When it was played, he disappeared into the dugout. As Delgado explained, "It's a very terrible thing that happened on September 11. It's also a terrible thing that happened in Afghanistan and Iraq. I feel so sad for the families that lost relatives and loved ones in the war. But I think it's the stupidest war ever."

Delgado's comments—more than a decade before football player Colin Kaepernick kneeled during "The Star-Spangled Banner" to protest police violence toward African Americans—reflect a long but little-known tradition of dissent and rebellion among professional ballplayers. Compared to their football and basketball counterparts, baseball players have been cautious about speaking and acting on controversial social and political issues, but throughout the sport's history, some players—alongside executives, sportswriters, and managers—have challenged the status quo.

Baseball's rebels, reformers, and radicals took inspiration from the country's dissenters and progressive movements, speaking and acting against abuses both within their profession and in the broader society: racism, sexism, homophobia, poverty, war, repression of civil liberties, undue corporate power, and worker exploitation.

Dissent has played a central role in American history. Every reformist crusade since the Boston Tea Party has drawn on this legacy: the abolitionists who helped end slavery; the populist farmers who sought to tame the banks, railroads, and other big corporations; the progressives who fought slums, sweatshops, and epidemic diseases; the suffragists who won the vote for women; the labor unionists who demanded an eight-hour workday, safe working conditions, and a living wage; the civil rights pioneers who helped dismantle Jim Crow; and other activists who have won hard-fought battles for environmental protection, women's equality, gay rights, immigrant rights, and decent conditions for farmworkers.

Ballplayers and owners, however, have often voiced skepticism and even opposition to progressive or radical movements. Hall of Famer (and Ku Klux Klan member) Rogers Hornsby claimed that "any ballplayer that don't sign autographs for little kids ain't American. He's a Communist." Ty Cobb, another hardcore racist Hall of Famer, chastised a shirking pitcher, "Don't you turn Bolshevik on me."

In the late 1940s, Brooklyn Dodgers president Branch Rickey condemned ballplayers' decision to join the Mexican League and reject MLB's stingy salaries as a "communist plot." In the 1950s, the Cincinnati Reds changed their name to the "Cincinnati Redlegs" to escape the nation's anticommunist hysteria.

In the mid-1970s, when ballplayer Rick Monday thwarted an American flag-burning attempt in the Dodger Stadium outfield, he was hailed as a hero. In the early 2000s, Dodgers manager Tommy Lasorda campaigned for an anti-flag-desecration amendment. Broadcaster and former major league pitcher Curt Schilling compared Muslims to Nazis and called for Hillary Clinton to be "buried under a jail somewhere."

America's battles for justice and progressive change have been reflected on the baseball field, in the executive suites, in the press box, and in the community. All Americans—whether or not they are baseball fans—can learn from this history. In *Major League Rebels: Baseball Battles over Workers Rights and American Empire*, we develop several themes. Baseball rebels have resisted labor exploitation both inside and outside the sport: challenging worker repression in the Gilded Age; fighting baseball's corporate monopoly; and inspiring labor resistance to the indentured servitude of the reserve clause.

Baseball has always paralleled economic struggles happening in the wider society. By the 1880s a few industrialists—Rockefeller, Carnegie, and Vanderbilt, to name just three—controlled most of the nation's wealth. Developing ruthless monopolies, these robber barons deployed every tactic, no matter how vicious, to enhance their power and profits—cutting wages, repressing unions, bribing politicians. This ushered in the Gilded Age: riches for the few, misery and exploitation for the rest.

A group of unscrupulous baseball club owners mimicked the industrial magnates' strategies. Parallel to a growing labor movement, pushing back against oligarchy, baseball players began demanding more rights and better pay. Later, during the post–World War II economic boom, the labor movement gained strength, lifting millions of workers into the middle class. But baseball players remained poorly paid and with little control over their working conditions until a courageous few fought back, suing MLB, organizing a serious baseball union, and sometimes risking their careers to produce the enviable position as workers that big leaguers have now enjoyed for several decades.

Baseball rebels have also resisted U.S. empire: challenging America's unjust wars, resisting the militarization and phony patriotism that owners try to link with the sport, and protesting U.S. imperialism in Latin America and elsewhere. The baseball establishment embraced America's military aggression in Vietnam even as the antiwar movement grew and MLB sheltered its players from combat. But baseball couldn't isolate itself from the growing anti-war dissent. Risking being labeled troublemakers and being dropped from their teams, a few spoke out against the war. Others followed with later protests against the Gulf War, the Iraq War, and the war on terrorism.

In a companion volume to this book (*Baseball Rebels: The Players, People, and Social Movements That Shook Up the Game and Changed America*, 2022), we profile baseball rebels who have resisted American racism: battling Jim Crow, building Black institutions, laying the foundation for breaking the color line, fighting against lingering discrimination after integration, and defending civil rights. The Civil War ended slavery but by the 1870s, segregation had been reestablished. For almost a century Black Americans and their white allies fought Jim Crow laws in all walks of life. Baseball had its own anti–Jim Crow rebels long before Jackie Robinson and decades after he broke the color line.

In the same companion volume, we explore the battles women fought, from the mid-1800s, to play organized baseball, including the pioneering women of the All American Girls Professional Baseball League of the 1940s and 1950s. In the 1970s, amidst the momentum of the feminist movement, women asserted themselves in positions both on and off the baseball field. Soon gay and lesbian movement activists and athletes joined them to pressure MLB for inclusion.

Baseball rebels include mavericks whose impact has spanned the sport's history and others who have stood up to confront America's current, most pressing problems. A few have helped confront a stodgy, conservative sport, introducing it to twenty-first-century realities. Sports both reflect and shape U.S. society. Athletes in other sports have responded to protest injustices, among them track stars Tommie Smith and John Carlos; boxer Muhammad Ali; soccer star Megan Rapinoe; tennis players Billie Jean King and Arthur Ashe; basketball players LeBron James and Steve Nash; and football players Dave Meggyesy and Colin Kaepernick. Since the late nineteenth century, baseball activists have challenged the status quo in baseball and in the country, contributing to the kind of dissent that creates a more humane society. These are their stories.

RESISTING LABOR EXPLOITATION

1

The Players' Revolt against Gilded-Age Baseball

Baseball became part of what historian Page Smith described as the "war between capital and labor." From the end of the Civil War through the end of the nineteenth century, America experienced four major trends: a significant concentration of wealth in the hands of corporate titans; a huge wave of immigrants; a huge increase in the population of cities; and a shift from agriculture to industry and from farms to factories. While 40 percent of Americans lived on farms in 1860, only 20 percent did so by 1900. The workers in overcrowded cities and factories came from abroad as well as from America's rural areas. As a sport and as a business, baseball reflected and was shaped by all these changes. Owners, players, and fans were caught up in the nation's transformation.

THE AGE OF LABOR EXPLOITATION

These trends changed the nature of work. Earlier, most workers who weren't running their own family farms toiled at workplaces where they knew the owner, who often worked with them side-by-side. In contrast, industrialized factories, mines, and railroads increasingly featured ruthless owners (capitalists) and impersonal management, who viewed workers as commodities to be treated like any other raw material.

Workers faced enormous competition for jobs, which made them ripe for exploitation. Wages were extremely low, working hours were long, and workplace conditions were unhealthy and unsafe. Between 1881 and 1900, an average of 35,000 lives were lost annually from preventable workplace accidents. Another 1 million workers were injured on the job each year. Business leaders blamed these deaths and other casualties on worker negligence. No legal recourse, government safety regulations, or workmen's compensation were available to prevent or repair the damage. Dangerous child labor was rampant, women were routinely fired if they got pregnant, and neither companies nor the government provided workers with benefits like health or unemployment insurance. Workers were anonymous, voiceless, and disposable parts in the industrial system. Organizers and activists who protested these conditions were typically fired as a warning to other workers.

Business owners often pitted workers from different ethnic, religious, and language groups against each other to weaken potential bonds of solidarity and common purpose. The capitalists' divide-and-conquer strategy—typically using recent immigrants and African Americans as strikebreakers—often succeeded, promoting resentment and hostility within the working class. This was particularly true among formerly skilled craftsmen who—as a result of the new factory system that turned workers into cogs in the industrial machine—lost the status, satisfaction, and self-respect their work had previously provided. Corporate owners and managers so thoroughly subdivided the work that workers had no transportable skills. They had nothing to sell except their physical strength and willingness to work long hours. No longer respected or needed for their skills, once proud cabinetmakers, mechanics, and shoemakers now had to compete with millions of unskilled workers. Unemployment was a constant threat.

Workers were crowded into urban slums. Families with five or more children crammed into one or two rooms in filthy and broken-down tenements. Poor plumbing, inadequate waste removal, and the manure of thousands of horses created tainted water, horrible odors, and persistent diseases, including epidemics. Medical care was primitive. Insects and vermin thrived. People reeled, unprotected from sweltering heat in the summers and freezing weather in the winters. Under these conditions, street crime flourished. Poverty and inequality escalated, and workers were constantly at the mercy of the ups and downs of business cycles.

This period, often called the Gilded Age, was an era of exploitation—of people, land, and resources. While an elite few benefited, most people suffered. The wealthy elite, along with some academics and theologians at the time, rationalized this dramatic gap in wealth and income by claiming it represented the "survival of the fittest," sometimes called "social Darwinism" after Charles Darwin, who popularized the idea of evolution. Steel mogul Andrew Carnegie claimed that capitalism rested on natural and divine laws: "In the long run wealth comes only to the moral man." Material prosperity makes the country "sweeter, more joyous, more unselfish, more Christ like."[1] But when all else failed, the corporate elite relied on brute force to suppress workers' movements to improve their lives. As railroad titan Jay Gould bluntly noted, "I can get one half of the working class to kill the other half,"[2] referring to capitalists' use of private militias as well as local police and the National Guard to break strikes and arrest activists.

Despite these justifications and threats, workers organized to improve working and living conditions. In 1866, the National Labor Union (NLU) became the first large-scale effort to unite skilled and unskilled laborers, farmers, and factory workers in different industries. Led by William Sylvis, the NLU fought for higher wages, shorter hours, and better conditions from employers as well as pro-labor candidates and legislation. Business owners resorted to using strikebreakers, blacklists, lockouts, goon squads, and yellow-dog contracts (banning unions as a condition of employment). The NLU lasted seven years until it was devastated by the panic of 1873, a financial crisis that triggered a long economic depression.

Even so, labor agitation persisted. Railroad workers, miners, factory workers, and others went on strike each year during the last three decades of the nineteenth century. Boycott campaigns and labor slowdowns were common. Another union, the Knights of Labor (KOL or KOFL), organized workers of all races, ethnicities, genders, and occupations. Begun in 1869 by Terence Powderly, the KOL lobbied government for an eight-hour day and restrictions on child labor. Instead of merely pressuring capitalists for better working conditions, the KOL promoted a cooperative model where workers could democratically own and run their own enterprises.

In 1877, a great upheaval in American labor emerged from the Great Railroad Strike. Amidst a continuing economic depression, railroad companies in West Virginia repeatedly cut their workers' pay. In response, workers struck and refused to let the trains move. The strike spread to Maryland but the railroad owners refused to negotiate. When Maryland's governor sent in the National Guard to suppress the strike, the soldiers and workers engaged in street fights. The action spread to Pennsylvania, and the violence escalated. New strikes emerged around the country, and the companies recruited Pinkerton detectives and other private militias to thwart the strikers. In the end, more than 100,000 workers went on strike, shutting down nearly half the nation's railways. At least 100 workers were killed and 1,000 were imprisoned. Many Americans were outraged at the repressive tactics used by the railroad companies and sympathetic government officials. It was the first mass strike to involve so many different workers across so much geography.

After the 1877 Railroad Strike, unions grew rapidly. By 1885, the KOL had 100,000 members. That year, when Jay Gould's Southwest Railway tried to break a local union, KOL members walked out in sympathy. The railroad system was paralyzed, and the company was forced to negotiate. The KOL was overwhelmed with new applications, and within a year its membership skyrocketed to 750,000 workers.

That success was short-lived, however, when a rally for an eight-hour day in Chicago turned violent. Someone ignited a bomb in Haymarket Square that killed several workers and policemen and wounded several dozen others. Despite a lack of evidence against them, eight radical labor activists, labeled anarchists, were arrested and convicted in connection with the bombing and several were then executed. Even though the KOL condemned the bombing, they were pilloried by the media. As a result of this guilt-by-association, the KOL lost about half its members. This was not unusual for that period. The newspapers, along with state and federal government officials, typically sided with the capitalists, who could also rely on favorable actions from police, judges, and the military against the workers.

The American Federation of Labor (AFL), led by Samuel Gompers, emerged in 1886 using a new approach to organizing workers. Rather than organizing all workers, the AFL focused on skilled, white, male craftsmen in the cities. Shunning the KOL's cooperative approach, the AFL sought to neither replace nor overthrow the capitalists nor lobby for social legislation but rather sought to secure the best conditions for a single segment of the working class. This was both a drawback and the key to its survival into the next century. By 1900, the AFL had more than 1 million members. Although representing only a fraction of the working class, the AFL nevertheless won significant victories against management in pay, hours, and other working conditions.

In 1892, a third major labor uprising resulted in a violent massacre. Workers at Andrew Carnegie's steel factories at Homestead, outside Pittsburgh, went on strike to oppose wage cuts and dangerous conditions. Carnegie hired hundreds of armed Pinkerton detectives to break the strike. Violence erupted, and many workers were killed. The Pennsylvania governor sent in seven thousand state militia while strikebreakers re-opened the factories. Public opinion initially favored the workers but then it swung against the strikers when an anarchist, unconnected to the strikers, attempted to assassinate Carnegie's henchman, Henry Frick. The Steelworkers Union was crippled by the incident. That same year, President Benjamin Harrison dispatched federal troops to Coeur d'Alene, Idaho, to put down a big miner's strike.

In 1892, railroad workers organized the American Railway Union (ARU). Almost everyone who worked for a railroad was eligible to join regardless of his specific job or skills; it was an industrial, not a craft, union. A year later, the ARU achieved its first major victory. Its three-week strike reversed the Great Northern Railroad's attempt to cut wages. But a much bigger labor action was looming in 1894. The Pullman Company made huge profits building railroad sleeper cars. Owner George Pullman required all his workers to live in the company town, called Pullman, that he had created just outside Chicago. Pullman described it as a paradise for workers but his employees regarded it instead as a kind of hell or exploitative prison, resenting the town's overbearing social control over their lives. The prices for housing, utilities, food, and other necessities were wildly inflated but workers had no choice but to pay them with the scrip they were given as wages instead of regular U.S. currency. The company cut wages by between 25 percent and 40 percent but didn't reduce rents or prices in the company stores. The frustrated and angry railroad workers responded by launching the Pullman Strike in May 1894.

Eugene Debs, an ARU founder, led the strike. Over twelve thousand Pullman employees refused to work, and train service ceased from Chicago to California. Pullman refused to negotiate, firing resisters and hoping to break the union. But from May to June 1894, more than 150,000 railroad employees across the country struck in sympathy with the Pullman workers. Railroad owners hired replacement workers and more than three thousand armed guards. But the revolt stretched into July when U.S. president Grover Cleveland sent federal troops to Illinois to stop the strike. The troops fired into a crowd of protesters, killing thirty of them and injuring many others.

When railroad companies placed bags of U.S. mail on trains that striking workers refused to move, the U.S. attorney general obtained an injunction against the ARU for illegally obstructing the mail. When Debs and other strike leaders violated the injunction, federal officers arrested them and they were quickly convicted and imprisoned. The U.S. Supreme Court upheld the conspiracy and mail obstruction convictions using a distorted interpretation of the recently passed Sherman Anti-Trust Act. Congress had designed the law to break up corporate monopolies and cartels. The court, however, began a three-decade campaign to instead apply the act against unions.

The failure of the Pullman Strike and the destruction of the ARU radicalized Debs. He emerged from his six-month prison sentence convinced that only socialism could effectively eliminate the evils of capitalism for workers and people generally. Debs and other socialists wondered why so many hard-working Americans should have so little while a tiny few profited from their sweat and toil. They decried persistent government support for the capitalist exploitation of the working class. He helped found the Socialist Party and ran for president five times between 1900 and 1920. At its peak, in 1912, about 1,200 Socialist Party members held public office in 340 cities, including 79 mayors in cities including Milwaukee, Buffalo, Minneapolis, Reading, and Schenectady. Eventually the public embraced and Congress passed many of the party's "radical" ideas: Social Security, women's right to vote, an end to child labor, a minimum wage, and consumer protection laws.

By the late nineteenth century, monopolies or oligopolies dominated virtually every industry. Their owners reaped enormous profits. Critics called the nation's wealthiest men, including John D. Rockefeller, J.P. Morgan, Cornelius Vanderbilt, Andrew Carnegie, and Jay Gould—the robber barons. They enjoyed fabulous lives of luxury while many of their workers were starving. They wielded power not only in the economic realm but also over the political system, routinely paying off politicians to adopt policies favorable to their continuing accumulation of wealth.

THE BASEBALL PLAYERS' REVOLT

Major league baseball arrived on the scene amidst this Gilded Age of great riches and great poverty and of repeated clashes between owners and workers. While MLB has designated 1876 as the official launch of the major leagues, they actually began in 1871 with the National Association of Professional Base Ball Players (NAPBBP). As baseball historian David Voigt explained,

> It was a player-run league, with a player president, and its stockholder 'owners' functioned mainly as patrons. That major league baseball was born of such parentage must have been anathema to modern owners and the sort of heritage one seeks to conceal.[3]

The NAPBBP featured a worker-owned cooperative model that baseball's capitalists couldn't tolerate. The NAPBBP survived from 1871 to 1875 when budding entrepreneurs William Hulbert and Albert Spalding launched a coup, which buried the NAPBBP in favor of a new league controlled by the owners: the National League of Professional Base Ball Clubs—the National League (NL) we know today. The baseball owners took over. They viewed themselves as business magnates in the emerging and lucrative baseball industry. Taking their cues and tactics from the robber barons in other industries, the baseball owners were determined to maintain their profits by controlling their primary costs: the wages they paid their workers; that is, their ballplayers.

Intimidated by the Gilded Age's culture and policies, ballplayers at first felt they had no choice but to conform to their restrictive contracts and working conditions. As skilled workers, they enjoyed higher-than-average salaries compared to many other Americans even if their wages and careers were precarious: typically short and solely at the whim of their owners. Only gradually did ballplayers recognize that their skills had real value and that owners could not easily replace them, especially when fans became devoted followers of teams and their popular players. Reflecting what workers were doing all over the nation in the late nineteenth century, ballplayers began to organize. As part of the wider war between capital and labor, several ballplayers stood out for challenging baseball's Gilded-Age magnates.

MONTE: JOHN MONTGOMERY WARD

Baseball players and other professional athletes today take for granted that they can offer their skills to the highest bidder just like employees in other professions. The fight for that freedom, won in 1975, began ninety years earlier, led by John Montgomery Ward, a ballplayer and renaissance man who knew the value of labor and who nearly succeeded in challenging baseball's ownership structure with a radical idea: a worker-owned league.

Ward was born in rural Bellefonte, Pennsylvania, in 1860. A precocious student, he entered Pennsylvania State University at age thirteen and in 1875 helped develop the school's first baseball team. He also threw a curve ball, a pitch he's sometimes credited with inventing. Although a good student, Ward was expelled for a fraternity incident. Failing as a traveling salesman, Ward returned to baseball, pitching for semipro teams in Pennsylvania towns that were hotbeds of the emerging labor movement.

In 1878 Ward received a major league contract from the Providence Grays in the two-year-old NL. The league's youngest player, he went 22-13, with a 1.51 earned run average (ERA). A year later, he pitched Providence to the pennant, going 47-19 with a 2.15 ERA. He also played outfield and infield positions. His pitching brilliance continued, including the second perfect game in history—and the last one in the NL for another eighty-four years. In 1882, he pitched an 18-inning complete game shutout, still the longest in MLB history. At age twenty, he became the Grays' player-manager. He continued to dominate on the mound until an arm injury from an awkward slide and from hurling 500–600 innings each year prematurely ended his pitching days.

Traded to the New York Gothams in 1884 (which became the Giants the following year), Ward taught himself to throw left-handed and became the team's starting centerfielder. The next year, his right arm healed, he became the Giants regular shortstop. He also switched from right-handed to left-handed hitting to shorten his run to first base and bolster his offensive output. Ward is the only player in history to both win more than 100 games as a pitcher (a 164-103 record) and get more than 2,000 hits. He also stole 540 bases, drove in nearly 1,000 runs and had the third-best WHIP (walks plus hits per inning pitched) in MLB history. He also managed the Giants, played on two more championship teams, and became a successful baseball executive.

The press described Ward as a ballplayer with "few equals and no superiors" and "by long odds the most popular player in the profession."[4] Ward was refined, handsome, elegantly tailored, and single, which—combined with his baseball exploits—made him prominent in New York's elite social circles. He courted and then married Helen Dauvray, the era's leading Broadway star, in the biggest baseball celebrity marriage until Joe DiMaggio wed Marilyn Monroe in 1954. Starting in 1884, the winner of baseball's championship between the NL and American Association (AA) pennant winners earned the Dauvray Cup; the World Series would come later. Motivated by a thirst for knowledge, Ward learned five languages, became a regular newspaper and magazine contributor, published a book, and completed a political science BA and a law degree at Columbia University—all while still a ballplayer.

THE BROTHERHOOD UNION

Although Ward didn't practice law for another ten years, he recognized—from his legal training—the unfairness of baseball contracts and conditions. A rival to the NL, the AA emerged in 1883. The AA lured players to the new league with better salaries but abruptly reneged on these agreements when it made peace with the NL. Both leagues exploited players, cut their pay, ignored their terrible working conditions, and undermined their value and mobility. In response, Ward organized the Brotherhood of Professional Baseball Players (BPBP) in 1885, the first sports labor union. Designed to help ill, injured, or destitute players, the BPBP rapidly developed into a union amid the extensive labor-owner conflict throughout America.

In the August 1887 *Lippincott's Magazine*, Ward published "Is the Base-Ball Player a Chattel?" accusing the baseball owners of "wage slavery." Organized baseball was a monopoly. The owners colluded with each other, primarily through the reserve clause. Contracts bound ballplayers to their teams, which could release them unilaterally without pay. Owners claimed the reserve system was essential to league stability but instead it was used to suppress wages. Tripling their profits in the 1880s, the owners nevertheless imposed meager salaries, extra unpaid duties, rent for uniforms, and meal-money fees.

To Ward, the reserve clause "was an inherent wrong, for by it one set of men seized absolute control over the labor of another . . . Clubs have seemed to think that players had no rights, and the blacklist was waiting for any man who dared to assert the contrary."[5] Ward sought the elimination of "baseball law" so that the "business of base-ball [would] rest on an ordinary business basis." He also threatened to organize a competing league: "Shall (change) come from the clubs, or from the players, or from both conjointly? If the clubs cannot find a way out of these difficulties, the players will try to do it for them."[6]

Only two decades after the Civil War ended, Ward compared players' situation to Black slaves before the war who, due to fugitive slave laws, couldn't escape their bondage. "In the eye of the baseball magnate the player has become a mere chattel," Ward said. "He goes where he is sent, takes what is given him, and thanks the Lord for life."[7] Not coincidentally, the BPBP promoted progressive race policies led by Ward's own forward-looking attitudes. Ward had lobbied to allow Black athletes to play in organized baseball during his Providence years, and he arranged for William Edward White, a light-complexioned African American, to play for the team in 1879. White was the first Black player in the major leagues but surreptitiously so (except to Ward) since he passed for a white man. After the 1879 season, Ward took a barnstorming team to the South and defied convention by playing against Black teams. After Black catcher Moses Fleetwood Walker threw him out in an 1887 exhibition game against an all-Black team, Ward lobbied New York Giants owner John Day to sign Black players but the Jim Crow color bar blocked the deal and MLB redoubled its baseball segregation.

Before the 1888 season, Ward authored a best-selling book *Base-Ball: How to Become a Player, with the Origin, History and Explanation of the Game.* The book explained baseball "for the benefit of those ladies whose escorts either cannot, or will not, answer their questions."[8] It was also the first book to explore the sport's history. Ward continued to star at shortstop for the Giants, who won NL pennants in 1888 and 1889 and then defeated the AA champions, the St. Louis Browns and Brooklyn Bridegrooms, for consecutive world championships. Ward hit .379 and .417, respectively, in those two postseason tournaments.

Responding to growing player frustrations, in 1887 Francis Richter, a writer for *Sporting Life*, proposed a Millennium Plan, a form of revenue-sharing among the teams to promote stability and equity. The baseball owners condemned the idea as "too socialist."

THE PLAYERS LEAGUE

In the off-season between 1888 and 1889, an incident significantly radicalized Ward and the BPBP. Albert Spalding—a former star pitcher who later owned the Chicago White Sox and became the NL's de facto president—organized a World Baseball Tour. Circulating the globe for nearly six months, Spalding sought to transplant "America's game" to foreign lands and—more importantly—expand his sporting goods empire. Spalding coaxed Ward to join the trip and to captain one of the teams. With Ward halfway around the world, baseball owners could easily plot against the players in his absence. To beat back the BPBP's modest labor activism, the NL and AA had already been mimicking the union-busting tactics used in other industries including penalties, collusion, intimidation, blacklists, and indiscriminately docking players' pay. One group of blacklisted players formed their own barnstorming team, calling themselves the Blacklisted.

When the world tour reached Cairo, Egypt, in February 1889, the players learned that the NL had adopted a scheme—the Brush Classification Plan—to undermine player wages. It set salaries in classes from A to E, ranging from $1,000 to $2,500. The system allowed players to be released with only ten days' notice while players could never break their contracts unless they wanted to be banned from playing professional baseball. The plan ranked not only on-field ability but also "conduct, both on and off the field." Like the owners of big corporations, the NL had already been using Pinkerton spies against players for a decade; now more were hired to further monitor them. The plan created classes among ballplayers to divide them so they'd fight each other rather than the owners, another typical divide-and-conquer tactic of the era.

Ward was incensed by the plan and by Spalding's duplicity. Spalding approached his role as a team owner like the captain of industry he had become. The players were employees and his job was to control his costs and workforce. Ward was further enraged when he learned the Giants were selling him to the Washington Nationals for a record price of $12,000. He left the tour early and told the Giants he would refuse to play for Washington unless he received a significant portion of his sale price, ultimately causing the Nationals to nullify the deal.

Back from the tour, Ward launched a protest but the NL owners refused to meet with him or the union. The tour provided excellent public relations for baseball, and the owners basked in the attention. Taking the owners' side, the media condemned the players for undermining baseball—now a global game—with their unreasonable demands. In the short run, Ward could do little to strengthen players' power vis-à-vis the owners. Despite his outrage at the owners' mistreatment, he kept focused enough to lead the Giants to their second straight championship in 1889. But during that season, Ward devised a radical remedy.

The Brush Classification Plan was only one of the many abuses the NL owners inflicted on ballplayers. At the start of the 1889 season, for example, they also charged players rent for their uniforms. These insults infuriated the players and led them to take more audacious action. *The Sporting News*, the voice of the baseball establishment, warned that the BPBP was ready to launch "a strike which will be the biggest thing ever heard of in the baseball world."[9] But Ward had even bolder ideas. Initially working in secret, he began building player support for a rival league. When word of the plan surfaced, the owners underestimated Ward and his connections in the business community.

In July 1889 Ward and other players founded the Players' League (PL) based on the revolutionary idea—both inside and outside baseball—that workers could run their own workplaces without the bosses. Their manifesto reflected the radical ideas circulating among labor activists around the country. They viewed sports leagues as cartels. While the players and their teams competed on the field, the owners colluded for common business interests off the field. They believed that players were contracted employees with no ownership interest in their teams, should have no voice in team or league operations, and could have their labor traded or sold to another team without their consent.

The PL promoted a radically different concept. It was a cooperative, where players owned and ran their teams, trades occurred only with players' consent, and outside investors divided profits equally with the players. In November 1889, the BPBP issued a statement, drafted by Ward, called "The Brotherhood Manifesto"—a kind of declaration of independence or emancipation proclamation for professional baseball players. It claimed,

> There was a time when the League stood for integrity and fair dealing; to-day it stands for dollars and cents. Once it looked to the elevation of the game and an honest exhibition of the sport; to-day its eyes are upon the turnstile. Men have come into the business for no other motive than to exploit it for every dollar in sight . . . Players have been bought, sold and exchanged as though they were sheep, instead of American citizens.[10]

The manifesto described an alternative approach:

> We believe it is possible to conduct our national game upon lines which will not infringe upon individual and natural rights. We ask to be judged solely by our

> business conducted more intelligently under a plan which excludes everything arbitrary and un-American, we look forward with confidence to the support of the public and the future of the national game.[11]

In 1890, when the PL began, Congress passed the Sherman Anti-Trust Act, challenging the growing scourge of corporate monopolization. The law made illegal any act that interfered with free competition between and among industries, businesses, and all interstate commercial ventures.

But a conservative U.S. Supreme Court quickly undermined Congress' intention of reigning in the growing power of corporate monopolies. For decades after Congress passed the Sherman Anti-Trust Act, it was rarely used against corporate monopolies in part because the court imposed a narrow interpretation of what constituted trade or commerce among states. The court was more willing to use the new law to thwart unions, which they often defined as "illegal combinations" that impeded commerce across state lines.

The agreement between the NL and AA clearly violated the anti-trust laws. As a monopoly, it restrained trade by blocking new companies in its industry. Its labor practices exploited players in ways that anti-trust laws sought to eliminate. But the conservative courts nevertheless upheld the reserve clause, which clearly restricted interstate commerce by limiting players' ability to determine whom to work for.

In this hostile political and legal environment, the players sought to own their own league. In each club in the PL, profits and management were shared. Eight-man boards—four players and four investors—ran the teams, and a senate governed the league, with a player and investor representing each club. Players owned team stock, and revenue was split evenly among the clubs. There was no reserve clause or classification plan. Player contracts ran three years, and trades required players' consent. Three-quarters of all NL players, including the top stars in both leagues (including fifteen future Hall of Famers such as Dan Brouthers, Hugh Duffy, Mike "King" Kelly, and Old Hoss Radbourne) jumped to the PL. Essentially the entire St. Louis Browns team of the AA became a new PL club. Ward ran the union; recruited financial investors; persuaded NL and AA players to switch to the PL; arranged to rent ballparks and created a league schedule; handled the media; managed the daily organizational challenges; and fought the NL counterattack—all while also acting as player-manager for the PL's Brooklyn Ward's Wonders. That season he hit .335, stole 63 bases, led the PL shortstops in assists, and piloted his club to a second-place finish.

The NL response was led by Albert Spalding who, like the era's other robber barons, pursued a cutthroat, survival-of-the-fittest strategy to undermine unions and other forms of dissent against corporate power. When the PL recruited NL players and began outdrawing it in attendance, Spalding and other owners filed suit, claiming the jumpers broke their contracts and violated the reserve clause. Ward was sued first. But in this and other cases against stars such as Jim O'Rourke and Roger O'Connor, judges ruled the contracts were unenforceable: they were vague and unfairly biased against the players. In January 1890, Justice Morgan O'Brien of the New York Supreme Court noted, "We have the spectacle presented of a contract which binds one party for a series of years and the other party for 10 days . . . This was rather absurd."[12]

The NL and AA owners threatened to hire strikebreakers. But soon they tried to lure the players back by offering more money. Although offered a blank check by Spalding to return, Mike "King" Kelly, who had jumped from the NL's Boston Beaneaters to the PL's Boston Reds, refused, saying, "My mother and father would never look at me again if I proved to be a traitor to the boys."[13] Curiously, three players who jumped—Charles Comiskey, Connie Mack, and Clark Griffith—eventually went from PL rebels to long-term and domineering baseball owners.

With the courts refusing to help, Spalding formed a "War Committee" to battle the BPBP. Relying on years of accumulated influence, Spalding bribed reporters and inundated the media with anti-union propaganda, turning them against the PL and poisoning public opinion against the players.

Just as the robber barons sought to discredit dissenters, Spalding and his allies accused the PL of being "hot-headed anarchists," "socialists," and "ultra-radicals." They claimed the PL was "an edifice built on falsehood" and its members were "overpaid players." Henry Chadwick, a renowned sportswriter who worked for Spalding, called the PL and its players "terrorists." He condemned Ward as the "mastermind" of the "secessionists"—still a provocative word so soon after the Civil War. The owners and their sympathizers also accused Ward of the "terrorism peculiar to revolutionary movements" and called him "Judas Montgomery Ward." But Ward got strong support from the nation's labor movement. Samuel Gompers, the AFL president, backed the new league, and some AFL unions fined members caught attending non-union games.

With three leagues competing against each other in 1890, all of them suffered at the gate. The PL outdrew and outplayed the NL and AA, yet Spalding wouldn't relent and his owners had deep pockets. The PL players, and particularly their investors, worried that the NL and AA owners could outlast them. Spalding wooed PL investors, even meeting with them in secret by excluding Ward and other BPBP leaders.

In the end, Spalding prevailed. He promised PL investors that they would be awarded new teams in a reconfigured NL. They capitulated, and Ward's revolution was over. As the *Sporting News* wrote, "Goodbye Players' League. Your life has been a stormy one. Because of your existence, many a man has lost thousands of dollars. And before long all that will be left of you is a memory—a sad, discouraging memory."[14]

With the PL's demise, the BPBP collapsed. The NL quickly killed off the AA and emerged with an exclusive monopoly. The NL owners drastically lowered player salaries (by 40 percent in three years), blackballed potential labor agitators, broke long-term contracts, reinforced the reserve clause, and commandeered the previously independent minor league teams for replacement labor to intimidate players from further agitation. The devastation for the players mirrored the economic hard times for most American workers in the 1890s. It also reflected the growing profits and riches of the country's robber barons, including the baseball tycoons.

Ward reluctantly returned to the NL as player-manager of the Brooklyn Grooms, leading them to two second-place finishes. In 1893 he returned to the New York Giants as their manager and second baseman. He hit .328, with 129 runs scored and 46 steals that year. In 1894, he led the Giants to a second-place finish, and then to a 4-game sweep of the pennant-winning Baltimore Orioles to win the postseason Temple Cup. After that season, Ward announced his retirement, even though he remained one of the NL's best players. All told, Ward completed 17 impressive major league seasons, compiling notable numbers as a pitcher, batter, and fielder. He won two world championships as a player and one as a manager, guiding his teams to a 412-320 (.563) mark.

The baseball barons pushed back the challenge posed by the BPBP and the PL. They likely also felt vindicated by the Supreme Court's 1896 *Plessy* v.

Ferguson decision, which officially endorsed the racial segregation the owners were already practicing. This closed baseball's door to African Americans and other dark-skinned players but it potentially left the door open for Native Americans. The first to walk through was Lou Sockalexis, a Penobscot Indian who joined the NL's Cleveland club in 1897 for a sensational but brief career as the first Native American in MLB. Ward first saw Sockalexis play at the College of the Holy Cross. Ward's attempts to break the color barrier for African American players had failed but the segregation doctrine was unclear when it came to Native Americans. While others have taken credit for elevating Sockalexis to the majors, it was Ward who received the call from Cleveland owner Frank Robison, thanking him for bringing Sockalexis to his club.

After retiring, Ward set up his law practice in Brooklyn and immediately rose to prominence defending players such as Amos Rusie and Fred Pfieffer against NL owners. In 1909, Ward sought the position of NL president but, not surprisingly, baseball's barons killed his candidacy.

Instead, in 1911 Ward became a part-owner and president of the NL's Boston Braves. Then in 1914 he became business manager of the Brooklyn Tip-Tops in the upstart Federal League, which provoked the next challenge to the NL and AL's reserve clause. He retired for good from baseball in 1915 then lived a prosperous life as a gentleman farmer on his two-hundred-acre Long Island estate while tending to several businesses (including an ice company, fuel company, and local newspaper), hunting and fishing, and winning several golf tournaments. He died on March 4, 1925, the day after his sixty-fifth birthday.

Ward's challenge to baseball's reserve clause failed, but the battle didn't disappear. Three years before Ward's death, the U.S. Supreme Court made one of the most controversial—and frankly absurd—rulings in its history when it declared baseball exempt from federal anti-trust laws, characterizing MLB as an "amusement" rather than a business and therefore not a monopoly. Another fifty years would pass before a new baseball union would overthrow the reserve system in favor of free agency.

With his accomplishments, Ward should have been an easy choice for the Baseball Hall of Fame. Yet he wasn't inducted into Cooperstown until 1964, seven decades after his last game and four decades after his death. As with players' union director Marvin Miller in recent times, Ward was punished for challenging the baseball establishment. His Cooperstown plaque makes no mention of his role in founding the BPBP or the PL or his groundbreaking fight against the reserve clause.

ORATOR: JIM O'ROURKE

While Ward may have been the general behind the nineteenth-century ballplayer revolt, he had plenty of help from enthusiastic lieutenants. One of those rebels was James "Orator" O'Rourke. Born in 1850 in Bridgeport, Connecticut, to Irish immigrants, after his father's premature death in 1868, O'Rourke had to stay close to home to help with the family farm. O'Rourke was a standout in local youth and semipro baseball leagues but he wouldn't sign his first professional contract, with the minor league Middletown Mansfields in 1872, until they provided a replacement worker for his farm. This characterized the assertive stance he took with management for his entire career.

The Boston Red Stockings tried to sign O'Rourke in 1873. Legend has it that Hall of Fame manager Harry Wright told him to change his name to "Rourke" to disguise his heritage because Boston's upper-class Brahmins "will not stand for the Irish."[15] O'Rourke refused, saying, "I would die first before I would give up any part of my father's name. A million would not tempt me."[16] Wright hired O'Rourke anyway and he helped lead the team to three straight pennants.

In *Orator O'Rourke: The Life of a Baseball Radical*, Mike Roer observed,

> In the new social order of America, with its class system of capitalists and workers, being "manly" (preserving one's dignity) required a worker to stand up for his rights, even if it meant losing his job. Jim would have to put his career on the line many times to defend his concept of justice for workers. For his spunk, he became a hero to the Boston Irish.[17]

In 1874, O'Rourke's team visited Great Britain, the first of many overseas baseball tours. Launched initially to promote goodwill, the tours quickly developed commercial and diplomatic objectives: to establish baseball's American (not English) origins, to open new markets for sporting goods firms, and to promote the American way. O'Rourke distinguished himself on the tour by winning a long-toss contest and by acquitting himself impressively in cricket games against British athletes. After returning home, however, the

Red Stockings owner imposed a $100 fee on the players to compensate for what he claimed were the losses he suffered on the tour. O'Rourke threatened to quit. Manager Wright persuaded him to pay the hated fee, but it would be the last time O'Rourke gave in to an owner.

In 1871, the Red Stockings were a charter member of the NAPBBP. Five years later the team became part of the new NL. O'Rourke became the first holdout. Not having received a raise in three years, he threatened to return to his Bridgeport business interests. O'Rourke risked being blackballed by NL teams, but he nevertheless prevailed, doubling his salary. This action emboldened other players to recognize that the owners weren't all-powerful. In the first NL game, between Boston and Philadelphia, O'Rourke got the first hit ever in the new league.

Albert Spalding's sporting goods company secured exclusive control over the sale of most equipment used by the NL. In 1877 he raised prices for his uniforms. The owner passed on the extra $30 to the players in addition to a new charge of 50 cents per day for meals on the road. O'Rourke rebelled, arguing against the monopolistic practices of both the company and the teams. He viewed this as part of the owners' endless quest to chip away at player salaries to enhance their profits. O'Rourke refused to pay, and the Boston owner finally relented.

In 1878, O'Rourke clashed with management again. Owner Arthur Soden had been housing the Boston team in fleabag hotels on the road, slashing their meal allowances, and even charging players' wives to attend home games. Then he imposed a $20 fee on players to have their uniforms washed. As biographer Roer put it,

> It wasn't about the $20. Jim was fighting for a principle, for the precedent of how a baseball player—indeed any worker—should be treated. The same struggle was being played out in coal mines in Appalachia, in factories in New England, and on farms in Georgia. If the workers did not resist, they would all end up owing their souls to the company store.[18]

O'Rourke refused the charge and sought offers from other teams.

After leading Boston to NL pennants in 1877 and 1878, O'Rourke joined the Providence Grays in 1879, leading the team to the championship. One of his teammates was Paul Hines, a hearing-impaired outfielder. To avoid collisions in the field and to allow Hines to keep the count while at bat, O'Rourke devised hand signals—the predecessors to those developed a decade later for the deaf-mute ballplayer William "Dummy" Hoy. It soon became standard procedure for umpires calling balls and strikes.

After the 1879 season, the NL, led by Spalding, imposed its first reserve clause on players. Uniform contracts were adopted, pay was made for "play" and not in advance, and five players were reserved by every club; that is, blocked from changing teams. Owners claimed they were responding to excessive "revolving" (player movement), but the reserve clause served instead to divide players (reserved versus not reserved) and especially to suppress salaries. As a result, owners' profits soared in the 1880s.

Since O'Rourke wasn't reserved by Providence and since his brother John now played for the Red Stockings, O'Rourke returned to the Boston team despite his past conflicts with owner Soden. The O'Rourkes each received a low-ball contract but rather than responding individually, Jim and John bargained jointly, posing the threat of the team losing both of these star players. The team gave both O'Rourkes contracts with a reserve exemption and much bigger salaries. (This anticipated the successful collaboration of Sandy Koufax and Don Drysdale in 1966, which began the reserve clause's destruction.)

In contrast to O'Rourke, the Providence team put its star shortstop, future Hall of Famer George Wright, on reserve and slashed his salary, despite his contribution to its championship season. Inspired by O'Rourke's holdout, Wright refused to sign. He sat out the 1880 season, arguing that the reserve clause bound players only for a single season. (Nearly a century later, in 1975, Andy Messersmith and Dave McNally successfully pursued this strategy to establish the current free agency system.)

But the Red Stockings weren't done. Player contracts ran from April 1 to October 31. To save money, owner Soden disbanded the team on September 30, 1880, to avoid paying October salaries. The O'Rourke brothers sued Soden for their month's pay and eventually got a settlement two years later. Fed up with Soden, John left baseball in 1881 for a job as a railroad baggage handler and Jim became player-manager of the Buffalo Bisons, leading a perennially losing team to four-straight winning seasons.

After the 1881 season, Spalding got the NL to adopt color-coded uniforms, purportedly to help fans identify the players. The plan increased the profits of Spalding's sporting goods company by forcing teams to buy new uniforms.

Again O'Rourke rebelled: "It is an insult to all of us to make a professional baseball player dress like a clown. If we are unfortunate enough to play near a lunatic asylum, we are likely to wind up inside looking out."[19] After two months, the league abandoned the new uniforms, which prompted another round of uniform orders and profits for Spalding.

In 1882 Soden became interim NL president and the league expanded the reserve from five to eleven players—essentially the entire team in this era. This sealed the players' bondage. The only other major league, the AA, adopted the same contract as part of its agreement with the NL. Players had nowhere else to go. Even so, O'Rourke rebelled and pressured Buffalo's owners to accept instead a gentlemen's agreement to maintain allegiance to the team. The NL objected, fearing other players would get the same idea, but the arrangement stood. Announcing that he would leave Buffalo after the 1884 season, O'Rourke nevertheless guided the team to another winning season and supervised the construction of Olympic Park, the Bison's new ballpark. With teammate Deacon White, O'Rourke also developed the first pneumatic chest protector for catchers, a version of which they still use today.

In 1885 O'Rourke agreed to join the New York Giants but only if he were exempt from the reserve clause and only if the team paid for his law school education in the off-season. Fulfilling a lifetime dream, O'Rourke then enrolled at Yale Law School, where he also coached the Yale baseball team to a winning season. O'Rourke had already been dubbed "Orator" for his grandiloquent language, but law school intensified the habit. To O'Rourke, manager Gus Schmelz's whiskers were "a phosphorescent trellis work of agitated hair." Not playing heads-up ball was an "ossification of the brainery." Arguing a call with an umpire, O'Rourke claimed, "I am conversant with the conglomeration of facts in this case, and as my optical eyesight is of extreme excellence, I am positive of your misinformation."[20]

O'Rourke's Yale legal studies escalated his activism for player rights. He joined his old Providence teammate John Montgomery Ward (also a lawyer) and Tim Keefe as leaders of the players' revolt, beginning with the first baseball union, the BPBP, triggered by a league-wide salary cap for the 1886 season. O'Rourke resisted, threatening to retire to Bridgeport and inspiring others to also rebel. While not all owners rigidly applied the cap, the well of owner-player relations had been poisoned. Ballplayers needed a united response.

What transpired following the 1886 season led to a further call-to-arms. Albert Spalding's Chicago White Stockings sold Mike "King" Kelly to Boston for $10,000. Not just the amount, but the sale itself, sent shockwaves through the league. The players knew the reserve clause bound them to their existing teams, but they now realized they could be bought and sold into a new "slave" contract.

After helping the Giants to the NL's 1888 pennant and a World Series championship over the AA's St. Louis Browns, O'Rourke and Ward realized that the BPBP needed a bolder approach. Some players favored a strike, but Ward wanted to go further. That was the catalyst for the idea of an employee-run PL. O'Rourke described his commitment to the cause as "uncoupled from all doubts, notwithstanding the warning of the master magnates and the snapping of their whip."[21]

Knowing that the players couldn't trust the media, O'Rourke took the lead in campaigning for the new league via his many ties to civic organizations such as the Elks Club. PL members were comforted by the fact that both Ward and O'Rourke had legal skills that they could employ in court if needed. While O'Rourke, Ward, and pitcher Tim Keefe were leading the Giants to a second straight NL pennant and World Series championship, the three teammates spent the 1889 season recruiting players to the PL.

According to Mike Roer,

> It was becoming clear even to the general public that the Baseball War was about much more than baseball—it was about the social structure of America. The Giants' [fans] refrain: "We are the People" was now a battle cry in the contest for worker rights, for the rights of the citizen against ruling magnates, who now had more control over their lives than did government or religion. In their stadia they were united, strong in number, a force to be reckoned with. They were *The People.*[22]

In 1890, Jim and John O'Rourke fought parallel battles for workers' rights. Jim worked feverishly to sustain the PL and the BPBP (while posting impressive numbers on the field). John was a union organizer with the Brotherhood of Railway Trainmen, which represented twenty thousand brakemen, switchmen, yardmasters, conductors, and baggage handlers. To combat the work hazards that killed two thousand men each year, John joined a brotherhood campaign in Hartford to lobby Congress for legislation mandating automatic brakes and couplers on freight trains. Then he helped lead a protest march of eight hundred BPBP members through the streets of Los Angeles.

But by 1891, both O'Rourkes had to face defeat. For John, corrupt elements had seized control of the railway union (and would soon support management against radical labor leader Eugene Debs during the Pullman Strike). For Jim, the PL had won the battle but lost the war to regain the baseball industry for the benefit of its workers. Despite the PL's outdrawing the NL and luring its best players, Albert Spalding outmaneuvered the baseball rebels by bribing the PL's financial backers. The league folded.

O'Rourke returned for two seasons to the Giants, who slashed all players' salaries. He ended his major league career in 1893 as the Washington Senators' player-manager. O'Rourke had played on eight championship teams, managed two other clubs, won the 1884 NL batting title, and finished with a .311 batting average over 21 seasons playing outfield and catcher. His 2,678 base hits were the second most by any nineteenth-century player.

After a brief turn as a major league umpire in 1894, O'Rourke returned to his hometown, where he created a new minor-league team, the Bridgeport Victors, as well as the new Connecticut State League (which eventually became the Eastern Association). Beginning in 1895, he was the club's player-manager for eight years while also practicing law and overseeing his real estate interests. In 1895, as a Democratic Party candidate, he lost a close election for the Connecticut state legislature. In 1898, he built a minor league stadium, Newfield Park, on his family's farmland in Bridgeport. It is still in use as a city park.

Like Ward, O'Rourke opposed the exclusion of African American players from MLB orchestrated by Spalding, Cap Anson, and other racist owners and players. He had batted against the great Black pitcher George Stovey and was angry when, in 1887, major league teams excluded him and other Black players. So when he led the Bridgeport Victors, he made sure to schedule games against Black clubs. More important, he hired a Black outfielder, Harry Herbert, for the Victors. By 1896, Herbert was one of the two African Americans left in professional baseball. He played for O'Rourke for four years until an injury ended his career.

In 1898, the Victors were renamed the "Orators" in O'Rourke's honor. In 1902, O'Rourke helped start the National Association of Professional Baseball

Leagues (NAPBL), a minor league protective organization, where his battles continued. The NAPBL sought to prevent player raids by the major leagues. In 1904, O'Rourke, at age fifty-four, was still playing for Bridgeport when Giants manager John McGraw summoned him to New York. One game away from clinching the club's first pennant since 1889, McGraw wanted a veteran of that championship team to catch Joe McGinnity for the title. O'Rourke caught the entire game and went 1 for 4 in the 7-5 Giants victory. For many years thereafter he was the oldest player to ever play in a major league game.

In 1912, at the age of sixty-two, O'Rourke played in his last professional game for the New Haven minor league club. It was his fifty-first season in baseball. In 1919, he caught pneumonia and died at the age of sixty-eight. O'Rourke was voted into the Cooperstown Hall of Fame in 1945, but his plaque makes no mention of his battles on behalf of players. In 2009, a movement arose to preserve O'Rourke's home overlooking the Bridgeport harbor, which city officials wanted to tear down to make way for a shopping development. The home was lost, but in 2010 a statue of O'Rourke was erected outside Bridgeport Bluefish Stadium. The inscriptions tell O'Rourke's history, including his enduring statement "Baseball is for all creeds and nationalities."[23]

SIR TIMOTHY: TIM KEEFE

Nicknamed "Sir Timothy" and "Smiling Tim" because of his gentlemanly and congenial behavior on and off the field, Tim Keefe was nevertheless "often blatant in his choice of words" according to his biographer Charlie Bevis, and "especially when he was defending issues that he was passionate about, such as the repressive activities pursued by the owners of the National League ball clubs."[24]

Keefe was born in 1857 to Irish immigrants living in Cambridge, Massachusetts. His father, Patrick, was a carpenter working on a construction job in the South when the Civil War broke out. When he refused to fight for the South, he was held as a prisoner-of-war for two years. Two of Patrick's brothers were killed in the war fighting for the Union.

After the war, Patrick moved his family in 1870 to the nearby working-class town of Somerville. As a carpenter, he was vulnerable to the emerging changes in the employer-artisan relationship. Increasingly he could get only piecework rather than whole jobs. He wanted to work for himself so he opened his own business as a master carpenter. Given his precarious experience, Patrick wanted Tim to focus on mathematics and engineering and to work with his head rather than his hands. But Tim shunned school and followed his father into carpentry as an apprentice. Even worse, in his father's eyes, Tim wanted to play baseball.

Despite his father's objections, Keefe understood that playing baseball had become a marketable skill. As the historian Warren Goldstein pointed out in *Playing for Keeps*, the "relative scarcity of baseball craftsmen earned them high wages and substantial freedom of movement."[25] Or so Keefe thought at the time. By 1877, Tim had been playing in amateur leagues for many years and was spending as much time on baseball as on carpentry. In the fall of that year, an incident convinced him to choose baseball as his profession. Keefe and three other carpenters had a verbal agreement to build a house for a Cambridge man for a fixed price for labor and materials. But when they completed the work the owner refused to pay, and Keefe was forced to sue. Keefe decided that if being a carpenter was this tenuous, he'd be better off as a professional ballplayer.

Keefe was drawn to the apprentice-journeyman-master system practiced by carpenters, which he believed should apply to the baseball profession. His biographer Charlie Bevis notes, "Keefe was driven by the principle of free labor, not negotiated labor."[26]

Keefe began playing baseball professionally in 1878, moving through five different minor league teams in the NA in the next two years, primarily as a third baseman. During the 1879 season, he debuted as a pitcher and played that position full-time when the NL's Troy Trojans signed him to his first major league contract in 1880. Keefe's rookie ERA of .086 set a major league single-season record that still stands today.

Keefe first met Ward playing winter ball in New Orleans in 1880. They not only discussed pitching strategy but their mutual frustration with the reserve clause, which the team owners had just imposed. This began their long partnership to promote workers' rights for ballplayers. Keefe felt that in moving from an amateur to a professional ballplayer, he had passed from the apprentice to the journeyman stage and he ought to be able, as Bevis put it, to

> negotiate his own employment deals, and once they were completed, move on to the next job without becoming encumbered by the previous job . . . If thrifty,

> the ballplayer could advance to the master stage by starting his own baseball club or other business that took advantage of his inherent artisanal skills.[27]

Keefe was one of the five players reserved by Troy for the 1881 season. Tim was forced to take the Trojan offer of $1,500 for both that season and the next. "I was considered a robber because I tried to hold out for $2,100," Keefe recalled. Keefe jumped ship the following season to the New York Metropolitans of the newly launched AA, which did not (yet) have a reserve clause. Keefe became the team's dominant pitcher, going 41-27 with 359 strikeouts in 1883, including a one-hit shutout and two-hit shutout in the same doubleheader. He went 37-17 in 1884, with 334 strikeouts, leading the Metropolitans to the AA pennant.

Earning far more with his Metropolitans salary than he could as a carpenter, Keefe began to wear tailored suits, attend the theater and other social activities, and generally emulate a well-heeled Cambridge citizen. He studied business and accounting on his own and spent hours alone in hotels on the road teaching himself shorthand, a valuable skill he used even before his retirement from baseball. As a professional baseball player, Keefe was able to overcome Irish stereotypes and get access to opportunities otherwise denied people with his ancestry.

For the 1885 season, Metropolitans owner John Day hatched a plan to transfer Keefe to the NL's New York Giants, which he also owned. To get around the AA's newly adopted reserve clause and to block other teams from signing Keefe after his release from the Mets, Day sent Tim out of the country, ultimately signing him to the Giants on a boat trip to Bermuda. Despite AA club objections, Keefe thus joined future Hall of Famers Ward, O'Rourke, Buck Ewing, Roger Connor, and Mickey Welch on an outstanding Giants team. Keefe went 32-13 that year, with a 1.58 ERA and 227 strikeouts. In 1886 he led the league with 42 wins, 62 complete games, and 535 innings pitched.

Ironically, Keefe fulfilled his father's wishes to have him use his head and not merely his hands in his chosen work. In 1885, the *Boston Globe* observed that "Keefe is said to be one of the most scientific pitchers in the country—that is, he uses his head as well as his hands while in the box."[28] Keefe adapted to continual pitching-rule changes in the 1880s. Besides his great fastball and curve, Keefe's main strength was deception: he was the first to master the change-of-pace pitch. Keefe said he owed his effectiveness to "outguessing the batter."[29] Fellow pitcher Mickey Welch claimed he "never saw a pitcher better than Keefe . . . He was a master strategist and knew the weakness of every batter in the league."[30]

Besides baffling batters with different speeds, Keefe used different arm motions, from overhand to submarine pitching. He used the entire pitcher's box, throwing from different angles rather than merely straight in to the batter. Keefe took multiple steps before releasing the ball, not always pitching from a set position. As a student of his craft, he wrote two book-length pitching manuals and was in demand as a college coach. In the off-season, he mentored pitchers at Harvard, near his Cambridge home, and eventually also at Amherst, Dartmouth, Williams, Princeton, and Tufts.

On the Giants team Keefe reunited with Ward, who had recently completed his Columbia University law degree. Keefe shared Ward's anger at owners treating ballplayers like livestock or slaves. Even though these two stars were relatively well-paid, they identified with the plight of the average player. Their frustrations pushed them to create the BPBP. Ward was made president, and partly due to his shorthand and accounting skills, Keefe became both secretary and treasurer.

While he operated more in the shadow of the publicity-oriented Ward, arguably Keefe played a more crucial organizing role. He bonded with the players, supervised recruitment and retention, and devised the profit-sharing plan behind the PL. According to Bevis, "Keefe was truly an unsung pioneer of ballplayer rights."[31]

Keefe believed, as in carpentry, that baseball should be both a craft and a trade. As Bevis explained, "The craft was the actual skills, tools, and logic of the work while the trade was control over the processes and products created by the craft."[32] The trade produced the kind of independence Keefe sought for himself and his fellow ballplayers but which the owners were impeding.

Keefe subscribed to what labor historians call artisan republicanism, a philosophy dating back to Thomas Jefferson's vision of a "nation propelled by yeoman farmers and urban mechanics." A republic of "small producers" was viewed as "essential to wise government and political stability." The intense industrialization of the 1880s challenged this practice as capitalists increasingly controlled businesses and maximized profits by hiring wage labor to replace artisans. As workers became economic captives of capitalists, they toiled under what reformers and radicals called "wage slavery." In response,

Keefe and others espoused a free labor philosophy where workers had opportunities to save money and then own their own enterprises.

According to Bevis, the BPBP took the position "that ballplayers' skills produced the game's profits, not the skills of management."[33] Therefore the players should share equally in the proceeds and profits and control their own destiny. Keefe, Ward, and other players were particularly outraged when the White Stockings sold Kelly to Boston for $10,000 after the 1886 season. In their eyes, Kelly was entitled to all or a significant portion of the value he had created. And when a team releases a player, they believed, he ought to be able to negotiate his own deal.

When Ward, Keefe, and other players formed the BPBP in 1886, they emphasized its role in protecting players' rights against greedy team owners through fair contracts and decent working conditions. Keefe initially viewed the union's efforts as helping the sport for both players and owners.

> The brotherhood was formed with the intention of fostering and elevating the game of base ball . . . We do not propose to work antagonistic to the League, and expect to do all we can toward bringing improvements in the playing rules. Our influence will also extend to players unjustly treated by clubs . . . In these cases we shall ask for satisfactory treatment, and that being refused, we shall be obliged to resort to extreme measures.[34]

But from the start, the BPBP had wider horizons that involved replacing, not just reforming, the baseball system. Owners' opposition to players' basic rights radicalized them further. After playing for the same salary for three years, Keefe resented the reserve clause that held him captive to the Giants and limited him to the small raise they offered him for the 1888 season: "It is not right to compel me to stay in New York and play ball for the money I get from the New York Club, when I have been offered one and one-half times more salary to pitch in another League city."[35] He held out for a month but went back to work on May 1. Despite the late start, he had perhaps his greatest season, leading the league in wins (35), ERA (1.74), and strikeouts (335), and capping 6 straight seasons of winning at least 32 games. Keefe led the Giants to its first "World Series" victory (and the Dauvray Cup), winning 4 games in the championship series. That year Keefe also won 19 consecutive games, a single-season record tied twenty-four years later by Hall of Famer Rube Marquard but never broken.

While playing for the Giants that season, Keefe designed the team's uniforms—his first foray into what turned into the sporting goods firm Keefe & Becannon the following year. Through his company, Keefe achieved his quest to become a "master" in his work by owning his own business where he could apply his skills. When Keefe held out again for a raise for the 1889 season, he observed,

> I have played good ball for the New York Club, the organization has made money, and I do not think that my demands are unjust . . . If my terms are not agreed to I will attend to my sporting goods business and give up the diamond until matters are arranged to my satisfaction.[36]

Keefe had a further buffer provided by his Cambridge real estate investments. Two weeks into the season, the Giants relented and Keefe got his raise.

When team owners imposed salary caps under the Brush Classification Plan, Keefe insisted,

> we are not going to sit idly by and allow the league to deal . . . unfairly by us . . . We won't assemble until next spring, but when our Houses of Parliament do assemble, let them tremble . . . Spalding and . . . the moneyed people may regret their step.[37]

He further protested, "This grading of players is all nonsense."[38] Keefe also challenged the owners' constant rule changes. He believed that as master craftsmen of their trade, ballplayers should determine the work process.

Despite the season's contentious BPBP distractions, Keefe still won twenty-eight games in 1889 and helped lead the Giants to their second straight "World Series." In September, Spalding refused to meet with the BPBP to discuss their differences. For Keefe, that was the final straw. It was, he claimed, the "crowning point to the arrogant despotism of these dictators, and the players will revolt against the contemptuous disregard for their rights as men and laborers."[39]

After the BPBP started the PL in 1889, Keefe bought stock in the new league and Keefe's sporting goods business became the PL's equipment supplier. He even got one of Spalding's top salesmen to jump to his new firm.

With jumping players (from the NL and AA) now having a stake in their own league and teams, a worker-owned cooperative seemed like a logical organizing structure. Cooperatives sold shares to their workers in exchange for a fixed dividend, a share of the profits, and a voice in management decisions. Cooperative members expected to set the price of their own labor and to receive the full value for their talent—an idea espoused by the KOL and socialists.

But the players lacked the money to fully own their teams so they had to rely on outside investors to provide some of the funding. Players comprised half of the PL's board of directors, but the outside investors had considerable influence and their ultimate goal was profit, not a player-run democracy. The investors of the more profitable teams were unwilling to share their profits with less-profitable teams, creating an unlevel playing field. This tension ultimately doomed the PL's cooperative model.

While Ward became the public voice of the PL and was properly credited for its initial success, Keefe played a much larger role in maintaining player solidarity and communications. He was a league officer and club representative and headed the grounds committee for constructing new ballparks. He also coordinated public relations with the baseball writers. "We expect to have obstacles thrown our way, but we are bound to win in the end. The League will no doubt flood us with injunctions, and there may be plenty of civil suits for damages, but we will be fully prepared for all of this."[40]

The suits against Keefe, Ward, and other players failed. When the NL decided to schedule its games directly opposite PL games, Keefe was confident: "I feel so strongly about the success of our cause that I would be eager to change the schedule to their dates if they make a single change. Why, bless you, we are not the weak side. We are the winners, we are the people."[41]

While the PL lured most of the NL players and while the PL consistently outdrew the NL at the turnstiles, problems emerged as the 1890 season unfolded. The Keefe & Becannon Company supplied the PL's baseballs but the balls were too lively, increasing errors and running up scores, which began turning fans away. Keefe had a sore arm and a mediocre season, and he began clashing with his team's financial patron, Edward Talcott. As the PL teams began slipping at the gate, their capitalist backers started to panic while Spalding worked to seduce them away. Keefe was indignant.

> It doesn't pay to fool with a buzz saw and the capitalists in this city ought to know this. The NL is very shrewd. The various club presidents sit back in the

> chairs and certain PL backers run all over the country to see them about a compromise. Why, the PL had the old organization "killed" three weeks ago. Now everything has changed.[42]

The collapse of the PL substantially weakened the BPBP. Keefe's sporting goods business encountered big debts and went bankrupt, and he was forced to sell it to Spalding. The PL and NL New York teams consolidated, and a much poorer Keefe was back with the Giants. There he faced repercussions for his strident unionism from the team's new owners, Edward Talcott and Spalding's brother Walter: a big salary reduction, limited playing time, staged failures on the field, and ultimately his release during the 1891 season.

Keefe ended his playing days with the Philadelphia Phillies. He finished his career with 342 wins (10th all time), a 2.62 ERA, and 2562 strikeouts. He was the first pitcher to achieve three 300-plus strikeout seasons, and he won games in 47 different major league ballparks—still the record. Keefe resumed his college coaching and umpired in the NL for two years and then another year in the minor leagues until he could no longer stand the abuse. When Harvard University dropped him as a coach for a younger pitcher in 1898, Keefe left baseball for good. He died in Cambridge in 1933. A plaque adorns Tim Keefe Square in that city in front of the house where he lived for the last two decades of his life.

When the first election to the Cooperstown Hall of Fame occurred in 1936, Keefe received only a single vote. His pitching dominance had been largely forgotten, or more likely, he was being punished, along with Ward, for challenging baseball's power structure. Long after his death, Keefe joined Ward in finally being inducted into the hall by the Veteran's Committee in 1964.

In the 1990s, a contractor discovered several boxes of PL documents in a vacant, crumbling, red brick building in upstate New York. Eventually, in 2017, he decided to find out if they were worth anything. Historians and auctioneers determined that the documents, along with the rare signatures of Hall of Famers Ward, Keefe, and Ewing, were quite valuable. They were sold at an auction for $136,000. As a result, these accomplished players achieved posthumous fame for their activist efforts to give ballplayers a stronger voice in organized baseball.

FIDO: MARK BALDWIN

Ward, O'Rourke, and Keefe performed key roles in baseball's organized worker rebellions of the late nineteenth century. The equally charismatic Mark Baldwin blazed his own defiant path. Nicknamed "Fido" because he was repeatedly in his manager's or his team owner's doghouse, Baldwin had a history of conflicts with management over player rights, including his own. He jumped major leagues twice and became a controversial recruiter for his new league each time. He took his rebellion to the nation's broader labor movement, playing a role in one of America's most famous labor struggles.

Born in Pittsburgh in 1863, Baldwin spent his formative years in nearby Homestead, where his father worked in the steel mills. Living in Homestead, the epicenter of America's steel industry, shaped Baldwin's view of labor and owners. Like Ward, Baldwin attended Pennsylvania State University and began pitching for amateur teams in the area in 1880. A talented athlete, when he wasn't pitching he played shortstop. Starting in 1883, he joined the professional ranks with minor league teams in Maryland and Pennsylvania before winning thirty-nine games for the Duluth (Minnesota) Jayhawks of the Northwestern League. Despite this stellar performance, the team owner fined him for allegedly poor defensive play, a ploy used to recoup player wages. In protest, Baldwin purposely played poorly until the fine was reversed.

At Duluth he struck out 18 batters in one game—12 of them in succession—and led the Jayhawks to the pennant. Albert Spalding's NL Chicago White Stockings signed Baldwin at the end of the 1886 season. Controversy arose when two Chicago pitchers were too ill to play in that year's "World Series" and Spalding put Baldwin into the rotation. The White Stockings' opponent, the AA's St. Louis Browns, protested, arguing that Baldwin was ineligible because he had not pitched for Chicago during the regular season. Browns manager Charlie Comiskey and owner Chris Von der Ahe prevailed and Baldwin was blocked from playing. Instead of Baldwin, the White Stockings put a shortstop on the mound who lost badly. The Browns captured the championship the next day.

Baldwin pitched for the White Stockings in 1887 and 1888 and quickly became known as the hardest thrower in the major leagues. The *Galveston Daily News* claimed, "No speedier man lives than Baldwin, and his terrific speed has made him a terror to opposing batsmen. He is an untiring worker and a good pitcher."[43] He was also quirky. As described by the *Daily*

Northwestern, Baldwin "goes through six different motions before he delivers the ball. He first passes his hand across his breast, then sizes up the ball, puts his right hand on the back of his head, looks at the ball again, closes his left eye and finally shoots the ball over the plate like lightning."[44]

Baldwin and the other White Stockings joined Spalding's World Baseball Tour after the 1888 season. When the tour ended, White Stockings captain Cap Anson released Baldwin and three other White Stockings, claiming he would "rather take eighth place with a team of gentlemen than first with a gang of roughs."[45] Baldwin was a free spirit, but Anson's real complaint was Baldwin's demand for a higher salary.

According to historian Brian McKenna, Baldwin thereafter wanted nothing more than to beat his former team. After his release, he was suspicious when no NL team picked him up. The *Pittsburgh Post* accused the NL clubs of collusion against Baldwin. Two weeks into the 1889 season, however, Baldwin was signed by the Columbus Colts in the rival AA. The team did poorly, but Baldwin led the league in games, innings, and strikeouts while winning 27 games. He also set an AA single-game record of 13 strikeouts. His catcher, the veteran Jack O'Connor, called him the "fastest pitcher I ever caught" and even faster than Cy Young, comparing how much his hands hurt after catching both pitchers' fastballs. Still sensitive to his and his fellow ballplayers' mistreatment by the NL, Baldwin claimed, "I like pitching in the Association much better than in the League. The salaries and treatment given the players are better, and there is more genuine fun and good fellowship among the players."[46]

After the 1889 season, Baldwin met with the BPBP and became the key recruiter for the Chicago team in the new PL. Having a change of heart, Cap Anson tried to get Baldwin to shun the PL and sign again with the Chicago White Stockings or some other NL team. Baldwin responded,

> I don't see where I will get the best of it. You had me once and you sold me. I have been doing so well this last season that you think my value . . . has increased. But suppose I go with you next season. If I don't happen to suit you, you and Spalding will dump me on a week's notice and I'll be without a job.[47]

Baldwin became an emissary for Ward on a recruiting mission to St. Louis, where he successfully signed Joe Quinn and Yank Robinson for the PL's Chicago Pirates and also lured recent Triple Crown winner Tip O'Neill. As labor historian Zachary Brodt has observed, it was "clear that Baldwin was a persuasive member of the BPBP who had his finger on the pulse of the labor issues of the day, much to the ire of National League owners."[48] Baldwin's old nemesis, Charlie Comiskey, and his Browns teammate Silver King also jumped to the Pirates. Meanwhile, during the 1890 season Baldwin led the PL in wins (33), strikeouts (206), and complete games (56).

The PL survived for only one season, after which the NL and AA agreed that the jumping players would revert back to their 1889 clubs for the 1891 season. Thus Baldwin would have returned to the AA's Columbus club, which offered him a contract. Instead, Baldwin signed with the NL team in his hometown of Pittsburgh. The Pittsburgh club, previously called the Alleghenys, soon became known as the Pirates. Rather than being a nautical reference for a team located far from the sea, the new name instead described the pirate-like raids on other teams the club initiated in 1891. St. Louis Browns owner Chris Von der Ahe believed that Baldwin was the chief recruiter for the Pirates and sought the pitcher's arrest on conspiracy charges. The battle would drag out for more than seven years. As Baldwin biographer Brian McKenna observed, "Von der Ahe's quixotic attack on Baldwin would be the magnate's downfall."[49]

In March 1891, claiming authority under Missouri law, Von der Ahe had Baldwin arrested at the Laclede Hotel's pool hall in St. Louis for bribery and for undermining pitcher Silver King's contract with the Browns. After Baldwin spent a night in jail, the charges were dropped, but when Baldwin went to leave, he was arrested again on new charges. In *The Beer & Whiskey League*, David Nemec writes that "Von der Ahe then pulled strings to have the case delayed so that Baldwin would be detained indefinitely in St. Louis and would be unable to continue his poaching for the League."[50] But when those charges were also dropped, Baldwin—according to baseball historians Harold Seymour and Dorothy Mills—"did not like being thrown into a jail infested with cockroaches and bedbugs, and he retaliated against Von der Ahe's harassment with a suit [in a Philadelphia court] for $20,000, charging false arrest and malicious prosecution." In response to NL president Nick Young's request that he drop the case, Baldwin claimed, "Now why should I? What has the National League to do with my personal affairs? The imprisonment was unjust. I suffered and I mean to go on with the suit. Why even after I was discharged . . . Chris had me run in again."[51]

Baldwin's 1891 season for Pittsburgh was only moderately successful. Although at one point he won 11 straight games, including both ends of a doubleheader, his season win-loss record was 21-28. Despite Baldwin's having a sore shoulder, Pittsburgh manager Ned Hanlon fined him $50 for skipping a game. When Baldwin demanded his release, Hanlon refused, instead putting him in the lineup more often.

Baldwin won twenty-six games the following season although his relationship with the Pittsburgh management and even some fans and the hometown press remained contentious. Baldwin resented the control owners had over him and other players. Having driven out the competing PL and in the prior off-season also the AA, the NL slashed salaries and re-imposed the reserve clause. But Baldwin would have even bigger troubles off the field.

In 1892, Andrew Carnegie's steel plant in Homestead was making increasing profits. Even so, workers were forced to endure unsafe plant conditions and a 22 percent pay cut. Carnegie and Henry Clay Frick, the virulently anti-union manager of the Homestead factory, sought not only to cut costs but to break the union, the Amalgamated Iron and Steel Workers. The company refused to bargain with the union and locked the workers out of the factory. Not only did the Homestead workers go on strike, but workers at Carnegie's other steel plants in Pittsburgh, Duquesne, Union Mills, and Beaver Falls struck in sympathy the same day. The workers picketed outside the plant to gain publicity and to stop Frick from hiring strikebreakers.

Frick hired 300 armed Pinkerton agents to brutally break the Homestead strike. Deputized by the Allegheny County sheriff, the hired guns were brought in on barges. When they landed, gunfire broke out and a 12-hour battle ensued, killing 9 workers and 3 guards. When the Pinkertons finally withdrew, 8,000 state militia soldiers arrived, clearly there to back the owners. The strikebreakers manned the factories, and martial law was declared in Homestead.

The public and some newspapers initially sided with the union. But a few weeks after the strike began, on July 23, 1892, anarchist Alexander Berkman barged into Frick's office and tried to assassinate him. Frick survived the attack, but the publicity undermined the public's support for the strike even though Berkman, who lived in Massachusetts, was not part of the union or the strike. The strike failed. Carnegie won, but the bloody results would provoke future worker agitation.

The strike leaders were charged with conspiracy, riot, and murder. Another 160 workers were also arrested. One of them was ballplayer Mark Baldwin, who was charged with aggravated riot. It isn't surprising that he was on the scene. Growing up in Pittsburgh and Homestead, Baldwin was exposed to the plight of workers and the brutality of the steel barons all his life. As historian Zachary Brodt observed, "These conditions led to a tight-knit community of workers' families within the small town [of Homestead]" to which Baldwin continued to return during the off-season.

> Baldwin's sense of community pride and labor solidarity were lifelong influences. As an employee during a period of heightened labor sensitivities, he knew the growing importance of trade unions to protect workers who were being exploited by those profiting from their efforts.[52]

Baldwin admitted he was at the Carnegie plant during the massacre but strictly as a spectator. He insisted that he left for his Homestead home without aiding or abetting the strikers or engaging in violence. According to Brodt, it's likely true that "Baldwin wasn't present during the deadliest portion of the struggle; however, his presence on the scene that day is still startling considering that he was to pitch in a game that very afternoon."[53] Right after the battle, the Brooklyn club—led by BPBP president John Montgomery Ward—came to town for a series against the Pirates. Ward and his teammates visited Homestead to demonstrate their solidarity with the striking workers. With Homestead citizens wary of any new arrivals after the clash with the Pinkertons, the players needed an escort, and Baldwin volunteered. According to the *Pittsburg Dispatch*, Baldwin "knows every man, woman, and child in the borough" and thus his endorsement carried weight. Another paper, the *Commercial Gazette*, reported that Baldwin "has resided at Homestead since childhood and always bore a reputation for being peaceful and law-abiding."[54]

Nevertheless Baldwin (identified as "Base Ball Pitcher") appeared on two witness lists during the coroner's inquest into the Homestead deaths. Baldwin avoided testifying at the inquest since he was on the road, playing ballgames. In the next few weeks, however, rumors implicated Baldwin in the Homestead events. Even though he pitched more games than anyone else on the Pirates staff, the club released him late in the season. On September 1, Baldwin responded to his arrest warrant. He faced preliminary charges of inciting and participating in the Homestead riot and was released on bail. Remarkably, the charges against Baldwin, and against all the workers, were filed not by the local prosecutor but rather by Carnegie company lawyers who had witnesses claiming that they "saw Baldwin in the mill yard participating in the conflict." The *Pittsburg Dispatch* cited rumors that Baldwin "furnished his fellow citizens with two Winchester rifles on the memorable morning of the battle."[55]

With his arrest behind him, Baldwin's suspension was rescinded and he rejoined the Pirates for a road trip to Cleveland. Baldwin was arrested again under more formal charges after pitching on September 23, but in the end he was never brought to trial. Brodt claims that Baldwin was likely more active during the Homestead Strike than merely a spectator.

> Given his reputation for being ill-tempered and his close ties to the community, it is easy to imagine him participating in the riot in some way as the Pinkertons threatened his friends and family. His role in bringing players into baseball's first trade union also indicates that Baldwin was sensitive to labor issues and an affront to striking workers in his hometown was sure to ignite his short fuse.[56]

The Pirates cut Baldwin early in the 1893 season. According to the *Massillon Independent*, "Baldwin's abilities are not disputed. His only failing is his ugly temper."[57] Such accusations would echo for another century against players who spoke out about their treatment or the nation's social conditions. Baldwin signed instead with the New York Giants and won sixteen games, but was again released at the end of the season, his major-league career over.

In 1894 Baldwin pitched for minor league teams in Allentown and Pottsville, winning nineteen games in the Pennsylvania State League, and also played briefly in the Eastern League. He signed an 1895 contract with the Philadelphia Phillies but never played and then bounced around the Eastern League and New York League. He organized a cooperative semipro club in Auburn, New York, in 1896, which was briefly successful.

Meanwhile, failing in his repeated attempts to get Browns owner Von der Ahe to appear in court, Baldwin refiled his suit in Pittsburgh. When Von der Ahe appeared in that city in March 1894, a local sheriff arrested him at the Pittsburgh ballpark and took him to jail. As a favor to a fellow owner, new Pirates president William Nimick posted a $1,000 bond to get Von der Ahe released. At trial, Baldwin reduced his suit from $20,000 to $10,000 but instead won a judgment for only $2,500. Still Von der Ahe wouldn't pay, and in February 1896 he was granted a new trial when he claimed that jury tampering tainted the original proceeding. On re-trial in January 1897, Von der Ahe lost again, this time owing Baldwin $2,525. The Browns owner's new appeal failed before the Pennsylvania Supreme Court in January 1898.

A month later, Von der Ahe still hadn't paid Baldwin and also hadn't repaid the $1,000 bond, but the judgments against Von der Ahe couldn't be enforced as long as he was outside the State of Pennsylvania. Thus, along with Baldwin's attorneys, Nimick (now no longer the Pirates president) obtained a warrant for Von der Ahe's arrest and hired private detective Nicholas Bendel to execute it in Missouri, where the Browns owner lived. A fraudulent telegram tricked Von der Ahe into a lunch meeting at the St. Nicholas Hotel in St. Louis. When he appeared, Bendel grabbed him, and kidnapped him back to Pittsburgh. Facing imprisonment, in September 1898 the St. Louis owner finally paid Baldwin $3,000 along with $1,200 in court costs.

By then Von der Ahe was in financial ruins and his team was in shambles. The owner had been a real showman. Earlier in the decade, he had built an amusement park around his ball field with a beer garden, a water flume ride, an artificial lake, and a horse track in the outfield. His facility became known as Coney Island West. His outfielders didn't appreciate the racetrack nor did the AA, which prohibited gambling. His victory fireworks featured flying shrapnel from tin mortars that seriously injured several spectators. According to historian Tobias Seamon, Von der Ahe was a "whirlwind of Falstaffian energies." Some fans and some in the press appreciated Von der Ahe. *Sporting Life* defended him against his accusers, lamenting the "wrongs afflicted upon a very worthy man, who has advertised St. Louis more than any citizen of that great city."[58] His game tickets were affordable for workers and he established the first Ladies Days at the ballpark.

But many people resented Von der Ahe, who went by the arrogant title "Der Boss President" and had an imposing statue of himself placed outside his ballpark. He was inclined toward booze-filled tantrums. Within a few years, he was sued by his son in a property dispute, sued by his wife for alimony, sued over a Cincinnati ballpark, and sued for breaking Missouri's blue laws by having his team play games on Sundays. In 1895 he assaulted and shot a Black stranger in the street and to deflect blame he then lied about Black neighbors stealing liquor deliveries (when actually he was sending booze to his mistresses and filing false theft reports). He was charged with assault with the intent to kill, but the charges were dropped on a technicality. In 1898, Von der Ahe's second wife divorced him and he was sued again for a fire at his ballpark, which some believed was set by one of his many enemies. This sent him shrieking into the streets and into a temporary nervous breakdown. His players routinely disliked him, and he resorted to selling off his best talent. He was driven from baseball for good in 1899, and his Browns became the St. Louis Cardinals in 1900. Von der Ahe was greedy like other baseball owners but he was also a victim of his own self-righteousness.

Baldwin was an excellent player but not Hall of Famer caliber. A real workhorse, he pitched 2,802 innings in 346 games over his seven-year pro career, winning 154 games and losing 165 with 1349 strikeouts. With his major league career ended, Baldwin pursued his dream of becoming a doctor, enrolling in the University of Pennsylvania's medical school in 1896. In early 1897, he helped coach the university's baseball team and pitched for Pittsburgh's Carnegie Athletic Club during the summer. After two years at the University of Pennsylvania he transferred to Bellevue Medical College in New York City to study dermatology and then to Roosevelt Hospital to learn surgery. In the fall of 1898 he moved to Baltimore Medical College, where he played baseball and football and completed his medical degree in 1899. Baldwin established a medical practice in Homestead but also assisted a New York City coroner, practiced briefly in Columbus, studied advanced surgical techniques at the Mayo Clinic in Minnesota in 1905, and was on the Johns Hopkins University Medical School faculty in 1914. Ballplayers were among his surgical patients. He died in Pittsburgh in 1929.

Baldwin was politically active for worker's rights—for himself, for his fellow players, and for working people in the broader society. As Jeff Kittel has observed,

> in the early 1890s a lot of forces [were] at work that were changing the business of baseball. Baldwin didn't create these forces. He represented the conflict that

existed between the players and the owners, and between the owners of the NL clubs and the AA clubs. Mark Baldwin was just a player who got caught up in all of this.[59]

Baldwin was much more than that.

2

Challenging Baseball's Corporate Monopoly

During World War II, union membership mushroomed to more than 10 million workers—one-third of the nonfarm labor force. But the nation's full-scale war mobilization meant that industry was producing fewer consumer products and almost no new housing. The major car companies built tanks, not cars. Gasoline was rationed, making driving more expensive. During the war's last year, the weekly wages of workers decreased by 10 percent. Soon after the war ended, rent and consumer prices increased. In 1946, workers and their unions responded with an unprecedented wave of strikes to demand their fair share of the nation's growing prosperity.

The United States ended the war in better economic condition than any other nation. It became even more affluent in the postwar years. Gross domestic product jumped from $102 billion in 1940 to $300 billion in 1950. The nation saw a boom in federally funded highway construction and federally subsidized homebuilding, which together promoted a dramatic exodus of Americans out of the cities and into the suburbs. More families owned their own homes and purchased new cars, refrigerators, lawnmowers, and other consumer goods. Thanks to federal government aid, more Americans could afford to send their children to college. Economist John Kenneth Galbraith described America as an "affluent society."

But not all Americans experienced this prosperity equally, particularly racial minorities and women, who still found themselves constrained by entrenched racism and sexism. Black Americans were shut out of most of the suburbs because of systematic racial discrimination by banks, landlords, and homebuilders. Women who had worked in factories to support the war effort lost their jobs and were encouraged instead to be housewives and mothers. Even when they did work, they were segregated into "women's jobs" and paid much less than men doing comparable work. Even many white males, particularly working-class men, felt shortchanged, watching their companies and executives get rich while their wages lagged behind.

POSTWAR LABOR CHALLENGES

Corporations made record profits in the postwar boom. Big business worried that the growing labor movement would get Congress to expand the New Deal, which meant higher taxes on corporations and the rich; bigger social programs like health care and Social Security; and higher wages and stricter rules on unsafe workplace conditions. In 1946, Republicans won a majority in Congress for the first time since 1930. They pushed back against President Harry Truman's Fair Deal ideas. A top priority was to weaken the National Labor Relations Act, which Congress passed in 1935 to give workers the right to unionize. In 1947, business lobby groups like the Chamber of Commerce and the National Association of Manufacturers persuaded the Republican Congress to pass the anti-union Taft-Hartley Act over Truman's veto. Truman described it as a "clear threat to the successful working of our democratic society."[1] Labor leaders denounced it as a "slave-labor bill." It restricted workers' right to strike, picket, and boycott, and it permitted states to enact "right-to-work" laws that blocked unions or allowed workers to enjoy the benefits of unionized workplaces without paying dues. As part of an expanding Red Scare, it also required union officers to deny under oath any affiliation with communist or left-wing organizations.

Baseball commissioner Kenesaw Mountain Landis died in November 1944, signaling a new era. As in the broader society, baseball would witness its own battles over workers' rights and civil rights. Contrary to common belief, MLB attendance didn't suffer greatly during the war. Although attendance decreased by about 1 million during the 1942 and 1943 seasons, by 1944 attendance equaled the record-setting numbers achieved in 1941. In the years immediately after the war, baseball teams, like other corporations, were highly profitable. Despite this, teams cut ballplayer salaries. Reflecting the labor turmoil elsewhere in America, some baseball rebels resisted, seeking not only more pay but also greater control over their own career.

OUTLAW: JORGE PASQUEL

Jorge Pasquel, a Mexican millionaire, was instrumental in freeing African American ballplayers from baseball segregation and liberating all professional ballplayers from the indentured servitude of MLB's reserve clause. He accomplished this through his ownership of the Mexican League and by using his political savvy to challenge MLB's twin evils of racism and worker exploitation.

Pasquel was born in 1907 in Veracruz, Mexico, into an affluent family. He and his four brothers took over their father's thriving cigar factory, cornering the Mexican market and launching an economic empire. Pasquel married the daughter of a former Mexican president, giving the Pasquels political ties and federal patronage that helped them control Mexican customs and the national lottery as well as their multiple banks, ranches, and shipping, publishing, automobile, and real estate businesses.

By the late 1930s, despite his wealth and luxurious lifestyle, Pasquel favored what he called an "intelligent socialism," inspired by the Mexican Revolution, which lasted from 1910 to 1920 and which ended the country's dictatorship, established a constitutional republic, and redistributed land to peasant farmers. Pasquel found other uses for his riches. Like many Mexicans, Pasquel was a rabid baseball fan. The professional Mexican League had existed since 1925, but he felt it could do much better. In 1940 he bought the Veracruz Blues team and held a minority ownership in the Mexico City Reds and a majority ownership in Mexico City's Delta Park. The other team owners wanted access to that stadium (the country's best), which gave Pasquel virtual control of the Mexican League even though he didn't become its official president until 1946.

Pasquel decided the key to the league's success was luring top-notch players to improve the quality of play. The league already had players from Cuba and other Caribbean nations, but American athletes were an untapped resource. Initially the most inviting targets were the Negro Leagues. Pasquel understood their precarious nature. Negro League teams couldn't pay very good wages, and their stars regularly jumped from team to team for better paychecks. In 1938, he snagged Satchel Paige, the Negro League's most famous player, whom he paid $2,000 per month, much more than the highest-paid Negro League player and more than most major leaguers were earning.

Pasquel launched a full-scale campaign to sign other Negro Leaguers. He had spent time in the United States, where he experienced anti-Mexican discrimination, and he empathized with Black Americans. By 1940 he had lured sixty-three Black players to Mexico. That year, Negro Leaguers Cool Papa Bell, Leon Day, Ray Dandridge, Martin Dihigo, Josh Gibson, and Willie Wells brought a Mexican League championship to Pasquel's Veracruz Blues. He made sure that other Negro League stars, like Willard Brown and Ted "Double Duty" Radcliffe, were spread around to other teams to make the Mexican League competitive and attract fans in the different cities.

Pasquel failed to lure Jackie Robinson, but he did recruit Negro League catcher Roy Campanella, who played in Mexico in 1942 and 1943 and later became a Hall of Fame catcher for the Brooklyn Dodgers. By 1946, 150 African American ballplayers had played in the Mexican League, 14 of them eventually enshrined in the Cooperstown Hall of Fame. Pasquel persuaded white ballplayers to manage the racially integrated Mexican League teams, including Hall of Famer Rogers Hornsby, despite his having been a member of the Ku Klux Klan.

Negro Leaguers raved about their Mexican experience. Unable to get a raise from the Newark Eagles, Monte Irvin jumped to the Mexican League in 1942, dramatically increasing his salary, along with having a free apartment with maid service. He hit .398 and won the Triple Crown. More important, he experienced equality. "It was the best move I ever made," Irvin reflected years later. "We were heroes . . . No Jim Crow laws . . . We could live anywhere, dine anywhere, go to movies anywhere, sit anywhere. It was wonderful. It was the first time in my life I felt free. I owe that to Jorge Pasquel."[2] Irvin was inducted into both the Mexican and Cooperstown halls of fame.

Negro League star Willie Wells said that he "found freedom and democracy [in Mexico], something I never found in the United States. I was branded a Negro in the States and had to act accordingly . . . Here in Mexico, I am a man."[3] Bill Wright was a Negro League star from 1932 through 1945 but jumped to the Mexican League for the 1940 and 1941 seasons, returned to the Negro League in 1942, played again in Mexico in 1943 and 1944, then spent the 1945 season playing for the Negro League Baltimore Elite Giants. By 1946 he'd had enough of American racism and rejoined the Mexican League, playing through the 1951 season. He stayed in Mexico after retiring, opening a restaurant, Bill Wright's Dugout, in Aguascalientes.

In 1942, two former Negro League ballplayers in the Mexican League, Theolic Smith and Quincy Trouppe, were drafted into the U.S. military. Pasquel got them back by arranging a trade. He used his government contacts to arrange a loan of eighty thousand Mexican workers to the United States in exchange for the two players. This was a little-known part of the U.S. government's Bracero Program, created to bring Mexican workers into the United States to keep American railroads, mines, and farms running at full capacity during the war.

The Negro League team owners resented the loss of their players to Mexico, but they lacked the resources to stop defections. Newark Eagles owner Effa Manley tried, but failed, to block the Wells and Dandridge departures by getting their draft exemptions revoked in 1944. In 1946, Alex Pompez, owner of the Negro National League New York Cubans, got three of his players—Sandy Amoros, Alex Crespo, and Silvio Garcia—to jump back from Mexico to his team. But Pompez wanted more. He approached MLB commissioner Happy Chandler with a proposal to make the Negro National League a separate part of organized baseball, hoping it would protect them from Mexican League raids. Chandler rejected the idea.

The exodus continued even after Jackie Robinson broke the MLB color barrier in 1947. Earl Taborn, a star catcher for the Negro League Kansas City Monarchs (1946–1951), played in the Mexican League from 1951 through 1961. His daughter Rose Maria described the attraction: "They had the chance to be real persons . . . to be considered human beings. I think that made a big difference."[4]

Although some tension arose among Black, white, and Latino players in the Mexican League, overall it was a successful experiment in racial integration. According to historian Cesar Gonzalez, Pasquel showed "Black baseball players that not only could they be treated as equals to whites, but that they could be better. The white players learned that they could share a clubhouse with Black players, and that colorblindness was the best way to win games."[5] Mexican sportswriter Angel Fernandez explained, "The Mexican League served as a bridge until Black players were able to go into the majors in 1947."[6] Yale professor Roberto Gonzalez Echevarria concluded that "Pasquel improved the quality of the Mexican game by developing a truly democratic, multi-ethnic league in which ability and the open market determined a player's worth."[7]

It would take many years before MLB achieved both racial integration and free agency, but the players experiencing it in the Mexican League helped pave the way.

POST–WORLD WAR II BASEBALL

As major leaguers returned from the war, competition for jobs with major league teams increased, leading owners to cut the players' already low wages. Observing that MLB paid "peon salaries," Pasquel announced that he was "ready to compete with organized ball, dollar for dollar and peso for peso, for the best talent"[8] and without the reserve clause.

Pasquel bristled when MLB owners and sportswriters called the Mexican League an "outlaw" organization: "I resent that and may take organized ball into the courts to make them prove that we are not operating fully within the laws of our land—Mexico."[9] But "outlaw" had another meaning for MLB owners: it meant that MLB—which they called "organized baseball"—didn't control the Mexican League. It threatened MLB's monopoly, particularly its ability to control player salaries and conditions. In 1944, Pasquel began attracting Latino major leaguers, luring Cuban-born Chicago Cubs catcher Chico Hernandez. The following year, he persuaded Cubans Roberto Ortiz of the Washington Senators and Tommie de la Cruz of the Cincinnati Reds. Strict wartime measures imposed by the United States convinced players born and raised in Latin America to play in the Mexican League rather than serve in the U.S. Armed Forces or work in U.S. defense plants.

In the 1940s, American businesses dominated the Cuban economy and the U.S. government essentially controlled Cuban politics. It wasn't difficult for MLB commissioner Chandler, anticipating an emerging Mexican threat, to gain control of the Cuban League, where many major leaguers played during the winter to earn extra pay and stay in shape. To deter American outlaw players from fueling Pasquel's raids, Chandler banned U.S. and Cuban players from participating in the Cuban Winter League if they also played in the Mexican League during the summer. This meant that Cubans who played in Mexico wouldn't be allowed to play in their own Cuban League each winter. MLB officials, including Brooklyn Dodgers president Branch Rickey, visited Cuba, Panama, Venezuela, and Puerto Rico—which all had popular winter baseball leagues—to warn them not to allow players who played in the Mexican League to participate in their winter games. Several major leaguers, including Mike Guerra, Gil Torres, Lou Klein, Sal Maglie, Dick Sisler, and Fred Martin, defied the Cuban ban and played there anyway.

In 1946, Pasquel stepped up his campaign. He targeted American stars such as Hank Greenberg, Johnny Pesky, and Joe DiMaggio, who rebuffed his offers. He reportedly offered Bob Feller $500,000 for five years and Ted Williams $360,000 for three but both rejected the deals. Pasquel made a bid for Cardinals star Stan Musial and Yankees infielders George Stirnweiss and Phil Rizzuto. None of them signed, but they did use the offers to get better MLB salaries. Rizzuto came the closest to leaving, ready to take a fat new, untaxed salary, a signing bonus, and a free Cadillac and luxury home until his wife vetoed the deal.

Even so, Pasquel did sign twenty-seven major leaguers and many more minor leaguers. The jumpers included genuine stars such as Sal Maglie, Max Lanier, Vern Stephens, and Mickey Owen as well as Danny Gardella, Lou Klein, George Hausmann, Roy Zimmerman, Adrian Zabala, Luis Olmo, Harry Feldman, Ace Adams, Roberto Estallela, Fred Martin, Roland Gladu, and Jean-Pierre Roy. Most players who signed with the Mexican League at least tripled their salaries, often for multiple years, besides receiving bonuses, free lodging, and other perks. As Maglie observed, "I will make as much the first year [in Mexico], including my bonus, as I would in five years at my present salary with the Giants. Why should players have to work for that cheap wage?"[10]

BACKLASH

Bolstered by the influx of major league and Negro League players, the 1946 Mexican League teams drew 700,000 fans in just the first twenty-four games. But amidst the Mexican League's ongoing raids, MLB fought back. It pressured U.S. sporting goods companies to stop selling equipment to the Mexican League. Commissioner Chandler created a blacklist and banned jumpers from the MLB for five years. It was the start of the Cold War, and Chandler found it useful to justify his decision by drawing on the patriotic rhetoric of the Red Scare era. He called the jumpers "disloyal" and urged American fans to "stand by the flag of Organized Baseball."[11]

Rickey was among many MLB owners who condemned Pasquel's raids, labeling the Mexican League an "outlaw league." In response, Pasquel noted that the major leagues had a long history of raiding competing leagues in the United States going back to the early 1900s. As Pasquel observed, "For many years, while our Mexican League was struggling, major league scouts, and Joe Cambria of the Washington Senators in particular, visited our cities and over our protests, stole our players [despite their] Mexican League contracts."[12]

Senators owner Clark Griffith acted like a corporate robber baron, stealing more Latinos—from Mexico, Cuba, and elsewhere—than any other major league owner, paying peanuts for great players. During Griffith's four decades as the Senators' manager and owner, he hired thirty-five Cuban players. The Chicago Cubs and Cincinnati Reds followed Griffith's lead, but when the Caribbean leagues complained to Commissioner Landis, he did nothing about it. By the mid-1940s, Rickey himself was stealing Negro League players for the Dodgers, beginning with Robinson, without offering the Negro League teams compensation for the athletes he lured away.

Some MLB owners tried to use the courts to deter Pasquel. The Yankees' Larry MacPhail, the Giants' Horace Stoneham, and the Senators' Clark Griffith could get only temporary injunctions against Pasquel and his Mexican scouts. In 1946 a Missouri circuit court judge dismissed Rickey's suit against *St. Louis Star Times* reporter Ray Gillespie for helping his friend, catcher Mickey Owen, jump to Mexico. When NL batting champion Pete Reiser was offered ten times his Dodgers salary, Rickey sued Pasquel and intimidated Reiser into refusing, convincing him "he didn't want to be a man without a country."[13]

Other owners worried about Pasquel's use of U.S. courts to test the legality of MLB's reserve clause and anti-trust exemption. Pasquel claimed MLB was an illegal monopoly. He was represented by a prestigious New York law firm, which handled other Mexican-American governmental affairs, suggesting the implied backing of the Mexican government. MLB was fortunate that no direct court test of the legality of its player contracts ever materialized.

Pasquel also pursued the public relations game. In May 1946, he brought Babe Ruth to Mexico and hosted him lavishly and visibly. He was exploiting the snub MLB had given Ruth, who had aspired to manage a major league team. It was rumored that the Babe would become a Mexican League manager or even president of the league despite his questionable health. Ruth gave speeches endorsing the Mexican League: "I think the Pasquels are doing a fine thing for baseball and for their country. How far they will be able to go is hard to say, but they have a good start."[14] Elsewhere, Ruth claimed MLB was a monopoly and that Pasquel's lawsuits would "expose organized ball's contracts and their controversial reserve clause in the courts."[15] Ruth's visit was a sensation, promoting Mexican pride at American expense. "Nobody really likes Jorge," as one Mexican observed, "but he's a national hero."[16] Pasquel even tried to lure Commissioner Happy Chandler, offering him the Mexican League commissionership and a huge raise of $50,000 a year.

Soon the Mexican baseball war was headline news. Pasquel tried to persuade the American press of the rightness of his cause, but reporters and editorial writers generally sided with the American owners. They labeled the defectors "Mexican jumping beans." The *Sporting News* consistently used the term "outlaw" to describe the Mexican League and ran a cover showing a stereotypical bandido with a six-shooter sticking up an honest-looking American in a business suit. The victim was labeled "Organized Baseball." A United Press International report indicated that: "Pancho Villa's raids over the border looked like pale stuff compared to the peso-happy caballero [Pasquel] promoting big-time baseball in Mexico and using bona fide Brooklyn Dodgers for bait."[17] In *The Mexican Jumping Beans*, John Phillips observed, "Mexico and the U.S. were allies during World War II. When it ended, the baseball hierarchies of the two countries went to war."[18]

Militaristic rhetoric permeated the 1946 season: wars, battles, besieged owners, and exploited American workers were hot topics. The U.S., Mexican, and Cuban governments were even drawn in. Mexican officials wanted their nation treated fairly. The U.S. State Department wanted to at least convey that appearance. Concerned that the baseball dispute was harming U.S.–Mexican relations, American officials urged MLB to settle its differences. One said, "Baseball is making it tough on us. We try to build up goodwill and this sort of thing tears it down." Mexican diplomats in Washington and at the United Nations claimed the big leagues had a chance to spread ideals: "We exchange students, professors, artists, workers . . . so why not ballplayers?"[19] Defending American baseball, Commissioner Chandler posed a revealing analogy: "Suppose the Mexican government did not recognize American oil concessions . . . Don't you suppose [the State Department] would put up a protest?"[20]

It was precisely this imperial attitude that also riled Cuban officials after Chandler imposed his Cuban League ban. It threatened to create an international incident, with familiar cries of "Yanqui imperialism." Luis Rodriguez,

Cuba's national director of sports, described MLB as a "commercial, imperialistic monopoly" and threatened a complaint with the U.S. State Department. A Havana broadcaster observed, "America wants to ration our baseball, and we will not submit."[21] This was more than a decade before Fidel Castro's revolution overthrew the Cuban dictator Fulgencio Batista.

In raiding MLB rosters, Pasquel was motivated by the prospect of big profits and a sincere desire to elevate Mexican baseball. A proud Mexican patriot, Pasquel was also driven by nationalism. He resented how MLB acted like the world's governing body for the sport when fine baseball was being played in Mexico and elsewhere. By labeling itself "organized baseball," MLB implied that everything else was chaotic and inferior. And if there were any outlaws, Pasquel claimed, they were MLB clubs, attempting to monopolize the game. How could the Americans hold a World Series without playing against foreign leagues and teams? The U.S. champion should have to play the Mexican League champion to win the crown.

But the dispute cut deeper. Like all Mexican children, Pasquel learned in school how in the Mexican-American War (or what the Mexicans call the War of U.S. Intervention, 1846–1848), the United States stole the richest half of Mexico. Then in 1914, in one of many other U.S. invasions of Mexico, the U.S. Navy bombarded and seized Veracruz, the hometown of Pasquel and his cousin Miguel Aleman. Experiencing the attack first hand, the boys cowered in a cellar to protect themselves. The bombing was retaliation for the Mexican government's decision to nationalize its oil industry to protect it from foreign corporations. Hundreds of Pasquel's fellow Mexicans were killed in the attack.

In late 1941 when Pasquel tried to enter the United States, he discovered he had been blacklisted by Washington. He was treated as a Mexican spy because his oil company had been doing business with Nazi Germany and thus he was viewed as trading with the enemy. Of course, many U.S. corporations, such as Ford and General Motors, were also conducting business in Germany and even supporting the Hitler regime before the U.S. entry into the war. Actually, Mexican oil companies were forced to deal with countries other than the United States, including Germany, because U.S. corporations were boycotting Mexican oil in retaliation for Mexican president Lazaro Cardenas nationalizing the oil industry in 1938. Pasquel was removed from the U.S. blacklist only after the intervention of the Mexican Embassy and his cousin Miguel Aleman, Mexico's minister of the interior.

Aleman had presidential aspirations, and after the war he launched his campaign. He relied on two things: Mexicans resented U.S. economic and military interventions, and they loved baseball. After his mistreatment by American political and business elites, Pasquel was determined to use baseball to help his cousin's election prospects. Luring U.S. players to the Mexican League was regarded as a national triumph. Aleman and Pasquel were not so much anti-American as pro-Mexican, and Pasquel's baseball raids helped fan the flames of Mexican nationalism. As Tom Gorman, one of Pasquel's pitchers put it, Pasquel was like "a bullfighter, a little guy taking on a huge beast—the Colossus of the North."[22] In the end, Aleman won the presidency and credited Pasquel's baseball initiatives for the victory.

AFTERMATH

During the 1946 and 1947 seasons, about one-fifth of the Mexican League's players had previously played in MLB or the high minors. But Pasquel couldn't sustain his efforts. High-profile players such as Vern Stephens and Mickey Owen broke their Mexican contracts and returned to the United States despite lawsuits against them. Pasquel's money was running out. Some white U.S. players (in contrast to Negro Leaguers) didn't like the playing conditions or the foreign food and accommodations. Max Lanier remained but was ineffective. Sal Maglie was a twenty-game winner two years in a row, but by 1948 the Mexican League was losing money and teams, and Maglie saw little future in Mexican ball.

In the end, Pasquel simply lacked the resources to effectively compete with MLB for the best players. Although Pasquel lost the battle, he did gain prestige for Mexican baseball and his nation, and he helped bolster the Mexican League in the long run. In 1954, some American politicians scapegoated Mexicans for competing for jobs with U.S. veterans returning from the Korean War. In response, the United States launched Operation Wetback, which rounded up 1 million Mexicans—a third of whom were U.S. citizens—and deported them to Mexico. Some claim that this was, at least in part, retaliation for Pasquel's Mexican baseball invasion.

By 1955, shortly after Pasquel died in a plane crash, the Mexican League had been reconstituted, and it was then formally added to organized baseball, first as a MLB Double-A league and then to Triple-A—a status it enjoys today. Pasquel was elected to the Mexican Baseball Hall of Fame in 1971.

Besides Pasquel's contribution to Mexican baseball, his campaign helped draw attention to MLB's horribly low salaries and exploitative reserve clause. Pasquel's brother Alfonso claimed, "If major leaguers had any guts, they'd make sure my brother Jorge was elected to Cooperstown for helping them gain their freedom."[23] That hasn't happened, but *Newark Star-Ledger* sportswriter Jerry Izenberg agreed, observing, "Major league players should erect a shrine to Jorge Pasquel. He set the stage for [Danny] Gardella's suit against the reserve clause. The end of the reserve clause flowed from Gardella's suit. Pasquel had a tremendous effect on baseball."[24] MLB owners were so worried they'd be targets of more court cases, they even began questioning whether Chandler's blacklist and five-year ban was excessive. Gardella's challenge would come soon, but as the owners feared, other lawsuits were already in the works.

SERVICEMAN IN HOLLYWOOD: TONY LUPIEN

The first consequential stirrings of professional ballplayer activism began right after World War II. While progress was slow and periodically interrupted, it created momentum for the dramatic changes in labor rights that emerged in the 1970s in the form of free agency. Unheralded in their own time, ballplayers Tony Lupien and Al Niemiec set this process in motion.

Ulysses "Tony" Lupien was born in 1917 in Massachusetts and grew up in Connecticut. He attended Harvard University, and while studying, he also played ball with the J. F. McElwain team, one of many top-notch company clubs at the time. Despite tough competition from college players and former minor leaguers, Lupien excelled. He further blossomed on the Harvard team, where he led the Ivy League in hitting in both 1938 and 1939, batting .442 in his senior year.

After Harvard, Lupien signed with the Boston Red Sox, which sent him to its Scranton, Pennsylvania, affiliate in the Eastern League for the remainder of the 1939 season. Hitting .319, he was selected as an All-Star first baseman. When the Scranton ballpark tried, as a promotion, to run an all-Italian infield for a game, Lupien was asked whether he was Italian. He was French-Canadian so he said no but then joked, "But I do eat spaghetti. Hey, just call me Tony."[25] The name stuck.

After spending most of the 1940 season with the Little Rock minor league team, Lupien earned a call-up to the Red Sox. In 10 games, he got 9 hits in 19 at-bats for a .474 average. The Red Sox returned him to the minors in 1941, where he hit .289 for Louisville. In 1942, he became the Red Sox's regular first baseman after slugger Jimmie Foxx was sold to the Cubs. Batting alongside Ted Williams and Bobby Doerr, Lupien hit .281 that season. He dipped to .255 for the 1943 season on a seventh-place Boston team depleted by military service.

The Red Sox sold Lupien to the Phillies for the 1944 season. He played in all but one of that last-place team's games that year, hitting .283 and ranking second in the NL in stolen bases. Despite supporting a wife and two small daughters, the twenty-eight-year-old Lupien was drafted into the Navy before the 1945 season. He served at Sampson Naval Base in upstate New York for most of the season, rejoining the Phillies for its last fifteen games, hitting .315.

Before spring training began in early 1945, Lupien was looking forward to resuming his career when the Phillies bought slugging first baseman Frank McCormick from the Reds. Phillies general manager Herb Pennock told Lupien he had been sold to the minor league Hollywood Stars of the Pacific Coast League (PCL). Lupien was shocked to both lose his job and be demoted to the minors, and he knew it violated the federal G.I. Bill of Rights, officially known as the Servicemen's Readjustment Act, which Congress had passed in 1944 to provide benefits to World War II veterans. Confronting Pennock, Lupien said, "Don't you know that a returned serviceman is allowed at least a year's grace at getting his old job back?"[26] Pennock claimed that it didn't apply to baseball, to which Lupien responded, "Who the hell are you to think that you're above the federal government?"[27]

Even MLB's own rules were being violated since they mandated that servicemen had at least thirty days in spring training before any decision was made about their future. Lupien had spent less than a month with the Phillies after his military service, hitting over .300, and wasn't even invited to spring training. Lupien wrote to Commissioner Chandler, laying out his claims, but the letter was returned unopened.

Getting no satisfaction, Lupien had to decide whether to file a lawsuit. While his attorney and his local Selective Service board assured him he had a claim under the G.I. Bill, Lupien was warned that a suit would be expensive and drag on for years and that teams might blacklist him from organized baseball in retaliation. Lupien instead chose to litigate his grievance through the media, for which he received some support. In February 1946, *Boston*

Record columnist Dave Egan wrote, "The law of the land gives Tony Lupien the absolute right to reinstatement as first baseman of the Phillies and not for fifteen days, as the barons of the racket contend, but for one year." Egan continued,

> Baseball players who are veterans did not fight for the dubious privilege of selling apples on the street corners and in common justice are entitled to the same rights as other citizens. This is the first recorded instance in sport of a war veteran being denied his rights, but I am sorry to say that it is not the last, for by the first of May the woods will be filled with veterans, wondering what happened to them and their supposed rights.[28]

In March 1946, the *Sporting News* gave full-page coverage to the controversy, quoting Lupien as saying,

> The G.I. Bill was designed to protect for at least one year the jobs of men who entered the service. Now that bill either applies to ballplayers or it doesn't. If the G.I. Bill does apply, then I may help many other veterans in the months to come by following through with my action.[29]

Lupien was surprised to receive a contract for $8,000 from the Hollywood Stars, about $3,000 more than the normal minor league salary, but he learned that despite organized baseball's rule that forbid a major league team from paying all or part of the salary of a minor leaguer whose options had expired, the Phillies were doing exactly that. As historian Lee Lowenfish observed in *Imperfect Diamond*, "The major leagues were planning to circumvent the Veterans Act by paying the banished servicemen their prewar salaries, thereby meeting at least the provision that the former soldier received his previous salary."[30] Even so, it was the job and the prospect of longer-term re-employment (in this case, in the major leagues) that was supposed to be guaranteed by the law. Still deterred from a lawsuit, however, Lupien decided to report to the Hollywood Stars and try to play his way back into the majors. But he didn't stop trying to publicize the injustice.

SERVICEMAN IN COURT: AL NIEMIEC

The PCL began each season with the two Northwest teams, Seattle and Portland, playing a home-and-home series against the Los Angeles Angels and

Hollywood Stars, with all four clubs riding back and forth on the Pacific Coast Special train. Using his access on the train to players, including returning servicemen on several teams, Lupien told them their rights under the federal law. Among them, Tony was reacquainted with fellow New Englander and former Red Sox infielder Al Niemiec, who was about to return from military service to play for the PCL's Seattle Rainiers.

Niemiec was born in Meriden, Connecticut, in 1911. He attended the College of the Holy Cross, where he was a star third baseman and outstanding student. The Red Sox signed him after his graduation in 1933 and he bounced back and forth between the majors and minors with the Red Sox and Phillies. He put up impressive batting numbers in the minors but struggled offensively in the majors, hitting .200 in 78 games in 1934 and 1936. In his one claim to fame, in 1937, Niemiec was dealt by the Red Sox, with an outfielder, to the PCL's San Diego Padres in exchange for future Hall of Famer Ted Williams.

Niemiec hit .304 in 130 games for the Padres in 1938 despite suffering a concussion. His average slipped to .279 in 155 games in 1939 perhaps from lingering effects of the injury. At season's end, Niemiec was claimed off waivers by another PCL team, the Seattle Rainiers, where he played three seasons, 1940 to 1942. Niemiec hit .274, .297, and .266, respectively, set a defensive fielding percentage record of .988 at second base in 1940, and led the league in fielding all three years as the Rainiers won three consecutive championships. After the 1942 season, Niemiec was inducted into the U.S. Navy despite having a wife and two sons at the time. He was assigned to a pre-flight program in California at St. Mary's College, whose baseball team was coached by future Hall of Famer Charlie Gehringer. Niemiec played third base and was promoted to lieutenant in 1944.

After his release from the Navy in January 1946, Niemiec signed a contract with Seattle and joined the team for spring training. Since the Rainiers had groomed a younger player, Bob Gorbould, for the second-base position, Niemiec was released twenty-three days into the new season.

Having been alerted to his rights by Lupien, Niemiec filed a protest with his local Selective Service office a week after being released, complaining that he'd been dismissed in violation of federal law. Niemiec gave the draft board the "letter of introduction" the Rainiers manager and vice president gave him upon his release. The letter praised Niemiec's past baseball service as "one of the most dependable ball players we have ever had." It claimed, however, that given a surplus of talent and the need to accommodate younger players, he had to be let go. The letter nevertheless recommended Niemiec as "the type who would be a credit to the game in years to come as a manager of some club."[31]

The Selective Service immediately sided with Niemiec, and in a letter to Rainiers president Emil Sick, it reviewed the team's obligations under the law, indicated that Niemiec was still capable of playing baseball at an acceptable level, and concluded that his dismissal was "without cause." Encouraged, but uncertain about the fate of his claim, Niemiec signed to play ball with the Providence-Cranston Chiefs in the New England League.

Owners, players, and sportswriters began to realize that the outcome of the Niemiec case could affect thousands of returning veterans. Jeff Obermeyer observed that baseball was riding "a wave of patriotism as the 'American game' during the Second World War" and was eager to keep cultivating that status. "It was," Obermeyer noted, "a time of record popularity and profits, and not a time to take an unpopular stance with respect to veterans who made up a significant portion of the game's fan base."[32] Organized baseball should have avoided the bad publicity, but money was a competing incentive to avoid losing the Niemiec case.

The Seattle Rainiers didn't have to face the situation alone. The PCL, the NAPBL, and MLB all got quickly involved, with the latter two agreeing to split the legal costs. Ironically, at a time when MLB was trying to block the raiding of its players by the Mexican League, Rainiers' vice president Roscoe Torrance proposed that the returning-veterans problem might be solved if two hundred ballplayers were sent to the Mexican League to make room on MLB rosters. That's not what Commissioner Chandler had in mind.

Leading the Rainers' defense was its attorney Stephen Chadwick, a surprising choice since he was a veteran himself and very active in veterans' rights groups. In fact, he had been national commander of the American Legion. Even so, in response to a second demand to reinstate Niemiec from the U.S. Attorney's Office, Chadwick defended organized baseball's own rules on returning veterans guaranteeing them their old jobs for a trial period of fifteen days of regular-season play or thirty days of spring training after which each team could cancel the contract at its discretion. Chadwick claimed that the Rainiers had re-employed Niemiec, that he had been given the reasonable and minimum playing time provided by league's rules, and that he had shown that he was "unable to meet the accepted standards of work performance and professional skill and proficiency required of our players and by clubs with which we were in competition."[33] The Rainiers claimed that the leg injury Niemiec suffered before leaving for the military in 1942 had probably slowed him down.

In court, the Rainiers claimed baseball wasn't covered by the veterans' law because they were a quasi-public institution not operated primarily for profit; because Niemiec was no longer able to perform acceptably; and because Niemiec had signed a contract with another team, which waived his rights under the G.I. Bill. In response, in June 1946 U.S. District Court Judge Lloyd Black argued, to the contrary, that the PCL was clearly a for-profit business and that non-profits weren't exempt from the law anyway. He claimed the team had provided no evidence that Niemiec couldn't perform skillfully and had inappropriately concluded that Niemiec wouldn't last the season. Black also observed that owners, not players, controlled contract language and that a reasonable reading of the contract suggested that players couldn't waive their legal rights. The reserve clause prevented players from selling their services to other teams. Black rejected the team's apparent claim "that if the baseball player be older when he comes back from service than when he entered it, his baseball club employer is given the right in its discretion to repeal the Act of Congress."[34]

Judge Black noted that Congress passed the veterans law "to enable the serviceman to render the best he had for his country unworried by the specter of no payment during his first year after his return to civilian life." He argued, "Baseball is no different than a store or machine shop. The law is simple. A veteran rates his old job back." Black reminded the Rainiers that

> professional baseball is a great American institution. Compared with many professional sports and entertainments it holds a very high regard of the people of the nation . . . There are few institutions in American life which ought to feel a greater obligation [to veterans].[35]

Black ordered Seattle to reinstate Niemiec and pay him a full season's salary. The money Niemiec made in his brief time with the Providence-Cranston club was deducted from Seattle's obligation. The Rainiers had to pay him, but they didn't have to play him or even restore him to the roster.

The team was owned by the Rainier Brewing Company, and Niemiec was instead given a job selling beer. Two other Rainiers player vets were also granted small awards.

A SMALL STEP FORWARD

Organized baseball wasn't happy with Black's ruling. Commissioner Chandler urged Seattle to appeal, offering to pay all expenses. The PCL directors similarly pushed an appeal, with the NAPBL now agreeing to help cover the costs as well as those for any new cases. These officials were concerned by a *Sporting News* report that as many as 143 major leaguers and 900 Triple A players alone might make claims against teams that violated their rights as military veterans.

But baseball officialdom was even more alarmed by the rest of Judge Black's decision. He observed that the terms "option" and "waiver" in the baseball contract were "reminiscent of chattels." Players were forced to sign an agreement that is "the contract of the employers" who demanded "loyalty" of the players, ordering them to report to spring training but empowered to end the contract at any time while not paying players until the start of the season. Black complained about the lack of an outside arbitration of grievances and questioned the MLB commissioner's authority over the PCL. Essentially, Black declared that the reserve clause in every player's contract was illegal. He ominously warned, "Professional baseball should not be too certain that some of the recent decisions by the United States Supreme Court would not be the basis for a re-examination of the interstate character of professional baseball."[36] In other words, the court could strip MLB of its anti-trust exemption, the central foundation of its business model.

Despite this threat, the Rainiers decided, by season's end, that it wouldn't appeal Black's decision. In theory, hundreds of ballplayers could sue for their jobs and pay. But in practice, in the absence of a baseball players' union, the players were on their own. They might, like the case of the Philadelphia Athletics' Bob Harris, be pressured by a local district attorney to settle their case. Or like Steve Sundra of the St. Louis Browns, they might actually lose their case in a court with an unsympathetic judge.

The MLB and the NAPBL backed off from appealing the decision when they realized how profitable the 1946 season had been in relation to the claims they might have to pay off. In a report by its steering committee, MLB falsely congratulated itself, saying, "No business has done a better job for its returning service men."[37] They worried that an appeal of the Niemiec decision might create more negative publicity. As Obermeyer observed, paying off claims helped organized baseball maintain complete control over the players. The player vets in World War II might have been

> fighting for a democratic society, but they returned to a game in which the owners held the power and the players had no say in their own careers, a status quo that remained in place for another twenty years until the rise of the Major League Baseball Players Association.[38]

Even so, the Niemiec decision was a step toward stronger players' rights—a battle that would intensify once the players revived the idea of having a union. The decision also allowed a number of veterans to receive the pay they were owed on coming back after the war, and some—like Hank Sauer, Frank Baumholtz, Danny Murtaugh, and Jim Konstanty—were able to resume their major league careers.

Niemiec returned to baseball in 1948 for only one year, serving as general manager of a Rainiers farm team, the Great Falls Electrics in the Pioneer League. He was little-known by the general public even in 1962 when he spoke out against what he viewed as the over-competitiveness in Little League. He became a golf pro at courses in the Pacific Northwest during the 1970s, and he died in Kirkland, Washington, in 1995.

Tony Lupien had two excellent years for the Hollywood Stars. He batted .295 in 1946 and the following season hit 21 home runs, batted .341, and won the PCL's MVP award. He was promoted back to the majors for 1948, playing every game for the last-place White Sox but with little success at the plate. He was traded to the Tigers in 1949 but was sent to their Triple A Toledo affiliate. With no prospect of an MLB return, he became the player-manager of the Claremont, New Hampshire, semipro team in 1950. He went on to manage 8 seasons in the minors and 21 seasons as baseball coach at Dartmouth College. He transformed Dartmouth's program. The team won the NCAA District One championship in 1970 and produced two major league pitchers, Chuck Seelbach and Pete Broberg. Lupien died in Norwich, Vermont, in 2004.

DAUNTLESS: DANNY GARDELLA

Despite fending off lawsuits from World War II veterans and fighting off Jorge Pasquel's Mexican League raids, MLB's troubles were not over. The inequities and inefficiencies of its business model would generate continued resistance and eventually become unworkable. In this regard, today's major league players owe Danny Gardella a million thanks but most have never heard of him.

Gardella was born in the Bronx, New York, in 1920. He and his brother Al grew up playing sandlot and club baseball. Gardella became a professional player at age seventeen, bouncing around the minors with teams affiliated with the Tigers, Indians, and Senators. While Gardella was very popular with the fans, he felt his chances of making the major leagues were slim, and he quit professional baseball after the 1940 season.

A punctured eardrum kept Gardella out of the military during World War II. He returned to New York, working for the next couple of years as an elevator operator and house detective at the New Yorker Hotel, a railyard freight handler, and a shipyard stevedore. He had a short amateur boxing career, reaching the Golden Gloves welterweight semifinals with four knockouts. Gardella kept playing baseball, first for the New Yorker Hotel team and then in the semipro Consolidated Shipyard League. His manager was a major league scout who recommended Gardella to the Giants. They signed him to a contract in 1944 mostly because many good players were in the military.

The Giants sent Gardella to their Jersey City minor league team, and he went back and forth between them and the Giants during the 1944 season. Despite his strong throwing arm, Gardella had trouble catching flies in the outfield. At one point, the *Sporting News* described one play this way: "Gardella caught Litwhiler's fly, unassisted."[39] Even so, he quickly became a favorite among Polo Grounds fans, who set up Gardella Gardens in the upper left-field balcony. In 47 games, Gardella hit .250 with 6 home runs. At the end of the season, however, Gardella was suspended for the remaining games for missing curfew. He told Giants manager Mel Ott he didn't believe in curfews.

Gardella was invited back to the Giants for the 1945 season, where his eccentric behavior competed with his playing skills. After one game, Gardella crashed a high school prom, befriended the band, and began singing "Indian Love Call" to his stunned audience before being kicked out. During spring training in Lakewood, New Jersey, Gardella walked the town nightly, loudly singing operatic arias in his strong, baritone voice. He continued such outbursts on trains and in the clubhouse. "I love music, particularly operatic music, and I would uninhibitedly burst out in song from time to time," he explained. "What the hell, why not sing and holler? You're young, you're healthy, and you're playing baseball."[40]

As his biographer Charlie Weatherby has noted, Gardella was articulate, colorful, and unpredictable and thus accumulated many nicknames: Dauntless Danny, Dangerous Danny, Desperate Danny, the Ignited Italian, the Mighty Midget, and the Little Philosopher. Gardella was an insatiable reader and regularly appeared with novels and books of poetry, psychology, or philosophy. He quoted Plato and other philosophers. He was also physically strong and gifted. Despite his troubles in the outfield, before an exhibition game he caught a baseball dropped four hundred feet from a Navy blimp. He performed one-armed handstands, walked up stairs on his hands, and would do triple midair twists while belting out a song. On train rides, he'd sometimes strap his 5-foot-7-inch body into a luggage rack for a nap.

Gardella was also known for his pranks. On one road trip, his roommate Napoleon Reyes was in the bathroom shaving when he noticed a strange silence since Gardella almost never stopped talking. Stepping back into the room, Reyes saw a note on the dresser: "I'm bored with life. So long. Danny."[41] The window was wide open and Reyes, horrified, ran over, expecting to see his teammate splattered on the pavement several stories below. Instead, he found Gardella hanging by his fingers from the window ledge, laughing at the frightened Reyes.

But Gardella could also hit a baseball. He began the 1945 season as a pinch hitter, but when he started getting game-winning hits, including late-inning home runs, the Giants put him into the lineup. The *New York Times* observed, "Dauntless Danny right now is going great guns no matter where you play him . . . The conviction is growing that . . . for all his queer antics and occasional mental lapses, [Gardella] has the makings of an excellent ball player."[42]

Gardella also had philosophical views on the state of the game: "Baseball today . . . is too stereotyped. Everything is precision play and while the technique improves, the individual dash and verve of players, which once made them standouts, has disappeared." On the field, playing first base as well as left and right field, Gardella finished the 1945 season batting .272, with 71 RBIs, and 18 home runs—eighth in the National League—in only 484 at bats.

With World War II over in time for the 1946 season, many major leaguers in the military headed back to their old teams. Although organized baseball wasn't honoring the job guarantee mandated in the G.I. Bill and the excess of talent induced MLB teams to curb player salaries, Gardella felt the Giants would offer him a decent raise because of his strong 1945 season. Instead, they offered him a $500 salary increase to $5,000, assuming that the reserve clause would force him to take it. Gardella returned the contract unsigned, claiming he deserved more. Although Gardella was living his boyhood dream of playing for the Giants, he was offered less money than he had made in the shipyards.

Gardella missed the Giants train to Miami for spring training. He claimed the team intentionally gave him the wrong departure time to punish his holdout. He paid his own way, but when he arrived, manager Mel Ott barred him from the hotel and workouts until he signed the contract. Then the Giants disciplined him for not wearing proper clothes to a team dinner at an upscale restaurant. Ott declared, "This fellow apparently has to be taught that players of his type are no longer of great importance in the major leagues, now that the war is over."[43] Gardella apologized to Ott and agreed to sign for the $5,000 he'd been offered, but instead the Giants told him they were trying to sell his contract to other clubs, including minor league teams.

During the off-season, before spring training, Gardella had been working at a New York City gym as a trainer and masseuse. Gardella was one of the first ballplayers to use weights for his own training. Coincidentally, one of his customers was Jorge Pasquel, who was in the United States trying to lure ballplayers to the Mexican League. Gardella and Pasquel were both physical fitness fanatics, and Gardella supervised the Mexican's workouts. Pasquel couldn't believe how little the Giants were paying Gardella, and he told Gardella to call him if he ever was interested in playing in Mexico. With the Giants about to drop him, Gardella contacted Pasquel, who offered him triple his MLB salary and a long-term contract.

In February 1946, Gardella was the first of twenty-seven players to defect from MLB to the Mexican League that year, accepting a position with the Veracruz Blues. When questioned by reporters, Gardella defiantly responded,

> I do not intend to let the Giants enrich themselves at my expense, by selling me to a minor league club after the shabby treatment they have accorded me. So I have now decided to take my gifted talents to Mexico. I would have accepted [the Giants'] figure if they had not started to push me around.[44]

It wasn't just the money but also the indignity of being trapped by the reserve clause that triggered Gardella's rebellion.

Arriving in Mexico City a few days later, Gardella claimed, "I'm mighty glad I'm no longer connected with the New York Giants. They are paying me more [here] so why shouldn't I play in Mexico?"[45] Gardella had a strong first half for Veracruz, batting .300 and hitting 2 home runs in the Mexican League All-Star game. Gardella's production fell off in the second half, but while some other U.S. players had already soured on the Mexican League, Gardella enjoyed most of the season. Since he spoke Italian, he picked up Spanish quickly and wasn't bothered by the living or playing conditions. He invited his girlfriend down to Mexico City and they were married there. But Veracruz underperformed, and soon even Gardella was grateful for the season's end. Gardella had a good year, hitting .275 with 13 home runs and 64 RBIs in 100 games. But then Pasquel announced the bad news that revenues had fallen short and he'd have to cut Gardella's and the other players' salaries for the 1947 season. While a few jumpers remained, Gardella and his wife decided to leave.

In June 1946, Commissioner Chandler announced his blacklist, which barred Mexican League jumpers from returning to organized baseball for at least five years. He cited the reserve clause, which bound a player to his team for life unless the club traded, sold, or released him. Since the ban included the MLB–affiliated Cuban Winter League, Gardella played instead in the Cuban Players (Federation) League in 1947, where he hit .250 and won a home-run championship. Back home in New York, he worked multiple blue-collar jobs while playing semipro baseball in his spare time. Then he joined eighteen other returning jumpers to form the Max Lanier All Stars, led by a one-time Cardinals ace pitcher who had spent the 1946 and 1947 seasons with the Veracruz Blues. The All-Stars barnstormed the country, winning all eighty of its games, with Gardella providing the entertainment, which featured renditions of the song "Danny Boy" and various operas he played over the team bus loudspeakers for local townspeople.

The barnstorming team lost money despite good fan turnouts. Chandler's ban ruled out professional ballparks for the games, and other fields were too small to draw bigger crowds. The commissioner intervened to prevent Lanier's team from even playing college and semipro teams. Chandler proclaimed that anybody playing with or against a jumper would be put immediately on the blacklist, and thus the All Stars dissolved.

Gardella was scheduled to play with the semipro Staten Island Gulf Oilers in the summer of 1947 but its opponent, the Cleveland Buckeyes, cancelled the game at the last minute. The Buckeyes were a Negro League team, and since Jackie Robinson had broken the color barrier, Black ballplayers hoped to join organized baseball. Chandler sent a telegram, to be read over the loudspeaker, reminding the players of the blacklist. When the game cancellation was announced, the spectators were asked "not to hold the action against the players of the Negro National League, because they could not afford to risk the penalty imposed upon players who played against an outlaw."[46] That outlaw was Gardella, who dropped out so the game could be played. Black players who had played in Mexico had already been at least informally blacklisted by MLB. Of the sixty-eight U.S. Black athletes who played in Mexico between 1945 and 1948, not a single player was signed by an MLB team until after the blacklist of white players was rescinded in 1949.

In 1947 there was no mercy for the returning jumpers. The most high-profile returnee was Mickey Owen, of whom Cubs general manager James Gallagher observed, "The spectacle of Mickey Owen languishing on a Missouri farm will do more to keep players from jumping this winter than anything Mr. Rickey or the rest of us could do."[47]

Gardella was disgusted and embarrassed by the Staten Island incident. It infuriated him that the "big-headed guys" who ran baseball would callously expel him from their game and humiliate him. Just as coincidental as Gardella's accidental introduction to Jorge Pasquel, a disgruntled fan at the Gulf Oilers game complained to his dentist the next day about the horrible treatment Gardella had received. The dentist mentioned it to one of his patients, Frederic Johnson. With family ties in baseball dating back to the 1880s, Johnson was a big baseball fan and an attorney who had published a legal treatise in 1939 in the *U.S. Law Review* predicting the fall of the reserve clause. Gardella hired Johnson as his lawyer, believing his situation could be a test case not only for the reserve clause but also for MLB's anti-trust exemption.

In October 1947, Gardella's suit was filed in federal court, charging MLB with a conspiracy to restrain free trade and seeking $300,000 in damages for having illegitimately deprived him of his livelihood through the blacklist and the reserve clause. Instead of playing baseball, Gardella was making $36 a week at a New York hospital. The response was outrage from the baseball establishment and beyond. The owners portrayed the challenge as the sport's death knell. Although Branch Rickey helped break baseball's color barrier, he regarded any challenge to management as a "bolshevik" conspiracy. Rickey claimed that "baseball cannot endure" without the reserve clause. Those attacking it had, he claimed, "avowed communist tendencies who deeply resent the continuance of our national pastime."[48] Senators owner Clark Griffith declared, "For the life of the trade [sport], you've got to keep the ball player in his own association [team]. If they are allowed to move around every fall, it would destroy their profession."[49] The implication was that the owners were colluding and profiting only as a benevolent gesture to their players.

Chandler went even further, suggesting that Gardella was a radical and claiming his suit threatened the American way of life as embodied in the traditions of the national pastime. Portraying Gardella and the other jumpers as deserters who abandoned the United States for Mexico during a time of national crisis, Chandler said, "I tried to get them to live up to their obligations and responsibilities . . . These players joined a group who said they were going to kill baseball in the United States."[50]

MLB had clout in Congress as well. A young Arkansas Congressman, Wilbur Mills (whose long reign in Washington would eventually end in a 1974 sex scandal), was eager in 1947 to introduce legislation to legalize baseball's reserve clause and affirm organized baseball's anti-trust exemption. Rickey's friend, Senator John W. Bricker of Ohio, implored MLB to combat communism by indoctrinating the nation's youth with American values. He declared, "While the marching hordes in China are spreading the doctrine of communism, officials of the national pastime are helping make democracy work in this country by giving every youth a chance to carve out his own career."[51] As the lawsuit dragged on, Congressional leaders scheduled hearings that furthered these views.

In 1951, the House Judiciary Committee's Subcommittee on Study of Monopoly Power began an investigation and held hearings on economic concentration in major American industries, including baseball. (This was the height of the Cold War, when Congress was also holding hearings to investigate and villify American dissenters as unpatriotic and subversive communists). The subcommittee discussed legislation to give Congressional approval to baseball's exemption from anti-trust laws and extend the exemption to other professional sports leagues, designed, said committee chair Cong. Emanuel Celler, a Democrat from Brooklyn, to "strengthen and fortify" baseball's legal position, which was under attack in court. Two little-known minor league players—Ross Horning and Seymour "Cy" Block—testified at the hearings. They described the miserable pay and working conditions of minor league players and testified against the reserve clause and baseball's exemption from anti-trust laws. After 16 days of hearings, 33 witnesses, and 1,643 pages of transcript, the subcommittee decided to do nothing.[52]

Not surprisingly, the press supported the owners. Typical was *New York Times* sportswriter Arthur Daley, who noted that "it was Doubleday who is accorded the distinction of inventing our great American game. Dauntless Dan could very well become the fellow who destroyed it."[53]

Given the media's stance, it's not surprising that public opinion was largely lukewarm toward Gardella. He was viewed as a marginal player. MLB owners pressured players to disavow Gardella, and when Chandler began hinting at amnesty for the other jumpers, they dutifully distanced themselves from Gardella. This mimicked broader developments in U.S. society, where Americans were naming names and dissociating themselves from radicals and protesters in the growing Cold-War Red Scare.

According to Ron Briley, "for baseball to maintain the fiction that it was a game and not a business, it was imperative that players not voice discontent, while asserting how fortunate they were to be playing baseball."[54] Gardella dissented from this view. He loved baseball and wanted to play in the majors. But he also did not want organized baseball to violate his basic rights. He was a working-class American trying to preserve his job in baseball and get a fair salary for his labor.

Gardella wanted a free labor market, which ironically, in the eyes of the baseball establishment, made him a communist. MLB used the same Red-baiting language that was becoming widespread during the Cold War. As Briley noted, the baseball moguls joined "Hollywood producers, business executives, university administrators, and conservative politicians, who suggested their critics . . . [represented] an alien communist ideology"[55] seeking to undermine American values. Just as actors and teachers were blacklisted for failing to cooperate with the House Un-American Activities Committee and its Senate counterpart, baseball jumpers were banned as disloyal for failing to support the reserve clause. America's virulent anti-communism choked off legitimate social reform and helped undermine baseball reform as well.

Despite all these social forces against him, Gardella did have some supporters. A New York state senator and an assemblyman introduced legislation to invalidate the reserve clause, calling the current system "akin to peonage." A few players spoke out. Marty Marion, the Cardinals' star shortstop, proposed a three-person salary arbitration system to reform the reserve system. Jackie Robinson supported Gardella, saying, "He simply wanted compensation for his inability to making a living as a result of the ban."[56] Gardella also received an unexpected boost when the U.S. Justice Department began an investigation of MLB under the anti-trust laws.

Gardella wasn't shy about explaining his motives: "It's too bad if my case is hurting baseball because I've been hurt pretty badly myself. They say I'm undermining the structure of the baseball contract . . . Let's say [instead] that I'm helping to end a baseball evil." Gardella denied he was a radical: "I was no communist for exercising my American rights . . . I feel I let the whole world know that the reserve clause was unfair. It had the odor of peonage, even slavery."[57]

Fred Johnson, Gardella's lawyer, was undeterred by MLB's patriotic and anti-communist rhetoric. He claimed that Rickey had had "dictatorial powers so long he [didn't] recognize the true principles of American life. Name calling is the last resort for a beaten man."[58] Reviewing the history of pennant winners, Johnson easily refuted MLB claims that the reserve clause had provided competitive balance. Aside from the obvious—that baseball teams were constantly crossing state lines—Johnson argued that the transmission of games via radio and television put MLB into interstate commerce, which made it subject to anti-trust laws. Through the reserve clause, baseball's owners had been collaborating for decades, violating the anti-collusion provisions of federal anti-trust laws, binding players to their teams, and blocking them from selling their skills to the highest bidder. The MLB farm system, Johnson said, allows "players to be signed during infancy without giving them the common law right to repudiate such contracts upon attaining their majority or exercise statutory rights for disavowing their contracts."[59]

Johnson believed that Gardella had a particularly strong case because unlike other jumpers, he hadn't signed (and therefore hadn't broken) a contract. Thus Gardella could only be accused of violating the reserve clause, which was suspect enough. On top of that, Johnson discovered that in the original U.S. Supreme Court case that granted MLB its anti-trust exemption, Garry Herrmann (president of the Cincinnati Reds and chairman of the three-man national commission that ruled MLB from 1903 to 1920) claimed the reserve was only for twenty-two players and not the entire roster or all farm team players. In addition, George Wharton Pepper, the chief MLB attorney in that case, indicated that the reserve clause was only an "honorary obligation" upon the player.

Even so, when the Gardella case reached the federal district court in July 1948, the court granted MLB's petition for dismissal. Ignoring the flaws in the 1922 decision *Federal Baseball Club of Baltimore* v. *National League of Professional Baseball Clubs*, the judge claimed he was bound by the anti-trust exemption granted by that case since it hadn't been overruled and since Congress hadn't acted. MLB was doing nothing different now than it had been in the 1920s, the court decided.

When Johnson decided to appeal, MLB offered Gardella a settlement, purportedly as high as $200,000. Johnson rejected the offer, perhaps more interested in overturning the landmark court ruling than in the money. In the short term, he succeeded. In February 1949, the federal appeals court overturned the lower court ruling and ordered a jury trial for Gardella. Besides the threat the trial itself posed to MLB, the court's reasoning alarmed baseball officials.

Implying that MLB was, indeed, operating in interstate commerce, federal appeals court Judge Learned Hand wrote,

> Whatever other conduct the [antitrust] Acts may forbid, they certainly forbid all restraints of trade which were unlawful at common-law, and one of the oldest and best established of these is a contract which unreasonably forbids any one to practice his calling.[60]

This was a direct challenge to the reserve clause.

Judge Jerome Frank went even further. The *Federal Baseball* decision was, in his mind, an

> impotent zombie . . . We have here a monopoly which, in its effect on ballplayers . . . possess characteristics shockingly repugnant to moral principles that, at least since the War Between the States, have been basic in America, as shown by the Thirteenth Amendment to the Constitution, condemning "involuntary servitude," and subsequent Congressional enactments on the subject.[61]

In response to MLB objections that its players were adequately paid, Frank declared,

> Only the totalitarian-minded will believe that higher pay excuses virtual slavery . . . The public pleasure [of watching the games] does not authorize the courts to condone illegality and . . . no court should strive to ingeniously legalize private (even if benevolent) dictatorship.[62]

The lower court was specifically ordered to explain how radio and television transmissions hadn't brought MLB into interstate commerce.

Johnson petitioned for an injunction to allow Gardella to be reinstated to MLB pending the outcome of his court case. An initial hearing was inconclusive but it raised another question: Would Gardella also be forbidden from playing amateur, independent, or semipro baseball? Without answering that question, the federal court soon rejected the injunction petition, but Gardella had other plans.

Gardella had left the country for Canada. He joined at least a dozen other jumpers to play in the independent Quebec Provincial League (QPL). They were dispersed among the six teams, earning higher salaries than they would have back in MLB. Gardella signed with the Drummondville Cubs with a provision allowing him to break his contract if he were accepted back into organized baseball. In 1949, Gardella had an excellent season, making the QPL All-Star team, and hitting .283 with 17 home runs and 80 RBIs.

Among his fellow QPL players were other MLB jumpers: Max Lanier, Fred Martin, and Sal Maglie. In March 1949, New York attorney John L. Flynn filed a new suit, initially for eight jumpers challenging the blacklist, although only Lanier and Martin ended up in court documents. They were seeking $2.5 million in damages. Then Maglie signed on to the case, seeking an additional

$1 million. Flynn argued that the unilateral MLB contracts "completely violate the liberty of the players." It was a case of "men against monopoly, [and] human rights against property rights."[63] In response, a federal court ordered organized baseball to show why it ought to be allowed to ban the jumpers, and U.S. marshals served papers on sixteen MLB clubs.

Although Giants owner Horace Stoneham claimed he welcomed Gardella's court test, other owners worried that Gardella in the courtroom would be far more damaging than Gardella in Mexico. Some of them began blaming Chandler for not dropping the ban sooner since the Mexican League threat had faded. While Chandler's predecessor, Landis, had kept MLB out of the courts, the blacklist-provoked suits put baseball in jeopardy of losing the reserve clause and its anti-trust exemption. MLB was lucky the cases hadn't reached the U.S. Supreme Court already. If they had, organized baseball would have been asking the court to overrule two of America's most esteemed judges, Jerome Frank and Learned Hand.

Thus in June 1949, Chandler cancelled the blacklist, about halfway into his five-year threat, and allowed reinstatement for jumpers who dropped their lawsuits. Each player and his MLB team would get thirty days to decide whether the player made the roster. A few jumpers were still playing in Mexico, several more were playing for QPL teams in Canada, and some were with Caribbean league teams. Lanier, Martin, and Maglie initially resisted but then dropped their cases and returned to MLB, but Gardella refused. "If I didn't sue," Gardella later recalled, "they would have destroyed my spirit."[64] In a pretrial deposition in September 1949, Johnson got Chandler to admit that MLB earned $750,000 from radio rights and $65,000 from television. Fearing that it might lose in court, MLB again offered Gardella a settlement.

Gardella didn't want to settle and he complained,

> It was baseball which was so wrong—so undemocratic for an institution that was supposed to represent American freedom and democracy. I thought it was quite wrong . . . If you sue someone for something, why should money appease you? It is like Judas taking money and saying, "I'm being bought off" . . . I considered the settlement a sellout, a moral defeat.[65]

Even so, Johnson convinced Gardella to take MLB's offer, warning his client that a court case and appeals would be costly and drag on for a long time—the same prospects that had deterred Tony Lupien from pursuing his battle with MLB.

Even if he won, Johnson predicted that MLB would find a way to keep Gardella out of the game. Damages would be difficult to collect since Gardella was making more playing in Mexico and Quebec than he would have in MLB. In the absence of a baseball union, Gardella had no institutional resources or organized backing. In October 1949, he settled for $60,000, half of which went to his attorney, and Gardella was allowed to sign with the St. Louis Cardinals.

JUST A WORKER AND BALLPLAYER

Gardella used his settlement to buy a home in Yonkers so he and his growing family could move out of his father-in-law's house. He joined the Cardinals in 1950 but had only one at bat before being demoted to their Houston Buffaloes farm team, where he was sometimes recruited to sing for fans before games. He was soon released. The Cardinals denied that he had been blacklisted again. Instead, the team executives made the unlikely claim that no other MLB teams could use his services.

In August 1950, Gardella was signed by the Bangor club in the North Atlantic League, where he hit .337 in 26 games. He played with the semi-pro Brooklyn Bushwicks to start the 1951 season, and returned to the QPL with the Trois-Rivieres Royals briefly before retiring from baseball for good. Gardella began a new career singing Broadway songs on the vaudeville circuit, but when it fell short, Gardella claimed MLB had scuttled his chances. He worked a variety of blue-collar jobs thereafter, including construction worker, warehouseman, truck driver, drill press operator, street sweeper, gym trainer, furniture mover, and hospital orderly. In 1961 he revealed the details of his settlement: "I felt like I was getting paid off, but being a poor man I felt more or less justified. It wasn't like I had a lot of money."[66] He never would.

When the Mexican League rebellion began to stall, Jorge Pasquel declared, "I cannot lick [the MLB owners] because they are big and belong to the biggest country in the world. But I am going to make them pay [ballplayers] two and three times the salary they now pay."[67] For a short period in the late 1940s, Pasquel's raids forced MLB to raise player salaries, but when the Mexican League was absorbed into U.S.-controlled organized baseball, the salaries quickly deteriorated. Having dodged a bullet, the owners proceeded with a false sense of security. Pasquel's prediction would eventually come true, however. Gardella's suit was the first blow for free agency, pursued again in the 1960s and finally achieved in the 1970s, first for baseball and then spreading to all professional team sports.

Pasquel pushed back against American and MLB imperialism and offered underpaid U.S. ballplayers, including Gardella, a decent standard of living. As Ron Briley observed, Gardella wasn't a labor agitator leading a collective challenge to MLB. He was just a worker and ballplayer who "appealed to the nation's democratic traditions of equal economic opportunity, which were essential to the civil rights movement and labor reform."[68] Gardella supported the Major League Baseball Players Association as it rose in his later years. But just before he died in 2005, he explained that he had jumped to the Mexican League "because I loved the game and wanted to play." He worried that "today's players make too much money to love the game. Their hero is Donald Trump, not Babe Ruth."[69] Many defenders of baseball's corporate monopoly, including Happy Chandler, Branch Rickey, Clark Griffith, Ford Frick, and William Harridge, are in the Cooperstown Hall of Fame. But few people have ever heard of Danny Gardella.

3

Ending Indentured Servitude

During the Great Depression (1929–1941) and World War II (1941–1945), the nation faced two overlapping domestic problems: racial segregation and labor unrest. Protests for civil rights and workers' rights were widespread during both periods. Baseball was not immune to having to confront both issues, but the reckoning came after the war ended.

During the Depression, millions of workers, consumers, students, farmers, and African Americans engaged in massive protests over economic hardship. This reflected the nation's mood, a combination of anger and fear. Franklin Delano Roosevelt's 1932 election as president, with 57 percent of the vote, added an element of hope. For most Americans, New Deal reforms—including Social Security, a minimum wage, workers' right to unionize, subsidies to troubled family farmers, a massive government-funded jobs program, and regulation of banks and other businesses—offered welcome relief to the suffering. Americans reelected FDR in 1936, 1940, and 1944.

Black Americans, 10 percent of America's population, were relegated to second-class status and denied basic civil and political rights, not only in the Jim Crow South. They faced discrimination in every facet of American life. The subjugation of Negroes, wrote sociologist Gunnar Myrdal in 1944, was "the most glaring conflict in the American conscience and greatest unsolved task for American democracy."[1] Black Americans were excluded from many New Deal programs and faced persistent discrimination.

In the 1930s and 1940s, civil rights activists fought against discrimination in housing and jobs; mobilized for a federal anti-lynching law; protested against segregation within the military; marched to open up defense jobs to Blacks during World War II; challenged police brutality and restrictive covenants that barred Blacks from certain neighborhoods; and boycotted stores that refused to hire African Americans.

Some African Americans had mixed feelings about the war effort when they faced blatant racism at home. When he was drafted, Nate Moreland, a Negro Leagues pitcher, complained, "I can play in Mexico, but I have to fight for America, where I can't play." Black leaders and Black newspapers enthusiastically supported the Double V campaign: victory over America's enemies overseas and victory over racism at home. As Black veterans returned home from the war, they expected America to be a more tolerant and inclusive society, helping to fuel the modern civil rights movement.

Thanks to massive wartime government spending, the country experienced full employment, but would the economy return to Depression-era levels without that stimulus? After the war, many Americans worried that there wouldn't be enough jobs for the influx of 10 million workers returning home. Eventually the federal government would start investing heavily in road-building, universities, and subsidized housing, particularly in the booming suburbs, while maintaining a large and expensive military that created new jobs and profits for defense contractors. But in the immediate postwar years, America's workers faced a severe housing shortage, skyrocketing inflation, and job insecurity. So in 1945 and 1946, more than 5 million American workers—in the steel, coal mining, electric consumer goods, meatpacking, railroad, automobile, oil, film, and other industries—were involved in the biggest strike wave in U.S. history.

On both the race and labor questions, the baseball establishment sought to maintain the status quo but mass movements around civil rights and workers' rights made it impossible for the baseball moguls to avoid addressing these intertwined problems.

Beginning in the 1930s, as part of that wider movement, the Negro press, civil rights groups, the Communist Party, progressive unions, and radical politicians waged a sustained campaign to integrate baseball. To keep the issue before the public, they published open letters to baseball owners, polled white managers and players (most of whom said that they had no objections to playing with African Americans), brought Black players to unscheduled tryouts at spring training camps, gathered signatures on petitions, and picketed ballparks in New York and Chicago. On opening day in 1945, activists carried picket signs at Yankee Stadium, saying, "If we are able to stop bullets, why not balls?"[2] That year both the New York State Legislature and New York mayor Fiorello LaGuardia formed task forces to investigate discriminatory hiring practices, including one that focused on baseball. Left-wing congressman Vito Marcantonio, who represented Harlem, called for an investigation of baseball's racist practices.

These activists believed that if they could push the nation's most popular sport to dismantle its color line, they could make inroads in other facets of American society.

Brooklyn Dodgers president Branch Rickey had wanted to break baseball's color line by hiring African American players, but he faced strong resistance from other team owners and from the powerful baseball commissioner Kenesaw Mountain Landis. Rickey believed, however, that he could carry out his idea after World War II was over, and he began making plans while the nation was still at war. The growing movement to end Jim Crow in baseball and Landis's death in 1944 boosted Rickey's efforts. Baseball's owners selected Albert "Happy" Chandler to replace him. As governor and then senator from Kentucky, Chandler echoed the segregationist views of most white Kentuckians. So when Ric Roberts, a reporter for the *Pittsburgh Courier*, a leading Black newspaper, asked Chandler about allowing Blacks in the big leagues, he was surprised to hear Chandler say that he didn't think it was fair to perpetuate the ban and that teams should hire players to win ballgames "whatever their origin or race."[3] The owners were as shocked as Roberts by Chandler's statement.

Rickey carefully scouted the Negro Leagues to find the right player to integrate the major leagues. Rather than pick one of the Negro Leagues superstars like Satchel Paige or Josh Gibson, he selected Jackie Robinson, who had just started playing for the Kansas City Monarchs.

Robinson was young, articulate, and well educated. He had grown up in Pasadena, California, outside Los Angeles. The city was rigidly segregated but Robinson had formed friendships with his white neighbors and classmates in high school and college. He had been a star athlete at Pasadena Junior College before enrolling at the University of California, Los Angeles, where he became its first four-sport athlete (football, basketball, track, and baseball), twice led basketball's PCL in scoring, won the NCAA broad jump championship, and became an All-American football player. He had also served in the Army during the war, where he faced racism on a daily basis. Rickey knew Robinson had a hot temper and strong political views but was also deeply religious. Rickey believed that Robinson could handle the emotional pressure and help the Dodgers on the field.

Rickey signed Robinson to a contract in October 1945 and assigned him to the Montreal Royals, its top minor league team, for the 1946 season. Rickey figured that Robinson would face less overt racism in Montreal than in most other minor league cities. During spring training and the season, Robinson constantly had to deal with racism from fans, opposing players, and even some of his own teammates. When the Royals traveled to segregated cities like Louisville and Baltimore, he couldn't stay in the same hotel or eat in the same restaurants as his white teammates. Despite these obstacles, he led the International League with a .349 batting average and 113 runs, finished second with 40 stolen bases, and led the team to a 100-54 season and a triumph in the Minor League World Series.

Rickey promoted Robinson to the Dodgers for the 1947 season. On April 15, he became the first African American on a major league team since the early 1900s when baseball drew its color line. In the majors, he still had to endure segregated hotels, buses, trains, movie theaters, and other facilities. He received a torrent of hate mail and death threats. On the field, he heard constant racist taunts from fans and opposing players. Throughout his rookie season, opposing pitchers threw fastballs at his head, brushed him back, and occasionally plunked him. Runners on opposing teams went out of their way to spike him when he was covering the bases. Robinson seethed with anger but he kept his promise to Rickey to endure the abuse without retaliating. But it took a toll. He developed stomach pains. His hair turned prematurely gray.

Robinson had an outstanding rookie season. He hit .297, led the NL with 29 stolen bases (including 3 steals of home), and led the Dodgers to the NL pennant. The *Sporting News* named him baseball's Rookie of the Year. That year the Dodgers set road attendance records in every NL park except Cincinnati's Crosley Field. In September Robinson appeared on the cover of *Time* magazine. At the end of the season, an Associated Press poll ranked Robinson second only to singer Bing Crosby as America's "most admired man."

Robinson quickly became a symbol of the promise of a racially integrated society. His actions on and off the diamond helped pave the way for America to confront its racial hypocrisy.

The dignity with which Robinson handled his encounters with racism drew public attention to the issue, stirred the conscience of many white Americans, and gave Black Americans a tremendous boost of pride and self-confidence.

Robinson spent his major league career (1947 to 1956) with the Brooklyn Dodgers. He won the Most Valuable Player award in 1949. An outstanding base runner with a .311 lifetime batting average, he led the Dodgers to six pennants and was elected to the Hall of Fame in 1962.

During and after his playing days, Robinson was an outspoken advocate for civil rights. He was the first well-known professional athlete in post–World War II America to use his celebrity to speak out against social injustice. He joined marches and picket lines, raised money for civil rights group, gave many speeches, and used his regular newspaper column to address racial injustice. Martin Luther King Jr. once told Dodgers pitcher Don Newcombe, "You'll never know what you and Jackie and Roy [Campanella] did to make it possible to do my job."

Despite Robinson's success on the field, most other major league teams were slow to bring other Black players onto their rosters. In 1952, five years after he had broken baseball's color barrier, only six of MLB's sixteen teams had a Black player. It was not until 1959 that the last holdout, the Boston Red Sox, hired its first African American player. But the movement to end baseball's Jim Crow system showed Americans, and ballplayers, that it was possible to pressure the sport's moguls to do things they were reluctant to do. It helped inspire the modern civil rights movement that began with the Montgomery bus boycott in 1955. A decade later, it helped embolden players to take action to secure their own rights by organizing a labor union.

The battle over racial segregation was only one aspect of the struggle to overcome baseball's system of indentured servitude after World War II. The other was the struggle to free players from the straitjacket of the reserve clause, which bound players to one team, severely limiting their freedom to decide for themselves which team they wanted to work for. As described in chapter 2, Tony Lupien, Al Niemiec, and Danny Gardella tried to challenge the baseball establishment as individuals, without the backing of a union.

They didn't win their battles, but their defiance reflected a growing sense of unease among many Americans following World War II.

Baseball was not immune to the growing class tensions across America, but few ballplayers thought that unionizing was a good idea. Most of them were simply grateful to get paid to play baseball. They didn't want to have to return to their hometowns and work in the farms and factories with their parents and siblings. They weren't about to cause any trouble with team owners, who had almost dictatorial control over their wages and working conditions.

It would take another two decades—until the mid-1960s—before major league players had their own labor union. And it wasn't marginal players like Lupien, Niemiec, and Gardella who led the revolution. It was superstars like Bob Feller, Sandy Koufax, and Don Drysdale who helped lay the groundwork, and superstars like Jim Bunning and Robin Roberts who persuaded their fellow athletes that only a union would give them the clout they needed to improve their working and living conditions and provide them with pensions to cushion their retirement when their playing days were over. They picked a union veteran named Marvin Miller without any experience in baseball to lead them into the promised land. In the 1970s, with the help of a courageous All-Star outfielder named Curt Flood, the union successfully challenged the owners' firm grip on their livelihoods by overturning the dreaded reserve clause. And in the 1980s and 1990s, when teams were reaping huge profits thanks to an influx of massive television revenues and increased attendance, the players went on strike several times to compel owners to share that abundance with the athletes who put the fans in the stands.

MONEY: ROBERT MURPHY

The first baseball union, the BPBP, and its breakaway PL, fell apart in 1890. Several other efforts to organize ballplayers—the Players Protective Association in 1900, the Fraternity of Professional Baseball Players of America in 1912, and the National Baseball Players Association in 1922—quickly died.

Players gained some leverage when new leagues emerged to compete with the major leagues for players and fan loyalty. These new leagues—the AL in 1901, the Federal League from 1914 to 1915, and the Mexican League in the 1940s—provided players with an alternative to the owners' despotism. But MLB quickly squelched or co-opted these threats.

Robert Murphy, a Harvard-educated lawyer who worked with the federal National Labor Relations Board (NLRB) and was an enthusiastic baseball fan, thought he had an answer. He knew that ballplayers had no minimum salary. The salaries were pitifully low compared to the profits they generated for owners. Players earned as little as $1,500 a year with no additional pay for spring training. Players were the property of team owners and thus unable to pursue other options. They could be fired without cause with only ten days' notice. They had no medical insurance.

Murphy visited spring training camps in early 1946, interviewing players and executives alike. He believed that MLB would never improve players' pay and working conditions on its own. Jumping to other leagues was not a viable option for most players. The only way for players to get a better deal was to form a union. So on April 17, 1946, Murphy registered the American Baseball Guild (ABG) as an official labor union. At a press conference the following day, Murphy said, "The Guild's purpose is to right the injustices of professional baseball and to give a square deal to the players, the men who make possible the big dividends and high salaries for stockholders and club executives."[4]

Murphy put together an eight-point program for ballplayers' rights. It included a $6,500 minimum salary (about $88,000 in 2021 dollars) with no maximum; salary arbitration if players and owners couldn't agree to final terms; and medical insurance. The plan also called for teams to give players half of the price when their contract was sold to another team. It also called for modification—if not elimination—of the reserve clause.

Not surprisingly, the team owners opposed the idea. One of the most vocal opponents was Washington Senators owner Clark Griffith, who claimed that what the union sought would "be fatal to the life of baseball." When Griffith forbid his players from reading ABG literature or discussing the union at the ballpark, Murphy filed an unfair labor practices claim against the owner's intimidation. But since the Supreme Court had long before ruled that MLB was exempt from the anti-trust laws, the NLRB's office in Washington, DC, didn't even respond to the complaint.

When Murphy made his dramatic announcement, he had no financial support or staff. Nor did he have a nucleus of rank-and-file ballplayers who embraced his idea. But he believed he could persuade and organize players to support his plan one team at a time. He initially chose the Pirates because the players were paid particularly poorly and because Pittsburgh was a union town led by the powerful United Steelworkers union. Murphy got the city's labor unions to support the ABG and to urge its members to boycott Pirates games until the team accepted the union. Andrew Federoff, regional director of the Congress of Industrial Organizations, proclaimed, "No red-blooded American man or woman carrying a union card will go to a ball game while there is a strike of players."

By May, Murphy believed that a significant majority of Pirate players would vote for the ABG so he petitioned the team management to allow the players to vote on whether to have the ABG represent them in collective bargaining. The team's owner, William Benswanger, refused, angering the players. Murphy gave him a deadline of June 5 to set a date for the vote. If he didn't agree, Murphy said, the players would go on strike, refusing to play the game scheduled for that day.

After Benswanger didn't respond on June 5, 1946, most of the players wanted to strike immediately, but on the day of the scheduled strike, Murphy made a tactical error, convincing the players to hold off. He was overconfident that public opinion would force the Pirates' hand. When it didn't, a contentious meeting took place before the June 7 game. Murphy was banned from attending, but Benswanger showed up and reminded the players that he had been a benevolent owner. One of the Pirates highest-paid players, pitcher Rip Sewell from Alabama, led the opposition, parroting the owners' line. To go through with the strike, the players decided a two-thirds majority would be required. Thus, although the tally was 20 to 16 in favor of the strike (including trainers and coaches), the vote failed.

Murphy filed another claim with the NLRB, this time in the local Pennsylvania office. The board rejected the Pirates owner's claim that it had an anti-trust exemption under Pennsylvania law. It ordered the Pirates to allow an official union election, but it wasn't scheduled until late August when the movement's steam would likely be gone.

Murphy filed similar NLRB claims against teams in Boston, Philadelphia, and New York. Meanwhile, Tony Lupien, who had decided not to sue MLB as an individual, led the effort to create a Players Guild among PCL players to demand a minimum salary, spring training pay, improved field lighting, and outside arbitration of disputes.

These initiatives, combined with the Al Niemiec court decision, Jorge Pasquel's Mexican League raids, and the threat of more lawsuits, finally pushed the owners to act. In early July owners from both leagues formed a committee to respond to the ABG's demands. The committee agreed to a minimum pay of $5,000, a 25 percent limit on any pay cuts, and, thanks to the initiative of Cardinals shortstop Marty Marion, a pension plan with contributions from both owners and players. The reforms also included $25 per day in spring training pay, still known to this day as "Murphy Money."

In August, the Pirates players voted again whether to have a union. This time the vote failed 15 to 3, with 12 abstentions. Most Pirate players favored the union, but many worried that Benswanger would seek revenge and demote pro-strike players to the minors or release them.

The ABG failed, and as Murphy had predicted, with the union threat gone, the owners began taking back many of their concessions. The minimum pay was immediately reduced to $4,500, and a new clause appeared in all player contracts giving teams the right to take players to court if they violated their contract's terms—affirming that baseball owners could treat their workers differently than workers in other industries. The owners also proposed expanding the season from 154 to 168 games but this failed as too obvious a scheme to pay for their salary concessions.

Sewell later received a gold watch from Commissioner Happy Chandler for undermining the strike. But Pirates infielder Lee Handley said,

> I don't think we gave Murphy a square deal. We let him down and I was one of those who did it. We're not radicals . . . We don't want to be affiliated with any labor organization. We want our own group, like the Professional Golfers Association or the Actors Guild . . . [but] we believe thoroughly in some plan for representation.[5]

It was precisely this failure to understand the real value of unionization that would thwart ballplayer rights well into the late-1960s.

While Murphy's crusade made some progress, it was far less than he had hoped for. Among other things, it left the reserve clause intact. The pension plan—which was supposed to be funded from receipts from World Series games and radio and TV revenues, and would apply to players with four or more years' major league playing experience, to start when they turned forty-five—was woefully underfunded from the start. Within three years it was almost bankrupt.

Murphy lamented the passivity of the players and their lack of labor consciousness. "The players have been offered an apple," he observed, "but they could have had an orchard." Murphy went on, "The players will eventually realize that the club owners who have had seventy years to change the one-sidedness of the baseball picture never acted until the American Baseball Guild threatened the very foundation—sometimes rotten—of their baseball empire."

FOUNDING THE MAJOR LEAGUE BASEBALL PLAYERS ASSOCIATION

The owners had tried to ward off the players' union by agreeing to set up a pension fund. But their efforts backfired when players quickly realized that the pension plan was a sham. Since the average player spent only four years in the majors, many of them understood the importance of providing some financial cushion for when their playing days were over. In 1953, when players began asking questions about how much money was in the pension fund, the owners stonewalled. Yankees hurler Allie Reynolds and Pirates slugger Ralph Kiner set up a meeting with owners after the All-Star game but they couldn't get a straight answer.

Each team picked a player representative to meet with the owners but they were not part of any formal organization that could take concerted action. Nor did most of the selected players know enough about economics and pensions to discuss, much less negotiate, with the owners.

In August 1953 the player representatives hired attorney Jonas Norman Lewis to serve as their liaison at the meeting with the owners. The owners took affront at the very idea of the players hiring their own lawyer. Dodgers owner Walter O'Malley, a fierce foe of unions, tried to talk Lewis out of working for the players. The owners should have been pleased because Lewis was a management-side attorney whose sympathies were more with the owners than the players. In fact, his law firm had represented the New York Giants for many years. One of his clients was the Harry Stevens concession firm that sold hot dogs, beer, and peanuts at major league ballparks. Lewis believed in baseball's reserve system and its exemption from anti-trust laws. He opposed strikes. The players' decision to hire Lewis demonstrated their naiveté in labor-management relations.

When Lewis arrived for the meetings, the owners refused to allow him in the room. This sent a clear message to the players that the owners didn't take them seriously. So when the owners held their annual winter meeting in Atlanta in December 1953, the player representatives organized their own meeting, where they formed the Major League Baseball Players Association (MLBPA). The Yankees co-owner Del Webb told Reynolds, his ace pitcher, that he wasn't pleased. "What are you attempting to do, start a union?" Webb asked. "That's the farthest thing from my mind," Reynolds responded, explaining that the players needed an organization to press the pension issue.[6]

In fact, many players were still wary of unions. So the players called their new organization an "association" just as they called the previous incarnation a "guild." But whatever they called it, their organization was a paper tiger. They elected pitcher Bob Feller, who was in the twilight of his illustrious career with the Cleveland Indians, as their first president, a position he held until 1959. The MLBPA had no full-time employees and no office. During the off-season, it had no means to communicate with the players. The organization didn't even have a way to collect dues, and some players were reluctant to pay dues anyway.

Even so, the formation of the MLBPA got the owners' attention. After a joint meeting with the players' representatives in 1954, the owners agreed to a funding formula for the pensions: 60 percent of all broadcast revenues from the World Series and All-Star game would go to the pension fund. "We were just infants," Kiner later recalled, "but we broke the ice."[7]

During its first six years, the MLBPA accomplished very little else. The organization's leaders hired Lewis on a part-time basis, didn't know what to ask him to do, and complained when he refused to tour spring training camps to meet with them. They fired him in 1959.

The players replaced Lewis with Frank Scott, a former traveling secretary for the Yankees, and gave him the title of executive director. At first he was hired on a part-time basis, but Scott suggested that the MLBPA set up an office with a full-time director. The players agreed, and Scott opened up headquarters in a New York hotel—the same office where he ran his business as a players' agent, helping them secure paid guest appearances and commercial endorsements. (The owners wouldn't allow him, or any other agent, to represent players in negotiations over salaries.)

Scott hired Judge Robert C. Cannon as the MLBPA's legal advisor. Cannon's father, also a lawyer, had represented Shoeless Joe Jackson during the infamous Black Sox scandal of 1919, but the younger Cannon was hardly a strong advocate for players. He told the owners that his "primary concern will be what's in the best interest of baseball. Second thought will be what's best for the players." Cannon's appointment was another example of the players' naiveté and inexperience. It soon became clear that Cannon was more interested in being the baseball commissioner than the union's lawyer, and he did little to offend the owners. When Commissioner Ford Frick retired in 1965, Cannon lobbied for the job but they passed him over.

DODGERS DUO: SANDY KOUFAX AND DON DRYSDALE

The MLBPA was stuck in a labor-management no-man's land. Many players were upset about their pay and working conditions but they had not yet embraced the idea of being part of a union. They felt powerless and didn't think they could challenge the team owners without undermining their careers.

But when superstar pitchers Sandy Koufax and Don Drysdale stood up for themselves against the Dodgers management in 1966, they showed other players that the owners weren't invincible in the face of collective action.

Drysdale and Koufax were both unlikely revolutionaries. Drysdale grew up in the Los Angeles suburbs, an outgoing golden boy from a middle-class family. He signed with the Dodgers in 1954 right out of high school. After two years in the minors, he was promoted to the Brooklyn Dodgers.

Koufax grew up in a working-class Jewish family in Brooklyn. His hero was his grandfather Max, a plumber, a socialist, and an intellectual. The young Koufax was shy and introspective.

In high school, Koufax was a better basketball than baseball player. In his senior year, he was Lafayette High's team captain and leading scorer. In the fall of 1953, he went to the University of Cincinnati hoping to become an architect and was a walk-on for the college basketball team, eventually earning a partial scholarship. He was only 6 feet 2 inches but he was a known as a "savage" rebounder and he could dunk. He was the freshman team's third-leading scorer with a 9.7 point average. His coach, Ed Jucker, thought Koufax could make it in professional basketball.

Junker was also Cincinnati's baseball coach, and he asked Koufax to join the team. In his only season, Koufax was 3-1 with a 2.81 ERA, 51 strikeouts, and 30 walks in 32 innings. He had a blazing fastball, and this attracted the attention of scouts. In 1954, after his freshman year in college, Koufax signed with the Dodgers for $6,000 with a $14,000 signing bonus. He intended to use the money to finish his college education if his baseball career failed.

Koufax and Drysdale met when they were teenagers at the Dodgers spring training camp. Koufax came to the Dodgers first, but Drysdale became a starter while Koufax was still struggling. After the 1957 season and before spring training in 1958, they both served in the Army Reserves at Fort Dix in New Jersey. They lived on the base and spent weekends together at Koufax's parents' home in Brooklyn. As their careers advanced, they remained friends but were not close. Koufax was single and mostly kept to himself. He liked to read and listen to music. His friends on the team were utility players like Dick Tracewski. Drysdale was married, owned a bar, and liked to go to the racetrack, occasionally hanging out with Dodgers general manager Buzzie Bavasi. Because they played in Los Angeles, both made extra money by making appearances on television shows made in and around Hollywood. Drysdale liked the limelight. Koufax didn't.

In 1957 the intimidating 6-foot-6-inch Drysdale led the club with a 17-9 record and 2.69 ERA. He continued to excel in subsequent seasons. In 1962, he won 25 games and the Cy Young Award. The next season he struck out 251 batters and won Game 3 of the World Series over the Yankees 1-0.

Under the rules at the time, teams who signed players for signing bonuses over $4,000 had to keep them on the major league roster for at least two years. Other Dodgers resented Koufax's presence on the team. He wasn't ready for the majors because he couldn't control his fastball. In his first six seasons with the Dodgers in Brooklyn and Los Angeles (1955–1960), he won 36 games and lost 40. In 1958 he led the league with 17 wild pitches.

During spring training in 1961, Dodgers catcher Norm Sherry noticed that the harder Koufax threw, the wilder he got. "Why not have some fun out there, Sandy?" Sherry suggested. "Don't try to throw so hard and use more curveballs and changeups."[8]

That advice changed Koufax's career. He had his first good season in 1961, going 18-13 and leading the league with 269 strikeouts. By 1963, he had eclipsed Drysdale as the team's best pitcher, going 25-5 with a 1.88 ERA and 306 strikeouts, earning both the Cy Young and Most Valuable Player awards. At that point, Koufax was clearly the best pitcher in major league baseball. In

1963, 1965, and 1966, Koufax and Drysdale carried the weak-hitting Dodgers to three pennants and two World Series championships.

By 1965, Koufax and Drysdale were perhaps the most dominant pitching duo in baseball history. That season Koufax won 26 games, had a 2.04 ERA, struck out 382 hitters, and earned his second Cy Young Award. Drysdale won 23 games with a 2.77 ERA and 210 strikeouts. He was the Dodgers' only .300 hitter and even banged seven homers. Together, they started more than half (85) of the Dodgers' games and pitched 44 percent of the team's innings, went 56-17, and had a combined 2.39 ERA. They led the Dodgers to a World Series victory over the Minnesota Twins. In the seven-game series, Koufax won two games, Drysdale won one game, and they each lost one game.

Given the team's mediocre hitting, this dynamic duo was mostly responsible for attracting more than 2.6 million people to Dodger Stadium that year, the highest attendance in baseball by far. The Dodgers estimated that an additional 10,000 fans showed up when Koufax was pitching while Drysdale attracted an additional 3,000 ticket-buyers when he took the mound. They put big profits in owner Walter O'Malley's bank account.

Koufax was angry at how O'Malley and Bavasi refused to negotiate seriously with him when he asked for a raise. After the 1963 season, Koufax asked Bavasi to raise his salary to $75,000. The Los Angeles newspapers reported that he had asked for $90,000. Koufax suspected that Bavasi had leaked the story to embarrass him and make him look greedy. Koufax recognized that despite his outstanding performances, he had no bargaining leverage. He wasn't allowed to hire an agent to negotiate on his behalf. Because of the reserve clause, his only options were to take what he was offered or quit playing MLB. He was a powerhouse on the mound but he felt powerless in his dealings with the Dodgers brass.

After leading the Dodgers to a World Series championship in 1965, Koufax and Drysdale expected big raises the next season. But when they met separately with Bavasi, he offered to raise Koufax's salary from $85,000 to $100,000 and Drysdale's from $80,000 to $85,000. They both thought they deserved more. The San Francisco Giants had signed Willie Mays for two years at about $125,000 per year.

One night the two met for dinner. In his autobiography *Once a Bum, Always a Dodger*, Drysdale recounted their conversation.

> "You walk in there and give them a figure that you want to earn," Sandy said, "and they tell you, 'How come you want that much when Drysdale only wants this much?'"
>
> "I'll be damned," I replied. "I went in to talk to them yesterday for the first time and they told me the same story. Buzzie wondered how I could possibly want as much as I was asking when you were asking for only this."[9]

Drysdale's wife came up with the idea of the two of them joining forces. "If Buzzie is going to compare the two of you, why don't you just walk in there together?" she proposed.

They thought it was a great idea. As *Los Angeles Times* sportswriter Bill Shaikin observed, "The duo effectively became baseball's first union—a union of two."[10]

In February 1966, a few weeks before the start of spring training, they asked the Dodgers for three-year contracts totaling $1 million, split equally, the equivalent of $167,000 a year ($1.3 million in 2021 dollars), which would have made them the highest-paid players in baseball. They told Bavasi to talk to their agent, entertainment lawyer J. William Hayes, who represented Koufax in his business dealings outside baseball. Both ideas were unheard of. No player had ever received a three-year contract. And no player ever had an agent negotiate on his behalf.

Koufax and Drysdale refused to go to spring training in Florida until Bavasi met their demands. They both signed a deal to appear in a Hollywood movie called *Warning Shot*—Drysdale as a TV commentator, Koufax as a detective—and appeared at a press event at Paramount Studios to show they were serious about their showbiz careers. They also agreed to appear on a TV variety show called *The Hollywood Palace*.

The news media wasn't friendly to the duo's hold out. The *Los Angeles Times* described their demands as a "double-barreled raid on the Dodger treasury." Other headlines included "Koufax-Drysdale Trade Looms, Bavasi Fed Up," "K-D Contract War Has Mates Uneasy," and "K and D Spurn Offer."[11] Given the press coverage, it wasn't surprising that most fans sided with the Dodgers against the two players. In his 1966 autobiography, Koufax wrote, "It was astonishing to me to learn that there were a remarkably large number of American citizens who truly did not believe we had the moral right to quit rather than work at a salary we felt—rightly or wrongly—to be less than we deserved."

Maury Wills, the Dodger's outstanding shortstop, also decided to hold out during spring training. He had singlehandedly revolutionized baseball with his base-stealing prowess. During the 1965 season he stole ninety-four bases.

"Mr. O'Malley scared me to death, saying I was in cahoots with them," Wills recalled. "He said, 'They might be able to get away with that, but you can't.'" Wills quickly reported for spring training and signed the contract O'Malley put in front of him. "I didn't even look at it," he remembered.[12]

Hayes, the duo's agent, warned them that their holdout would only work if they were willing to carry out their threat and quit baseball if necessary. Koufax was willing. His socialist grandfather had taught him to act on his principles, and Koufax believed that the Dodgers had violated his basic rights. During the holdout, Koufax told the *New York Times*,

> The negotiations have reached the point where they came down to basic principles. The ball club is defending the principle that it doesn't really have to negotiate with a ballplayer because we have no place to go. You might say Don and I are fighting for an anti-principle—that ballplayers aren't slaves, that we have a right to negotiate.

Koufax knew that 1966 would be his last season. For several years, he had been constantly in pain with arthritis in his left elbow, his pitching arm. Many of his teammates wondered how he could withstand the agony. He didn't want to risk permanent injury and was going to retire after the season anyway. He'd be willing to forgo that final year to take a stand on principle. Drysdale was more ambivalent. He had a wife and kids to support. On March 25, four weeks into their holdout, the *Los Angeles Times* published a photograph of Drysdale in uniform, working out at a local college. Once that photo appeared, it was clear that Drysdale wasn't going to prolong the strike much longer.

Koufax gave Drysdale permission to negotiate for both. Five days later, Bavasi agreed to pay Koufax $125,000 and Drysdale $110,000. Koufax objected. "I thought we're supposed to get the same thing," he said.[13] But Drysdale was willing to accept the lower amount. Only Mays had a higher salary that year.

Koufax and Drysdale's teammates knew that without them, the team had little chance to win the pennant and get that extra check for playing in the

World Series. The two pitchers joined the team in Arizona for the final exhibition games before the regular season began.

Their hold-out was groundbreaking—a major turning point in baseball's labor wars.

Bavasi acknowledged that their holdout was possible because they were the two best players on the team and indispensable to the Dodgers' success on the field and financially.

But he warned, "Be sure to stick around for the fun the next time somebody tries that gimmick. I don't care if the whole infield comes in as a package; the next year the whole infield will be wondering what it is doing playing for the Nankai Hawks."

What Bavasi misunderstood was that eventually not only the whole infield but every player in the majors could beat the owners if they stuck together. Koufax and Drysdale had demonstrated the power of players joining forces. For rank-and-file players without their star power, that meant seeing a union as their best form of leverage.

Koufax and Drysdale not only won substantial raises, they also forced the Dodgers to negotiate with their agent. In an article in *Sports Illustrated* in 1967, Bavasi explained that doing so "set a precedent that's going to bring awful pain to general managers for years to come because every salary negotiation with every humpty-dumpty fourth-string catcher is going to run into months of dickering."[14]

On this point, Bavasi was right. Eventually even the lowest-rank players would have their own agents but only after the MLBPA won that right through collective bargaining.

UNION REPS: JIM BUNNING AND ROBIN ROBERTS

Two other All-Star pitchers—Jim Bunning and Robin Roberts—had to overcome a lot of skepticism among their fellow players—not only to embrace the idea of joining a union but also to hire a New York–bred labor radical with no ties to baseball: Marvin Miller.

Bunning pitched for the Detroit Tigers from 1955 to 1963, making the All-Star team in six of those years. For much of that time, he was the Tigers' player representative to the union. Although Detroit was a strong union city, its sportswriters criticized Bunning's involvement in the MLBPA. Bunning suspected that the Tigers management planted some of these stories.

A reporter for the *Detroit News*, for example, labeled Bunning a "briefcase ballplayer" for his MLBPA activism. And when the Tigers traded him to the Phillies after the 1963 season, the *Detroit Free Press* ran a story headlined "Was Player Rep Bunning Too Busy?" warning that the trade "should serve as a lesson to the rest of players on the Tigers [not to waste time on union activities]."[15]

Once he joined the Phillies, Bunning discovered that the team made the players pay for parking spaces at the ballpark. He complained to team executives, who soon allowed Bunning and his teammates to park for free. In 1965, still in his pitching prime, he wrote an autobiography, *The Story of Jim Bunning*, in which he expressed his concern about the sport's unfair economic playing field. "We're an entertainment providing relaxation for people," he wrote, pointing out that while the teams were highly profitable, players were being shortchanged. He worried that the owners would hoard almost all the teams' expected TV revenues for themselves rather than increasing the share going to the players' pension fund. In 1990, when he was serving as a Republican congressman from Kentucky, Bunning recalled, "We would take our requests to the owners at a joint meeting and then they would just laugh at us and say, 'Sure, we'll look at it,' and that was the end of it. We didn't know labor law. We didn't know collective bargaining."[16]

With a BA in economics from Xavier University, Bunning was one of the few college graduates among pro players in the 1950s and 1960s. He saw that more and more teams were being purchased by big corporations, replacing local families. "The nature of ownership groups was changing dramatically," he recalled. "We wanted to make sure we knew where we were going even if management didn't."[17]

Bunning joined forces with Roberts, another future Hall of Fame pitcher and college graduate (Michigan State, where he starred in basketball and baseball), in trying to transform the union into a real bargaining force. Playing for the Philadelphia Phillies, Roberts was the best right-handed pitcher in the NL from 1950 to 1955, making the All-Star team each year. In his best season, 1952, he was 28-7 with a 2.59 ERA. He was at the 1953 meeting in Atlanta when the owners refused to meet with the players' lawyer, a rebuff that led to the MLBPA's founding. In 1954, his fellow players elected him the NL's MLBPA player representative. After being traded to the Baltimore Orioles in 1962, he remained active in the union. That experience, like Bunning's, opened his eyes to the MLBPA's weakness vis-à-vis the team owners.

In the fall of 1964, Roberts realized that the owners were about to sign a lucrative new television contract, and like Bunning, he was worried that the players wouldn't get their fair share for their pension fund.

Both Roberts and Bunning suspected that the owners weren't being honest about the amount of money in the MLB pension fund by low-balling the size of the revenues they received from radio and TV contracts. The teams contributed 95 percent of the revenue from the annual All-Star game (which the players didn't get paid for) and 40 percent of the broadcast fees from the All-Star and World Series games.

The two pitchers recognized that their fellow players harbored widespread distrust of the owners but lacked the knowledge or skills to challenge the owners' grip on the pension fund, licensing rights, and the basic economics of the baseball business. Roberts and Bunning persuaded the other union representatives that the MLBPA needed a full-time executive director who could help players understand the business side of baseball and go toe-to-toe in negotiations with the owners. The MLBPA set up a search committee consisting of Roberts, Bunning, Pirates pitcher Bob Friend, and Giants infielder Harvey Kuenn.[18] Former MLBPA president Bob Feller actively campaigned for the job. Friend's initial favorite was Judge Cannon. Bunning was partial to Tom Costello, a Detroit lawyer who had helped him with his personal matters. They also considered former Detroit slugger Hank Greenberg and Giants vice president Chub Feeney. Roberts asked his friend George Taylor, a professor at the University of Pennsylvania's Wharton School of Business, who worked with unions, for advice. Taylor had approached Lane Kirkland, a top official (and later president) of the AFL-CIO, about the job, but Kirkland wasn't interested. He next talked with Miller, then a high-ranking official with the United Steelworkers. Miller said he was willing to put his hat in the ring.

WHOLE NEW BALL GAME: MARVIN MILLER

Born in 1917, Miller grew up in Brooklyn as a Dodgers fan. He was a decent ballplayer in neighborhood pick-up games but not good enough to make the baseball team at James Madison High School (where Greenberg had graduated six years before him).

Miller's parents made sure he understood the importance of labor unions. At a young age he walked a picket line with his father, a clothing salesman who joined a fledging union organizing drive, which led to paid holidays and sick days. His mother was active with the New York City Teacher's Union. He spent summers at a camp run by the left-wing Workman's Circle organization.

After graduating from high school in 1933, he took several menial jobs, took some college classes at night, and then spent several years at Miami University in Ohio, where he was shocked by students' casual racism and anti-Semitism. He returned to New York to finish his degree at New York University.

As a teenager, Miller saw many of his neighbors and family members fall on hard times. His return to New York put him in the middle of a whirlwind of union and political activism. He determined to devote his career to making the world a more humane place.

Miller graduated from New York University in 1938 with a degree in economics. As the country was still trying to dig its way out of the Great Depression, he survived on temporary jobs until he landed a job as an investigator with the New York City Welfare Department. The work put him in close contact with the city's most indigent and desperate residents, which further radicalized him. He got heavily involved with the State, County and Municipal Workers of America, the union that represented his agency's employees, and participated in their efforts to help elect progressive candidates, from city council contenders to FDR. He also enrolled in graduate school at the New School for Social Research, a hotbed of radicalism. Between his job and his graduate classes, he realized that his New York University economics training had not prepared him to understand the real world of social injustice and human suffering.

In 1944 the FBI began a "loyalty" investigation of Miller as part of its efforts to root out communists and radicals from government, education, the labor movement, Hollywood, and other institutions. Its surveillance of Miller continued at least through 1949 and probably longer.

The probe was triggered by the activities of his wife, Theresa, who, according to FBI informants, had been literature director for the Olney Club in Philadelphia, an alleged Communist Party front group, in 1944. In 1948, she ran for the New York State Assembly on the American Labor Party ticket, which was heavily influenced by communists. Miller was also involved in radical circles. He had attended benefits for organizations that raised money for war relief to Russia, America's ally in World War II. In 1948 he supported the campaign of former vice president Henry Wallace, who was running for president on the left-wing Progressive Party ticket. Like Wallace, Miller spoke out for unions, workers' rights, and racial integration, which the FBI identified as left-wing causes. But the FBI could not substantiate that Miller was a communist or a threat to national security. If they had, he wouldn't have gotten a job with the federal National War Labor Board, resolving labor-management disputes during the war.

Miller eventually decided that unions were the key engine for creating social justice. After he left the labor board, he took jobs with the International Association of Machinists, the United Auto Workers (UAW), and the United Steelworkers of America (USWA).

Miller joined the USWA in 1950 as a staff economist in the research department. He rose through the ranks, eventually becoming the union's chief economist and assistant to the president. When he worked for the USWA, it was one of the largest and most powerful unions in the country, with 1 million members. As a member of the union's negotiating committee, Miller was constantly strategizing with union leaders on how to outmaneuver industry executives to win better pay, benefits, and working conditions for the steelworkers. He was frequently in meetings with the steel company honchos, honing his skills across the negotiating table.

In 1965, Miller's boss and mentor, USWA president David McDonald, lost a bitter election battle. McDonald's successor, I. W. Abel, asked Miller to stay on, but the election had exposed the union's internal divisions, and so after fifteen years with the USWA, Miller began looking for another job. He was offered positions with the Carnegie Endowment for International Peace and at Harvard University and was trying to decide which to take when George Taylor talked to him about the MLBPA position.

Miller was impressed that Roberts, whose pitching prowess he admired, was a key member of the search committee. He agreed to be interviewed for the job. Roberts, Bunning, and Kuenn met with Miller. Friend didn't show up for the meeting, having already decided that Judge Cannon was the right man for the job.

Miller was flabbergasted when Roberts asked him how he'd feel about appointing former vice president Richard Nixon as the union's legal advisor.

Miller knew that Nixon, a conservative Republican, was not very fond of labor unions, and Miller was surprised at Roberts's naiveté. He wondered if Nixon was Roberts's idea or whether Roberts was simply relaying the views of other members of the steering committee. Miller told the hiring committee that whoever they pick as executive director should be allowed to hire his own legal advisor. When he came home that day, Miller told his wife that he'd blown the interview and wouldn't get the job.

But he had let Roberts know that he was interested in the job, explaining that his background and experience and the MLBPA's needs were a perfect fit. He tried to soothe the fears of some players, and perhaps Roberts, that someone like him who had spent his life in the labor movement might encourage hostility between owners and players and even encourage the players to go on strike.

Some of Miller's close friends, as well as his son Peter, encouraged him to accept Harvard's offer to join its faculty. In his autobiography, Miller explained,

> The opportunity in baseball would never come again. The Players Association was a totally ineffective organization, and anything I did would be an improvement, and a big one. Other academic opportunities would likely be available down the road. And, if truth be told, the chance to lead an organization after years of toiling in the background was quite attractive.[19]

The hiring committee recommended Judge Cannon. At a January 1966 meeting of the player representatives from the different teams, the players unanimously endorsed the recommendation. As further evidence of the players' naiveté, the meeting was overseen by Baseball Commissioner William Eckert and his assistant Lee McPhail, who owed their allegiance to the owners not the players. Once the rank-and-file players voted to support Cannon, he would have the job.

But Cannon began having second thoughts once he realized that he wouldn't be getting his judicial pension if he took the MLBPA job. He asked the hiring committee to renegotiate his contract and raise his pay to make up for the loss of his pension benefits. He also told the union leaders that he didn't want to move to New York, where the MLBPA had its office.

The owners clearly wanted Cannon in the job. Pirates owner John Galbreath even offered to reimburse Cannon for his lost pension. By then, however, key players had soured on Cannon's candidacy. Even Bob Friend, Cannon's biggest booster, changed his mind, offended by the judge's greed. They withdrew the offer. Roberts called Miller to tell him that the job was his. Despite his wounded pride at not being the players' first choice, he told Roberts that he'd accept the offer if the players voted for him.

Once word got out that the union leaders wanted Miller, the owners mounted a full-scale lobbying campaign to persuade the players that he was the wrong guy. They feared having to deal with an experienced and skilled union man. The owners could rely on baseball writers—who depended on the owners to pay their travel costs and provide them with access for interviews and inside knowledge—to do their bidding. The owners got coaches and managers to warn the players—individually and at team meetings—that Miller would hurt the game and their livelihoods, warning that he would encourage them to strike, which the players couldn't survive on their modest salaries. The owners even enlisted Cannon in their campaign to discredit Miller. He distributed pamphlets to every clubhouse warning that Miller would bring mob-like goon squads and corruption into the players' union. The owners also recruited players willing to tell major newspapers that they objected to a radical union man in the job.

To bolster his chances, Miller went on a tour of spring training sites to talk with players on every team. His first meeting was with the Angels at their Palm Springs, California, camp. The day before Miller was scheduled to meet with the team, the Los Angeles *Herald-Examiner* ran a story headlined "We Don't Want Any Labor Boss in Baseball," quoting player rep Buck Rodgers (who had been talking with Cannon) and veteran outfielder Jimmy Piersall criticizing Miller.[20] Miller traveled to Arizona and met with the Giants, Cubs, and Indians. Those meetings did not go well. Miller was met with little enthusiasm and some hostility. In the Cleveland clubhouse, manager Birdie Tebbetts constantly interrupted Miller (who was supposed to be talking with the players, not the manager and coaches), even asking him, "How can the players be sure you're not a Communist?"[21] It appeared that the owners' anti-union, anti-Miller smear campaign was working.

At these meetings, the voting was conducted by the managers, and the players had to vote in public by raising their hands yes or no. Even players who may have supported Miller didn't want to vote for him in front of their managers. The Giants players voted unanimously (27-0) against Miller and the other teams also opposed him by lopsided margins. In total, the four teams opposed Miller by a 102-17 margin.

Miller next traveled to Florida, where most of the teams had their spring training camps. The tide began to turn, in part because the owners were going overboard in their hostility to Miller. Roberts, fearing that Miller would face the same hostile reaction in Florida he confronted in California and Arizona, made sure that the players ran the meetings, that team executives (including managers), were excluded, and that the voting was done by secret ballot. At these meetings, Miller reminded players that he wasn't a labor "boss" but that he would be working for them. The players would decide what concerns to raise and whether they wanted to go on strike.

When Miller arrived in Vero Beach to meet with the Dodgers, Koufax and Drysdale were still holding out. The players weren't sure whether their hold out was brave or foolhardy, but it got their attention. The day after Miller visited the Dodgers training camp, Bavasi called a meeting to talk with the players. As Jim Lefebvre, a second baseman who had been the 1965 Rookie of the Year, recalled, "Bavasi said, 'We can't have this guy. This means strike. Strike means no money, no food to feed your family.' We all looked at each and said, 'He's in.' Anybody Buzzie was that scared of had to be good for you."[22]

All the Florida meetings went well. The Florida teams voted for Miller by a landslide 472-34 margin, with five teams voting unanimously for him. In total, the rank-and-file players supported Miller by a 489-136 margin. On April 12, 1966, two days short of his forty-ninth birthday, Miller became the union's full-time executive director.

Once Miller's appointment was a sure thing, the owners worked hard to undermine his ability to do the job. The union's assets totaled $5,700, some used furniture in a rented New York office, and a single filing cabinet. The players' dues—a ridiculously low $50 a year—didn't come close to covering the MLBPA's expenses. Before Miller arrived, the owners had diverted some of the players' pension fund to support the union, which was illegal under the federal Taft-Hartley Act, but nobody noticed or cared. After Miller joined the union, all of a sudden the owners realized that they had been violating the law and ended the arrangement. Undaunted, Miller came up with a plan to finance the union by getting Coca-Cola to pay a licensing fee to put the players' images on the underside of their bottle caps. The owners tried to sabotage the deal by refusing to allow the soda company to use the teams' logos. So Coke airbrushed the logos off the caps and paid the MLBPA $60,000 for the privilege, enough to tide the union over. Over time, Miller negotiated more and much larger licensing agreements that benefited the players and the union.

Miller was shocked when, in June of 1966, the owners refused to negotiate with the union over the soon-to-expire pension agreement. Instead, the owners decided to unilaterally announce a new pension plan without meeting with the union. When Miller reminded Commissioner Eckert that this was another violation of federal law, they called off the press conference. The owners also refused to show Miller the owners' highly profitable new deal with TV rights to broadcast the All-Star game and World Series. The owners didn't want to share their new-found wealth with the players. Miller was particularly outraged when he learned that the owners had already broken the law by siphoning $167,440 from the pension fund and putting it in their own pockets. Miller used this revelation of the owners' greed and lawlessness as a bargaining chip to renegotiate the pension deal. He got them to redirect the players' previous contributions to the fund ($344 year) as dues to the union and to agree to a higher annual contribution to the pension fund. The owners agreed to funnel $4.1 million into the pension plan each year instead of tying the deal to World Series and All-Star game money. This new arrangement amounted to doubling the benefits for all players, coaches, managers, and trainers active since 1957. Miller also negotiated increased life insurance, health insurance, and widow's benefits. Over 99 percent of the players subscribed to the dues check-off, a remarkable show of support for Miller and the union.

Miller reminded the players that since most of them would have short major league careers—typically four or five years in the majors—they needed to stick together to support the union's effort to consolidate their pensions. Increasing payments and shortening the number of years needed to qualify for a pension became critical issues.

Before Miller, players had no right to determine the conditions of their employment. They were tethered to their teams through the reserve clause in every player's contract. Those contracts were limited to one season. The contracts reserved the team's right to retain the player for the next season. Each year, the team owners told players, Take it or leave it. The players had no leverage to negotiate better deals. Even superstars went hat-in-hand to owners at the end of the season, begging for a raise.

Before the union could seriously challenge the owners, Miller had to get the players to stand up for themselves. "People today don't understand how beaten down the players were back then," Miller recalled. "The players had low self-esteem, as any people in their position would have—like baggage owned by the clubs."[23]

"We had to get players to understand that they were a union," he recalled. "We did a lot of internal education to talk to players about broader issues."[24]

Miller instructed ballplayers in the ABCs of trade unionism: fight for your right to be treated as more than property; stick together against management; work on behalf of players who came before you and who would come after you; prepare yourself—professionally and financially—for life after your playing days are over; and don't allow owners to divide you by race, income, or your place in the celebrity pecking order.

By the end of his first year as MLBPA's head, Miller had put the union on a firm financial footing with the increased dues and the Coca-Cola deal. He shed the union's financial dependence on the owners. He replaced owner-friendly Judge Cannon as the union's legal advisor with Richard Moss, who had worked with him at the steelworkers' union.

Miller's second year with the union was nothing short of revolutionary. He negotiated the first basic collective bargaining agreement (CBA) in the history of professional sports. The contract, signed in February 1968, included a dramatic 67 percent increase in the minimum salary from $6,000 (roughly $45,000 in 2021 dollars) to $10,000 (about $76,000 today). It also included increases in cash allowances for incidentals such as meals and spring training.

Ballplayers were not immune to the spirit of rebellion animating the civil rights and anti-war movements. In April 1968, Roberto Clemente led a players' revolt, demanding that MLB cancel its games the day of Martin Luther King Jr's funeral. In June, Mets players forced the Giants to postpone a night game to honor the funeral of Senator Robert Kennedy, who had been assassinated in Los Angeles during his presidential campaign. That Sunday, an official day of mourning for Kennedy, the Reds' Milt Pappas; the Astros' Dave Giusti, Rusty Staub, and Bob Aspromonte; and the Pirates' Maury Wills refused to play. All of them were fined. Pappas was traded a few days later. Giusti, Staub, and Aspromonte were traded after the season. Wills was left unprotected in the expansion draft.

On issues large and small, players began to recognize how Miller operated and stood up for them. In the summer of 1968, for example, Pappas, the Reds' union player representative, complained that the team had bumped the players out of first-class airplane seats in lieu of the reporters even though the CBA required first-class seating. Miller met with Reds president Bob Howsam, who relented. The word of Miller's efforts spread quickly throughout all the teams' locker rooms.

Before Miller's arrival, player grievances could only be heard by the commissioner, who was selected by team owners—a paternalism that players had never challenged. The second CBA, in 1970, established players' right to binding arbitration over grievances and permitted players to hire agents to negotiate on their behalf. By 1973, salary demands were subject to go to neutral and binding arbitration as well.

During his fifteen years as the MLBPA's executive director, Miller used the owners' obvious greed, duplicity, and disregard for players' well-being to galvanize the players' support for the union.

CHALLENGING THE RESERVE CLAUSE: CURT FLOOD

The biggest hurdle the union had to overcome was the owners' fierce opposition to eliminating the reserve clause. Miller believed it was possible but that it would take time, and he quickly began setting the stage.

The reserve clause restricted the right of players to move from club to club. That undermined their bargaining power to improve their pay and working conditions. A player could only negotiate with the team that had him on its reserve list. He could not talk with other clubs for a better contract. A team could sell, trade, or terminate his contract without his consent, but otherwise he remained the property of the team until he retired.

In 1969 Miller and the MLBPA pressured the owners to participate in a Joint Study Committee on the Reserve System. The three MLBPA representatives on the committee were Miller, Moss, and Bunning along with five representatives of the owners, who insisted that ending the reserve clause would destroy professional baseball.

At the committee's first meeting, Bunning mentioned the union's proposal to allow a player to leave his team if his salary did not reach a certain level. The owners' rejected this idea, claiming it "would create an incentive to do poorly," to which Bunning responded, "No one tries to have a bad year."[25]

During negotiations over the 1970 CBA, the MLBPA proposed giving players the option of becoming free agents once every three years. The owners rejected the idea, claiming that it attacked "the heart of the game and the reserve system."[26]

Curt Flood was only thirty-one when he stood up to baseball's establishment by challenging this feudal system. He was in his prime—an outstanding hitter, runner, and centerfielder with potentially Hall of Fame statistics. His protest destroyed his career.

Born in 1938, Flood, an African American, grew up in Oakland, California. During World War II, his father worked in various defense-related jobs while his mother ran a small cafe and mended parachutes to help the family make ends meet. After the war, they both found menial jobs at Fairmont Hospital.

Growing up, Flood pursued two passions: art and sports. As a teen, he created the artistic backgrounds for school proms and plays and earned extra money designing storefront window displays and advertising signs for a local furniture store. From the time he was nine, local baseball coaches recognized that Flood was a gifted player. He played at Oakland Technical High School and led his local American Legion team to the 1955 state championship, hitting .620 in 27 games. After graduating in 1956, he signed a $4,000 contract, with no bonus, with the Cincinnati Redlegs (the name they used for several years to avoid being called the "Reds" during the height of the Cold War). When he showed up at spring training in Tampa, Florida, he was ushered out a side door of the Redlegs' hotel and sent across town to a boarding house where the Black players stayed.

The team sent Flood to its High Point–Thomasville team in the Class B Carolina League for the 1956 season. He was prohibited from staying in the same hotels or eating in the same restaurants as his white teammates. He couldn't use the bathrooms when the team bus stopped at gas stations. Many Southern fans were not happy with Flood's presence on the diamonds.

"One of my first and most enduring memories is of a large, loud cracker who installed himself and his four little boys in a front-row box and started yelling 'Black bastard' at me," Flood recalled.[27]

Flood had difficulty adjusting to the segregation and hostility not only from fans but also from his white manager and teammates. He frequently returned to his hotel and cried. But as he explained, "I solved my problem by playing my guts out."[28] He led the league in batting with a .340 average, set a league record with 133 runs scored, led the league with 388 putouts, and set a team record with 29 home runs. He was named the league's Player of the Year.

The Redlegs called him up at the end of the 1956 and 1957 seasons. After playing winter ball in Venezuela, he got a telegram informing him that he'd been traded to the St. Louis Cardinals, the most Southern team in the major leagues. He began the 1958 season with the Cardinals' Double-A team in Omaha, but after hitting .340 in 13 games he was called up and became the Cardinal's starting center fielder.

Between 1958 and 1969, Flood was one of baseball's best players. (He didn't play in 1970 and played only 13 games in 1971.) Overall he played in 1,759 games, had a .293 lifetime average, won seven Gold Gloves, and was a three-time All Star (1964, 1966, and 1968). He hit over .300 six times. He had 1,861 hits but had he been able to remain in baseball, he would have reached 2,000 hits and perhaps even 2,500 hits. He played on the Cardinals teams that won pennants in 1964, 1967, and 1968 and won the World Series in 1964 and 1967. *Sports Illustrated* put a photo of Flood making a leaping catch on the cover of its August 19, 1968, issue with the caption "Baseball's Best Center Fielder." In 1965 he and Tim McCarver were named team co-captains, an honor he retained until 1969.

Flood was one of the first ballplayers to get involved in the burgeoning civil rights movement. In February 1962, at the invitation of his hero, Jackie Robinson, the twenty-four-year old Flood traveled to Jackson, Mississippi, to speak, along with Robinson and African American boxers Floyd Patterson and Archie Moore, at a protest rally against segregation organized by civil rights leader Medgar Evers. He told the crowd of 3,800 at a Masonic Temple that the rally helped him realize that he had a personal responsibility to fight racial injustice.[29]

Flood knew that bigotry wasn't confined to the South, but he was shocked by his experience trying to move into an all-white neighborhood in the Oakland suburb of Alamo. In October 1963, Flood put down a deposit to rent a three-bedroom house for himself, his pregnant wife, and their four kids. Once the property owner learned that Flood and his family were Black, he threatened to shoot them if they arrived to integrate the all-white neighborhood. Flood filed suit in Contra Costa County and won a temporary restraining order allowing his family to occupy the home. They arrived accompanied by eleven sheriff's deputies, several highway patrolmen, and two representatives from the state Fair Employment Practices Commission along with many print and TV reporters. About a dozen white supporters—local women and their children—showed up to welcome the Floods to their neighborhood. After the law enforcement officials determined that the house was safe to enter, Flood addressed the crowd, "It doesn't make any difference whether I'm a professional athlete or a negro or whatever. I'm a human being. If I have enough money to rent the house, I think I ought to have it." He told the Baltimore *Afro-American* newspaper, "You don't do these things if you scare easily, and this time I knew I was legally and morally right."[30] After the Floods moved in, white neighbors brought them meals, took them shopping, and invited Flood to play golf and bridge but the Floods continued to get racist phone calls and the Flood children confronted racist taunts.

"For Curt, players' rights and civil rights were part of the same idea," recalled his widow, actress Judy Pace Flood. Even before the MLBPA had any influence, Flood was an eager trade unionist. "On our first date, over dinner in 1964, he quizzed me about the Screen Actors Guild," Pace Flood remembered. He was particularly interested in the fact that SAG members had their own agents and lawyers, could negotiate with film studios over salaries, and could move to different studios—all things prohibited in major league baseball at the time.[31]

Flood played for the Cardinals for twelve seasons. After the 1969 season, the Cardinals traded him to the Phillies but Flood didn't want to move to Philadelphia, which he called "the nation's northernmost Southern city."[32] The Phillies offered him a $100,000 salary for the 1970 season, a $10,000 boost from his Cardinals salary. But for Flood, it was a matter of principle. He objected to being treated like a piece of property and to the reserve clause's restriction on his freedom.

Flood talked with Miller about the possibility of suing MLB in order to overturn the reserve clause and baseball's 1922 exemption from the Sherman Anti-Trust Act, which was intended to prevent collusion and monopolistic practices by business. It was as if, as Miller once observed, "the courts were saying, 'Yes, you're an American and have the right to seek employment anywhere you like, but this right does not apply to baseball players.'"[33]

Miller warned Flood that the odds were against him. He pointed out that a lawsuit would be expensive and could take two or more years. Moreover,

Miller said, even if Flood won the lawsuit, the owners would probably blacklist him as a player and as a future coach or manager. Miller recalled, "I said to Curt, 'Unless some miracle takes place and the Supreme Court reverses itself, you're not going to win,' and Curt, to his everlasting credit, said, 'But would it benefit all the other players and future players?' And I said, 'Yes.' And he said, 'That's good enough for me.'"[34]

Miller invited him to a MLBPA Executive Committee meeting in San Juan, Puerto Rico, in December to ask for the union's financial and moral support. They voted unanimously to back the lawsuit. Miller recruited Arthur Goldberg—his former colleague in the steelworker's union, President John Kennedy's secretary of labor, a former associate justice of the U.S. Supreme Court, and former U.S. ambassador to the United Nations—to represent Flood.

On December 24, 1969, Flood sent a letter to Commissioner Bowie Kuhn.

> After twelve years in the major leagues, I do not feel I am a piece of property to be bought and sold irrespective of my wishes. I believe that any system which produces that result violates my basic rights as a citizen and is inconsistent with the laws of the United States and of the several States. It is my desire to play baseball in 1970, and I am capable of playing. I have received a contract offer from the Philadelphia club, but I believe I have the right to consider offers from other clubs before making any decision. I, therefore, request that you make known to all Major League clubs my feelings in this matter and advise them of my availability for the 1970 season.[35]

Kuhn immediately rejected Flood's request so Flood made the letter public and sued MLB.

Most baseball writers opposed Flood's suit. They viewed him as a whining, spoiled brat, making $90,000 a year. He alienated many baseball fans when, during an interview with Howard Cosell on *ABC's Wide World of Sports* on January 3, 1970, he said that "a well-paid slave is, nonetheless, a slave."

The case known as *Flood v. Kuhn* began on May 19, 1970, in federal court in New York City. Flood's lawyers recruited four prominent baseball figures to testify on his behalf: Jackie Robinson, Hank Greenberg, Bill Veeck, and Jim Brosnan. Both Robinson and Greenberg had been traded by their long-time teams (the Dodgers and Tigers, respectively) against their will. Robinson chose to retire rather than play for the Giants. Greenberg played for the Pirates for a year then retired as a player, eventually becoming White Sox general manager.

He knew that testifying at Flood's trial meant he'd never work in organized baseball again. Veeck, the maverick owner, had always battled his fellow owners to democratize professional baseball. Brosnan had been a major league relief pitcher from 1954 through 1963. In 1959 he wrote *The Long Season*, based on his baseball diary, followed by *The Pennant Race*, based on his 1962 diary. Both the Reds and the White Sox told him he could no longer write about his experiences without their permission. Brosnan complained to Commissioner Ford Frick, who didn't bother to respond. By the time of Flood's trial, Brosnan had become a full-time writer and sports commentator.

On the witness stand, Robinson testified, "Anything that is one-sided in this country is wrong, and I think the reserve clause is a one-sided thing in favor of the owners, and I think certainly it should at least be modified to give a player an opportunity to have some control over his destiny." He predicted that if the reserve clause weren't changed it would "lead to a serious strike in terms of the ballplayers."[36]

After three weeks, the judges ruled in favor of the owners. Flood's lawyers appealed to the U.S. Court of Appeals, which in April 1971 also ruled against Flood. The Supreme Court agreed to hear the case and heard oral arguments on March 20, 1972.

Goldberg was not well-prepared and made several mistakes during his oral argument before his former Supreme Court colleagues. He lost his place, repeated himself, failed to answer the justices' questions, went past his allotted time, and recited Flood's year-by-year batting averages for no apparent reason. His friend, Justice William Brennan, cringed from the bench watching Goldberg struggle to make the case. Goldberg later acknowledged, "[I was in] over my head." But given the make-up of the court, it was unlikely that Goldberg would have prevailed even if he had been at the top of his game.

On June 19, 1972, the Supreme Court ruled against Flood by a 5-3 vote. Writing the majority decision, Justice Harry Blackmun admitted that baseball's exemption from federal anti-trust laws was an "aberration" but declared that it was up to Congress, not the court, to fix the situation.

Flood paid a huge financial and emotional price for his crusade. Not only did he give up his $100,000 salary, but—as Miller warned him—he was blacklisted by major league owners despite his talent. Instead, he spent years traveling to Europe and devoting himself to painting and writing, including his autobiography *The Way It Is*. Looking back, Flood explained,

> I guess you really have to understand who that person, who that Curt Flood was. I'm a child of the sixties, I'm a man of the sixties. During that period this country was coming apart at the seams. We were in Southeast Asia. Good men were dying for America and for the Constitution. In the southern part of the United States we were marching for civil rights and Dr. King had been assassinated, and we lost the Kennedys. And to think that merely because I was a professional baseball player, I could ignore what was going on outside the walls of Busch Stadium was truly hypocrisy and now I found that all of those rights that these great Americans were dying for, I didn't have in my own profession.[37]

Flood died of throat cancer in 1997 at age fifty-nine. The following year, with the support of Jim Bunning—by then a Republican U.S. Senator from Kentucky—Congress passed the Curt Flood Act, apparently intended to overturn baseball's anti-trust exemption, which the Supreme Court had three times upheld. But the bill "carved out so many exclusions" in "almost every conceivable situation" that it was "basically pointless."[38]

In 1999, *Time* magazine named Flood one of the ten most influential people in sports in the twentieth century. Upon Flood's untimely death, Miller said,

> At the time Curt Flood decided to challenge baseball's reserve clause, he was perhaps the sport's premier center fielder. And yet he chose to fight an injustice, knowing that even if by some miracle he won, his career as a professional player would be over. At no time did he waver in his commitment and determination. He had experienced something that was inherently unfair and was determined to right the wrong, not so much for himself, but for those who would come after him. Few praised him for this, then or now. There is no Hall of Fame for people like Curt.[39]

THE MLBPA DISMANTLES THE RESERVE CLAUSE

When the players were deciding whom to pick as their union's first executive director in 1966, the owners, most sportswriters, and some players warned that hiring a career union guy like Miller would lead to strikes. That year, New York City's sanitation workers had gone on strike and shut down the city's vital subway system for twelve days. Over the next few years, the United States experienced major work stoppages by sanitation workers in 1968 in

Memphis (where Martin Luther King Jr. had gone to support the strikers and was murdered); Chrysler auto workers (1968); New York City and Florida school teachers (1968); California farm workers (1970); postal workers across the country (1970); New York City police officers (1971); and longshoremen at fifty-six west coast ports (1971). The longshoremen got most of what they wanted: a significant pay increase, improved medical benefits to include dental and prescription medicine for workers and their families, better pensions, life insurance, and a retirement age lowered from 69 to 65.

For some players, these and other strikes represented their worst fears. For others, it demonstrated the necessity that workers use strikes to improve their lives against greedy and recalcitrant owners. Miller made it clear that only the players, by a rank-and-file vote, could decide whether to strike.

Not surprisingly, it was a pension issue that triggered the players' strike in 1972—the first strike in the history of American professional sports. Players wanted an increase based on inflation. The owners saw it as a chance to break the union. "The perception on our side was that the union was still weak," said John Gaherin, the owners' chief negotiator. "This was the time to take it on."[40]

But the owners hadn't reckoned that Miller would prepare the players for this by reminding them how rich the owners were getting from their labor. He informed the players that the owners had reneged on their written agreement to increase their funding of the players' health and pension plan. The owners hadn't counted on how unified the players were.

Miller and union leaders visited the teams at their spring training camps to explain the situation. On March 30, the players authorized a strike by a 663 to 10 vote. The next day, the forty-eight-member executive board (two from each team) voted 47-0 for an immediate strike, with Dodger representative Wes Parker abstaining.

The owners, realizing that they were losing more money from lost attendance than they would have to pay to meet the union's pension demands, conceded after thirteen days. The owners agreed to increase their contribution to the pension fund from $5.45 million to $5.94 million. (It had been $2.85 million in 1966.) During the strike, eighty-six games were cancelled and never played.

The next year, it was the owners who went on strike. In September 1972, negotiations began for a third CBA. The players wanted neutral salary arbitration and veteran players to be able to refuse trades (as Flood had not been able to do). On February 8, 1973, negotiations stalled, and the owners announced that they would lock players out of spring training. They hoped to exact revenge for their humiliating defeat the previous year. But once again the players and their union prevailed. The MLBPA and the owners agreed to a new three-year contract that included neutral binding salary arbitration for players with at least two years' service time. It allowed players who had ten years of service in the majors—and five with their current team—to veto trades. It prohibited teams from sending players who had five years of service with that team to the minors without their consent, increased spring training allowances, and boosted the minimum salary to $15,000 for 1973–1974 and $16,000 for 1975.

On March 27, 1973, pitcher Jim Perry approved the sale of his contract with Minnesota to Detroit—the first use of the players' new rights. (After the 1973 season was over, Cubs infielder Ron Santo vetoed his trade to the Angels, the first player to do so.)

In 1974 the union filed a grievance, under the new binding arbitration rule, on behalf of that season's Cy Young Award winner Jim "Catfish" Hunter after Oakland Athletics owner Charlie Finley refused to pay the $50,000 insurance annuity that was part of Hunter's contract. Hunter used the union's newly won right to a three-person board to hear all grievances. Miller represented the union, Gaherin represented the owners, and both sides agreed to hire Peter Seitz, an experienced arbitrator, as the third member. Everyone knew that Seitz would be the deciding vote. Seitz agreed with the union that Finley had violated the contract and that Hunter could become a free agent—the first in modern baseball history. Two weeks later, after twenty teams had bid for Hunter's services, he signed a five-year, $3.5 million contract with the Yankees, by far the richest contract in baseball and more than double that of the next-highest player. Players soon realized how much they were being underpaid.

But Miller wanted a wider ruling on behalf of free agency and found a weakness in the owners' cherished reserve clause. At the close of the 1975 season, Miller persuaded Dodgers pitcher Andy Messersmith and Expos pitcher Dave McNally to refuse to sign contracts with their teams, claiming that they were free agents. Miller viewed this as a way to challenge the clause that gave owners the right to renew a player's contract without his consent.

Miller, Gaherin, and Seitz again formed the three-person grievance board. Seitz tried to convince the union and the owners to resolve the matter without his intervention but the stakes were too high for either side to concede.

Miller pointed out that based on the contract language, the reserve clause allowed a team to renew a player's contract on the same terms for one year. To Miller, "one year" meant "only one year."[41]

On December 23, 1975, Seitz ruled in favor of Messersmith and McNally, agreeing with Miller that owners didn't have the right to perpetually renew contracts, that renewals could only be a one-time thing, and that players should be free to negotiate with another team.

This momentous decision reversed almost a century of labor-management relations in MLB. The owners were shocked and appalled. Commissioner Bowie Kuhn quickly fired Seitz as the permanent neutral arbitrator, accusing him of having had "visions of the Emancipation Proclamation dancing in his eyes."[42] MLB appealed the ruling, arguing that ending the reserve clause would be a catastrophe for baseball, but in February 1976 the Eighth Circuit Federal Court upheld Seitz's ruling. The reserve clause was history.

The union and MLB went back to the bargaining table to negotiate the fourth CBA. Still smarting from their huge defeat, the owners locked players out of spring training for the first few weeks of March, hoping to get the union to establish a weak free agency policy as part of the next agreement. But the players pushed back and forced the owners to back down. The two sides agreed to a four-year contract (1976–1979) that allowed players to become free agents after six years. That six-year provision helped the players. If every player went on the market after each one-year contract, it would reduce their leverage to maximize their salaries. By restricting the number of players who came up for free agency each year, the auction price would increase. The six-year rule has remained in place ever since.

In April, Messersmith became the first free agent under the new contract, signing a three-year, $1 million deal with the Braves. After the season was over, Orioles slugger Reggie Jackson, another free agent, signed with the Yankees for five years and $29 million, making him the game's highest-paid player.

In July 1978 the owners replaced Gaherin with Ray Grebey, formerly a negotiator for General Electric, as their chief negotiator. This signaled that the owners were gearing up for fight when the CBA expired in December 1979. In response, the MLBPA voted to raise money for a strike fund just in case. As expected, in 1980 the owners sought to regain control over the players by demanding that each team receive compensation for free agents, a move designed to weaken the free agency system.

The owners knew that their demand could provoke a players' strike but they figured they could outlast the players. They miscalculated. After Miller toured the spring training camps to meet with the players, they voted 967 to 1 to authorize a strike if the two sides couldn't agree on a new contract. On April 1, the union's executive board voted 27-0 to cancel the remainder of the spring training games and set a strike date of May 22. In negotiations, the owners refused to budge. So the players walked out, in the middle of the season, on June 12, 1981.

With the union keeping the players informed about the ongoing talks, they stuck together, from superstar outfielder Dave Winfield (who lost roughly $7,770 for each day of the strike) to players earning the minimum salary of $32,500 (about $180 a day). On August 10, after 50 days and 712 cancelled games, the owners caved in.

"From the standpoint of labor, it was the most principled strike I've ever been associated with," recalled Miller, who took himself off the union's payroll during the strike to demonstrate his own solidarity.

> Many of the players struck not for a better deal for themselves but for a better deal for their colleagues, and for the players who would be coming into baseball in the future . . . There were veterans on every team who remembered how it used to be and the role of union solidarity in changing things.[43]

Even after Miller retired, the spirit of solidarity he brought to the organization remained. In 1982 for example, Brooks Robinson, the former Orioles star third baseman, was a color commentator for games broadcast on WMAR-TV when station employees went on strike, picketing outside the building for two months before the start of the baseball season. Robinson refused to cross the picket line, which put pressure on management to settle. The strike ended the next day.

THE MLBPA AFTER MILLER

Miller outmaneuvered baseball owners and their hired commissioners throughout his tenure with the MLBPA. He and the union didn't lose a single important battle in their crusade to improve pay, conditions, and benefits for superstars and rank-and-file players alike.

By the time Miller retired in 1982, the players had gained the right to arbitration for disciplinary issues and salaries and increased the size of their pensions. Minimum salaries increased from $6,000 to $33,500 (a doubling of annual income in inflation-adjusted dollars) while average salaries grew from $19,000 to $241,497 (more than a fourfold increase in inflation-adjusted dollars). It established players' rights to binding arbitration over salaries and grievances. Players also won the right to hire agents for contract negotiations; increased per-diem allowances; improvements in travel conditions; and better training facilities, locker room conditions, and medical treatment.

Eventually Miller and the union persuaded the owners to fund the pension from their national TV contract. By 1980, that was bringing $15.5 million a year into the fund. Even baseball players who had short and less-than-illustrious careers would receive good retirement benefits.

When Miller retired, the union hired his top legal advisor, Donald Fehr, as its new executive director. The owners hoped that without Miller, the union might not be as formidable a foe. Under Fehr, the MLBPA consolidated its economic victories with one exception: During the 1985 CBA negotiations, the union agreed to raise the required service time for players seeking salary arbitration from two years to three.

During those negotiations, the owners claimed that they were losing money—in fact, they falsely claimed that MLB had shown a profit only once since 1972. Under the CBA, the owners had to make their financial data available to the MLBPA. Stanford economics professor Roger Noll examined the data and determined that the owners had made $24 million in 1984. The alleged losses, he discovered, were the result of shady bookkeeping (for example, lowballing revenue from TV and radio, parking, and owners' other businesses) and excessive executive salaries.

Meanwhile the owners were engaged in an illegal war against free agency and increasing salaries. In 1984, after replacing the incompetent Kuhn with Peter Ueberroth, a businessman who had organized the successful Olympic Games in Los Angeles, the owners conspired against the players, refusing to sign free agents to multiyear contracts. Not only utility players but also superstars like Tim Raines and Andre Dawson received one-year offers at salaries lower than they, and most baseball experts, expected. In most cases, players received offers only from their own team, indicating that the owners were colluding with each other to avoid bidding wars for players. In 1985, only four of the sixty-two free agents switched teams.

Fehr recognized the collusion and was determined to challenge the owners' illegal conspiracy. In February 1986, the union filed its first of three arbitration cases charging the owners with illegal collusion. The neutral arbitrator, Thomas Roberts, ruled against the owners. The owners fired Roberts and replaced him with George Nicolau, an experienced arbitrator in sports and other industries. After seven months of hearings, fifty witnesses, and 8,500 pages of testimony, Nicolau also determined that MLB teams had colluded to restrict bidding for free agents. "By common consent, exclusive negotiating rights were, in effect, ceded to former clubs," he wrote in his 81-page opinion. The union kept filing grievances as new information on the owners' collusion emerged. In 1988, Nicolau ruled that the owners had devised another way to collude against the players by creating a databank so they could compare salary offers to free agents. In 1990, based on Nicolau's ruling, lawyers for the players and owners negotiated a $280 million settlement for the aggrieved players.[44]

Players who previously may have given owners the benefit of the doubt now realized that they could not trust baseball's barons. After Ueberroth resigned as commissioner in 1989, the owners replaced him with former Yale University president Bart Giamatti. He served for only five months before dying of a heart attack. The owners picked Fay Vincent to fill the position but soon determined that he was too weak to deal with the union. In 1992, Milwaukee Brewers owner Bud Selig helped lead a coup that ousted Vincent. They owners installed Selig—who had participated in their collusion—as acting commissioner.

After the owners were found guilty of collusion, players' salaries began to increase, and the gap between large- and small-market teams, and especially their ability to compete for free-agent talent, widened. Under Selig, the owners included several proposals in the 1994 CBA negotiations that they knew would antagonize the union. This included elimination of salary arbitration and a restriction of free agency. The owners also insisted that as a quid pro quo for introducing a new revenue-sharing plan among teams and in order to help franchises in small-market cities, the players agree to a salary cap. After fighting for almost three decades to improve their wages, the players would not accept a salary cap under any circumstances. In July 1994, in a move that further angered the players, the owners withheld a $7.8 million deposit into the players' pension fund.

Both the owners and the players expected the other side to back down in order to avoid a strike. Both sides misjudged the other side's resolve.[45]

On July 27, 1994, the players voted to give the union's executive board the authority to set a strike date. On August 12, the players went on strike. Two weeks later, the MLBPA released a study by Roger Noll reporting that "baseball is financially healthy" and "the claim of widespread disaster in the sport is pure fiction." In September, the union sent out the first checks from its $200 million strike fund.

The players stuck together. The remainder of the reason was cancelled as was the post-season. The World Series was cancelled for the first time since 1904. Negotiations continued throughout the rest of 1994 and into the following year. President Bill Clinton assigned former Labor secretary Bill Usery Jr. to help resolve the strike—to no avail.

The owners threatened to hire replacement players if the strike was not settled before spring training in 1995 and began recruiting minor leaguers and former major leaguers to serve as strikebreakers. Owner Peter Angelos of the Orioles—a former labor lawyer—refused to field a team of strike-breaking players despite threats of fines and suspensions from his fellow owners. Tigers manager Sparky Anderson announced that he would refuse to manage a team of replacements. "There ain't no place in our game for replacement players," he said. "The one thing I have that will never leave me is integrity. That is the one thing I have that money can't buy."[46]

The union challenged the owners' strikebreaker plan. The National Labor Relations Board and then federal judge (and future Supreme Court justice) Sonya Sotomayor, thwarted the owners' strategy. The strike ended on April 2, 1995, after 232 days, and nearly a month after the regular season was supposed to begin.

The contentious negotiations continued for more than another year. The two sides didn't reach an agreement until December 1996, setting terms through 2000. The new CBA included a luxury tax on team payrolls—a form of revenue-sharing—but did not include any of the owners' proposed changes that had triggered the 1994 strike.

But the strike had repercussions that neither side had anticipated. The cancelling of the World Series, in particular, soured many fans on the game. Baseball writers and TV commentators took a "pox on both your houses" perspective, but when play resumed in April 1995, many fans expressed their anger by verbally abusing the players in stadiums around the country. Even though the union had won the strike, Fehr and the other union officials did little to win the fans' loyalty although a few players stepped into the breach. After the strike ended, for example, Dodgers catcher Mike Piazza donated $100 for every home run he hit to the union that represented the concessionaires, who lost considerable pay when 921 games were canceled. It was an individual gesture of empathy for Dodger Stadium's working class—ushers, ticket takers, parking-lot attendants, and food vendors—that generated goodwill among the Dodgers' fan base.

In the 2002 agreement, Fehr and the MLBPA allowed the owners to institute revenue sharing and a luxury tax. Although the owners had to pay the tax, it gave them an additional incentive to limit pay raises because the tax kicked in if a team exceeded a certain total salary figure. Although minimum salaries continued to increase, arbitration continued, and free agency remained intact, the union was gradually resting on its laurels rather than staking out new frontiers.

MILLER'S LEGACY

"The difference between a ballplayer's being required to accept whatever a club offered him, as had been the case almost from the beginning of professional baseball, and the new system of salary arbitration was like the difference between dictatorship and democracy," Miller wrote in his 1991 autobiography *A Whole Different Ball Game*.[47]

After Miller retired in 1982, the union continued to make advances for players in terms of wages, benefits, and working conditions. By 2019, the minimum salary had jumped to $555,000, the average salary to $4.4 million, and the median salary to $1.5 million. The major stars—the best-paid 25 percent of the players—earned 75 percent of the total salaries. Many Americans believe that major league players have become spoiled millionaires but don't realize that the typical player spends only five years in the majors. It is a hard perception to shake particularly since the union has done little in recent decades to influence public opinion.

Since Miller arrived on the scene, the owners had warned that a strong players union would destroy MLB. That proved to be a misguided prediction (or empty threat), an example of the owners crying wolf. Attendance and television revenues soared, overall team revenues increased, new teams were added in different cities, and the value of major league franchises skyrocketed. In 1967, the year after Miller joined the MLBPA, attendance at MLB games averaged 15,005. In 2019, it was 28,199. League revenue reached a record-breaking $10.3 billion in 2018. The major difference was that players were getting a larger share of MLB's prosperity. Miller was baseball's Moses, leading them out of indentured servitude.

When pitcher Gerrit Cole signed his $324 million, nine-year contract with the Yankees in December 2019, he paid tribute to Flood and Miller. "Challenging the reserve clause was essential to the blossoming sport we have today," Cole said, later adding, "I just think it's so important that players know the other sacrifices that players made in order to keep the integrity of the game where it is, and so I hope everybody has that conversation about Curt Flood on the bus."[48]

Despite Cole's statement, few contemporary ballplayers understand how big a revolution Miller started and how much they owe their prosperity to the solidarity created by the union. The MLBPA often issues statements in support of workers in other industries, but compared to Miller's day, the union does little to educate players in the broader labor movement or even the MLBPA's own history, although the union began taking steps in that direction during the past few years under executive director Tony Clark, a former player.

Miller urged players to respect other union's picket lines, as Brooks Robinson demonstrated back in 1982. Miller would have been galled that the MLBPA sat on its hands while the Yankees and Dodgers crossed a union picket line at Boston hotels where workers were on strike during the 2018 postseason. He would have urged the MLBPA to insist that their contract requires teams to stay in union hotels and boycott hotels where workers are in a labor dispute with management.

The baseball establishment hated Miller. As former Yankee pitcher Jim Bouton, author of the classic *Ball Four*, observed, "Marvin Miller kicked their butts and took power away from the baseball establishment—do you really think those people are going to vote him in? It's a joke."

Indeed, the Hall of Fame has long been controlled by anti-union team owners and executives along with friends and business associates of Jane Forbes Clark, the hall's conservative chair and the granddaughter of its founder. One longtime board member, David Glass, a former Kansas City Royals owner and CEO of Walmart, is a virulent foe of unions. Even though Miller retired in 1982, the Hall of Fame refused to put him on the ballot until 2003. It rigged the elections by appointing enough owners and executives to the Veterans Committee and Modern Baseball Era Committee to guarantee that he didn't get the required votes. Miller was snubbed seven times while second-rate owners and executives like Barney Dreyfuss, Pat Gillick, and the colluding Bud Selig made the cut. The Hall of Fame demonstrated its disdain in 2007 when it inducted former commissioner Bowie Kuhn but rejected Miller, who had outmaneuvered Kuhn many times in contract negotiations. In 2017, the sixteen-member committee included six owners and executives—in other words, more than enough to keep Miller from gaining the twelve of sixteen votes needed for induction.

In 2008 Miller wrote a letter to the Baseball Writers Association of America saying he no longer wanted to be considered for the Hall of Fame. He criticized its "anti-union bias" and the "rigged veterans' committee whose members are handpicked to reach a particular outcome while offering the pretense of a democratic vote." He added, "It is an insult to baseball fans, historians, sports writers and especially to those baseball players who sacrificed and brought the game into the twenty-first century. At the age of 91, I can do without farce."[49]

But as *New York Times* columnist William Rhoden wrote at the time, "With all due respect, this issue is larger than the individual." Like others, Rhoden noted that the Hall of Fame was diminished by Miller's absence.[50]

Hall of Fame broadcaster Red Barber once said that Miller, Jackie Robinson, and Babe Ruth were the three most important figures in baseball history. Over the years, many baseball luminaries urged the Hall of Fame to include Miller. Hank Aaron wrote that "Miller should be in the Hall of Fame if the players have to break down the doors to get him in." Joe Torre agreed: "Marvin Miller should be in." According to Joe Morgan, who became a member of the Hall of Fame Board of Directors, "They should vote him in and then apologize for making him wait so long." Brooks Robinson, who was also on the Hall of Fame Board of Directors, said, "What! Marvin Miller is not in the Hall of Fame? How can that be? I don't believe it!" Jim Bunning said, "The Hall of Fame is about players, and Marvin did more for the players than anyone else." Tom Seaver called Miller's exclusion "a national disgrace." When he was inducted into the Hall of Fame in 1999, Nolan Ryan paid tribute to Miller, recalling that when he broke into the majors in 1966, he spent the winter months working at a gas station while his wife worked at a local bookstore to make ends meet. Because of Miller's efforts, Ryan said, "we brought that level up to where the players weren't put in that situation."

Duane Kuiper—a second baseman for the Cleveland Indians and San Francisco Giants from 1974 to 1985—told the *San Francisco Chronicle*, "I don't think any of us really appreciated Marvin until we all got older." Said Rusty Staub, who played in the majors from 1963 to 1985, "Every time somebody signs one of these wonderful contracts, and there are so many of them out there, I think before they get the first check they should have to write an essay on Marvin Miller." In 2010, former major league pitcher Bob Locker started www.thanksmarvin.com to promote Miller's accomplishments. Another one-time major league pitcher, Bob Tufts, even taught a course at New York University on Miller's role in American trade unionism.

Former baseball commissioner Fay Vincent said in 2009, "It's preposterous that Marvin Miller isn't in the Hall of Fame. It's an embarrassment." Even Ray Grebey, who went toe-to-toe with Miller as the team owners' chief negotiator during the 1981 players strike, publicly supported his former nemesis in a letter to the Hall of Fame board of directors in 2009.

Miller died in 2012 at ninety-five. Even after his death, baseball's plutocrats rejected him several more times for Hall of Fame membership. In 2000, the union began bestowing a Marvin Miller Man of the Year Award on a player "whose on-field performance and contributions to his community inspire others to higher levels of achievement." But the union never waged a campaign to get Miller into the Hall of Fame. They didn't mobilize living Hall of Fame players to issue a statement, call a press conference, or threaten to boycott the annual induction ceremonies.

Hall of Fame pitcher Dennis Eckersley served on the 2017 committee that gave Miller only seven of sixteen votes—far from the twelve votes needed to get into the Hall of Fame. He thought that a positive vote for Miller "was going to be a slam dunk," but "then I figured it out when I got into the room. There are only 16 people there. There are six owners there. Do the math."

But in 2019, the Hall of Fame relented. Eckersley also served on the committee that year, when Miller got the necessary twelve votes. All six of the former players on the committee took part in the 1981 strike led by Miller. What had changed? "You got fresh people in there" who had not done battle with Miller, observed Eckersley, referring to the executives in the group. "It wasn't just old school folks."[51]

The Hall of Fame was scheduled to induct Miller in 2020, but the ceremony was canceled due to the coronavirus pandemic. He was inducted posthumously at a ceremony in Cooperstown on September 8, 2021. Don Fehr—who served as MLBPA general counsel under Miller and then succeeded him as executive director from 1983 until 2009—accepted the Hall of Fame plaque on Miller's behalf.

"Marvin's induction is bittersweet," said Tony Clark, the MLBPA's executive director. "He had been shunted aside for so long and now he's no longer alive, and not able to offer his own thoughts and feelings at the ceremony. But I'm grateful he's being recognized for his significant contributions to our game."[52]

II

CONTESTING THE AMERICAN EMPIRE

4

Resisting War, Fighting for Peace

Since the American Revolution, the United States has been constantly at war. In its 245 years, the United States has averaged more than one military intervention per year, often occupying other nations in the aftermath.[1] The American military has more than eight hundred bases abroad in more than one hundred nations, and about one-half of discretionary federal spending devoted to military spending each year.

We think of war as conflicts that involve combat troops—on land, on sea, and in the air. The United States has fought in an endless stream of "hot" wars, including the War of 1812; multiple Indian Wars; the Mexican-American War; the Civil War; the Spanish-American War; the Filipino War; the Mexican Border Wars; World War I; World War II; the Korean War; the Vietnam War; low-intensity Central American wars; the Gulf War; the Bosnian War; the War on Afghanistan; the War on Iraq; and drone wars on Syria, Yemen, Somalia, Libya, and Pakistan. Only five of these wars have been officially declared by Congress, and none since World War II. The United States has also been engaged in numerous quiet wars in which American spy organizations (such as the Central Intelligence Agency) try to destabilize or overthrow governments considered unfriendly to the United States or to American business overseas. From the 1950s through the 1980s, the United States secretly helped overthrow democratically elected leaders in Guatemala, Iran, the Congo, Brazil, Chile, and Nicaragua because they obstructed

American corporate interests. Few Americans knew about these covert wars at the time.

Historically wars have been popular with the U.S. public. Politicians and plutocrats have had no trouble rallying Americans to fight our wars, conjuring threats and enemies—real or imagined—to routinely mobilize, if not manipulate, public support. With the constant specter of threats to national security, elites can divert attention from domestic troubles or wrongdoing while the nation braces itself to confront real or imagined adversaries.

Thus it might be surprising that most of our wars have also generated opposition and sometimes significant dissent and resistance. Although American pacifists and radicals might predictably oppose American participation in wars, we generally don't expect dissent from the sporting world. American sports have a history of cozy relations with the U.S. military and of jingoistic, even violent, displays of support for America's wars and aggressive foreign policies. For more than a century, organized baseball has been a cheerleader for America's many wars and interventions. One of MLB's founding fathers, Albert Spalding, backed the U.S. attack in the Spanish-American War of 1898, repeatedly connecting it to the national pastime. Employing the rhetoric of empire, he wrote approvingly, "Baseball is war! It has followed the flag to the Philippines, to Porto Rico, and to Cuba."[2] Spalding supported America's wars for expansion and enlisted baseball in the cause.

In such circumstances, it's difficult for professional ballplayers or others in organized baseball to protest our wars even if they privately oppose our military policies. Baseball is supposed to wave the flag, not challenge the nation's far-flung escapades. Even so, some ballplayers have dissented or resisted America's past wars despite the risks that entailed.

By 1911, for example, pitcher Floyd Kroh left his Louisville team for an unusual reason. The United States had been committing American troops in the Mexican border wars. Their engagement escalated when U.S. industrialists demanded protection of their corporate operations in Mexico. Meanwhile, Kroh had been pegged as a budding star, but he developed a "bad boy" reputation and had been bouncing back and forth between the majors and minors with the Boston Red Sox and Chicago Cubs. Then, according to New York American reporter Harold Levine, when the U.S. army amassed in Texas for an attack, Kroh left baseball to fight with the Mexican Insurrectos. His fellow rebels viewed not only the Mexican but also the U.S. government as their enemy: Mexicans for undermining the Revolution and the Americans for their long-standing imperialism in their country. A weathered photo from that era, labeled "Mexican Insurrectos and White Recruit," shows Kroh, marked with an X, on horseback amidst a group of Mexican irregular soldiers.

RESISTING THE GREAT WAR—WORLD WAR I

In 1916, President Woodrow Wilson successfully campaigned for reelection by promising to keep the United States out of World War I. After his election, however, Wilson got the nation into the war, claiming it would "make the world safe for democracy." *New York Times* writer Benjamin DeCasseres claimed that "the world ought to be made safe for baseball."[3] DeCasseres meant that the sport should help the war effort because baseball and democracy go hand in hand. But many critics viewed U.S. involvement in World War I as making the world safe for American corporations, not democracy.

The baseball establishment had its own imperial ambitions. Major league teams organized several global tours to introduce the game around the world. By early 1917, baseball's leaders had agreed to "join hands with the government in arousing the patriotism of its civilians."[4] MLB supported the war by providing baseball equipment to U.S. military camps. It sponsored large martial parades and extravaganzas at ballparks, benefit games for soldier charities, military drills performed by ballplayers, and Wake Up America days to encourage military volunteers. Teams admitted soldiers to games for free.

Team owners hoped these gestures would spare the sport from the military draft, but the U.S. government's 1918 Work or Fight order subjected all American men to conscription except those with a legitimate deferment. Uncle Sam might have had in mind Chicago Cubs pitcher Harry Weaver, who requested a deferment on the dubious grounds that his team had a good chance to win the pennant. To the contrary, the U.S. government classified professional baseball as a non-essential occupation.

MLB appealed, claiming that baseball was productive employment. Its hopes were raised when an Ohio draft board told Brooklyn Dodgers outfielder Hy Myers to finish his season and then find war-industry work. Other states followed Ohio's lead, but then the Washington, DC, draft board ruled against another ballplayer, Eddie Ainsmith, despite his and the Washington Senators' claim that baseball was a unique business likely to be destroyed without its players' unusual skills. Secretary of War Newton Baker declared that ballplayers were not exempt from the draft.

Although baseball wasn't ordered to shut down, nine of ten minor leagues were suspended and major league rosters began to shrink. More than 440 major and minor leaguers either enlisted, were drafted, or found defense work, including 27 future Hall of Famers. But when some players, including Babe Ruth and Joe Jackson, pursued stateside war-production work, they were criticized as draft dodgers or slackers even though Ruth, as a married man, was actually exempt from any kind of service. *Stars and Stripes*, the military newspaper, complained, "It seems beyond belief that any well trained athlete . . . should be guilty of such yellow-hearted cowardice, traitors to their country's good, and worse than traitors to their own souls."[5] Even AL president Ban Johnson condemned "shipyard slackers" who played in "Shelter Leagues" although he and the baseball owners were less concerned with patriotism and more with ballplayers escaping the reserve clause system to play (and often get better pay) in the industrial leagues.

In fact, according to sportswriter William Phelon, organized baseball furnished a greater percentage of its personnel for military service than almost any other industry. Six major leaguers died in World War I and at least one player, the popular New York Giants pitcher Christy Mathewson, died prematurely from inhaling poison gas.

But even baseball was not immune to significant opposition to the war elsewhere in American society. The dissent came from pacifists, anarchists, labor unions, the Socialist Party, women's organizations, religious groups, and civil libertarians. Opponents included prominent Americans such as Eugene Debs, Helen Keller, Jane Addams, Samuel Gompers, Robert LaFollette, William Jennings Bryan, and even Henry Ford. Many condemned U.S. participation, claiming World War I was mostly a war to determine which nations would emerge dominant over Asian, African, Middle Eastern, and Latin American colonies and their vast resources. American and other soldiers would merely be cannon fodder for a rich man's imperialist war.

BATTLING THE DRAFT: FRED TONEY

Many ballplayers found ways to avoid serving in the World War 1 military. But the government tried to make an example of major league pitching star Fred Toney. Born and raised in Nashville, Tennessee, Toney was discovered by a minor league scout who stumbled upon Fred in the countryside killing squirrels with rocks he threw with his powerful and accurate arm. After pitching for semipro teams in Nashville and Bowling Green, Toney joined the Winchester Hustlers of the Class D Blue Grass League in 1908, his fastball garnering comparisons to future Hall of Famer Walter Johnson. Toney soon put his name in the record books, pitching a 17-inning no-hitter for Winchester, still the longest in professional baseball history.

Toney quickly drew major league attention, but he was a reluctant star, skeptical about the pressure of being a big leaguer. Even so, he signed with the Chicago Cubs in 1911. He appeared in only eighteen games, moving between the Cubs and the minors before being released. He returned to the majors in 1914 with the Brooklyn Dodgers but left for Cincinnati after a contract dispute. In 1915, a more confident Toney went 17-6 for the Reds, compiling the NL's second-best ERA (1.58). He followed that with a 14-17 season with a 2.28 ERA and then went 24-16 the following year (second in wins to the great Grover Cleveland Alexander) with a 2.20 ERA.

In May 1917, Toney faced Chicago Cubs ace Hippo Vaughn and entered the record books again. After both hurlers had pitched no-hit baseball for 9 innings, Vaughn gave up a hit and a run in the 10th and Toney ended the game with another no-hit inning. In July, Toney won both games of a doubleheader against the Pittsburgh Pirates, allowing only 6 hits and 1 earned run in 18 innings.

Despite this stardom, Toney was headed for a fall. He was married with a child and had received a military deferment for World War I. But in December 1917 he was arrested and charged with dodging the draft. Toney was accused of falsely swearing that his wife and child were dependent on his salary when actually he had been separated from his family for three years. The charges were described as the "first black eye on the national pastime."[6] If Toney were convicted of "conspiring to make fraudulent representation of dependencies," it would mean a year in prison followed by military service.

At the March 1918 trial, prosecution witnesses claimed Toney wasn't providing family support, but his estranged wife, Alice, testified that Toney had been sending her $70 a month. Toney also swore to the judge that not only his wife and sister but also his mother, stepfather, brother, and niece depended on his income and would suffer if he were imprisoned or drafted.[7] The trial ended with a hung jury, and a retrial was scheduled.

During the trial, however, Toney was indicted for another crime: violating the Mann Act. Otherwise known as the White Slave Traffic Act, the Mann Act forbade the transporting of a woman, other than one's wife, across state lines for the purpose of having sex. Even though Toney and his girlfriend's relations were consensual and not for pay, Toney had still violated the laws of America's puritanical society.

Toney rejoined the Reds for the 1918 season but the club put him on waivers, concerned about negative public opinion from his alleged disloyalty and Mann Act violation. No other team selected him so he remained with the Reds, winning his first start against Pittsburgh. Some fans gave Toney a rousing reception. According to *Cincinnati Enquirer* sportswriter Jack Ryder, "the fans had finally [understood] his case and realized he was simply the victim of circumstances and not an intentional slacker."[8] But other fans voiced their disapproval.

The Reds sold Toney to the New York Giants in July. He protested the deal, provoking *New York Telegram* sportswriter Dan Daniels to complain, "While the major league officials are trying to talk the Secretary of War into granting them a respite [from losing players to the draft], Fred Toney balks at being sold by Cincinnati to the Giants."[9] Daniels ignored the basis for Toney's objections: not the sale itself but rather being deprived, via the reserve clause, of any portion of the sale price—his value as a worker. Dropping his threat to go home to Nashville, Toney joined the Giants in August 1918, losing his first two games but winning the next six.

Toney was acquitted in his second draft trial but pleaded guilty to the Mann Act charges even though he had since married the woman he transported across state lines. He served four months in federal prison and considered retiring from baseball. But Giants manager John McGraw insisted Toney could be the best pitcher in the NL if he got back in shape. A slimmed-down Toney rejoined the Giants in May 1919, posting a 13-6 record with a 1.84 ERA, fourth-best in the NL. In 1920 he was 21-11 and then helped the Giants win the 1921 pennant with an 18-11 season.

The fallout over the 1919 Black Sox scandal ensnared Toney. Eight Chicago White Sox players were accused of throwing the 1919 World Series and were banned from organized baseball for life, casting a huge shadow over the game. Toney wasn't a White Sox player, but one of the gamblers, Sleepy Bill Burns, testified that Toney had attended meetings between players and gamblers during the 1919 World Series. But it seemed that it wasn't Toney's alleged gambling but his alleged draft dodging that made him a marked man. NL president John Heydlar deemed it a false accusation and cleared Toney of the gambling charges.

Toney began a rapid decline during the 1922 season. Nursing a sore arm and broken finger, he won only five games for the Giants and was volatile in the dugout, including clashes with manager McGraw. In July the Giants sold him to the last-place Boston Braves. When he refused to report, he was picked up by the St. Louis Cardinals on waivers. But Toney wouldn't budge even after talking to Branch Rickey, who thought enough of his skills to visit him at his Nashville home. Toney did report in 1923, however, but was released again by St. Louis before the 1924 season. Toney returned to the Nashville Volunteers in the Southern Association in 1925, but after his teammates kicked away three straight stellar pitching performances, he left the mound without a word, walked to the clubhouse, knocked the lock off his locker, dressed, and went home, never to pitch professionally again.

Toney ended his MLB career with a 139-102 record, a .577 winning percentage, and a 2.69 ERA. But he never shook the accusations that he lied to avoid military service. In a 1923 article, a *Sporting News* sportswriter reflected that sentiment, calling Toney a "large, fat draft dodger."[10]

We don't know Toney's true motivation for avoiding the draft. It may have been for the legitimate reasons he claimed about his family responsibilities. Or it might have been fear of combat or opposition based on political, religious, or philosophical grounds. What *is* clear is that his unwillingness to serve tarnished his reputation and provided an example for other Americans that refusing military service was widely viewed as disloyalty, a stigma that could hurt one's status in society.

OPPOSING THE GOOD WAR: TOM ANANICZ AND MIKE BALAS

When World War II began in Europe in 1939, many Americans remained isolationist. Some felt it wasn't America's war. Others, most famously the aviator Charles Lindbergh, were German sympathizers. He lead the America First Committee, a xenophobic, pro-German, and anti-Semitic organization that opposed U.S. involvement in the war. Not until the Japanese bombed Pearl Harbor on December 7, 1941, did most Americans back the war. With the United States now attacked, and with German, Italian, and Spanish fascism spread across much of Europe, most Americans accepted the nation's moral responsibility to enter the war. World War II became known as the Good War.

Once the United States had entered the war, baseball was fully on board. In *Baseball Goes to War*, historian William Mead notes, "No institution voiced [patriotic jingoism] more loudly, nor identified itself more with the war effort, than organized baseball." It was one of the institutions American soldiers "were fighting to preserve."[11]

Baseball embraced the war with more than patriotism. It was fighting to survive. Baseball moguls remembered the sport nearly being shut down during World War I. They had to justify keeping baseball alive during World War II when the government and business and civic groups were pushing all eligible Americans to enlist in the military or take defense-oriented jobs.

Publishers, sportswriters, and baseball officials all had a financial stake in maintaining the game. When Commissioner Landis wrote President Franklin Roosevelt in January 1942 asking what baseball should do, FDR penned the Green Light letter, claiming "baseball would help win the war" and boost the nation's morale so it would be "best for the country to keep baseball going."[12] He assumed all players eligible for military or government service would enlist but felt the game would still be worthy even with depleted ranks.

As during World War I, baseball enthusiastically supported the war effort. Teams organized exhibition games at military bases. Military personnel were admitted free to ballgames, which featured military bands, tank parades, and ballplayers drilling with bats (instead of rifles). Military dignitaries and veterans were recognized along with soldiers. Teams held scrap metal and rubber recycling drives. Phil Wrigley, who owned the nation's largest chewing gum company as well as the Chicago Cubs, rerouted the foil used to wrap his gum to war production. Bat companies made wooden stocks for military rifles. Sporting goods companies donated baseball equipment to soldiers playing ball abroad in their free time. Ballplayers sold war bonds at ballpark rallies. Ballparks became bomb shelters. Player uniforms featured American flag patches and other patriotic insignia. In spring training, pitchers threw at cardboard caricatures of Japanese soldiers instead of throwing to catchers. Radio broadcasts brought baseball to the troops. "The Star-Spangled Banner" was incorporated not merely into the World Series but into every ball game.

Business groups and labor unions promised to work together to help America win the war. Unions promised not to strike and businesses reluctantly agreed to allow the federal government to enlist them in producing tanks, guns, airplanes, ships, food, clothing, and other tools for prosecuting the war. Many businesses used the no-strike pledge to take advantage of their employees, blocking the renegotiating of wages and workplace conditions. Some companies used patriotic appeals to convince workers to take "voluntary" pay cuts despite their continuing profits. Despite the no-strike pledge, 7 million American workers engaged in 14,000 strikes during the war anyway to protest unfair practices, mostly wildcat actions not authorized by the unions. Many businesses made significant profits producing for the war effort. Some were accused of being war profiteers.

Major league teams pursued the same ends in their own industry. Owner Ed Barrow used the war to justify salary freezes for his 1941 World Series champion New York Yankees, including Joe DiMaggio, on the heels of his record 56-game hitting streak. St. Louis Cardinals owner Sam Breadon chastised star pitcher Mort Cooper for returning his contract unsigned: "I do not think it makes very good reading for persons who have their boys on the fighting fronts."[13] Rather than exceeding the pay of typical American workers, ballplayers' wages fell below the average. Yet it was the owners rather than the players who were applauded for their wartime financial contributions.

More than 1,700 major leaguers (and 3,700 minor leaguers) served in the military during World War II. Many were in combat and were wounded; some were killed. Major league teams publicized their and their players' sacrifices to substantiate the sport's contribution to the war effort. In *Playing for Their Nation*, historian Steve Bullock described them as a "highly visible aspect of the military war machine."[14] When star ballplayers like Hank Greenberg, Bob Feller, and Ted Williams joined the military, it was front-page news while other ballplayers were criticized for not joining the military or for delaying or reducing their service. Players who did join the armed forces were sometimes accused of having easy assignments—such as playing military baseball.

And as historian Robert Burk observes in *Much More Than a Game*, each team "retained its own officer specifically charged with keeping players out of the draft."[15] Some players, such as Sal Maglie and Lefty Gomez, avoided the military through war-production work, which was sometimes secured by teams to keep players out of the service. Other players were medically ineligible. Detroit Tigers pitcher Hal Newhouser, a two-time Detroit Tigers MVP, had a bad heart but had to constantly fend off slacker accusations. Some believed that ballplayers actually suffered worse treatment because they were highly visible athletes. The draft took Yankees pitcher Red Ruffing even though he was missing four toes. Players initially classified as 4F (unfit for service) were sometimes drafted later even after failing one or more physicals.

Thousands of Americans resisted military service as a matter of principle. There were 12,000 conscientious objectors (COs) who refused to serve in the military on religious grounds. Most of them were sent to Civilian Conservation Corps work camps. Another 25,000 COs agreed to alternative service (such as working in hospitals), and 6,000 COs refused to even register because of their opposition to all wars. Most of them were imprisoned. A few resisters included pacifists, socialists, anarchists, isolationists, theologians, college students, African Americans protesting Jim Crow, and Japanese Americans protesting their wartime incarceration as allegedly disloyal Americans based solely on their ethnic background. Only a handful of dissenters sympathized with America's German or Japanese enemies.

Organized baseball showed little tolerance for dissent against the war. Four days after the Pearl Harbor attack, the *Sporting News* editorialized,

> Born in America, propagated in America, and recognized as the National Game . . . All those engaged in the sport are Americans first, last, and always . . . In all the history of baseball there never was a conscientious objector, or a slacker in its ranks.[16]

To the contrary, one ballplayer, Tom Ananicz, had declared his CO status even before the war began. Ananicz, a graduate of St. John's University in New York, opposed the war for religious and philosophical reasons. While pitching for the Kansas City Blues of the American Association, he received CO status as a pacifist but agreed to work in a munitions factory if needed. Rather than being called up for civilian duty, however, Ananicz was allowed to continue playing baseball during the war. Although he experienced some backlash against his CO status, few newspapers even mentioned his CO status while reporting on his baseball performance even after the United States entered the war. He compiled a 40-42 record over 7 seasons in the minors, retiring at age 27 in 1945 without ever making the majors.

While Ananicz escaped any great scrutiny for his anti-war stance, Mike Balas (originally Balaski) wasn't as fortunate. He bounced around the minors between 1929 and 1940 with one brief appearance in the majors, pitching one game for the NL's Boston Bees (later renamed Braves) in 1938.

When his baseball career ended in 1940, Balas returned to his hometown of Billerica, Massachusetts. He was a Jehovah's Witness, a religious doctrine that asks members to refrain from acts of violence against people of other nations, whom they should regard as neighbors they should love not fight. They also believe their allegiance belongs to God's kingdom and thus they refrain from saluting the flag of any country or singing nationalistic songs.

With the nation whipped up for war, most Americans scorned COs. The *New York Times* condemned war resisters for accepting "safety instead of service in the midst of a war for survival" and for believing "that they know better than their government how a man should meet the Axis attack."[17] To make matters worse, Jehovah's Witnesses were already unpopular in America for their unconventional beliefs and were sometimes viewed as unpatriotic. In 1940, in *Minersville School District* v. *Gobitis*, the U.S. Supreme Court ruled that despite their beliefs, Jehovah's Witness children could be forced to salute the flag in school. When they still refused, they were taunted and even attacked. Although the court reversed itself in its 1943 *West Virginia Board of Education* v. *Barnette* decision, many Americans disdained Jehovah's Witness COs like Balas.

In November 1942, when Balas refused to report to a CO work camp, he was prosecuted for violating the Selective Service Act. Besides reiterating his beliefs against participating in the war, Balas startled the courtroom with claims that Jehovah would convert Adolf Hitler and halt his aggression. The judge disagreed and sentenced Balas to three years in federal prison. It's not clear how much time he actually served, however. After his release, Balas returned to Massachusetts, ran a construction company, and retained his Jehovah's Witness beliefs.

ANTI-WAR OBJECTOR: BILL ZUBER

While Tom Ananicz and Mike Balas only flirted with big league careers, another baseball dissenter, Bill Zuber, was a major leaguer for nearly a dozen years. Born in 1913 in Middle Amana, Iowa, Zuber grew up in an Amana colony, a religious sect known as a Community of True Inspiration. The colonists were German-speaking Christian communalists who practiced self-denial. They prohibited sports and other entertainment, which made Zuber perhaps the most unlikely man to ever make it to the major leagues.

During his childhood, Zuber broke all four limbs and his collarbone, suffering some permanent damage. In the 1920s, Amana youth rebelled against the sect's strictures. Zuber and others began playing music and baseball, and the sport soon became popular in the colony. Zuber never attended high school but he emerged as a standout third baseman on the Amana sandlots.

With his strong throwing arm, however, Zuber had more potential as a pitcher. He attracted the attention of Casey Stengel, who was managing the Toledo Mud Hens minor league team in 1931. Stengel later recalled that "Zuber and the strike zone [had] never been introduced," but he was impressed by Zuber's fastball. Stengel alerted Cleveland Indians scout Cy Slapnicka (who would later sign Bob Feller) about Zuber's prowess. Slapnicka met Zuber on his farm in 1932, saw an onion on the ground, and asked him if he could hit a distant barn. Zuber picked up the onion, threw it over the barn, and was immediately on Slapnicka's radar.

Zuber pitched inconsistently and at times wildly in the Indians farm system, securing limited action with the parent club. Besides his pitching woes, Zuber was frequently targeted by his teammates for being a rural hayseed with limited English and a thick accent. Sportswriters also taunted him. Not impressing Indians manager Ossie Vitt, Zuber was put on waivers. The Washington Senators signed him after the 1940 season.

Zuber compiled a 6-4 record for Washington in 1941, mostly as a reliever. Manager Bucky Harris praised him. "When Bill Zuber joined the Senators, he and he alone did more to boost the team's morale and confidence than I did."[18] Zuber's trouble with English sometimes made him unintentionally funny, and he kept the clubhouse lively with his quick wit.

When the United States entered World War II in December 1941, team rosters began to shrink. While many ballplayers enlisted, Zuber filed for CO status based on his religious beliefs. The Selective Service rejected many CO petitions, and thus Zuber faced a possible prison sentence for refusing to fight. Instead, his draft board classified him 2-B, designating him for work in war production. This meant he didn't have to see combat, but Zuber believed that even participating in the war effort by working in a civilian defense job violated his religious beliefs.

A clash was avoided, however, because of Zuber's physical condition. Some ballplayers were fit enough to be professional athletes but had injuries making them unfit for military service. Zuber was one of them. His childhood history of broken bones disqualified him. Thus this would-be CO was instead reclassified 4-F, and his baseball career continued.

In 1942, Zuber won 9 games for the Senators, with a 3.89 ERA. His fastball, which sometimes reached 100 mph, terrorized batters. AL umpire Art Passarella and future Hall of Famers Joe Cronin and Ted Williams believed that Zuber threw faster than Bob Feller. Zuber had also developed a slider and change up.

Despite his promising prospects in Washington, in January 1943 the Senators traded Zuber to the New York Yankees, where he went 8-4 with a 3.84 ERA both as a starter and in relief. Zuber went 5-7 in 1944 and 5-11 in 1945. In one 1945 game, he pitched a 1-hitter through 9 innings, only to lose the game. After only 3 games for the Yankees in 1946 Zuber was sold to the Boston Red Sox, where he began with a shutout performance and then compiled a 5-1 record with a 2.54 ERA, helping the team to a pennant. Zuber had only a single victory for Boston in 1947, losing most of the season to a dislocated shoulder. He was optioned to the Triple A Louisville Colonels in the American Association in 1948, pitched poorly, and never returned to the majors.

Zuber was no Hall of Famer but he did compile a 71-58 minor league record and a 43-42 record in eleven years in the big leagues with a respectable 4.28 ERA, two pennants, and a World Series ring. Zuber returned to Amana and purchased the Homestead Hotel with his wife. They renovated the restaurant, rechristened it Bill Zuber's Dugout in 1949, and filled its walls with photographs and other memorabilia from his baseball career. Zuber died in 1982 but his family continued operating the popular restaurant until 1998.

INTERNMENT RESISTER: KENICHI ZENIMURA

If conscience prevented several ballplayers from participating in World War II, another kind of dissent occurred behind the barbed wires of the detention camps to which Japanese Americans were forcibly evacuated in 1942. Kenichi Zenimura was born in Hiroshima, Japan, in 1900. When he was a young child, his family moved to Hawaii, where he grew up playing baseball, ultimately for the Mills Institute for Boys from 1915 to 1918. Since baseball had already become Japan's national pastime by the late 1800s, transplanted Japanese brought their love of the game with them. The first American team of Japanese immigrants, the Excelsiors, formed in Hawaii in 1899. The first U.S. mainland team of Issei (first-generation) Japanese immigrants was organized in 1903.

The early 1900s witnessed an upsurge in anti-Asian sentiment in the United States, including the Asiatic Exclusion League's efforts to ban Asian immigration. In 1922, in *Takao Ozawa v. United States*, the U.S. Supreme Court disqualified Asian immigrants from becoming naturalized U.S. citizens, and in 1924 Congress passed the Immigration Act to end all future Japanese immigration to the United States.

As with African Americans, Japanese players were kept out of white teams. In response they formed their own professional leagues. After playing for and coaching the Hawaiian Islands championship team, Zenimura moved to Fresno, California, in 1920, where he helped launch the Golden Era of Nisei (second-generation) baseball, reaching from Seattle to San Diego. Excelling as a player at all nine positions, Kenichi broke the color line for Asians, starring and managing in the previously all-white, semipro Twilight Leagues in California.

Zenimura was also an adept administrator. He established a ten-team Nisei League in Fresno. He turned his Fresno Athletic Club into a baseball powerhouse, beating teams from the Negro Leagues, the PCL, the California Winter League, and college clubs such as Stanford, St. Mary's, Fresno State, and the University of Southern California. When Babe Ruth and Lou Gehrig arrived in Fresno for a barnstorming tour in 1927, the highly regarded Zenimura was invited to join the team.

Zenimura promoted baseball diplomacy between the United States and Japan. Aside from hosting Japanese teams in the United States, he led barnstorming tours to Japan, Korea, and Manchuria in 1924, 1927, and 1937, including games against Japan's Big Six universities. During the 1927 tour, Zenimura arranged a classic series, pitting his All Stars against a powerful Negro League team, the Philadelphia Royal Giants. In 1934, Zenimura organized the tour that brought Babe Ruth to Japan and helped launch the Japanese Professional Baseball League.

For these initiatives, Zenimura became known as the Father of Japanese American Baseball. According to historian Samuel Regalado, he "saw in baseball a mechanism to help unify the American Japanese community and as a means to build bridges between American and Japanese cultures."[19] This would be greatly tested, however, after the outbreak of war between the United States and Japan in December 1941.

Xenophobic sentiment arose after Pearl Harbor, and the U.S. government took drastic measures. In February 1942, Zenimura and 120,000 Japanese

Americans were sent to internment camps. Stripping Japanese Americans of their jobs, rights, and property, this forced evacuation was rationalized as a war measure but has long since been condemned as one of the worst violations of civil liberty in American history. Kenichi and his family were first interned at the Fresno fairgrounds, where families were put up in animal stalls, and then transferred to the desert wasteland of the Gila River War Relocation Center in Arizona, where detainees were surrounded by barbed wire and watchtowers.

Camp conditions were harsh. Provisions were meager and inferior, and the hastily built barracks gave little protection from the cold nights and blisteringly hot days. Recognizing the power of baseball, Zenimura wasted no time supervising the construction of ballparks in both camps and inspiring ballparks in other detention facilities. Lacking official approval, he initially acted surreptitiously at Gila River then resourcefully thereafter. Despite the limited materials available, the stadium (later named for Zenimura) contained not only an impressive field but also covered dugouts, a grandstand, an outfield wall, and an irrigation system to keep the grass green.

Zenimura organized a thirty-two-team league between his camp and four other camps in the area. This allowed ballplayers to leave the camps for games while other detainees remained imprisoned. He raised money to purchase better baseball equipment from a Fresno sporting goods store. He placed ads in local newspapers challenging local semipro teams, which were permitted into the camp to play games. In one challenge, Zenimura's team dealt the three-time state champion Tucson Badgers high school team their only defeat in fifty-three games. A Tucson player recalled,

> I saw the fence and said, "God, this is like a prison." It was a game that most of us will never forget. I realized that these people were Americans, just like myself . . . What a big mistake we made by putting these people in this relocation camp.[20]

Zenimura no doubt had several motives for promoting camp baseball. Certainly it helped counter the heat and boredom. Thousands of prisoners used baseball as their main entertainment, either as players or fans. It provided a gathering place for displaced members of the community. It bolstered morale during their imprisonment. As detainee George Omachi recalled, "It was demeaning and humiliating to be incarcerated in your own country. Without baseball, camp life would have been miserable."[21] Baseball brought a sense of pride, making life more bearable during this unjust incarceration. According to historian Kerry Yo Nakagawa, "For Japanese-Americans interned during World War II, playing, watching, and supporting baseball inside of America's concentration camps brought a sense of normalcy to very 'abnormal' lives and created a social and positive atmosphere."[22]

In 2017—the seventy-fifth anniversary of FDR's Executive Order 9066, which authorized the removal and incarceration of Japanese Americans—the Cooperstown Hall of Fame finally recognized the injustice of the camps and baseball's significance behind barbed wires. After obtaining the home plate from Zenimura Stadium, Hall of Fame curator Tom Shieber described it as

> much more than a corner of a dusty baseball diamond, or the shape that helped define a batter's strike zone. It was (and is) a vibrant symbol of hope for those who were denied their freedom, and an expression of what it meant to be an American for those who were stripped of their civil rights.[23]

Through internment camp baseball, the detainees both showed their loyalty to the United States by embracing its national pastime and protesting the terrible living conditions they were forced to endure. Zenimura used baseball to expose America's racism and cruelty toward loyal citizens.

After the war, Zenimura returned to Fresno and continued playing, managing, and organizing baseball for another two decades. He used baseball to help rebuild relations between the United States and Japan and to temper the animosities of white Americans. He helped negotiate professional contracts for several Japanese Americans to play in Japan's Central and Pacific leagues. Besides being featured in the Hall of Fame's permanent exhibit on Japanese American baseball, Zenimura was also inducted into the Baseball Reliquary's Shrine of the Eternals and became the first Japanese American enshrined in the Fresno Athletic Hall of Fame.

PROTESTING THE VIETNAM WAR

Compared with the limited dissent against World War II, the Vietnam War catalyzed a massive protest movement. The antiwar activism started with a handful of pacifists and radicals in the early 1960s but grew dramatically later in that decade. The crusades for and against the war reverberated in baseball.

As part of a global anti-colonial movement, Vietnamese nationalists sought to force France to relinquish its control over the country's political, economic, and cultural life. When the French suffered a major defeat at Dien Bien Phu in 1954, the Geneva Agreements negotiations divided Vietnam in half at the seventeenth parallel. Ho Chi Minh led a nationalist and communist government centered in Hanoi in the north (the Democratic Republic of Vietnam), and President Ngo Dinh Diem led a new Republic of South Vietnam in Saigon. The French left Vietnam, and the United States assumed support for South Vietnam, providing arms and assistance to defeat North Vietnam and unify the country within America's geopolitical orbit. U.S. political leaders pushed the domino theory, claiming that if one Southeast Asian country fell to communism, many others would follow. U.S. involvement escalated under President John F. Kennedy with sixteen thousand American advisors sent in 1963. American pacifists, radicals, and student activists—led by groups such as the National Committee for a Sane Nuclear Policy, the Quaker American Friends Service Committee, and Students for a Democratic Society—organized the first significant antiwar rallies in 1964, demanding U.S. withdrawal from Vietnam.

After Kennedy's assassination in 1963, new president Lyndon Johnson quickly escalated the U.S. war in Vietnam, justified by the false claim that American boats had suffered an unprovoked attack by North Vietnamese ships in the Gulf of Tonkin in July 1964. Based on this lie, Congress granted Johnson the authority to begin open warfare against North Vietnam, vastly increasing the number of U.S. troops in March 1965 with solid support from the American public. By 1966, more than 200,000 troops had been dispatched to Vietnam. America's effort to shore up several corrupt South Vietnamese regimes continued under Johnson and then, after the 1968 election, under President Richard Nixon.

By the late 1960s, however, public opinion had begun to shift in response to increased antiwar protests, the growing number of Americans killed and severely wounded, and the emerging awareness that the United States and its South Vietnamese allies were losing the war. Black, Latino, and low-income soldiers were disproportionately among U.S. combat troop casualties. But as draft calls dramatically increased, threatening to enlist college students, white middle-class families began to stir.

By the mid- and late-1960s, new and larger protests had emerged. Prominent leaders began to speak out. Draft resistance surged, inspired in part by the courage of boxer Muhammad Ali, who refused to serve in the military as a CO due to his religious beliefs. In 1967, half a million protesters demonstrated against the war in New York. Tens of thousands of Americans engaged in nonviolent civil disobedience at the Pentagon, induction centers, troop trains, and draft boards. In 1967, Martin Luther King Jr. publicly expressed his opposition to the Vietnam War. "The bombs in Vietnam explode at home," he said at a Chicago rally that year. "They destroy the dream and possibility for a decent America."[24]

Domestic crises, such as escalating protests, urban race rebellions, the assassination of King and Senator Robert F. Kennedy in 1968, and the riot by Chicago police at the Democratic National Convention that year made the war untenable, and yet it persisted. In November 1969, the media revealed an incident prompting global outrage—the massacre by U.S. troops of hundreds of unarmed Vietnamese in the village of My Lai in 1968. Many Black Americans and college students rebelled against the war after police and National Guard troops killed protesters at Kent State University in Ohio and Jackson State University in Mississippi in 1970.

By the early 1970s, most Americans wanted the United States to "bring the boys home" from Vietnam. Soldiers who had returned home were traumatized, disillusioned, and often drug addicted. Vietnam Veterans Against the War joined the protests. A handful of small revolutionary groups occasionally resorted to violence to protest the war and the military-industrial complex. In 1971, the *New York Times* published the classified Pentagon Papers, which revealed the history of America's secret and illegal war in Southeast Asia, and Nixon's covert war in Laos and Cambodia was also uncovered. Scientists spoke out against the U.S. military's use of toxic defoliants such as Agent Orange. As antiwar sentiment rose, and as Americans elected more antiwar candidates, Congress began to oppose allocating more money and troops.

Despite the upsurge of antiwar protest and public opinion, Nixon expanded the war through 1972, relenting only after his reelection, and signed the Paris Peace Accords in 1973 to finally end U.S. military involvement even though American military aid to South Vietnam didn't end until 1975 when North Vietnamese tanks rolled into Saigon. More than fifty thousand Americans and more than 1 million Vietnamese died in the war.

Amidst the protest, where did organized baseball stand? According to historian Ron Briley, "to many Americans baseball remained a symbol of traditional values in a confusing world."[25] To better tap this sentiment and to toughen its exterior, baseball turned to the military for new leadership. In 1965, seeking a new commissioner, the owners selected General William "Spike" Eckert, whom the media quickly dubbed the "unknown soldier" since he was unheard of, a poor leader, and knew essentially nothing about baseball. Along with his lieutenants, AL president Joe Cronin and NL president Warren Giles (a former infantry officer), Eckert strongly supported the Vietnam War.

The *Sporting News* urged ballplayers to enlist in the military and MLB to reassert itself amidst the growing protests against the war. Eckert adopted the slogan "Where soldiers and veterans are, baseball will be." General William Westmoreland, commander of U.S. forces in Vietnam, honored Eckert for a tour he arranged to war zones featuring major leaguers Harmon Killebrew, Brooks Robinson, Joe Torre, Hank Aaron, and Stan Musial. In 1967 the Air Force presented Eckert with its meritorious award for sending more ballplayers—including Ernie Banks, Pete Rose, Tony Conigliaro, and Joe DiMaggio—to entertain the troops. As U.S. involvement in the war grew, Eckert and AL triple-crown winner Carl Yastrzemski visited the White House, where a beleaguered President Johnson commended the commissioner for supporting the war. In 1968, as public opinion began turning against Johnson, he told a *New York Times* reporter, "They booed Ted Williams, too, remember?" referring to the Red Sox slugger's hot-and-cold relationship with Boston fans.[26]

Although it denied the accusations, MLB began interfering with local draft boards to protect players from serving in combat. It secured National Guard positions for its players to avoid the draft. Service with the guard or the reserves typically lasted only six months stateside; thus players avoided service abroad. A 1967 Defense Department report found 360 athletes serving in draft-exempt units, 311 of them joining after turning professional. As the body bags returning from Vietnam piled up, ballplayers with deferments embarrassed MLB as well as the Pentagon.

To avoid the appearance of favoritism, U.S. Secretary of Defense Robert McNamara ordered all reserve and guard vacancies filled on a "first-come, first-served basis" but most ballplayers got deferments when they wanted them anyway. Organized baseball's close military-government relationship helped it protect its primary investment: the players. Some ballplayers were actually drafted, but most were not top players or prospects and few had their careers seriously interrupted. Only a handful actually went to Vietnam. No major leaguers were killed in the war although a dozen minor leaguers died in the conflict.

Commissioner Eckert couldn't cope with the increasing pressure on baseball, and after only three years MLB replaced him with longtime NL attorney Bowie Kuhn in 1968. Kuhn, a Naval Officer Training Program graduate, joined NL president Charles Feeney and AL president Lee MacPhail, both of whom had served in World War II. Kuhn encouraged ballplayer excursions to Southeast Asia to boost soldier morale and demonstrate MLB's patriotism. Ernie Banks led a 1968 post-season delegation, and Kuhn joined additional players sent to visit Vietnam in 1969, including Tug McGraw, Reggie Jackson, Milt Pappas, and Denny McLain. In 1970 four MLB groups toured the war zone including Bob Feller, Waite Hoyt, Bud Harrelson, Willie Stargell, and Phil Niekro. Following the 1971 season, two more ballplayer groups visited Vietnam and hospitals in Japan, Guam, and the Philippines, including Bob Gibson, Graig Nettles, Dock Ellis, and Bobby Bonds.

Cincinnati Reds Pete Rose, a reservist who avoided the draft and Vietnam, lauded troop morale. Chicago Cubs Ernie Banks cheered the soldiers. St. Louis Cardinals executive Al Fleishman claimed the "clean-cut young men" in military uniforms knew "why they were fighting in Vietnam."[27] He didn't mention the reason nor did many others in baseball seem to understand American foreign policy. Most were simply awed.

Kuhn aligned baseball with President Nixon, who fashioned himself the sport's number 1 fan. To revitalize the connection between baseball and patriotism during the ongoing war, Nixon encouraged teams to invite American soldiers who had been prisoners of war to toss out the first pitch on opening day. Several ballparks hosted Prisoner of War days with armed services color guards and huge American flags unfurled in the outfield. Embracing the president and his war, MLB sided with patriotic nationalism against growing popular dissent.

Although the baseball establishment seemed united, not all the ballplayers were. In the late 1960s, some ballplayers were influenced by the social and political currents occurring in society—campus antiwar protests; civil rights activism and Black power movements; a widening counterculture of hippies, drugs, and a "do your own thing" mentality; and a growing skepticism toward big business fostered by social critics and consumer activists like Ralph Nader. In baseball's defense, the *Sporting News* editorialized, "If you think the hippies and yippies represent young America, you're wrong. For every rabble-rouser on a college campus, there are hundreds of other students finding a wholesome outlet in sports."[28] Unsure how to deal with a growing number of players with unconventional views and lifestyles, the baseball establishment doubled down to defend conventional standards, including support for the Vietnam War.

The *Sporting News* admitted the 1969 World Series champion New York Mets had caught "the spirit of a youth rebellion sweeping the world . . . [But] the sports version seems highly preferable to the forms of revolt available elsewhere, including college campuses."[29] Yet the Mets had more players who spoke out against the war than any other team. At a spring training rally, St. Petersburg's mayor proclaimed the Mets "a symbol of Americanism in the battle against hippies and demonstrators."[30] In response, Mets pitcher Tug McGraw, a veteran of a USO Vietnam tour, flashed a peace sign to signal his solidarity with the protesters.

During the Vietnam War, Commissioner Kuhn claimed, "There was no comprehensive support of the war effort through anything baseball did."[31] Yet in *America through Baseball*, historian David Voigt noted that players who spoke against the war received the "chill of official disapproval" and were deterred from joining peace movements.[32] Players who engaged in small, subversive actions were often sanctioned by managers and coaches. According to Ron Briley, while dissent permeated American culture, organized baseball was "less tolerant of those who questioned authority or military policy."[33]

In 1968, popular guitarist Jose Feliciano played a Puerto Rican soul version of the national anthem in Detroit before game five of the World Series. It drew hot criticism, charges of subversion, and calls for his arrest for treason. Although mild-mannered Hall of Famer Tigers broadcaster Ernie Harwell had arranged the innovative performance, one critic claimed, "Anybody who'd let that long-hair hippie ruin our Star Spangled Banner has got to be a Communist."[34]

A new patriotic push in baseball during the Vietnam War mandated that all teams play only traditional versions of the national anthem at every game. According to spokesman John Holland, the Chicago Cubs endorsed this policy "due to the situation in Vietnam and the world."[35] The ritual cemented "the implicit link between patriotism and sport," explained sportswriter Russell Crawford.[36]

Thus it was a bit surprising when Kansas City Royals owner Ewing Kaufmann limited performances of the national anthem at his ballpark in 1972, reserving it for Sundays, holidays, and special occasions. Kaufmann received a flood of criticism, including protests from the Veterans of Foreign Wars. Kauffman claimed it was disrespectful to play the anthem every day, but the protests persisted.

Among Kaufman's few supporters, *Sports Illustrated* writer Robert Creamer declared,

> Indiscriminate flag-waving [isn't] evidence of patriotism. When I was a boy, playing the "Star Spangled Banner" and raising the flag were thrilling moments [reserved] only for major events . . . and many loyal, patriotic citizens were distressed it was chosen [as the national anthem] instead of the more stirring "America the Beautiful" . . . During World War II baseball . . . began to play the anthem and raise the flag before every game . . . to equate baseball with patriotism . . . Now the flag and anthem . . . have about as much significance as shaking hands . . . We need less flag-waving and more attention to the Constitution.[37]

Nevertheless, Kaufman was forced to reinstate the anthem.

Although Jackie Robinson had been a strong supporter of the Vietnam War, he changed his views about the war and about America's commitment to addressing racial injustice. In 1972, right before his premature death, Robinson wrote, "I cannot stand and sing the anthem. I cannot salute the flag; I know that I am a Black man in a white world."[38]

ROCKY: RON SWOBODA

Signed by the Mets in 1963, Ron Swoboda was sent to their Double-A club in Williamsport, Pennsylvania. Promoted to the Mets in 1965, he became a Topps Rookie All-Star. Swoboda was a home-run threat but he earned his nickname "Rocky" for being unreliable in the outfield. His slugging in September 1969 lifted the Mets into the playoffs. And in the World Series, he made a spectacular catch, unexpectedly, in the outfield to stifle a Baltimore Orioles rally and preserve a Mets win in game four. He had the winning RBI in game five as the Miracle Mets took the series. Still remembered for "the Catch," Swoboda was traded to the Montreal Expos in 1971 and played briefly with the New York Yankees and Atlanta Braves before retiring in 1975.

Not only the Mets but also the U.S. Army recruited Swoboda. But he was determined not to go to Vietnam. "Not that I had anything against the army. I'm as patriotic as the next man," Swoboda explained. "But my patriotism was colored by the sense of whether what my country was up to was right. I knew I didn't want any part of the war in Vietnam. The reasons were many, [including my] fundamental belief that this war business is deadly, expensive, and not to be trusted."[39] He found the domino theory unconvincing and believed, correctly, that President Johnson had used the Gulf of Tonkin incident as an excuse to expand the war. "No one was ever going to convince me that North Vietnam could be an existential threat to the United States," Swoboda said.[40]

Swoboda recalled his options.

> You could, like Muhammad Ali, declare yourself a conscientious objector, which I was not. You could run to Canada, which I would not; I wasn't going to renounce my citizenship. You could join a National Guard or Reserve unit, like George W. Bush . . . or get a medical deferment for bone spurs, like Donald Trump, or go to Paris for the Mormon Church to counsel the French against extramarital sex and alcohol, as Mitt Romney managed to do. Or, like Dick Cheney, you could say "I had other things to do," and wangle a student deferment. I suppose I could have stayed at [the University of] Maryland and done that.[41]

The remaining option was only available early in the war. If you were married by 1965, you'd be deferred. Swoboda was engaged to Cecilia Hanna, and they moved up their wedding date. "Were I not a ballplayer, were I not in love, were I not seriously questioning the politics of this war, I wouldn't be chasing a deferment. But I was all of those things."[42]

During the 1968 off-season, Swoboda surprised himself by agreeing to join baseball commissioner Bowie Kuhn, Joe DiMaggio, and Larry Jackson on a USO tour of Vietnam. It only confirmed his concerns about the war. "Outside the hospital," Swoboda recalled, "a doctor ranted for fifteen minutes about what insanity, what madness, this whole Vietnam thing was . . . Hearing it there, from someone so deep into it, left me feeling rattled."[43] He saw soldiers, variously crying, drunk, or whipped up into a frenzy. "Souls were being tried by the struggles over the Vietnam War and the civil rights movement," Swoboda observed.

> Outside the bubble [of Major League Baseball] . . . huge antiwar demonstrations broke out all over the nation. While we were in the midst of a pretty thrilling World Series [1969], a lot of the country had its mind on another matter

> . . . The Mobilization Committee to End the War in Vietnam had called for a national Moratorium—stopping all activities to protest the war—and in cities and on campuses, millions of people heeded the call.[44]

Like many other Vietnam War opponents, Swoboda distinguished between supporting the troops and supporting the war. Swoboda explained, "Nixon prolonged the war because he wasn't ready to accept terms . . . and by escalating he took more lives." Swoboda viewed the war as an expensive waste of American and Vietnamese lives.

> I don't think anything has changed us as a country more in squandering our living capital and living assets—young people, and not just the people who died—but the money wasted that could have gone somewhere else . . . and we just decimated the [Vietnamese] culture. I feel a big guilt about that.[45]

TERRIFIC: TOM SEAVER

After only a single season with the Jacksonville Suns farm team in the International League, Tom Seaver joined the New York Mets in 1967. He quickly became an All Star, winning sixteen games in his first season for the perennial last-place team and earning the NL's Rookie of the Year Award. In 1968 the Mets finished ninth in the NL, but the following year Seaver won 25 games, led the "Miracle Mets" to a World Series victory, and won the Cy Young Award. He also joined the ranks of the antiwar movement—a stance overlooked by many of the media obituaries when he died in 2020. He did so within a baseball culture that was the most conservative and traditional of the nation's major sports.

By most measures, Seaver was an all-American boy. His father was a business executive and his mother a homemaker. He had joined the U.S. Marine Corps Reserves after high school. But Seaver claimed, "I hated the Marine Corps boot camp."[46] Punished, often physically, for petty infractions, Seaver remembers being repeatedly kicked by a drill instructor for whispering to a fellow soldier while eating in the mess hall.

After six months of active duty, he enrolled at Fresno City College then transferred to the University of Southern California, one of the country's most conservative campuses. He posted a 10-2 record his sophomore year before signing a contract with the Mets. He remained a part-time member of his reserve unit until 1970. He displayed no counterculture affinity in his hair, dress, rhetoric, or personal style. He often visited wounded Vietnam veterans in hospitals and, according to Steven Travers's biography *The Last Icon*, Seaver was "aghast at the loss of American life, the suffering of the wounded." He had a strong social conscience, regarding himself as a role model for young people. Seaver was a "wide-eyed idealist who thought he could change the world."[47]

Because of his military service, Seaver had credibility on the war that other players did not, but his public stance against it triggered controversy. Seaver was scheduled to pitch the first game of the 1969 World Series against the Orioles in Baltimore on October 11. That morning, the *New York Times* ran a story headlined "Tom Seaver Says U.S. Should Leave Vietnam" in which Seaver expressed his opposition to the Vietnam War. "I think it's perfectly ridiculous what we're doing about the Vietnam situation," he told the *Times*. Seaver said that if the Mets won the World Series, he would buy an ad in the *Times* saying, "If the Mets can win the World Series, then we can get out of Vietnam."[48]

Seaver lost the first game of the series and was slated to pitch the fourth game at Shea Stadium in New York. That day, October 15, hundreds of thousands of protesters gathered in cities around the country propelled by the Moratorium to End the War in Vietnam. Despite President Nixon's promise to find an honorable peace, discontent with his policies had moved far beyond the campuses and into the mainstream.

In the Mets clubhouse before game four, Seaver's teammate Tug McGraw showed him a pamphlet being distributed outside the ballpark by antiwar protesters under the banner "Mets Fans for Peace." Headlined "Tom Seaver Says U.S. Should Leave Vietnam," the pamphlet reprinted part of that morning's *New York Times* article.

Seaver claimed that he hadn't been asked for permission to use his name in the pamphlet. But before the World Series, the antiwar Vietnam Moratorium Day Committee, a major antiwar group, had asked him to sign an ad opposing the war. Seaver agreed, explaining that "the war was not helping the American image abroad, was splitting the country apart at home, and was not adding much to our national security." Seaver was also asked to wear a black armband in the game but he "declined because it would disrupt his team. He felt an obligation to concentrate on baseball but also express his rights as a citizen."[49]

The political atmosphere inside the ballpark was another story. New York City Mayor John Lindsay, a war opponent, had decreed a day of mourning, ordering city flags to be flown at half-mast, including those at city-owned Shea Stadium. That idea clashed with an honor guard of 225 wounded veterans who were scheduled to participate in the game's opening ceremonies. They told city officials and Mets brass they would physically resist any effort to fly the flag at half-mast. Commissioner Kuhn intervened, ordering the flag flown at full staff.

When the public address announcer identified Seaver as the starting pitcher, the fan response was less enthusiastic than usual. Some fans even booed the team's best pitcher. According to sportswriter Ray Robinson, there were "too many [pro-war] hawks fluttering around in their expensive seats at Shea."[50]

Seaver beat the Orioles in that game, and the next day the Mets clinched the series in five games. After the game, Seaver reminded reporters, "I am against the war and want us to get out as soon as possible without endangering lives." Two months later, on December 31, 1969, he and his wife, Nancy, placed an antiwar ad in the *New York Times*, as he had promised, although it wasn't as forceful as his previous antiwar statements, reading, "On the eve of 1970, please join us in a prayer for peace."

Seaver's outspokenness ran counter to baseball's prevailing ethos and to the common belief that professional athletes should just play and keep their political opinions private. Seaver continued building his Hall of Fame career, winning twenty games four more times and leading the Mets to another World Series in 1973. Despite being a New York icon, Seaver endured a salary dispute with the Mets in 1977 and was traded to the Cincinnati Reds. Seaver won seventy-five games for the Reds in six years before his unsuccessful return to the Mets for the 1983 season. He pitched two years for the Chicago White Sox and won his 300th game. After a subpar year with the 1986 Boston Red Sox, Seaver retired the following year as a Met.

A first-ballot, nearly unanimous Hall of Famer, Seaver compiled eye-popping pitching statistics. Besides winning more than 300 games, he had 3,000 strikeouts and a 2.86 lifetime ERA, a combination matched only by Walter Johnson. He pitched the second-most shutouts in MLB history, was a 12-time All Star, won 3 Cy Young Awards, and a World Series ring.

SIMBA: TED SIMMONS

In 1967 the St. Louis Cardinals selected switch-hitting catcher Ted Simmons as its first-round draft pick out of the University of Michigan, which was a hotbed of political activism in the 1960s and the birthplace of the radical Students for a Democratic Society. While Simmons wasn't a political activist, he had absorbed the campus culture, shared many progressive beliefs, and wasn't afraid to express them. A serious thinker, his hero was Sir Thomas More, who was willing to die instead of putting the king ahead of God. "Now that's what I call sticking with your convictions," Simmons once observed, "no matter what the consequences."[51]

At age nineteen, Simmons debuted with the Cardinals late in their 1968 pennant-winning season. He spent the 1969 season with their Triple A Tulsa team before returning to the majors for good in 1970 after finishing his Army Reserve duty. Becoming the full-time Cardinals backstop in 1971, Simmons emerged as one of the best hitting catchers in major league history.

After hitting .304 in 1971 while earning $17,500, Simmons was dissatisfied with the contract the Cardinals offered him for 1972. He asked for $30,000 and when the Cardinals balked, he refused to sign. He announced his intention to become a free agent. The head of the players union, Marvin Miller, recalled, "Simmons refused to be bluffed into signing a new unsatisfactory contract in order to be 'allowed' into uniform."[52]

Simmons played out much of that year without a contract. His threat worried the baseball establishment. MLB's general counsel John Gaherin told Cardinals general manager Bing Devine, "Get a hold of this. We don't want to test it [the reserve clause]. Sign him. Don't let him go through this year without a contract." Devine lectured Simmons on duty and loyalty, but Simmons shot back, claiming Devine owed those same things to his players. He refused to budge. He had an outstanding year, hitting .303 with 16 homers and 96 RBIs. The Cardinals and other team owners worried that the fans would get behind the popular Simmons. Right before the All-Star game in Atlanta, Devine finally offered Simmons a two-year contract—$30,000 for 1972 and $45,000 for 1973. Had it not been for the pressure the NL put on the Cardinals to give him his asking price, Simmons could have completed the season and been released from the reserve clause. He could have pioneered free agency three years before the players' union orchestrated its demise in 1975.

Simmons remained with the Cardinals eight more seasons and played eight more with the Brewers and Cubs. He ended his career with a .285 average, 248 home runs, 1,389 RBIs, and 2,472 hits. He was the all-time hits leader for MLB catchers and second all-time leader in RBIs, doubles, and total bases when he retired. He was an eight-time All Star and hit over .300 seven times with 90 or more RBIs in eight seasons. *The Bill James Historical Baseball Abstract* ranked him the tenth best MLB catcher of all time. Thereafter, Simmons became a coach, scout, and executive for several major league teams. He also became an expert antiques collector and St. Louis Art Museum trustee.

These numbers should have made Simmons a strong and immediate candidate for the Hall of Fame. But the Baseball Writers' Association of America put him on their ballot only once, in 1994, and he garnered only 3.7 percent of the votes, falling short of the 5 percent required to remain on future ballots. It took the Veteran's Committee to get him inducted, in 2021, decades after his retirement. The delay no doubt had something to do with his political views.

Simmons pressed his fellow athletes to develop a sense of social responsibility for their country while combatting what he viewed as false stereotypes about "dumb jocks." He rebelled against traditional values, and his outspoken views didn't sit well in conservative St. Louis. Because he grew his hair long and often resembled a lion roaring his defiance, he was nicknamed "Simba." Variously called a "rebel in shin-guards" and the "counterculture catcher," he always seemed to "march to the beat of a different drummer."

But Simmons voiced not only a cultural critique but also a political protest. He was a vocal activist for civil rights and protested against the Nixon administration and the Vietnam War. For this both the press and the fans targeted him despite his stellar play. In the end, Simmons reflected, "It was nice to be right about some things, but I didn't really pay much of a price for my convictions, not like Jane Fonda or Tom Hayden or a lot of others. All I got was a few boos."[53]

ACID: DOCK ELLIS

In 1964 the Pittsburgh Pirates signed Dock Ellis out of Los Angeles Harbor College. The Pirates sent him to pitch for the Batavia Pirates of the New York–Penn League, the Kingston Eagles of the Carolina League, the Asheville Tourists of the Southern League, and the Columbus Jets of the International

League. He made his major league debut with the Pirates in June 1968 in relief and made the starting rotation the next year.

Ellis was an All Star and won nineteen games for the Pirates in 1971, remaining with Pittsburgh until he was traded to the New York Yankees after the 1975 season. In 1976 he won seventeen games for the Yankees. Between 1977 and his 1979 retirement he pitched for the Oakland Athletics, Texas Rangers, New York Mets, and again for the Pirates. Ellis's drug dependence undoubtedly cut his career short although he did compile a 138-119 record with a 3.46 ERA, 1,136 strikeouts, a World Series ring, and a Comeback Player of the Year Award in his twelve years in majors. He was inducted into the Baseball Reliquary's Shrine of the Eternals in 1999. He successfully completed drug rehabilitation and became a drug-abuse counselor after his retirement but died prematurely of liver disease in 2008.

Ellis's career was marked by controversy. He experienced frequent racial discrimination. Called a "spear chucker," he was demoted and penalized for his "big" hair and his hair curlers; he was maced by a Cincinnati Reds security guard; and he endured repeated conflicts with white managers and owners. In June 1970, Ellis pitched a no-hitter against the San Diego Padres, allegedly while under the influence of LSD, one of the many drugs he used during his career. The feat has been repeatedly memorialized in pop culture.

In *Dock Ellis in the Country of Baseball*, U.S. poet laureate Donald Hall observed that Ellis was determined to speak his mind and act freely without concern for the consequences. To some people, he was too outspoken and militant. He was frequently targeted with hate mail, mainly from fans who, Hall explained, "prefer their athletes to be docile, humble, grateful, clean-cut, and white."[54] As Jackie Robinson warned Ellis, "The news media, while knowing full well you are right and honest, will use every means to get back at you . . . There will be times when you ask yourself is it worth it all? I can only say, 'Dock, it is.'. . . You have made a real contribution."[55]

As Hall observed,

> All over the country, Dock [was] a roguish and spirited celebrity among Black people . . . He [was] popular because he upset white racists. He [was] popular like Muhammad Ali because he [did] what he pleased and [got] away with it. He [was] popular because he [was] brave and stylish . . . [and] because he [was] loyal to Black brothers and sisters everywhere, and [spent] his leisure . . . work-

> ing for the rehabilitation of convicts, fighting sickle-cell anemia, and working with Black youth.[56]

In 1971, Ellis joined an MLB–USO tour to Vietnam. "My friends were coming back from Vietnam," Ellis recalled, "and they were telling me different things . . . I wanted to see what it was."[57] Ellis arrived with only one other Black player, Bobby Bonds. They were separated into different groups, supposedly because they were the only two stars. It wasn't long before Ellis realized what was going on in Vietnam. His group met with General James Adamson, and "he was telling us all sorts of shit. He was trying to tell me how the [military] service was going to be voluntary. I say, 'Wow. That's a trip. Now we're going to be nothing but a military police state.' And it's coming about."[58]

Adamson and other officials were "talking about how there wasn't much drugs over there." Ellis observed, "Bullshit, I'm looking right at it." Ellis saw the capsules of heroin around and was offered drugs many times when he was there.

> Several dudes, they got high on heroin in the hooch [barracks] while I sat there . . . They were shooting and snorting both . . . in one place . . . I walked around the perimeter and it was all caps [of heroin]. At night, everyone who was supposed to be on guard was high.

Ellis felt similarly deceived about race relations, such as when he

> went out to a lookout post and they had this brother and this little white dude . . . both . . . from Mississippi [trying to] convince me they were close, how they were not like they used to be. Bullshit . . . They were protecting each other in wartime.[59]

After Ellis returned to the United States, the U.S. military's public relations brass asked him to go on television to discuss what he had seen in Vietnam. Ellis told the captain, "You're pretty cool. In order to protect you, I'm going to tell you what I'm going to say. I was going to talk about dope. I saw drugs all over Vietnam. And I was going to tell about the black market—soldiers selling jeeps and batteries and things like that. I wasn't going to say what they wanted me to say."[60] The Army withdrew its request.

BULLDOG: JIM BOUTON

In 1969, the Vietnam Moratorium Day Committee contacted New York Yankee pitcher Jim Bouton along with other athletes. Bouton was known for supporting student antiwar protesters and for signing antiwar petitions. He spoke against the war at a rally in New York's Central Park. Eager to participate and to recruit other athletes, Bouton observed,

> What I'm doing now, with the Moratorium group, is no major concerted effort. I'm just feeling some players out. But it is not like Jim Bouton is trying to rouse guys. A lot of them feel the same way I do, about the war and about other types of involvement. And there are many who want to express these feelings.[61]

When he got involved in the peace movement, however, Bouton was seen as a radical by the baseball establishment, most sportswriters, and many fans. "Oh, you are a ballplayer," they'd say, according to Bouton.

> You have to keep quiet. Others say we aren't qualified, that we aren't experts . . . Well, we're always being used for telling kids to stay in school, to brush their teeth. Why can't we tell them how we feel about things like the Vietnam War? And athletes do have influence.[62]

Bouton had trouble just trying to talk to other players. He explained,

> You could raise the topic of Vietnam, but you had to say something like: "Look at those crazy kids marching in the street. Why don't they take a bath?" Or you could say, "What right does [prominent antiwar activist] Reverend James Groppi have to go out in the streets like that? He should be in the pulpit where he belongs." Saying those things, no one would accuse you of talking politics, because you were *right*. If, however, you said: "We've got no right to be in Vietnam," or that "Reverend Groppi is certainly making his religion relevant up there in Milwaukee," then you shouldn't be talking about things like that, because you were *wrong*.[63]

Bouton admired Muhammad Ali who, he said,

> was one of the great men in history, and I don't mean sports history . . . He was internationally beloved for all the right reasons. He took a risk with his career,

> with his life . . . Here was a guy willing to go to prison for his beliefs. How many of those are there around?

Reflecting on the response of others to the Vietnam debacle (as well as the illegal Iraq War), Bouton later observed,

> today we have absolutely gutless politicians . . . I read about [JFK's defense secretary] Robert McNamara going to Vietnam to find out what went wrong. He was what went wrong. Him personally. He doesn't need to go anywhere to discover that. All those lives lost to find an "honorable" way out. It's disgusting to think of those lives lost.

Bouton further observed, "It just doesn't seem right that a member of my fan club should be fighting in Vietnam. Or that anybody should be."[64]

Long before football player Colin Kaepernick protested American racism by taking a knee before an NFL game, Bouton expressed similar views. He denied that flag waving constituted real patriotism, noting, "The whole anthem-flag ritual makes me uncomfortable . . . I'd usually be in the dugout toweling sweat off during the anthem."[65]

In 1970, Bouton's blockbuster book *Ball Four* revealed far more than the ballplayers' wild personal lives. It accused organized baseball of hypocrisy: by portraying a squeaky-clean image while ignoring burning social issues such as the Vietnam War. Bouton condemned the war and baseball's support for it. He attacked icons such as the Reverend Billy Graham, disputing his claim that communists had organized the antiwar protests. While Commissioner Kuhn said he couldn't remember any cases of players being ostracized for antiwar statements, Bouton claimed he was repeatedly heckled for his antiwar views by players and fans: "They wanted to know if I was working for Ho Chi Minh," the North Vietnam leader. While Bouton's book became a bestseller, he paid dearly in baseball since he was blacklisted from playing and even excluded from many ballparks. "Baseball, football—they've always felt the need to be patriotic," Bouton observed, "to be on the side of America and might, supporting wars no matter what, and so going against that conservative bent, to have a break in their ranks: This was a little too much for them."[66]

John Montgomery Ward. *Benjamin Edwards Collection, Library of Congress*

Jim O'Rourke. *Benjamin Edwards Collection, Library of Congress*

Tim Keefe. *Benjamin Edwards Collection, Library of Congress*

Mark Baldwin. *Benjamin Edwards Collection, Library of Congress*

Jorge Pasquel (r). *Rucker Archive*

Tony Lupien. *Bowman Gum*

Danny Gardella. *National Baseball Hall of Fame*

Sandy Koufax and Don Drysdale. *National Baseball Hall of Fame*

Marvin Miller. *National Baseball Hall of Fame*

Curt Flood. *National Baseball Hall of Fame*

Bill Zuber. *National Baseball Hall of Fame*

Tom Seaver. *National Baseball Hall of Fame*

Martin Dihigo. *Unknown*

Connie Marrero. *National Baseball Hall of Fame*

Roberto Clemente. *National Baseball Hall of Fame*

Ozzie Guillen. *Keith Allison*

Magglio Ordoñez. *Keith Allison*

Carlos Delgado. *National Baseball Hall of Fame*

Susan Sarandon. *Courtesy of Everett Collection*

Tim Robbins. *Courtesy of Everett Collection*

Bill Veeck. *National Baseball Hall of Fame*

Jim Bouton. *National Baseball Hall of Fame*

Bill Lee. *National Baseball Hall of Fame*

Sean Doolittle. *Keith Allison on Flickr*

5

The Latino Battle against Baseball Colonialism and Racism

In 1947 when Jackie Robinson broke the MLB color barrier, less than 1 percent of major leaguers were Latino. All of them, at that time and in MLB's previous history, were light-skinned and able to pass for white. By 2020, Latino ballplayers comprised nearly three of every ten major leaguers and half of all minor leaguers.

Besides the Latino pioneers who broke both ethnic and color barriers in baseball, some Latino players also challenged America's domestic and foreign policies, and racist prejudices, which oppressed nations and peoples "south of the border" and blocked Latinos from playing professional baseball in America for so long.

THE CUBAN EXPERIENCE

Organized baseball in Cuba began in 1864 with the Havana Baseball Club. In 1871, Esteban Enrique Bellan, a Cuban, became the first Latino ballplayer to play in MLB. A third baseman for the Troy Haymakers through the 1872 season, he then played a year with the New York Mutuals. Bellan pioneered a slow influx of Latinos into MLB in the early- and mid-twentieth century.

Meanwhile the sport of baseball became increasingly embroiled in the Cuban independence movement against Spanish and then U.S. colonialism. The Cuban Professional League, founded in 1878, had a startling political purpose beyond playing baseball: team meetings and practices fomented revolutionary fervor, profits were funneled to guerrilla groups, and many of the league's top players joined the revolutionary army as officers. At least two ballplayers (and future Cuban Hall of Famers), Jose Pastoriza and Ricardo Cabaleiro, gave their lives as rebels. In 1894 Augustin Molina, a Cuban émigré living in Key West, Florida, traveled to Cuba ostensibly to play baseball. He was actually a spy, carrying secret documents to the rebels. In 1895 Emilio Sabourin, a Cuban Baseball League founder and active in the independence movement, was arrested by Spain and died in prison in 1897.

While exiled in the United States, Jose Marti, who led the Cuban revolutionary movement in the 1890s, wrote approvingly of baseball's revolutionary role. Back in Cuba, baseball contests raised funds for Marti's movement. In 1897 on the eve of the Spanish-American War, Abel Linares—a Cuban League official—also served as the secretary of the Marti Society, which fronted Cuba's independence movement. He led an all-white Cuban team on a public relations campaign, disguised as a U.S.-baseball barnstorming tour, to secure American support for Cuban independence.

In 1898 in the Spanish-American War, the United States drove Spain out of Cuba and occupied the country. Baseball became more entrenched. As a result, most Latino major leaguers were Cuban—although only light-skinned Cubans were permitted on big league rosters. In 1911 the Cincinnati Reds signed two Cubans, Rafael Almeida and Armando Marsans, both veterans of integrated Negro League teams. Almeida played third base for the Reds through the 1913 season. Marsans played outfield for the Reds through 1913 then jumped from the NL to the upstart Federal League, playing for the St. Louis Terriers in 1914 and 1915. While his switch to the new league was described by *Baseball Magazine* as "one of the mysteries of the summer, but not to anyone who knows the Latin temper," it really wasn't so surprising.[1] Marsans came from a family of Cuban freedom fighters, and he bristled at the stereotyping of Latinos and the reserve-clause contracts he faced in the NL. Marsans finished his MLB career in the AL, playing for the St. Louis Browns and New York Yankees from 1916 to 1918.

Cuban catcher Miguel "Mike" Gonzalez debuted with the Boston Braves in 1912, left for Negro League teams, and then returned to MLB with the Cincinnati Reds in 1914. He played sixteen major league seasons through 1932 for the Reds, New York Giants, Chicago Cubs, and St. Louis Cardinals—for whom he also became a coach and interim manager. The first Latino star in MLB was Adolfo Luque, a Cuban pitcher signed by the Boston Braves in 1914. Traded to the Cincinnati Reds in 1916, he pitched for them for twelve seasons, winning a league-leading twenty-seven victories in 1923 with a 1.93 ERA. From 1930 to 1935 he played for the Brooklyn Robins and the New York Giants and then coached in the majors for another seven years. Luque compiled 194 career wins, a 3.24 ERA, and two World Series rings. Both Gonzalez and Luque promoted Latinos in MLB, but progress was slow.

In the 1920s the U.S. government backed dictator Gerardo Machado because he supported American corporations' control of much of the Cuban economy. A Cuban ballplayer, Baldomero Acosta, had been signed by the Washington Senators but he left the team to lead rebel forces in western Cuba against Machado. When the uprising began to succeed, U.S. Marines arrived to suppress the revolt and "protect American interests." When Machado's support faltered in 1933, the United States replaced him with another dictator, Fulgencio Batista, who launched a military coup to tighten the repressive clampdown.

In the 1930s the Washington Senators signed several Cuban players, and during World War II the team added more Cubans, and other Latino players, to fill rosters depleted by players in the military. A few other MLB teams began to tap the Cuban market as well as signing the first players from other Latin American, Central American, and Caribbean nations. All of them passed the light-skin criterion of American segregation.

Dark-skinned Cubans played and often starred in leagues less tainted by racial segregation including the Cuban League, the Mexican League, and the Negro Leagues. In 1908, when the Cincinnati Reds barnstormed in Cuba, Jose Mendez—one of the best pitchers in Cuban history—shut them out three times. But the Reds wouldn't sign him because he was Black. That pattern continued, robbing MLB of what could have been among their greatest players, including not only Mendez but also Luis Tiant Sr., Cristobal Torriente, Alejandro Oms, Lazaro Salazar, and Silvio Garcia.

EL IMMORTAL AND THE CUBAN COMET: MARTIN DIHIGO AND MINNIE MINOSO

Another player lost to major league baseball was Martin Dihigo. Born in 1906 in Matanzas, Cuba, Dihigo began playing professionally in 1923. Major Leaguers (such as John McGraw) and Negro Leaguers (such as Buck Leonard) who saw him play claimed Dihigo was likely the greatest talent to ever play the game. He excelled at virtually every position except catcher. He hit for average and power, was a superb fielder with a rifle arm, and starred as a pitcher, throwing no-hitters for several teams in the Cuban, Mexican, and Venezuelan leagues. After debuting with the Havana Reds as a sixteen-year-old, he joined the Cuban Stars in the Negro National League, primarily playing second base and outfield for five seasons. By 1926 he had emerged as one of the top Negro League players, leading in home runs and batting over .400. He later played for the Homestead Grays, the Philadelphia Hilldale Giants, and the New York Cubans.

Dihigo spent most of the 1937 season with the Aguilas Cibaenas in the Dominican League. He tied for the league lead in homers, hit .351 (third) and went 6-4 (second in wins to Satchel Paige). He also played for the Mexican League's Veracruz Eagles, going 4-0 with a 0.93 ERA, while hitting .357. In 1938, he led Veracruz to the Mexican League pennant with 18 wins while hitting .336. In 1939 Dihigo won another 15 games for Veracruz with 202 strikeouts. After batting .365 for Veracruz in 1940, he won 22 games and batted .319 the following season with Torreon Algodoneros in the Mexican League. Except for a short stint with the New York Cubans (again) in the Negro National League, Dihigo continued playing in the Mexican League for the next seven years before retiring in 1947. Dihigo never hesitated to speak out against the racism he experienced but integration came too late for him.

In 1949 Cleveland Indians owner Bill Veeck signed Cuban Minnie Minoso, the first Black Latino in MLB. Born in 1925, Minoso spent his early years dirt-poor on a plantation, was orphaned, and then raised by two sisters. He excelled at baseball, and the New York Cubans in the Negro League signed him in 1946 at age twenty-one. After joining the Indians, he was sent to the San Diego Padres of the PCL for the 1950 season then traded to the Chicago White Sox in 1951.

Minoso was beloved in Chicago and widely regarded as "Mr. White Sox." Although segregation robbed him of a few more years in MLB at the beginning of his career, he nevertheless had a lifetime .298 batting average with more than 1,000 RBIs, 9 All-Star appearances, 3 stolen base awards, and 3 Gold Gloves. About every ten years the White Sox invited him back to suit up, making Minoso the only person to play in a MLB game in seven different decades. The Cuban and Mexican Baseball Halls of Fame both inducted

Minoso, but the Baseball Hall of Fame committees have never admitted him to the Cooperstown shrine.

As with other Black players in the post-integration period, Minoso experienced racist taunts and discrimination. He reflected, "Racial segregation was rampant in the South, so there were only certain places we were allowed to get off the bus and buy things."[2] Yet Minoso claimed, "I never let the world hurt me. They used to call me terrible things. I let it go in one ear and out the other. I never wanted them to know my feelings on the inside. On the outside, I just gave them my smile." Like other Latino players, he had to deal with both racism and a language barrier. "Sure it made this more difficult," Minoso explained, "but never impossible."[3] Hall of Famer Orlando Cepeda called Minoso "Our Jackie Robinson."

Minoso never returned to Cuba. He became a U.S. citizen and was critical of the Castro-led revolution that began in 1959. When he put on his baseball uniform, he once said, "To me, it was like defending the American flag."[4] Minoso's hero, Martin Dihigo, pursued a different path. Ending his career in 1947, Dihigo compiled a remarkable pitching record of 288-142, often also leading leagues in home runs and batting average and never hitting below .300. He also managed championship teams in Cuba, Mexico, and Venezuela, umpired in both Cuba and Mexico, broadcast Cuban League games, and became a powerful goodwill ambassador for Cuba and especially for Negro leaguers coming to the island. Dihigo is the only ballplayer ever elected to the Hall of Fame in five countries: Cuba, Venezuela, Mexico, the Dominican Republic, and belatedly, Cooperstown in 1977.

Blocked from playing in the major leagues, Dihigo had little use for the United States or for MLB even after integration. Dihigo opposed the decades-old U.S. occupation, then domination, of his native Cuba. A strong supporter of the anti-Batista socialist cause, Dihigo left Cuba in protest. While umpiring and managing in Mexico, he met Che Guevara, who captivated him with his passionate vision of overthrowing the U.S.–backed military dictator. Soon Dihigo helped Fidel Castro and his rebel forces, helping to finance their boat *Granma* and the rebel army when it was still a rag-tag band of outmanned insurgents camped out in the Sierra Mountain foothills.

After the rebels overthrew the Batista dictatorship in 1959, Dihigo became the country's minister of sports. He engineered newly established programs institutionalizing amateur baseball on the island. Dihigo died in

1971, triggering a country-wide mourning befitting the national idol he had become. A bust of Dihigo was erected at Havana's Estadio Latinoamericano, where he's known as *El Immortal*. The public ceremony featured the country's number one fan, Fidel Castro, who lauded Dihigo as a fallen hero of the revolution.

BASEBALL FAN: FIDEL CASTRO

Many myths about Fidel Castro's baseball prowess endure. One of them claims he was good enough to be offered a major league contract. He once attended a Washington Senators tryout camp but wasn't good enough to get a second look.

Even so, Castro was definitely a big baseball fan. Joe Black, a Negro League pitching star and 1952 NL Rookie of the Year, met Castro when playing in the Cuban Winter League in 1950. Castro was a young lawyer and a budding politician who often attended games. One day he asked Black why he was warming up from ten feet behind the rubber. When Black explained that it stretched his muscles and helped him with his control, Castro said, "You're loco." Another time, Black played a one-on-one basketball game with Castro, who later wrote Black friendly letters when he joined the Dodgers in 1952.[5]

The Cuban Revolution—which Castro led to overthrow the U.S.-backed Cuban dictator Fulgencio Batista in 1959—has been mired in controversy. The series of U.S.-backed dictatorships in Cuba for the first half of the twentieth century brought political repression and economic misery to the Cuban people while promoting the dominance of the U.S. government, military, corporations, and an American-based Mafia, which controlled much of the island's tourism industry, including the hotels, gambling casinos, and prostitution. In 1961 the United States broke off diplomatic relations with Cuba and forbid American travel to the island. The United States refused to recognize the new government and began a boycott to strangle the Cuban economy, which had relied heavily on exporting sugar to the United States.

The CIA helped fund and train Cuban exiles seeking to overthrow the Castro government, including its failed invasion of the Cuban Bay of Pigs. In response, Castro escalated the nationalization of U.S. companies—including banks, oil refineries, and sugar and coffee plantations. With those interests threatened, the United States imposed an embargo on Cuba in 1962, prohibiting all economic activity between the two nations. The CIA sponsored at least five unsuccessful assassination plots against Castro. Over the next half century, the Castro government restricted political and civil rights, and suppressed political opposition. With financial support from the Soviet Union, it also dramatically improved the economic well-being of the Cuban people. According to human rights organization Amnesty International,

> Castro's achievements in improving access to public services for millions of Cubans were tempered by a systemic repression of basic freedoms [but] Castro oversaw dramatic improvements in access to human rights such as health and housing. This was accompanied by an unprecedented drive to improve literacy rates across the country.[6]

After the Soviet Union collapsed in 1989, it could no longer afford the subsidies that helped Cuba's material progress, and the island's economy and living standards suffered.

The first game played at Gran Stadium after Castro's 1959 triumph celebrated the Cuban Revolution. Rebel soldiers attended the game for free and the crowd and players gave them a stirring ovation. Castro formed a barnstorming team, *Los Barbudos* (the Bearded Ones), which toured the country to help solidify the revolt. Before an International League game in Havana, *Los Barbudos* played a Cuban military police team. Castro pitched and had two strikeouts in two innings.

When the MLB–affiliated Havana Sugar Kings began having money problems in 1959, Castro didn't shun the team as merely a "capitalist tool." Instead he backed it financially. In the end the Sugar Kings won the International League pennant and then faced the American Association winners, the Minneapolis Millers, for the minor league championship. Before the games in Havana, Castro proclaimed, "I want to see our club win . . . After the triumph of the revolution, we should also win the Little World Series."[7]

The Sugar Kings did win but the triumph was short-lived. In July 1960, the team was yanked from Cuba without notice and relocated to New Jersey. MLB commissioner Ford Frick blamed security concerns. The driving force behind this decision came from pressure put on MLB by U.S. Secretary of State Christian Herter. Castro denounced the Sugar Kings removal as aggression against the Cuban people. Cuban baseball became a victim of the Cold War.

In *Baseball and the Cold War,* Howard Senzel observed that the Kennedy administration and its successors repeatedly shunned opportunities for a baseball detente between the United States and Cuba because of persistent "anti-communist paranoia." In the *Sporting News,* Dan Daniel suggested, "Commissioner Frick should bar all players in Organized Ball, even natives of Cuba, from competing in the Cuban [winter] League."[8] Frick took this advice, prohibiting foreign players from playing outside their native country during the off-season. This made Cuban professional baseball nearly impossible.

Unable to compete with the United States economically or militarily, Castro turned sports into a political tool. Determined to beat the United States at its own game, Castro put the quintessential American sport—baseball—at the service of the Cuban Revolution. The Cuban government officially ended professional baseball but invested heavily in expanding the country's youth and amateur baseball leagues. Referring to MLB's reserve clause, Castro called professional baseball *la pelota esclava* (slave baseball) where athletes were sold or traded like simple merchandise.

Like many so-called amateur leagues around the world and in the United States, however, Cuban players were paid in various ways, including no-show, non-baseball jobs. In response to the U.S. boycott of the island, the Castro government restricted Cuban players from playing for MLB teams although some Cuban players managed to leave the island to sign MLB contracts.

Cuban national teams have been very successful in international competition despite the country's small population of about 11 million people. It's typically assumed that the heyday of Cuban baseball occurred before the revolution. Since the early 1960s, however, Cuban baseball has won 3 of 4 Olympic gold medals, 25 of 28 World Cups, and 9 of 12 Intercontinental Cups. While MLB calls its sport the national pastime, enthusiasm for baseball runs far deeper in Cuba than in the United States. Castro elevated the sport rather than the business.

HAVANA PERFECTO: CONRADO MARRERO

While most Cuban ballplayers never left the island and most Cubans who made the major leagues never returned to Cuba, Conrado Marrero was an exception. A light-skinned Cuban, Marrero was born in Sagua la Grande in 1911. After a late start, he joined the Cienfuegos club in the Cuban Amateur League at age twenty-seven in 1938, becoming a pitching sensation and winning 128 games and several MVP awards through 1945. In 1946, Marrero began playing winter ball in the Cuban League, where he again starred, compiling sixty-nine victories for several clubs after age thirty-five. In 1947, Marrero signed with the Havana Cubans, a Washington Senators farm team in the Florida State League. In three years, he won seventy games and an MVP award.

In 1950 Marrero debuted in MLB with the Senators when he was nearly thirty-nine, joining other Cubans, including Sandy Consuegra, Camilo Pasquel, Roberto Ortiz, and Julio Moreno. In his five years with the Senators, Marrero had three winning seasons and a 3.67 ERA. In 1951, when he was the oldest player in the majors, he made the AL All-Star team. He returned to Cuba to pitch part time for the Havana Sugar Kings in the International League for three more winning seasons, ending with an 80-29 minor league record. Tommy Lasorda claimed that Marrero had such good control he could "throw the ball into a tea cup."[9] According to Felipe Alou, Marrero's pitching motion was "a cross between a windmill gone berserk and a mallard duck trying to fly backwards."[10] But it worked. He retired from pitching in 1957, coached for the Sugar Kings, and scouted for the Boston Red Sox.

After the 1959 Cuban Revolution, Marrero could have returned to the United States but chose to remain on the island and became a supporter of the revolution. He joined the Cuban Communist Party and worked for six decades to develop and foster amateur baseball. In press interviews he advocated a socialist, government-run baseball system. "In Cuba," Marrero observed, "players are better now than they were before the Revolution."[11] After he'd been a pitching coach for several years for the Havana Industriales and a roving pitching instructor, the *Estadio Latinoamericano* memorialized him in a mural and Cuba honored him—along with Dihigo and Dolf Luque—with his picture on a Cuban postage stamp.

For years MLB's Baseball Assistance Team (BAT) denied Marrero a pension and assistance because of the U.S. embargo of Cuba and because he refused to renounce his communist homeland and move to Miami. Although Marrero lived modestly in a room in a relative's Havana apartment, a BAT official dismissed his claims, observing that "Marrero has made his bed (by choosing to remain with his family in his homeland) and now he can lie in it."[12] Marrero explained, "I'm Cuban and I came back to the place where I was born but I wish our countries could be united again, just like the way they used to be."[13] In 2013 he finally received a $20,000 pension payout from MLB at age 102. He died the next year, just shy of 103, thus becoming the second-longest-living player in MLB history.

CUBAN EMBARGO RESISTER: PETER ANGELOS

The last major league teams to visit Cuba were the Cincinnati Redlegs and Los Angeles Dodgers in 1959. After the Castro regime took power and the United States began its Cuban boycott, some Americans sought to build bridges between the two countries. In the early 1970s, Cuban-born San Diego Padres manager Preston Gomez wanted to take an American All-Star team to Cuba but the U.S. government blocked the effort. In 1975 Fidel Castro hosted U.S. Senator George McGovern, who returned from his Cuban visit recommending baseball diplomacy. Cuba invited the New York Yankees to play in Havana. Commissioner Bowie Kuhn endorsed the idea as a potential goodwill effort, promising the U.S. team wouldn't try to recruit Cuban players, but then backed off. Kuhn blamed Secretary of State Henry Kissinger, whom Cuba had angered by sending troops to Angola to fight U.S.–backed right-wing forces there.

In 1977 President Jimmy Carter, seeking to ease U.S.–Cuban tensions, proposed a spring training game between a U.S. All-Star team and a Cuban team. But Kuhn called this off as well, dropping all pretense and claiming that if Cubans kept blocking their players from signing U.S. contracts, then there would be no game.

In 1978 Carter's State Department gave Cleveland Indians general manager Gabe Paul permission to arrange a game. Things looked promising when Castro agreed to do a live interview with ABC sports broadcaster Howard Cosell. During the interview, Castro again proposed playing baseball with the Americans. But ABC Sports kept interrupting the interview to cover a speed-skating competition at the Lake Placid Olympics. Castro was predictably insulted. Commissioner Kuhn made it worse when he cabled the Cuban sports director, "We are unable to schedule exhibition baseball . . . Our principal incentive has been to facilitate the availability of star Cuban players to American baseball,"[14] a raid the Cuban government obviously would not allow.

In the mid-1980s the Toronto Blue Jays offered to sign Cuban Omar Linares and skirt U.S. embargo policies by having him play only home games in

Canada. Linares declined, however, saying, "We are not going to be overrun by the U.S. We prefer to die in our country before we submit."[15] Other U.S.–Cuba games were planned but they were all blocked either by the State Department or MLB, including a contest slated for Minneapolis and even one proposed for Mexico between the Seattle Mariners and the Cuban national team.

In 1995 Baltimore Orioles owner Peter Angelos sought to arrange contests between his team and the Cubans. As a labor lawyer, Angelos had enraged both Commissioner Bud Selig and other owners by siding with the players' union during the 1994 strike and refusing to use replacement players. With regard to Cuba, Angelos observed,

> I always felt the embargo was a mistake and did not work . . . I felt we had to put all that aside and re-establish the dialogue. I felt the two countries could get together and put their differences behind, and what better way to start than through baseball, the national sport of both countries? I only wanted to go there because I felt the Cuban people were our friends and someone was always stoking animosity between our two peoples.[16]

To explore the possibilities, Angelos took several other owners to Havana, where Fidel and Raul Castro hosted them at a state dinner. "Castro," Angelos worried, "had been characterized as a communist and in all kinds of negative ways . . . For crying out loud, Kennedy tried to invade the island and tried to kill him." The gathering "confirmed what I was hoping for," Angelos said. "The assumption that we could not get together was simply not correct."[17]

The Havana trip strengthened Angelos's opposition to America's Cuban policies. "What we witnessed was the capital of Cuba that was literally crumbling in the dust from the embargo that we had imposed upon the country." The Cubans, he observed, "were people who were just like our people. They . . . loved baseball and there was nothing they wouldn't do for us while we were there."[18] *Baltimore Sun* reporter Peter Schmuck, who accompanied the owners to Cuba, observed, "Being there and meeting the people, it changed my view of the embargo."[19] Angelos returned determined to arrange U.S.–Cuban ballgames. But the Clinton administration rejected the idea, claiming it would violate the U.S. Trading with the Enemy Act.

Angelos persisted and finally succeeded in 1999 when the Clinton administration loosened restrictions against Cuba. According to Sandy Alderson,

MLB's point man in talks with Cuba, "MLB wouldn't have done it without Peter [Angelos] really pushing it. It ended up costing him a lot of money because he had to cover all the losses."[20] Clinton wanted to grant permission without appearing to approve or sponsor the games. Instead of staying neutral, however, U.S. Secretary of State Madeleine Albright almost sabotaged the series when she described it as a Clinton policy to "provide the people of Cuba with hope in their struggle against a system that for four decades has denied them even basic human rights."[21]

While Castro had to be placated, the Clinton administration gave permission only after reassurances that profits would go directly to humanitarian groups and not to the government. Castro bristled at Clinton's thinly disguised tactic to support dissidents. Even so, he went along. In *A History of Cuban Baseball*, historian Peter Bjarkman observed,

> There was no moment attached to the long anticipated and politically charged contest that was more poignant than the one which witnessed a still-fit 88-year-old ex-big leaguer poised on the pitching rubber in Havana's March sunshine, determined to bridge the existing gulf of four decades of uneasy separation between two baseball-loving nations. Conrado Marrero took the mound for a celebratory game-opening ceremonial "pitch" and was not about to quickly release his moment of relived glory . . . It was pure theater—the stuff baseball used to be made of.[22]

According to reporter Jeff Stein, "The games were supposed to break the ice between Havana and Washington but apparently the first game, in Cuba, went so smoothly (with the Orioles winning by a run) that the State Department got frightened about its implications and decided it would make trouble for the second game."[23] A group of anti-Castro Cuban exiles called Brothers to the Rescue sought to sabotage the game by "booting" the tires of the airliner that would carry the Cuban ballplayers to Miami. The U.S. government blocked these efforts but it nevertheless permitted the organization's hostile flyovers and allowed anti-Castro protesters to buy blocks of seats close to the field. Initially it denied visas for much of the Cuban delegation and greased the way for any Cubans who wished to defect by asking Baltimore police to set up a system to process them. Despite this, anti-Castro forces in the United States viewed this baseball diplomacy as capitulating to the communist government. Florida Representative Ileana Ros-Lehtinen claimed the games were part of "an anti-democratic festival the Clinton administration is putting on in honor of Castro."[24]

Angelos was accused of using the games to unfairly promote the Orioles in Cuba so that Cuban ballplayers would want to play for his club. Yet when he pledged not to pursue Cuban players or encourage defections, the U.S. media criticized Angelos for kowtowing to Castro. The *Washington Examiner* sarcastically noted, "That's a man of principle: he'll sacrifice a chance for more wins in order not to offend a Communist dictator by not encouraging people to flee the dictatorship!"[25] Baseball agents who represented defectors were particularly upset since this deprived them of potential business. U.S. Senator Jesse Helms, a North Carolina Republican and a lifelong opponent of racial equality, claimed that by not signing Cuban defectors, the Orioles were discriminating in violation of the 1964 Civil Rights Act—legislation Helms had opposed.

At the second game in Baltimore, the Cubans avenged their loss with a 12-6 win over the Orioles. Political demonstrations riddled the contest, with Castro haters and defenders trying to out-duel each other with chants and placards. The clashes reached the field when a Cuban umpire body-slammed an anti-Castro demonstrator who came out of the stands holding a sign that read "Freedom—Strike Out Against Castro." But for baseball fans who cared to see, the game showed just how good the Cuban players were.

Sportswriter Dave Zirin observed,

> To stage such a home-and-home series was courageous and, if it was going to happen, only Peter Angelos amongst the fraternity of owners, would have done it. The elder Angelos has been subject to a great deal of criticism for his baseball moves over the years, but . . . as a sports owner, he is a bird of a different feather . . . a political progressive in an ownership fraternity where to be anywhere to the left of John McCain is tantamount to calling for a dictatorship of the proletariat.[26]

The games could have been a breakthrough in U.S.–Cuban relations if it hadn't been for the attack on the World Trade Center on September 11, 2001. Instead the George W. Bush administration escalated the U.S.–Cuban conflict, even trying in 2002 to implicate Cuba in the terrorist attacks. In 2006, in its attempt to supplant the Olympics, MLB launched the World Baseball Classic. In the finals, Japan beat Cuba, which had almost been barred from the tournament. The United States had tried to block Cuba's participation, again invoking the Trading with the Enemy Act. The Bush administration claimed that Cuba would use the games for spying, and the State Department said Cuba's inclusion would be rewarding a dictator. The media, including the sporting press, also chimed in, such as ESPN's repeated claims that Cuba was the "only country here that is under a dictator,"[27] conveniently ignoring China's participation in the World Baseball Classic.

In response, the International Baseball Federation threatened to rescind its endorsement of the World Baseball Classic; Puerto Rico vowed to withdraw as a host; and the International Olympic Committee warned that Cuba's exclusion could jeopardize America's ability to host a future Olympics. Even MLB protested U.S. policy in a rare departure from its collaboration with the American government. According to Peter Angelos, "once again the U.S., this huge colossus, is picking on a tiny country of 11 million. And for what? For their participation in an international baseball event? That makes us look like the big, bad bully our non-admirers say we are."[28] The United States finally relented and let the Cuban team compete but only if Cuba donated its game proceeds to a humanitarian cause. Ever the political tactician, Fidel Castro chose the U.S. victims of Hurricane Katrina, which had devastated New Orleans and the Gulf Coast in 2006.

Reflecting on the return of Cuban baseball to the United States after his father's initiative, Angelos's son and Orioles COO John Angelos said, "There is still more work to be done to bring our two peoples together, and let's hope the momentum continues . . . to a full and open relationship unfettered by government policy prohibitions of any kind."[29]

THE PUERTO RICAN–NICARAGUAN NEXUS

Baseball in Puerto Rico began in 1897 with two clubs: the Almendares and Borinquen teams. They played the first organized game in early 1898 in San Juan shortly before the United States launched the Spanish-American War. The sport expanded after the U.S. military occupied Puerto Rico when it took the island from Spain at the war's end and made it a U.S. territory.

As with other Black players, MLB barred dark-skinned Puerto Ricans until 1947 so some of them found work in the Negro Leagues as well as the professional leagues in Cuba, Venezuela, and Mexico. Emilio Navarro was the first Puerto Rican to play in the Negro Leagues when he joined the Cuban Stars in 1928. Other Black Puerto Ricans followed, but perhaps the island's best player in the mid-twentieth century, Perucho Cepeda, refused to play in the United States because he was so fiercely alienated by American racism. Cepeda, the father of future Hall of Famer Orlando Cepeda, played in Puerto Rico between 1938 and 1950. Known as the "Babe Ruth of Puerto Rico," he played shortstop and first base, hit for power, and batted over .400 several times in the Puerto Rican League, competing with Negro League stars Josh Gibson, Monte Irvin, Roy Campanella, and Buck Leonard.

When he joined the Chicago Cubs in 1942, light-skinned Hiram Bithorn became the first Puerto Rican player to break into MLB. He won eighteen games pitching for the Cubs in 1943, spent two years in U.S. military service, and returned to the majors for 1946 and 1947, ending with a lifetime 34-31 record and a 3.16 ERA. In 1962, Puerto Rico named its biggest ballpark after him.

THE GREAT ONE: ROBERTO CLEMENTE

If Minnie Minoso was the pioneer in 1949 for Black Latinos in the majors, Roberto Clemente was their crusader and patron saint. Born in 1934 in Carolina, Puerto Rico, Clemente starred as an all-around athlete in high school. His arm was so strong that he became an Olympic prospect throwing the javelin. But he loved baseball and attracted the attention of Brooklyn Dodgers scout Al Campanis at a San Juan tryout in 1952. After his outstanding 1953 season with the Santurce Crabbers in the Puerto Rican League, the New York Giants and Milwaukee Braves offered Clemente a contract but he signed with the Dodgers instead in 1954. Under MLB rules, Clemente received a contract that required the Dodgers to keep him on their major league roster or risk losing him in the off-season draft. Bonus players often just sat on the big-league bench when otherwise they could be gaining further experience playing in the minors.

The Dodgers took a chance on losing Clemente by sending him to their Montreal Royals farm team in the International League for the 1954 season. The Royals only put Clemente in the line up for 87 of its 154 games. Some argue that they did so to hide his skills from other clubs, especially the Dodgers' arch-rival, the Giants, which might claim him at the end of the season. Others speculate that Clemente wasn't elevated immediately to Brooklyn because they had a quota for Black players.

Clemente struggled initially in Montreal but his performance had improved by the season's end. The Dodgers knew that the Pittsburgh Pirates—now run by former Brooklyn general manager Branch Rickey—had their eye on Clemente. Dodgers general manager Buzzie Bavasi struck a deal with Rickey (his former boss) to have the Pirates draft another player from the Royals roster. Since each minor league team could lose only one player, Clemente would be protected. But the deal fell through and Clemente became a Pirate after all. In the off-season, Clemente returned to the Santurce Crabbers, joined by Willie Mays in the outfield. Clemente enjoyed a sensational season and the two players led the team to the Caribbean Series championship. Near the end of the winter season, an automobile accident damaged Clemente's back. It would hinder him for the rest of his baseball career.

Clemente made his MLB debut in April 1955. Besides his solid hitting as a rookie, he performed exceptionally on the base paths and defensively in the outfield, routinely throwing out runners. Clemente introduced an exciting, rambunctious style of play that endeared him to the fans but made him more susceptible to injuries. By 1956, his hitting (a .311 batting average) matched his sterling defense but Clemente was frequently hurt, sometimes requiring surgery. He suffered damaged discs, bone chips, pulled muscles, a strained instep, a thigh hematoma, tonsillitis, malaria, stomach problems, and insomnia. Even so, between 1955 and 1972 he played more games than anyone in Pirates history.

Yet sportswriters, teammates, and managers repeatedly accused him of being lazy or faking injuries if he missed a game. To the contrary, Clemente repeatedly played through pain and excelled nevertheless. According to Pirates trainer Tony Bartirome, Clemente "wasn't a hypochondriac, he was a fighter." When a white player pushed through injuries, he was regarded as a hero. "Mickey Mantle is God," Clemente observed, "but if a Latin or Black is sick, they say it is in his head."[30] Clemente fought constantly against negative stereotypes of emotional and lackadaisical Latinos.

In 1958–1959, Clemente served six months in the U.S. Marine Corps Reserves. In 1960 he was selected for his first of fifteen All-Star appearances and helped lead the Pirates to the World Series and to their upset victory over the Yankees. Despite his stellar play, he placed only eighth in the MVP balloting for an award bestowed on his white teammate Dick Groat. Given the racism he'd experienced throughout his time in the majors, he couldn't help feeling that it influenced the voting. Clemente wasn't a hometown favorite like Groat. He spoke Spanish, and some baseball writers viewed him as brash and moody for speaking his mind. Clemente believed Latino players like him didn't receive the recognition they deserved, and he publicly complained about it.

Clemente won the first of his four batting titles in 1961 (with a .351 average) and an MVP in 1966. Meanwhile he continued playing in the Puerto Rican League most off-seasons, eventually moving to the Senadores de San Juan, which he also managed in 1964. He felt obliged to play for his Puerto Ricans fans. As biographer Stew Thornley has noted, Clemente was "perhaps the most inspirational figure the island has ever known, and he took that responsibility seriously."[31] In 1968 he injured his shoulder and had such a hard time swinging the bat he thought he'd have to retire. He rallied, however, making a comeback in 1969, hitting an NL third-best .345.

In the 1970–1971 off-season, he managed the Senadores again, competing against Santurce, managed by future Hall of Famer Frank Robinson. Both were top candidates to be the first Black manager in the major leagues. In 1971, Clemente again led the Pirates to the World Series. He starred in the seven-game upset of the Baltimore Orioles, hitting .414 and winning the series MVP. In 1972, battling more injuries, Clemente reached his goal of 3,000 hits in his last game of the season, a feat surpassed by only ten major leaguers at the time. For his career, Clemente hit over .300 13 times and ended his career with a .314 average, 240 home runs, 1,305 RBIs, and 12 Gold Gloves.

Clemente bristled over the racist way sportswriters covered him. They called him "Bobby" or "Bob" instead of his preferred name "Roberto." Baseball card companies and other merchandisers followed suit even through the end of his career. White players were always asked what they wanted to be called. Sportswriters made fun of his accent, quoted him in broken English, and paid little attention to his powerful intellect and social conscience. He knew little English when he joined MLB and naturally spoke with a Spanish accent. After winning the 1961 All-Star game for the NL, for example, Clemente was quoted, "I get heet . . . When I come to plate in lass eening . . . I say I 'ope that Weelhelm [Hoyt Wilhelm] peetch me outside."[32]

Reporters corrected grammatical mistakes in English for white players all the time but routinely made Latinos look ignorant, even a highly intelligent thinker like Clemente. The sportswriters thought nothing about not speaking Spanish themselves despite the growing presence of Latinos in MLB.

Clemente refused to be treated as a second-class citizen, repeatedly protesting Jim Crow segregation. He didn't merely tolerate the racism and stereotypes he encountered as a Black Latino. He fought back vocally and visibly even when that made him a bigger target. As MLB columnist Joe Posnanski recalled, Clemente "did rage. In this way, he was like one of his heroes, Jackie Robinson. He was unwilling to simply accept what he saw as injustice."[33] Clemente refused to remain silent. "You writers are all the same," he shouted at one critical reporter. "You don't know a damn thing about me."[34] Clemente didn't want to merely represent Latin Americans; he wanted to improve their lives. He always said, "Remember who paved the way for you," and he paid tribute to Puerto Rican pioneers in MLB such as Hiram Bithorn and Luis Olmo.[35] Black players for the Pirates during Florida spring training in the late 1950s and early 1960s could not enter restaurants. White teammates had to bring their food out to the team bus. Clemente refused to sit and wait on the bus. He demanded that the Pirates provide Black players with another vehicle so they could drive to Black restaurants where they would be served.

During Clemente's playing days, Pittsburgh had a large Black population but few Latinos. The prejudice against Latinos came not only from the fans and the media but also his teammates, who used racial slurs when referring to Clemente and other Latino players. He occasionally confronted his bigoted white teammates. The racism he faced turned "a mild, kind man into a blunt and angry one."[36] Clemente said, "I don't believe in color; I believe in people. I always respect everyone, and thanks to God my mother and my father taught me to never hate, never to dislike someone because of their color. I didn't know about racism when I got to Pittsburgh."[37]

Clemente pushed back when a reporter called him a "chocolate-covered islander" or when sportswriters otherwise mocked him personally or questioned his abilities. He was confident of his abilities, insisting that "nobody does anything better than me in baseball."[38] Whites resented his directness but he demanded their respect.

According to his wife, Vera, Clemente talked "a lot about how being a Black Latin coming into baseball meant you had two strikes against you. He wanted the Latino players to get their fair share of the money. He wanted them to be managers . . . to get respect."[39] According to Pirates trainer Tony Bartirome, Clemente saw his quest to improve things for the Latin and Black players as "his small way of changing the country for the better."[40]

Double standards always angered Clemente: "When the sportswriters write about a Black or Hispanic player, it's always something controversial. When they write about white players, it's usually nice—human interest stuff." He liked to think he made some progress against that practice.

> I believe that every human being is equal, but one has to fight hard all the time to maintain that equality. Always, they would say you'd really have to be something to be like Babe Ruth. But Babe Ruth was an American player. What we needed was a Puerto Rican player they could say that about, someone to look up to and try to equal.[41]

In 1970, at Roberto Clemente Night at Three Rivers Stadium, Clemente declared, "I have achieved this triumph for us, the Latinos. I believe it is a matter of pride for all of us, the Puerto Ricans as well as others in the Caribbean because we are all brothers."[42] Clemente pushed the Pirates to hire more players of color and they listened. By the early 1970s, half the Pittsburgh roster was either Black, Latino, or spoke Spanish, and in 1971, for the first time in MLB history, the Pirates fielded an all-Black and Latino lineup, thanks largely to Clemente.

Clemente played his entire career with the Pirates, from 1955 to 1972, during the peak of civil rights activism. He closely followed the movement and identified with its struggles. He admired Martin Luther King Jr. and became his friend. They met often, including a long visit on Clemente's farm on the outskirts of Carolina, Puerto Rico, where they discussed King's philosophy of nonviolence and racial integration. Clemente voiced these ideas both inside and outside the clubhouse. As teammate Al Oliver recalled, "Our conversations always stemmed around people from all walks of life being able to get along. He had a problem with people who treated you differently because of where you were from, your nationality, your color; also poor people, how they were treated."[43]

King was assassinated in Memphis on Thursday, April 4, 1968, during the last week of baseball's spring training. His funeral was scheduled for Tuesday, April 9, the day after opening day. Immediately, the NBA and NHL suspended their playoff games. Racetracks shut down for the weekend. The North American Soccer League called off games. But MLB waffled. After many players sat out the last few games of spring training to honor King, several owners insisted that baseball commissioner William Eckert penalize them for refusing to play. But Eckert was more concerned about the start of the regular season.

Clemente was upset that Eckert announced that each team could decide for itself whether it would play games scheduled for opening day and the day of King's funeral. Some team owners, torn over what to do, approached their Black players to feel the pulse of their employees.

In response, Clemente observed, "If you have to ask Negro players, then we do not have a great country."[44]

King's murder triggered riots in a number of cities with major league teams. Two teams—the Washington Senators and Cincinnati Reds—postponed their home openers because their stadiums were near the protests. But Houston Astros owner Roy Hofheinz, a businessman and former Houston mayor, insisted that his team would play its opener against the Pirates—the third game scheduled for April 8. "Our fans are counting on it," explained Astros vice president Bill Giles.[45]

Under baseball rules, as the visiting team, the Pirates were required to play if the Astros wanted the game to go on. But veteran third baseman Maury Wills urged his Pirates teammates to refuse to play on opening day and the following day when America would be watching or listening to King's funeral. At the time the Pirates had eleven Black players (six of them also Latino) on their roster, more than any other major league team.

After Clemente, the team leader, urged his teammates to support Wills's idea, they took a vote. It was unanimous. Clemente and Dave Wickersham, a white pitcher, contacted Pirates general manager Joe L. Brown and asked him to postpone the season's first two games. The two players wrote a public statement on behalf of their teammates: "We are doing this because we white and Black players respect what Dr. King has done for mankind."[46] Pirate players Donn Clendenon and Willie Stargell walked into the Astros locker room and persuaded the Black players to join the protest. The other players agreed and informed the Houston brass: They would not play the first two games until after King was buried.

St. Louis Cardinals pitcher Bob Gibson and some of his teammates had the same idea. They met in first baseman Orlando Cepeda's apartment and then told Cardinals management that they wouldn't play on April 9, the opening day for most of the teams. Players on other teams followed their lead. The Los

Angeles Dodgers' Walter O'Malley was the last owner to hold out, but when the Phillies players refused to take the field against the Dodgers, his hands were tied. Commissioner Eckert, his back against the wall, reluctantly moved all opening day games to April 10. No sportswriter at the time described the players' action as a strike. But that's what it was—a two-day walk-out, not over salaries and pensions, but over social justice.

Clemente didn't limit himself to advocating for Blacks and Latinos. He observed, "If you have a chance to help others and fail to do so, you are wasting your time on this earth."[47] Besides sponsoring philanthropies to distribute food, medical supplies, and baseball equipment, Clemente focused on children. He routinely visited sick kids in hospitals and held frequent baseball clinics for low-income children. He campaigned to use sports to counter drug problems in Puerto Rico and elsewhere. Most ambitiously, he began building a Sports City in Puerto Rico, seeking to replicate it throughout the United States to provide athletics and counseling, and also intercity and interracial exchanges to challenge all forms of discrimination.

A lasting bond between Clemente and the Nicaraguan people also began in the 1963–1964 off-season when Clemente played winter ball for the Senadores de San Juan, which represented Puerto Rico in the International Series in Managua, Nicaragua. Clemente became a fan favorite during the series, making many friends and pledging to return.

In 1971, West Point graduate Anastasio Somoza Jr., the third in a succession of U.S.–backed Somoza dictators, canceled Nicaraguan Winter League baseball. However, the Nicaraguan national amateur team thrived. The following year, in front of euphoric home crowds in Estadio Nacional, the amateur team led by future major leaguers Dennis Martinez and Tony Chevez captured a bronze medal in the World Amateur Baseball Championships, winning upsets over perennial champions Cuba and the United States. Those victories sparked a national celebration. But one of Nicaragua's proudest and most memorable moments was upended three weeks later when a massive earthquake struck Nicaragua, killing nearly ten thousand people and destroying half of Managua.

Clemente had just been in Nicaragua, managing the Puerto Rican team at the World Amateur Baseball Championships games and making more friends in the country, many of whom were poor and needed help. Back home in San Juan, he decided to help the recovery, using the media to organize a massive campaign of food, clothing, and medical assistance. Funded by Clemente, two cargo planes and a freighter began delivering the Puerto Rican aid. But soon word got out that Somoza was siphoning off the international aid flowing into Managua (including $30 million from the United States) and stockpiling it for his corrupt government. President Nixon dispatched a battalion of U.S. paratroopers to Managua, which only further helped Somoza loot the country. Nixon claimed he didn't want the earthquake to provide opportunities for communists.

Clemente learned that when a private American medical team arrived in Managua, it had to fight local Somoza officials from confiscating the supplies they brought. When Clemente discovered Somoza was diverting other aid, he was enraged and vowed to personally deliver the relief he had gathered. Well-known and respected in Nicaragua, Clemente believed his presence would ensure the aid would get to the people who needed it. On December 31, 1972, the thirty-eight-year-old ballplayer boarded a poorly maintained and overloaded plane. Some warned him against making the trip, but he said, "Babies are dying. They need these supplies." Claiming "the people in charge know what they're doing," Clemente may nevertheless have suspected something was wrong with the plane, but he said, "I have to go. I have to make sure everything's okay in Nicaragua."[48] Several minutes after takeoff the plane crashed into the Atlantic Ocean, killing Clemente and four others.

After Clemente's death, Nixon proposed a Roberto Clemente Memorial Fund even though the president's support for the dictator Somoza and U.S. foreign policy's longstanding oppression of Nicaragua led indirectly to Clemente's death. In 1973, Nixon hosted the Clemente family survivors in the White House, posthumously bestowing the first-ever Presidential Citizen's Medal on the fallen star. Clemente would have likely bristled at Nixon's words: "The best memorial we can build to his memory is to contribute generously . . . to those he was trying to help . . . in Managua in Nicaragua, one of our friends to the south. That is the way Roberto Clemente would have wanted it."[49]

As his biographer David Maraniss observed, Clemente became "universally loved and admired . . . But it wasn't like that in his playing days."[50] It was "glorification after the fact." Clemente's memory was coopted not only by Nixon, but by other politicians he would have likely despised, including George W. Bush (who posthumously awarded him the Medal of Freedom) and Rudy Giuliani (who hypocritically hailed his humanitarianism). More genuinely, the Pirates retired Clemente's number in 1973 and the Baseball Writers of America waived the normal five-year waiting period to elect Clemente to the Cooperstown Hall of Fame in 1973, the first Latino player ever inducted. MLB established an annual Roberto Clemente Award (for community service) and a Roberto Clemente Day. In 1974 Roberto Clemente Sports City opened in Puerto Rico and has since served hundreds of thousands of kids, including future MLB stars Juan Gonzalez, Bernie Williams, and Ivan Rodriguez. In 1998, the sports center unveiled a bronze cenotaph such as usually reserved for fallen military heroes, describing Clemente as "Son of Carolina, Exemplary Citizen, Athlete, Philanthropist, Teacher, Hero of the Americas and the World." Clemente has been honored by dozens of schools, hospitals, coins, stamps, post offices, bridges, parks, housing developments, ballparks, streets, and museums in his name in the United States, Puerto Rico, and Nicaragua.

For all his posthumous veneration, Clemente was, as Maraniss observed, "no gentle giant or saint" but instead a "fierce critic of both baseball and American society."[51] Clemente's crusade should not be sanitized: "He ranks only behind Jackie Robinson among players whose sociological significance transcended the sport itself." He raised issues that remain relevant and unresolved to this day. "With the nativist strain in American politics resurgent," wrote Maraniss in 2016, "I wish Clemente were around to respond to . . . Donald Trump and those who promote fear based on geography and language and race."[52]

SANDINISTA AL: ALBERT WILLIAMS

Opposition among Nicaraguans to the harsh poverty and repression imposed by the Somoza regime grew rapidly. Increasingly they blamed such conditions on the United States, which had been propping up the dictatorship for over four decades. Led by the Sandinista National Liberation Front (FSLN), the revolutionary movement was gaining steam. Signaling the U.S. response, President Jimmy Carter cut economic aid to the destitute nation but increased military aid.

Nevertheless, the Sandinistas overthrew the Somoza government in 1979. Somoza fled Nicaragua with much of the nation's treasury, leaving the new government with an almost bankrupt country, much of which was in ruins from years of civil war and the 1972 earthquake. By 1982 the U.S.-funded

Contra forces had begun assassinations of members of the revolutionary Nicaraguan government. To tighten the noose on the Sandinistas, the CIA helped the Contras plant mines in Nicaraguan harbors in 1984 (for which the International Court of Justice awarded Nicaragua $18 million, which the United States never paid), and in May 1985 the Reagan administration imposed a trade embargo on Nicaragua.

According to Roger Burbach,

> The Sandinista movement comprised Nicaragua's urban masses, peasants, artisans, workers, Christian base communities, intellectuals, and the *muchachos*—the youth who spearheaded the armed uprisings. The revolution transformed social relations and values, holding up a new vision of society based on social and economic justice that included the poor and dispossessed. The revolution was multiclass, multiethnic, multidoctrinal, and politically pluralistic.[53]

The Sandinista government persevered, establishing sweeping programs for land reform, literacy programs, housing projects, worker benefits, food and farm support, local elections, and dozens of other initiatives to promote political and economic democracy, all of which Washington regarded as signs of communism. Despite the grim situation, the Sandinistas nevertheless incorporated baseball—which was extremely popular among Nicaraguans—into the national budget.

As with Cuba, rather than supporting the overthrow of a dictatorship, the United States instead declared war on the revolutionaries. The CIA organized the surviving Somoza military forces and National Guard into a counterrevolutionary army (the Contras) and helped them launch a civil war to overthrow the Sandinista government. Under the Reagan administration, Nicaragua became another target for U.S. low-intensity warfare, arming and financing the Contras—terrorists who conducted a dirty war, assassinating educators, farmers, women, children, and church leaders.

To Reagan, however, the Contras were freedom fighters. Reagan and most American business leaders worried that the Sandinista success in overthrowing the U.S.-backed Somoza regime would inspire other nations dominated by the United States, which might get the idea that they could launch a successful revolution too. But when liberal members of Congress and then the American media began exposing the atrocities perpetrated by the American-funded Contras—including mass killings of innocent civilians—Congress passed the Boland Amendment to force the White House to cut its support for the Contras. The Reagan administration violated that amendment by secretly arming the Contras, which was eventually exposed in the Iran-Contra scandal.

Under Fire, Hollywood's portrayal of the Nicaraguan uprising, includes a scene of a young boy, a Sandinista soldier wearing a Baltimore Orioles cap, who throws a hand grenade into a building occupied by President Somoza's troops. "You see Dennis Martinez, you tell him my curveball is better than his," he tells an American photographer played by Nick Nolte. "I like the Sandinistas, and I like the Baltimore Orioles."[54]

The real Martinez did not participate in the civil war between the Sandinistas and the Somoza dictatorship. He left Nicaragua before the Sandinistas and the Contras began to ask young men to fight. In 1976 he became the first Nicaraguan to play in the major leagues. He joined the Orioles that year and played in the majors for twenty-three years, leading the AL in wins in 1981 and leading the NL in ERA in 1991. He was selected to four All-Star teams and finished his career with a 245-193 win-loss record.

Another Nicaraguan, Albert Williams, who was born in 1954—the same year as Martinez—took another path. During the revolution against the Somoza dictatorship, he sided with the Sandinistas. He was born in Pearl Lagoon, Nicaragua, on the country's English-speaking east coast, grew up on a farm, and fished in the nearby Pacific Ocean. He didn't pick up a baseball until age seventeen because he really wanted to be a rodeo rider, emulating the Spanish rodeos he observed as a boy. Later he recalled, "I rode some broncs and didn't realize until years later how dangerous they can be. But I compare it to pitching in the big leagues. The broncs and the other team are both trying to get rid of you. The broncs are bucking this way and that, and you have to ride with the moves. It's like working on hitters."[55]

In 1975, the Pittsburgh Pirates signed Williams as a pitcher, assigning him to their Charleston, South Carolina, farm team, where he played for two years. Back home in Nicaragua, he was denied a visa to continue playing in the United States, and the Pirates released him. In 1977, he took up arms with the FSLN and fought with them for sixteen months. "I didn't care much for politics, still don't," Williams reflected, "but the [Somoza] government gave me a reason to fight, so I fought. I was fighting for my country, my family, my mother, my brothers and sisters. I was fighting for democracy."[56]

In 1979, shortly before the Sandinistas overthrew the Somoza regime, Williams was forced into exile and smuggled out of the country to Panama. There he began pitching again, this time for the Panama Banqueros in the Inter-American League. Then he moved to Venezuela, joining the Caracas Metropolitanos. The Minnesota Twins spotted and signed him. He began the 1980 season with their Toledo farm team. In May he made his MLB debut with the Twins and pitched for them for five years, including an opening-day start in 1984. He also played six seasons in the Venezuelan Winter League. Once considered as having one of the MLB's best arms and despite having several winning seasons, stardom eluded Williams, who endured elbow surgery and ended his MLB career with a 35-38 win-loss record for mediocre Minnesota teams.

Dubbed by teammates "Sandinista Al," Williams no doubt had stories to tell about his guerilla years but hesitated revisiting those exploits. Asked about his cloak-and-dagger escape from Nicaragua, Williams responded, "That's in the past. I live for the future."[57] In 1984, when a reporter pushed him to discuss the fighting he did in the jungles of Nicaragua, Williams claimed, "I don't want to talk about it. I haven't talked about it since 1980."[58] In the mid-1980s, with his family still in Nicaragua in the early days of the revolution and the counterrevolution against it, Williams was likely cautious about publicly reminiscing.

Twins manager Billy Gardner observed about Williams,

> After jungle fighting, baseball is like going to the beach. And you see his toughness on the mound. He never gets rattled. If he gives up a couple of base hits, and maybe someone boots one behind him, he just takes it in stride. A lot of guys have a tendency to give in. Williams battles them.[59]

Reflecting on his pitcher's unusual experience, Gardner said, "Ever see Williams handle a knife? He takes a big cake knife and peels an orange off in one big curl. And then he flips the knife—choo! It sticks in the wall!"[60] Asked where he learned to handle a knife like that, Williams responded, "At home."

Rather than rejecting baseball as an "imperialist game," the Sandinista government embraced the sport. It treated ballplayers as national resources who exemplified values such as equality, community, and sacrifice. During the 1980s, two other Nicaraguan players—David Green and Porfi Altamirano—made it to the majors. As Nicaraguan sports editor Edgardo Tijerino indicated, "Baseball doesn't just belong to the United States. It's our game, too." And Defense Minister Humberto Ortega proclaimed, "The only way we want to compete with the United States is through baseball. If the U.S. presence has left us something beautiful, it's baseball."[61]

But rebellion against the United States had a cost: by 1986 at least 170 Nicaraguan ballplayers had been killed by the Contras. Had Albert Williams remained in Nicaragua to defend the revolution he had fought for, he might have been one of the casualties.

The Sandinistas governed Nicaragua from 1979 to 1990. Throughout that period, they were weakened by the destructive war with the U.S.-backed Contras and the troubled economy. In 1990 they were defeated in free elections. After that election, President George H. W. Bush immediately announced an end to the U.S. embargo of Nicaragua and promised economic assistance to the new government. "During the next 16 years, three Nicaraguan presidents backed by the United States implemented a series of neoliberal policies, gutting the social and economic policies of the Sandinista era and impoverishing the country."[62] Daniel Ortega, who led the Sandinista movement and was the country's president while the Sandinistas governed the country, "ran in every election, drifting increasingly to the right, while exerting an iron hand to stifle all challengers and dissenters in the Sandinista party."[63] Ortega was reelected president in 2006 but by then his movement was no longer a leftist democratic force.

Throughout all the political turmoil, baseball has remained a Nicaraguan passion. Since the 1990s, ten more Nicaraguans—Marvin Benard, Vicente Padilla, Oswaldo Mairena, Devern Hansack, Everth Cabrera, Wilton Lopez, Erasmo Ramierz, J. C. Ramirez, Cheslor Cuthbert, and Jonathan Loaisiga—have made it to the major leagues. In recent years, Williams has helped promote baseball in Nicaragua through Project Baseball's Home Run for Equality campaign, a collaboration of MLB and the Nicaraguan Federation of Associated Baseball, which provides baseball clinics and seminars on gender-based violence for hundreds of Nicaraguan boys and girls.

THE VENEZUELAN EXPERIENCE

While Venezuela began playing baseball in the 1890s, the first Venezuelan didn't play in the majors until Alex Carresquel was signed by the Washington Senators in 1939, pitching for them until 1946. When the Senators sold him to the Chicago White Sox, he rejected the move and made a better deal with Jorge Pasquel's Mexican League. Carresquel pitched in Mexico through the 1948 season. When Commissioner Chandler rescinded the blacklist against the Mexican jumpers, Carresquel joined the White Sox for a year before ending his MLB career. More Venezuelans began joining MLB in the 1950s, including stars Chico Carresquel and Luis Aparicio. Venezuela has sent more than four hundred players to the majors, more than any other country except the Dominican Republic.

KING OF VENEZUELA: OZZIE GUILLEN

Ozzie Guillen followed in a long line of Venezuelan All-Star shortstops including Carresquel, Aparicio, Dave Concepcion, and Omar Vizquel. Born in Ocumare del Tuy, Venezuela, in 1964, Guillen signed with the San Diego Padres in 1980, playing for their minor league clubs until he was traded to the Chicago White Sox in 1984. The following year he was selected AL Rookie of the Year. He became one of the White Sox's star players, mostly for his fielding and base running. He later played for the Orioles, Braves, and Devil Rays before retiring in 2000 with a .264 batting average. In his sixteen-year career, he won a Gold Glove and was a three-time AL All-Star.

Guillen knew baseball history, particularly Latino baseball history. In his home, he created not only a shrine to his hero Roberto Clemente but also revealed, "I have a room just dedicated to him. My second kid is named Roberto."[64] On his uniform, Guillen wore number 13 to pay tribute to his Venezuelan shortstop predecessor, Dave Concepcion, who had the same number.

Considered an insightful student of the game, Guillen coached for the Montreal Expos (2001–2002) and Florida Marlins (2003) before the White Sox made him MLB's first Venezuelan-born manager in 2004. The next year he led the team to their first pennant since 1959 and then their first World Series championship since 1917. Voted AL Manager of the Year, he became a hero not only in Chicago but also in Venezuela. The first Latino manager to win a World Series, Guillen managed the White Sox for eight years to a .524 winning percentage before piloting the Miami Marlins in 2012 to end his managerial career.

Known for being outspoken, Guillen often provoked controversy. "In the country I come from, we can talk about anything . . . Here [in the United States] you have to be real, real careful what you say."[65] On the one hand, he seemed anything but a rebel. He was a stickler for the national anthem.

> If you're not from this country, you should respect the anthem even more than Americans because you should feel pleased you're here. And if you're from this country, you should have respect for people who are dying for it . . . I can't wait to see the planes fly over our field in the World Series . . . It gives me goose bumps just thinking about it.[66]

Guillen became a U.S. citizen, observing, "This doesn't mean I'm not Venezuelan. But you think this [the United States] is not the greatest country in the world? Prove me wrong."[67]

Besides these patriotic gestures, Guillen expressed his appreciation of George W. Bush when his Florida Marlins team visited the White House in 2003 to celebrate their World Series championship. But in 2005, after managing the White Sox to the World Series crown, Guillen skipped the traditional White House visit with Bush. He claimed he had to attend to family responsibilities but some suspect it had more to do with the United States' attempted coup against Venezuelan president Hugo Chavez.

Beginning in 2010, Guillen became a very vocal critic of the United States' treatment of Latino immigrants and ballplayers. Arizona's anti-immigrant law, SB 1070, allowed police to racially profile Latinos and criminalized the failure to carry immigration documents. Guillen defended immigrants as

> workaholics . . . And this country can't survive without them. There are a lot of people from [the United States] who are lazy. We're not . . . A lot of people in this country want to be on the computer and send e-mails to people. We do the hard work. We're the ones who go out and work in the sun to make this country better.[68]

Guillen claimed most Americans didn't realize that farm workers "arose at 4 a.m. and worked until 6 p.m. picking all kinds of stuff. Nobody complains about that. Leave those guys alone. Help them . . . [We need to] do something different to maintain these guys here . . . This problem should have been resolved a long time ago."[69]

Michael Weiner, former executive director of the players' union, announced, "We hope that the [Arizona] law is repealed or modified promptly. If the current law goes into effect, the Major League Baseball Players Association will consider additional steps necessary to protect the rights and interests of our members."[70] But Arizona Diamondbacks owner Ken Kendrick, while feigning concern about the controversy, substantially funded the Arizona Republican Party that created the law. He wasn't alone among baseball owners in sharing anti-immigrant attitudes. Rather than sending a message, MLB held its 2011 All-Star game in Phoenix as planned. Guillen claimed he would refuse to attend the game. "I'm upset about it. I wish I could do more than I'm doing."[71]

Guillen expressed specific concerns about MLB's treatment of Latino ballplayers. With more Latinos entering organized baseball, he claimed they were exploited and subject to double standards. He complained that Japanese and Korean players received special privileges, such as translators, that weren't available to Latino players. The 2008 film *Sugar* illustrates the problem as it follows a promising Dominican ballplayer to a farm team in Iowa, where his inability to communicate takes a traumatic toll and he washes out as an MLB prospect.

As sportswriter Dexter Rogers observed,

> Latino players . . . will play for less money, work hard, and not put up a fuss because they have to take care of their families back home. They won't rock the boat and the baseball establishment knows this. Hence this creates an atmosphere for players to be exploited.[72]

As Guillen told the *New York Times*, "We're abused. [Latino ballplayers are] cheaper, or they can't say no. They are underpaid and they are still working."[73]

MLB's low-cost investments in Caribbean academies draw players who believe baseball can pull them out of poverty. But according to the Council for Hemispheric Affairs,

> Globalization and the incredibly magnetic and financial appeal of American baseball have created direct links between the Dominican Republic's cheap labor market of brilliant and talented baseball players and Major League teams. These links mimic the more prosaic forms of exploitation when it comes to outside producers taking advantage of the cheap labor upon which the island's sugar and textile industries are based.[74]

Guillen's home country of Venezuela has also been a target. In *Stealing Lives: The Globalization of Baseball*, Arturo Marcano Guevara and David Fidler tell the story of Venezuelan Alexis Quiroz.[75] Alberto Rondon, a Chicago Cubs representative in Venezuela, signed Quiroz to a contract in 1995 at age seventeen. According to Quiroz, the contract was in English, which neither he nor his parents could read. (Since 2000, MLB has required clubs to give Latin players copies of their contracts in Spanish.) Quiroz accused Rondon of paying himself $2,000 of his $6,000 bonus, an exorbitant percentage. Rondon promised him a three-year contract starting in the United States, a guarantee that Major League clubs never make. In fact, the Cubs immediately sent him to the Dominican Republic, where he and about two dozen other players lived in a house with a single toilet and often no running water in the village of Santana. They were given little to eat, certainly not sufficient for young athletes. The quantity and quality of the food only improved when Cubs executives visited. That season he lost fifteen pounds. His career ended when he ripped apart his left shoulder diving for a line drive and received terrible medical treatment. He still lacks full movement of his arm. He was cast aside after years of largely uncompensated service.

According to sportswriter Dexter Rogers, when it comes to cases like this, "Guillen is raising issues that Major League Baseball avoids. If there's an injustice, there's nothing wrong with bringing it to the masses . . . Good for Guillen in having the strength to consistently speak his mind when others fear rocking the boat."[76]

But rocking the boat has consequences. In 2008, Guillen told the *Chicago Sun-Times* that Castro is "a dictator and everybody's against him, and he still survives, has power. Still has a country behind him. Everywhere he goes, they roll out the red carpet. I don't admire his philosophy; I admire him."[77] In 2012, as the newly hired Miami Marlins manager, Guillen told *Time* magazine, "I love Fidel Castro. I respect Fidel Castro. You know why? A lot of people have wanted to kill Fidel Castro for the last 60 years, but that motherf****r is still here."[78] Guillen was referring to the many CIA assassination attempts against Castro. The latter comments unleashed a storm of protest from the conservative Cuban-exile community in Miami, which was adamantly opposed to improving U.S.–Cuban relations until the communist government was overthrown.

Guillen apologized profusely, calling his comments "stupid and naïve." In a lengthy news conference, he claimed, unconvincingly, that he was misquoted. "What I meant in Spanish . . . was that I cannot believe that somebody who hurt so many people over the years is still alive." Whether he was really contrite or realized that his survival as Marlins manager required a different tack, Guillen said, "I am willing to do everything in my power, the Marlins power, to help the Cuban community, the Latino community, like I always do."[79] The Marlins suspended Guillen for five games without pay. The team issued a statement acknowledging "the seriousness of the comments attributed to Guillen. The pain and suffering caused by Fidel Castro cannot be minimized, especially in a community filled with victims of the dictatorship."[80] Others might disagree with that description, but not the one hundred protesters who gathered outside the Marlins stadium waving Cuban and American flags, calling Guillen a communist, and shouting in Spanish, "Get rid of him." The Marlins claimed the Guillen incident, rather than the team's subpar roster, caused their attendance to flat-line, and Guillen was fired at the end of the season.

ENDORSING CHAVISTA BASEBALL

In the late 1990s, not content with merely fighting Cuban president Fidel Castro, the United States manufactured another nemesis for itself: Venezuelan president Hugo Chavez. Unlike Castro, however, Chavez became president through democratic elections. He was elected president of Venezuela in 1998 with 56.2 percent of the vote, reelected in 2000 with 59.8 percent of the vote, reelected again in 2006 with 62.8 percent of the vote, and won a fourth term as president in 2012 with 55.1 percent of the vote. He was to be sworn in again on January 10, 2013, but the inauguration was postponed due to his cancer treatment and he died on March 5, 2013.

Chavez instituted bold reforms as part of a new Bolivarian Revolution, including nationalizing key industries, creating participatory democratic Communal Councils, and implementing far-reaching social programs to expand access to food, housing, education, and healthcare. His presidency coincided with record-high oil revenues, which provided the funding for his programs. The country experienced a decline in poverty, inequality, and illiteracy. His effort inflamed the country's wealthy elite and some of its upper-middle-class professionals. Democratic elections lifted Chavez into office but he constantly feared being overthrown by a U.S.-backed coup and resorted to repression to stifle his domestic critics.

Like Castro, Chavez was a revolutionary leader and a baseball fan. Growing up, Chavez wanted to play for the San Francisco Giants, the team with the most Latino players. "It was my dream," Chavez reflected, "I would have preferred, personally, to do that." It's doubtful he had the talent but it didn't matter because an injury cut short his career. Instead, Chavez continued, "I became a soldier . . . But I am still the young baseball player who wanted to play in Yankee Stadium."[81] During Chavez and Castro's mutual visits, they routinely attended ball games together. Regaining control over Venezuelan baseball became part of Chavez's struggle to return his nation to the Venezuelan people, out of the clutches of Americans and local Venezuelan elites.

One indication of Venezuela's baseball resurgence was the triumph of its Maracaibo team, which won the Little League World Series in 2000. In 2002, however, Venezuela had to cancel its Winter League season because of a U.S.-sponsored coup attempt against Chavez. Chavez survived amidst popular acclaim, and in the 2004 presidential elections he campaigned against U.S. imperialism, claiming that he "would hit a home run that would soar over Cuba and land on the White House."[82] When he won the election, despite U.S. efforts to prevent it, his supporters chanted, "Home run, home run." When conservative TV evangelist Pat Robertson called for the United States to assassinate Chavez, Guillen called him "an idiot."[83]

In 2005 the Cooperstown Hall of Fame created the Baseball/Beisbol: Latin American Baseball Project to highlight Latino contributions to America's national pastime. But the hall shelved the exhibit and its travel plans, at least temporarily, because its main sponsor was the Citgo Petroleum Corporation. Owned by Venezuela, the company had embarrassed President George W. Bush by completing a deal, in the absence of U.S. federal assistance, to provide Massachusetts residents with low-cost heating oil for the winter. President Chavez addressed the United Nations, where he called President Bush "the devil." Because of the politics, the Hall of Fame shuttered the Baseball/Beisbol project, even though it went ahead with its exhibit on baseball and the U.S.-Afghan war.

In October 2005, when the White Sox won the World Series, Guillen wasn't shy about showing his pride in his native Venezuela and its president Hugo Chavez. Reflecting on the president's congratulatory call, Guillen said,

"To me it's an honor . . . I say I like the man because I think he works hard for the country and I feel proud to represent my country."[84] Chavez called Guillen a national hero, commenting, "You are like the King of Venezuela. Your triumph is a triumph for all of Venezuela. The whole nation is waiting for you."[85] Guillen promised to bring the trophy to Venezuela. He appeared on Chavez's television program after the series while the streets of Caracas overflowed as much as those on Chicago's South Side. Speaking for his country, Guillen observed, "People say that because we don't have a good relationship with George Bush, that's the thing. Everybody talks about Chavez; but you've got to look at yourself [the United States] first. . . Nobody has to think the way the U.S. thinks."[86]

Nevertheless, in 2006 U.S. Ambassador William Brownfield began using baseball to taunt Chavez. Claiming he needed to counter "anti-American messages," Brownfield began touring Venezuela, distributing funds and equipment to repair baseball fields. Knowing it would infuriate his host government, he had himself photographed throwing a baseball with a local boy in Chavez's hometown. Venezuelans shouted down Brownfield at his baseball media events, however, with signs and chants of "Get out, gringo!" and "No more imperialist intervention!" One Venezuelan baseball fan asked, "Since when does the mighty U.S. give out baseballs? Do they think they will buy us that easily?" Larry Birns of the Council on Hemispheric Affairs claimed Brownfield was "a mischief maker . . . resorting to theatrical actions to undermine the regime."[87]

After MLB launched the World Baseball Classic, Chavez often called Venezuelan team manager Luis Soto to discuss tactics. "He was a man of baseball," Soto observed. "He was always aware of the team and who was on it. He was the first call I got in the morning during the tournaments in 2006 and 2009. He lived for baseball."[88] But Chavez resented organized baseball's exploitation of Venezuelan ballplayers, its violation of the nation's labor and minimum wage laws (due to its exemption from federal anti-trust laws), and its failed promises for reform. In 2007, with at least fifty Venezuelans playing in the majors, Chavez demanded a better deal for the one thousand additional Venezuelans in the minor leagues or the MLB–sponsored baseball academies in Latin America. He proposed better pay and conditions, claiming MLB should return to Venezuela 10 percent of the signing bonuses given to its players to help maintain his nation's leagues and infrastructure.

Chavez observed, "If George Bush and I survive all of this and we are old men, it would be good to play a game of . . . street baseball."[89] But Washington shunned the overtures and MLB sought baseball as usual—with maximum profits and itself firmly in control. In response, although Venezuelan players remained a bargain compared to U.S. players, some Major League clubs left Venezuela, focusing instead on their Dominican operations. Fearing "another Cuba" and baseball's nationalization, the number of U.S. teams in the Venezuelan Summer League declined from eleven to four between 2007 and 2015. The following year, MLB teams pulled the plug, ending the league.[90]

CHAVISTA SOCIALIST: MAGGLIO ORDOÑEZ

Although he expressed mixed support for Castro and Chavez, Guillen was no socialist. Such was not the case for Magglio Ordoñez, another Venezuelan ballplayer. Born in Caracas in 1974, Ordoñez was signed by the White Sox in 1992 and made his MLB debut late in the 1997 season. Ordoñez quickly became one of the team's leading batters, hitting for average, home runs, and RBIs.

Already a four-time All-Star, Ordoñez became a free agent in 2004. He accepted a big contract from the Detroit Tigers, where he continued to star from 2005 to 2011. Besides his three Silver Slugger Awards, two more All-Star selections, and the 2007 AL batting title, Ordoñez posted a .309 career batting average with 2,156 hits, 294 home runs, and 1,236 RBIs during his fifteen-year career.

In 2009, while still playing for the Tigers, Ordoñez did the unthinkable. He vocally supported Hugo Chavez and his socialist revolution. He campaigned with the president for a constitutional amendment to end term limits, appearing in a television ad and at campaign-sponsored softball games. He told fellow Venezuelans that "the best of the revolution is yet to come."[91] The backlash against these activities occurred during the World Baseball Classic that year in Miami. Playing for the Venezuelan team, Ordoñez was greeted with a rain of boos from Venezuelans in the crowd when he was introduced and before each at-bat. After he struck out and left the game in the seventh inning, cheers erupted from the stands. Some called for Ordoñez's expulsion from MLB. In contrast to their attitude toward Ordoñez, fans loudly cheered his Venezuelan teammates, including Bobby Abreu and Miguel Cabrera. This wasn't surprising. Venezuelans who were wealthy enough to travel to

Miami or who already lived in the United States were disproportionately anti-Chavez.

Ordoñez didn't retreat. "I support the government," he said. "So that's why they boo me, they heckle me, they criticize me, because I made a personal decision . . . But [their views] are not the reality in Venezuela."[92] Polls and repeated elections showed that most Venezuelans supported Chavez and his socialist programs. Ordoñez said, "If you don't like Chavez, then go vote [against him]." Ordoñez wasn't shocked by the boos. "I have nothing against the fans. I just don't think they're well-informed," he said. "I love everyone. But that's not respecting the country . . . I carry the name of Venezuela on my chest. It's an honor for me to represent my country."[93]

Ordoñez appreciated the support he received from teammates who came off the bench to try to quiet down the negative crowd. Venezuelan Sports Minister Victoria Mata condemned the "Venezuelan worms in Miami." According to Mata, "The hostility from those fans against a player who is defending Venezuela with courage and dignity is shameful."[94] Chavez also weighed in, wishing Ordoñez luck in the games and claiming, "Everyone has the right to think about politics. Viva Magglio and all our patriots."[95]

When Chavez died from cancer in early 2013, Vice President Nicolas Maduro succeeded him, attempting to perpetuate the revolution in the face of rising internal and U.S. opposition. That year Ordoñez became a co-owner of Caribes de Anzoategui, the professional Venezuelan baseball team he played for before coming to the United States. Shifting his support from Chavez to Maduro and campaigning as a United Socialist Party candidate, Ordoñez became the socialist mayor of Sotillo, an eastern Venezuelan city with 250,000 residents.

In addition to Ozzie Guillen and Magglio Ordoñez, several other Latino ballplayers entered politics in their home countries. Second baseman Bobby Avila—a three-time All-Star who played in the majors from 1949 to 1959 and led the NL in batting (.341) in 1954—served as mayor of Veracruz and as a representative in the Mexican National Legislature. Pitcher Aurelio Lopez spent several years in the Mexican League, then eleven seasons (1974 and 1978–1987) with four teams in the majors, most of it with the Detroit Tigers. In 1990 he was elected mayor of his hometown, Techamachalco, serving until his death in 1992. In the Dominican Republic, pitcher Melido Perez (1987–1995) became mayor of San Gregorio de Nigua. Another Dominican, outfielder Raul Mondesi (who played in the majors from 1993 to 2005), was elected to the Dominican Chamber of Deputies in 2006 and was then elected to a six-year term as mayor of San Cristobal in 2010.

The U.S. government has persistently sought to undermine left-wing governments in Venezuela, Nicaragua, and Cuba. U.S. policymakers have imposed embargoes to short-circuit popular and successful economic initiatives, supported minority political opposition, and subverted elections. It has planned and carried out military and other coups to topple socialist governments in these three nations. The Obama administration sought to renew diplomatic relations with Cuba but Trump reversed the initiative. All three nations have faced dire circumstances because of these efforts to disrupt their political and economic systems that could easily return the countries to the right-wing dictators or military regimes the United States has always favored in Latin America.

This has consequences for MLB. In 2019, the Trump administration annulled an agreement between MLB and the Cuban Baseball Federation that would have allowed Cubans to compete in the United States without defecting from their country. MLB also blocked its players from participating in the Venezuelan Winter League to comply with the Trump administration's intensified embargo. Challenging such policies may be the task of the next generation of Latino baseball rebels.

6

Protesting America's War on Terrorism

On September 11, 2001, foreign terrorists attacked America—hitting targets in New York City and Washington, DC—producing catastrophic death and destruction. In total, the attacks killed 2,977 people and injured more than 25,000 people. It was the first foreign attack on American soil since the Japanese invaded Pearl Harbor in Hawaii in 1941. Most nations in the world immediately sympathized with America and offered their support. But that backing quickly evaporated when less than a month after 9/11, the United States launched an attack on Afghanistan to oust the Taliban regime.

THE WAR ON TERRORISM

While the presumed masterminding of the terrorist violence came from Al Qaeda, a group operating in Afghanistan, none of the terrorists themselves were Afghani. Among the terrorists, nineteen were from Saudi Arabia, two were from the United Arab Emirates, and one each came from Lebanon and Egypt. Nevertheless the Taliban, a radically militant Islamic movement, controlled most of Afghanistan at the time and the Bush administration held it responsible for harboring Al Qaeda. Even though American foreign policy had helped create Al Qaeda and its leader Osama bin Laden in the 1980s, the United States blamed the Taliban for not apprehending the group and turning over its members. As a result, America pursued what became the longest war in its history. The war ended in 2021 when the United States withdrew its troops and the Taliban took over the country.

In 2003 the United States launched another war, on Iraq, as part of what the White House called the War on Terrorism. To justify its invasion, the Bush administration falsely claimed that Iraq perpetrated the September 11 attacks and that it was harboring weapons of mass destruction even though United Nations inspectors had verified that it was not. The White House further claimed it acted to remove Iraqi dictator Saddam Hussein, whom the United States had helped gain power and then helped maintain his dictatorship for decades.

Evidence also emerged that the Project for a New Century (PNC), a conservative organization with close ties to the Bush administration, had prepared plans to attack Iraq long before September 11. The September 11 attack served the purpose of justifying the U.S. invasion in order to assert U.S. dominance in the oil-rich region. Ten PNC members had joined the Bush administration, including his closest foreign and military policy advisers Dick Cheney, Paul Wolfowitz, and Donald Rumsfeld.

Immediately after 9/11, American public opinion was solidly behind the idea of the United States seeking revenge. But as millions of people in cities around the world, and in the United States, began participating in anti-war protests, and when Americans began to doubt that the Bush administration was telling the truth about 9/11, the protests widened and public opinion began to shift toward opposition to the costly U.S. invasion and troops in both Afghanistan and Iraq. There was plenty to protest. But how would MLB react?

SHELTER DURING THE STORM

The attacks shocked the entire country, but the most serious emotional, physical, and financial trauma was centered in New York City. "This tears at who we are," said Yankees outfielder David Justice on the day of the attack. "Our lives have been changed. We'll never be the same after this."[1] Within an hour of the 9/11 attacks, MLB commissioner Bud Selig announced that the day's games had been postponed. Selig and the team owners then had to decide when it would be appropriate to resume playing games. "We're talking about life and death. We're not talking about wins and losses," said the Arizona Diamondbacks Cy Young Award–winning pitcher Randy Johnson, who won his third consecutive Cy Young Award that season. "It's completely understandable if all sports shut down for a while."[2]

Selig and the owners were eager to resume the season but they had to wait to see what NFL commissioner Pete Rozelle would do. When, on September 13, the NFL announced it was postponing all games for that weekend, MLB followed suit. Selig announced that MLB would get back to work on Monday, September 17, that teams would make up the ninety-one postponed games during the week of October 1, and that the World Series would be played in November for the first time in history. Selig claimed that baseball was "woven so deeply into the national fabric. It means so much to so many people, although what happened September 11 certainly trivializes it."[3]

But Selig did more than cancel games and then invoke baseball's place in American history and culture. He and the rest of the baseball establishment embraced an upsurge of nationalism and super-patriotism that emerged in the wake of 9/11. It took many forms, but the scale and intensity of baseball's rallying around the flag reflected the sport's double standard. In the midst of a controversial war triggered by political calculations, baseball's officialdom had no qualms about embracing the Bush administration's war policy, but players who expressed concern or even opposition to the war were labeled unpatriotic and told to avoid making political statements.

According to sociologist Rebecca Kraus, baseball served as a "shelter during the storm . . . [bearing] much of the burden for healing the nation after September 11."[4] As Baseball Hall of Fame's John Odell observed, each game "became a kind of village green where people could talk and deal with their fears."[5] When the games resumed, they supplied the primary stage for stirring displays of patriotic unity. Curt Schilling, Arizona Diamondbacks pitcher, indicated, "We will proudly wear the great flag of this country on our uniforms and it's something I hope baseball will adopt forever. When the nation sings 'God Bless America,' we do so because men and women have died so we can continue on as a free nation."[6]

Virtually every major league ballpark was awash with patriotic gestures. American flags were provided for fans and moments of silence were religiously observed. Fields were blanketed with red, white, and blue, from flags to people's faces to ribbons painted on the outfield grass. Silent auctions were held, contributions were asked for relief efforts, unions and companies donated funds and services, and benefit games were played for the Red Cross. Flag days and community days were punctuated by patriotic music.

At Pittsburgh's PNC Park, the Mets and Pirates wore caps honoring New York's police, firefighters, and emergency crews. At San Francisco's Pac Bell Park, fans held candles and flags, prayed and sang, and chanted, "USA! USA!" Yankee Stadium hosted a memorial service, and manager Joe Torre took his players to shelters and fire stations. At Shea Stadium, Liza Minelli turned "New York, New York" into a fight song. New York Mets players hosted families of victims at their annual holiday party and joined other players in raising money for the Twin Towers Relief Fund. They also donated one game's salary to the New York City Police and Fire Widows and Children's Benefit Fund. Arizona Diamondbacks players visited ground zero wearing New York City Fire Department hats to honor rescue workers.

Broadcast by Fox Network, images of U.S. flags and tanks and the national anthem's almost non-stop performance framed the 2001 World Series games between the Yankees and the Diamondbacks. The network scripted the series as "nationalist patriotism in support of U.S. military action in the [emerging] campaign, Operation Enduring Freedom."[7] When the series moved to New York for game three, President Bush arrived to throw out the first pitch. He walked to the top of the mound, threw a perfect strike, and then heard the roar of "USA! USA!" WBUR sports broadcaster Bill Littlefield said he didn't mind having politicians showing up at ballgames, where they "are less likely to engage in dangerous mischief . . . Nobody's ever called an air strike from the pitcher's mound, the proximity of military jets notwithstanding."[8] But President Bush's World Series appearance did just that, immediately launching the Operation Enduring Freedom attack on Afghanistan.

"The game of baseball," according to historian Lara Nielsen, "was narrated by an image that consolidated the moral victory of war, [promoting] the popular conclusion that military retaliation . . . was the appropriate course of action." It undermined any script that might have allowed fans to debate the subject. "The sanctioned exhibition of violence and trauma most commonly associated with a militarized society emerged again on the athletic field."[9] Baseball's central role in pulling New York and the nation out of the 9/11 catastrophe and in priming the country for war cannot be denied. As captured in the 2004 film *Nine Innings from Ground Zero*, so profound was the connection that even the widely hated Yankees suddenly became America's team.

Patriotism reigned on opening day in April 2002 and the military hoopla only escalated. Comparing the situation to World War II's early days, *Wall*

Street Journal reporter Robert Hughes claimed, "Whether it is 1942 or 2002, baseball and U.S. military history will always blend together."[10] According to sportswriter Dan Wachtell, "Baseball went on, because . . . if we stop playing, the Taliban Terrorists win."[11] Virtually every professional ball game began with salutes to the troops, and baseball telecasts routinely ran photos of soldiers in war zones watching their favorite teams. MLB clubs dressed their players in desert camouflage uniforms and gave away military bucket hats at ballgames. Military appreciation days proliferated, although to enlist others, and not ballplayers, in the war. As Bob Herbert observed, "Gone are the days when a Ted Williams would interrupt a flourishing baseball career to fight the enemy . . . War is something for other people to fight. Waving a flag is one thing; dodging bullets is something else."[12]

At 9:11 pm on September 11, 2002, the first anniversary of the attacks, MLB paused to commemorate the tragedy. Bud Selig gave a moving tribute. ESPN broadcast twelve continuous hours of baseball. Yankee Stadium dedicated a new monument. In a letter read at every major league game, President Bush observed, "During the past year baseball helped bring Americans together. In the aftermath of the attacks, an exciting pennant race and World Series were important [to] the healing process."[13] A few days earlier, Bush had hosted members of the Texas Rangers, a team he had previously owned. Later that day he met with top lawmakers to plan his next battle: a war on Iraq. Opposing the new intervention, protesters soon flooded the streets of America and cities around the world. At one demonstration, the signs read, "Impeach Bush; Dusty Baker for President" and "Baseball, Not Bombs." But MLB officially supported the new war.

In March 2003 with the U.S. attack on Iraq looming, Yankees pitcher Roger Clemens addressed the Seventeenth Military Police Battalion and the 810th Military Police Company during a mobilization farewell at Tampa's Legends Field, the Yankees spring-training home. Reprising the oft-repeated Vietnam-era canard, Clemens recalled his brother Richard's return: "He came home and it was difficult because, as you guys know, they weren't really well received." Clemens concluded by saying, "After 20 years of playing the game I love, I consider myself a true team player. But you guys are the ultimate team. You're protecting our freedom."[14] Not everyone agreed.

SITTING IN PROTEST: CARLOS DELGADO

While MLB didn't contribute soldiers to the war on terror, it nevertheless provided considerable institutional backing for U.S. military policies, both symbolic and tangible. Public relations–conscious MLB owners had institutionalized "The Star-Spangled Banner" at every game decades ago to make sure no one questioned their patriotism or support for America's wars. Most baseball people fell in line but with occasional exceptions, particularly during the Vietnam War (see chapter 4).

Still, "The Star-Spangled Banner" persisted as a baseball institution. After 9/11, however, baseball commissioner Bud Selig decided it wasn't enough. Selig believed that the traditional pregame singing of the anthem didn't reflect sufficient nationalistic fervor so he decreed that "God Bless America" must also be sung during every game's seventh-inning stretch, often replacing the traditional "Take Me Out to the Ball Game" altogether. Explaining his decision, Selig said, "I don't honestly think [it] politicizes the issue. After all, we do have troops in Iraq and Afghanistan."[15]

Of course, Selig was clearly making a political statement. In her retrospective on the song, historian Sheryl Kaskowitz shows that the composer, Irving Berlin, "initially perceived 'God Bless America' as a homage to peace, but increasingly the song became an anthem for military intervention in World War II—an association with militarism that was carried into the Cold War and the Vietnam War." "God Bless America" promotes a sense of "otherness" for those who do not share the song's core principles: "The song became an imperative, an important marker of patriotism and loyalty, and those who did not participate were seen as dangerous."[16]

After September 11, one ballplayer fit that description. Born in Aguadilla, Puerto Rico, in 1972, Carlos Delgado soon became an outstanding baseball player. By age sixteen he had been scouted by several MLB teams, and in 1988 the Toronto Blue Jays signed him. In 1996, his first full season in the majors, he clubbed 25 home runs and drove in 92 RBIs. This began a run of nine years with Toronto during which Delgado became one of MLB's most feared hitters while also mastering defense at first base. In September 2003 he became only the fifteenth major leaguer to hit four home runs in one game.

In 2005 Delgado signed as a free agent with the Florida Marlins, but despite his great season, they dealt him to the New York Mets in a cost-cutting move for 2006. He starred with the Mets through 2009, when he experienced debilitating hip injuries. Unable to make a comeback, he retired after the 2011 season. For his outstanding seventeen-year career, Delgado hit .280, with 2,038 hits, 473 home runs, and 1,512 RBIs, as well as two All-Star selections, a World Series ring, and induction into the Canadian Baseball Hall of Fame. But Delgado would also be remembered for something else.

Delgado's hero was Roberto Clemente, a fellow Puerto Rican, who had used his baseball celebrity to express his views on social and political issues. Soon after 9/11, Delgado expressed his horror at the tragedy and provided support for first-responders. He donated $25,000 to New York City firefighters and another $25,000 to the police. But he was increasingly disturbed by America's war on terrorism. "Who are [we] fighting against?" Delgado asked. "[We're] just getting ambushed now [in Iraq and Afghanistan]. We have more people dead now . . . [We've] been looking for weapons of mass destruction. Where are they? [We've] been looking for over a year. Can't find them. I don't support that . . . I think it's just stupid."[17]

Delgado wasn't alone. Long after his protest against the Vietnam War, the irrepressible Jim Bouton had a new war to oppose. Commenting on the Iraq War's failure, Bouton observed, "I'm not any kind of expert or genius about this stuff. I'm just a regular guy and I could see this clearly. What's happened over there is exactly what ordinary people like me predicted . . . Any politician who didn't see what would go wrong in Iraq isn't worth (bleep). Their actions are disgraceful."[18]

During the 2004 season, a dozen years before San Francisco 49ers quarterback Colin Kaepernick refused to stand for "The Star-Spangled Banner" and a year after the United States invaded Iraq, Delgado sat in baseball dugouts to protest American military policy by refusing to stand and sing "God Bless America" during the seventh-inning stretch. "I don't stand because I don't believe it's right," Delgado explained. "It's a very terrible thing that happened on September 11. It's also a terrible thing that happened in Afghanistan and Iraq. I feel so sad for the families that lost relatives and loved ones in the war. But I think it's the stupidest war ever."[19]

Blue Jays president Paul Godfrey strongly supported the Iraq War and publicly criticized the Canadian government for not sending troops. But in response to Delgado, he indicated, "I have no problem with what Carlos did. Carlos didn't hold a placard and stop traffic. He didn't impede the game because he's not that kind of guy. He's been total class in the community almost from the day he arrived."[20] Another Iraq War supporter, Toronto catcher Geoff Zaun, vowed he'd never again buy a Dixie Chicks CD—to protest the singing group's criticism of President Bush and his military policies. Even so, Zaun supported his teammate Delgado's right to dissent.

When the Blue Jays went to New York to play the Yankees in July 2004, Delgado got a different reception. At Yankee Stadium, "God Bless America" was not an option; it was required of fans as well as the players. Under orders from Yankees owner George Steinbrenner, ushers strung up chains during each seventh-inning stretch to keep people standing and secured—and blocked from leaving for the bathroom or concessions—until "God Bless America" was finished playing. During each of Delgado's at bats, fans greeted him with boos and then derisive shouts during each game's seventh-inning stretch. When he was at the plate and made an out, chants of "USA! USA!" went up in the crowd.

Some fans questioned the boos, but they were in the minority. As one Yankees fan said about Delgado, "It's totally disrespectful. It's a slap directly in my face as a New Yorker and an American."[21] Predictable howls also came from right-wing sports fans and commentators who labeled him "un-American" and unfit to collect his paycheck. One critic said Delgado turned his back on the country that made him rich and that he ought to be paid in "Cuban pesos or Iraqi dinars until he starts singing along." Another claimed that Delgado's protest "makes him a terrorist and he should be jailed."[22]

Some sportswriters defended Delgado. *Seattle Intelligencer* sportswriter Steve Wilstein claimed that "the Puerto Rican slugger is not being anti-American by showing his disagreement with President Bush's policy. He is not disrespecting the soldiers or . . . slapping every New Yorker and American in the face."[23] Instead Delgado is "exercising the most fundamental of our rights, freedom of speech, or . . . in this case, freedom to sit silently while his teammates stand on the dugout steps." *New York Times* columnist William Rhoden observed that since MLB had made "God Bless America" a political statement, "a player like Delgado became free to express his own political views."[24] Sportswriter Dan Wachtell asked, "What about those of us who get all our patriotism out during the traditional pre-game 'Star Spangled Banner?' Enough already."[25]

Delgado, an American citizen, wasn't anti-American. "I say God Bless America, God Bless Miami, God Bless Puerto Rico, and all countries until there is peace in the world," Delgado said.[26] He explained that he wasn't trying to make anyone mad or draw attention to himself. Some fellow athletes supported him but others wanted to rip his head off, saying, "Go back to Puerto Rico." Delgado knew people would hate him.

> I felt people booing me [but] when you do [something like this], you do it because it is the right thing to do . . . The most important thing is to stay true to your values and principles . . . It takes a man to stand up for what he believes . . . Sometimes you've just got to break the mold. You've got to push it a little bit or else you can't get anything done . . . Athletes, who have this platform where they can reach millions of people, should use it.[27]

Delgado also supported a longstanding campaign against the U.S. Navy presence in Vieques, a Puerto Rican island used as a weapons-testing ground for sixty years. Remembering older residents telling horror stories about uranium-depleted shells and the bomb explosions, Delgado viewed the military as waging a kind of war on the tiny island, using the nine-hundred-acre site for bombing exercises. After a civilian was killed by an errant bomb in 1999, Delgado joined Puerto Rican Socialist Party leader Ismael Guadalupe in demonstrations against the navy in the United States and Puerto Rico. The navy finally pulled out but left behind poverty, unemployment, and pollution. "It's still in the environment, it's still in the ground, it's still in the water," Delgado said. "That's why we've got the highest cancer rate of any place in Puerto Rico."[28]

Delgado, along with many other Puerto Ricans protesting in the early 2000s, "did not consider the occupation benign."[29] He wanted the United States to clean up its mess. Rallying other celebrities, including actor Martin Sheen and the Dali Lama, Delgado contributed hundreds of thousands of dollars to the campaign. He joined singer Ricky Martin and boxer Felix Trinidad in taking out full-page ads about Vieques in the *New York Times* and *Washington Post* and got fellow major leaguers Roberto Alomar, Juan Gonzalez, and Ivan Rodriguez to sign on.

According to activist Ismael Guadalupe, Delgado "wanted to help out with more than just the situation with the Navy. He wanted to help the people there."[30] His donations have been used to fund youth sports leagues in Vieques and a permanent peace and justice protest camp. "You'll need millions and millions of dollars to clean up Vieques," Delgado observed. "So we try to make the money as effective as we can. We make it work for kids. I can't clean up Vieques by myself. It's going to take a lot of people."[31]

As sportswriter Dave Zirin noted, Delgado "viewed the people of Vieques as casualties—collateral damage—from the war on Iraq, because they served as guinea pigs for weapons that have wreaked havoc throughout the Persian Gulf."[32] Thus Delgado had little patience for the "flag-waving, pro-military pageantry seen at major league games since the September 11 attacks and U.S.-led invasion of Iraq."[33] Vieques and Iraq are interconnected. Geoff Baker observed,

> That's because the fishermen, farmers and shopkeepers of this island unwillingly paid a huge price so the United States could certify the weaponry used in Iraq. Delgado was already "anti-war" before being involved in Vieques and now has some choice opinions about U.S. foreign policy and the Iraq conflict.[34]

After being traded to the Mets in 2006, Delgado ended his protest. As Dave Zirin reported, "The team made it clear that freedom of speech stops once the blue and orange uniform—their brand—is affixed to his body" and that standing for "God Bless America" wasn't optional.[35] Mets manager Willie Randolph claimed, "I'd rather have a man who's going to stand up and say what he believes. We have a right as Americans to voice that opinion," yet nevertheless he expected Delgado to abide by Mets rules.[36] As Mets COO Jeff Wilpon put it, "So he's going to have his own political views, which he's going to keep to himself."[37] Delgado claimed he "[would] not cause any distractions to the ball club . . . Just call me Employee Number 21."[38]

Writing about the song "God Bless America," historian Ron Briley explained,

> Whether it was [Irving] Berlin's intention or not, his song became associated with global military intervention during World War II, the Cold War, and Vietnam. Following 9/11, "God Bless America's" connection with militarism was extended to the war on terror and U.S. military operations in Afghanistan and Iraq as MLB embraced the song.[39]

While Delgado backed off about "God Bless America," he did not stop speaking out on social issues, including MLB's poor record in hiring Latino managers. "It's really sad," observed Delgado. "With all the players that come from Latin American countries, you'd want to see more managers."[40]

A dozen years after his "God Bless America" dissent, Delgado had no regrets and spoke out to support NFL quarterback Colin Kaepernick's national anthem protest in 2016. "It's not that he doesn't respect the anthem," Delgado claimed. "Just as, in my era, it wasn't that I didn't respect 'God Bless America.'" Kaepernick is

> tying [the anthem to] what he thinks [it] should represent for the African-American community . . . especially given all the things that have happened lately with African-American victims of beatings by white police. I don't think it is any secret that in the United States there is a problem with racism.[41]

As with his own experience, Delgado acknowledged that Kaepernick "has to know that he has a legion of followers and a legion of people who will hate him until his death. That is what democracy is about. You have the liberty to express how you feel and [other have] the liberty to say what they think about it."[42]

Delgado has linked his activism with philanthropy. He started the Extra Bases Foundation in Puerto Rico to assist ill and disadvantaged children, to promote local hospitals, and to publicize the island's education crisis. In 2006 he received MLB's Roberto Clemente Award, bestowed on a ballplayer who best exemplifies humanitarianism and sportsmanship.

In 2017, when Hurricane Maria tore through Puerto Rico wreaking untold devastation, Delgado led the response. Besides being directly involved in the backbreaking work of the recovery, he again mobilized his Extra Bases Foundation, turning this charity into a humanitarian relief agency. But Delgado realized that the storm was more than a natural disaster. The damage was particularly harsh because of the island's poverty and the U.S. government's failure to help provide basic infrastructure that would have minimized the suffering. "It was such a humbling experience, and it showed that Puerto Rico needed a lot of help before the hurricane," Delgado observed. "You saw a lot of the poverty . . . I guess it was masked behind the vegetation. When Maria blew everything out, it was worse than what we thought."[43] The humanitarian response became a campaign for justice.

ACTIVIST ACTORS: SUSAN SARANDON AND TIM ROBBINS

Actors Susan Sarandon and Tim Robbins never played professional baseball, but Sarandon nevertheless was "Baseball Annie" and Robbins was a cinematic pitching sensation. Sarandon played that role as Annie Savoy and Robbins portrayed Nuke LaLoosh in the 1988 baseball film *Bull Durham*. Depicting a season with the minor league Durham Bulls team, the movie traced the brash and erratic LaLoosh's maturation under the tutelage of Annie Savoy and veteran catcher Crash Davis (played by Kevin Costner). The film was directed by Ron Shelton, a former minor league ballplayer.

The film became one of the most popular baseball movies of all time. The Baseball Hall of Fame scheduled an event in Cooperstown to celebrate the film's fifteenth anniversary in 2003 and invited Sarandon and Robbins to participate. That event became controversial because the baseball establishment objected to the actors' opposition to the Bush administration's war on terrorism.

Sarandon and Robbins are best known as actors, movie stars, and sometime film directors. Both have Academy Awards and many other movie and theater honors. Among their other films, Sarandon starred in *Thelma and Louise*, *The Rocky Horror Picture Show*, and *Dry White Season*, and Robbins headlined *The Shawshank Redemption*, *Jacob's Ladder*, *Catch a Fire*, and *Mystic River*. The actors collaborated not only in *Bull Durham*, but also in *Dead Man Walking*, *Bob Roberts*, and *Cradle Will Rock*.

Sarandon and Robbins are also both political activists. In the 1960s, Sarandon (the older of the two) began protesting at civil rights marches and anti–Vietnam War rallies. Between the two of them, the actors have participated in dozens of protests and advocacy groups since then. They demonstrated against Congressional cuts in the National Endowment for the Arts (as Creative Coalition members), protested in Central Park against nuclear weapons, marched for abortion rights (in Washington, D.C.), and demanded serious anti-AIDS policies (for Act-Up, Housing Works, and the People with AIDS Coalition). They protested the Reagan administration's low-intensity warfare and Contra funding in Nicaragua (for MADRE), marched against racial profiling and police brutality in New York City (with the Center for

Constitutional Rights), fought attempts to censor controversial art (at the Brooklyn Art Museum), and were unofficially boycotted by Hollywood for protesting at the Academy Awards against U.S.-quarantined Haitian AIDS patients.

They've marched in rallies for gun control, demonstrated for the Equal Rights Amendment, supported farm communities (for the Heifer Project), promoted a recycling project (for We Can) to help the homeless, protested the criminalization of drug users, and lobbied Congress on the medical benefits of marijuana. Sarandon and Robbins supported a lawsuit against the Los Angeles Police Department for illegal spying, as well as the Screen Actors Guild strike. They've helped fund groups such as the American Civil Liberties Union, Film Aid, Emily's List, Cinema for Peace, the Right to Play, and the Plastic Pollution Coalition. Sarandon traveled to India and Tanzania as a Goodwill Ambassador for both UNICEF and the UN Food and Agricultural Organization. Robbins's Actor's Gang Education and Outreach Program provided free after-school, in-school, and summer programs for Los Angeles youth. Its Gang Prison Project provides art workshops in California prisons to reduce recidivism.

Sarandon has been a prolific documentary narrator, addressing political themes such as free speech (*The Need to Know*), the Seattle World Trade Organization protests (*This Is What Democracy Looks Like*), the U.S. export of human rights abuses (*School of the Americas*), the U.S. supported Guatemalan dictatorship (*When the Mountains Tremble*), women rebels (*Cool Women in History*), gay media portrayals (*The Celluloid Closet*), and U.S. Contra terrorism in Central America (*Talking Nicaragua*). Robbins cofounded the Actor's Gang, an experimental and nonprofit theater group, focused on politically relevant productions, including a Robbins-directed adaptation of George Orwell's *1984*. The group's other productions addressed themes such as wrongful convictions (*The Exonerated*), anti–nuclear weapons protests (*The Trial of the Catonsville Nine*), televangelism hypocrisy (*Carnage*), immigrant rights (*The New Colossus*), and coopted war reporting (*Embedded*).

Besides their earlier protests against the Vietnam War and the Reagan administration's wars in Central America, Sarandon and Robbins broke ranks with the Hollywood jingoism that supported the 1990 Gulf War. They joined the anti-war Military Families Support Network to oppose the war, demonstrating in Washington, DC and elsewhere. In the late 1990s, they protested the plight of the Kosovo refugees in the Clinton's administration's Bosnian War.

Not surprisingly, Sarandon and Robbins also opposed the Bush administration's the War on Terror and the U.S. invasion of Iraq. Sarandon argued that Americans "do not want to risk their children or the children of Iraq" for an "illegal, pre-emptive strike."[44] At a Washington, DC, demonstration, Sarandon observed, "In the name of fear and fighting terror, we are giving the reins of power to oil men looking for distraction from their disastrous economic performance, oil men more interested in the financial bottom line than a moral bottom line."[45] At a rally in New York's Central Park, Robbins said,

> This past November the American people sent a resounding signal to Washington, DC, and the world. We want change. We want this war to end. And how did Bush respond? Twenty-one thousand, five hundred more will risk their lives for his misguided war. Is impeachment still off the table? Let's get him out of office.[46]

Elsewhere Robbins reflected, "My children were young when 9/11 happened, and that was a traumatic experience. And they saw how [it] was turned into using manipulated information to produce another catastrophe, which was the [Iraq] war."[47] He claimed he didn't regret speaking out, even though conservatives denounced him as a "terrorist supporter" and "Saddam [Hussein] lover." But this was not the only criticism the actors would face.

In 1999 the Baseball Hall of Fame Board of Directors hired Dale Petroskey as its president. The board was (and still is) comprised primarily of business-oriented Republicans with close ties to the family of Jane Forbes Clark, the granddaughter of the hall's founder. Petroskey had been assistant press secretary for the Michigan House Republican caucus, chief of staff for Republican Congressman William F. Goodling of Pennsylvania, and President Ronald Reagan's assistant press secretary from 1985 to 1987. From 1988 to 1999 he was a senior executive at the National Geographic Society.

Soon after he began running the Hall of Fame, he invited Bush White House press secretary Ari Fleischer to give a non-baseball speech at the hall. Petroskey said, "We are thrilled to hear his perspective on life in the White House and the current political scene which, of course, includes the war on terrorism."[48] Petroskey gave President Bush a lifetime museum pass and had the hall install a special baseball exhibit in the White House. Every new Hall of Fame employee was required to watch a video of a Bush political speech.

Petroskey began militarizing the hall soon after he became its president. He hired his longtime mentor Bill Haase, an ex-Marine, as the hall's vice president. Haas quickly created a boot-camp atmosphere within the institution. Employees endured strict, military-style dress and grooming codes and a rigid, top-down hierarchy of command. Free admission was offered to all active and retired military although not to others dedicated to service such as teachers and firefighters. Installed on a large podium guarding the main Hall of Honor Gallery, a permanent plaque was unveiled in a 2002 Memorial Day ceremony to honor Hall of Famers who were military veterans. Special plates were inserted under the individual plaques of every Hall of Famer who had served in the military. According to Eric Enders, a former researcher at the Hall of Fame Library, it left some fans questioning whether they were visiting the Baseball Hall of Fame or the U.S. Military Hall of Fame.[49] Anything that might question the military's relationship with baseball—such as the unjust court martial of Jackie Robinson in 1944 or MLB's efforts to protect major league players from the Vietnam War draft—was nowhere to be found.

After 9/11, Petroskey became a visible cheerleader for the Bush administration's military policies. His machinations came to a head in 2003 when Petroskey cancelled the celebration of *Bull Durham* because Robbins and Sarandon had been visible and vocal opponents of the Iraq War.

When cancelling the *Bull Durham* event, Petroskey wrote Robbins and Sarandon that "your very public criticism of President Bush at this . . . sensitive time . . . helps undermine the U.S. position, which ultimately could put our troops in even more danger. As an institution, we stand behind our President and our troops in this conflict."[50] All but calling them traitors, Petroskey further claimed their anti-war criticism would politicize the event. Petroskey, of course, did not acknowledge that he had been politicizing the hall since he became its president.

Robbins quickly responded to Petroskey's censorship, declaring, "Long live democracy, free speech, and the '69 Mets—all improbable, glorious miracles that I have always believed in."[51] At an event at the National Press Club and in print, Robbins noted,

> I had been unaware that baseball was a Republican sport . . . You invoke patriotism and use words like "freedom" to intimidate and bully. In doing so, you dishonor the words . . . and the men and women who have fought wars to keep this nation a place where one can freely express their opinions without fear of reprisal . . . To suggest that my criticism put the troops in danger is absurd. . . I wish you had . . . saved me the rhetoric and talked honestly about your ties to the Bush and Reagan administrations.[52]

None of the sixty living Hall of Famers offered any dissent to Petroskey's mixing baseball and Republican politics. But Petroskey's cancellation of the *Bull Durham* event generated enormous media attention and catalyzed a flood of protests elsewhere, including 28,000 emails. Roger Kahn, the prominent baseball writer, dropped his hall appearance scheduled later that year, indicating, "By canceling the *Bull Durham* [event] for political reasons, you are, far from supporting our troops, defying the noblest of the American spirit."[53] *Detroit Free Press* reporter Mitch Albom asked,

> Where do you begin with such misguided patriotism? . . . It's the Baseball Hall of Fame, not the Pentagon . . . Who decided [its] position on the Middle East? A couple of Hollywood types expressing their opinions does not put bullets in our troops. Half the world already spoke out against the war.[54]

Albom accused Petroskey of McCarthyism and observed that "hugging the flag is simple. Hugging what it stands for is harder . . . These new 'super-patriots' are more un-American than the people they criticize."[55]

San Francisco Chronicle sportswriter Gwen Knapp used her critique of Petroskey to challenge baseball's broader militarism, including the Air Force flyovers at ballgames since 9/11.

> The ritual is fundamentally disrespectful to military operations . [Having] those planes at a sporting event trivializes their real purpose . . . Baseball pretends to be honoring the military . . . [But] it's really . . . aggrandizing itself, a commercial entity exploitatively wrapped in red, white, and blue . . . It's patriotism as a marketing tool.[56]

Actor Kevin Costner—Sarandon and Robbins' *Bull Durham* costar—defended them, observing, "I think Tim and Susan's courage is the type of courage that makes our democracy work . . . Pulling back this invite is against the whole principle about what we fight for and profess to be about."[57]

Even so Petroskey stuck to his decision, only later apologizing under pressure. Prominent baseball figures such as Jules Tygiel—author of a much-praised history of baseball integration—called for Petroskey's resignation. But the Hall of Fame's board of directors kept him on the job until 2008, when he was forced out for financial wrongdoing.

Sarandon and Robbins became inadvertent baseball rebels in response to a conservative baseball establishment that included not only MLB but also the Cooperstown Baseball Hall of Fame. Their actions as accomplished actors and seasoned activists challenged the status quo in organized baseball and especially its blind support of America's wars and interventions.

DISSENTING SOLDIER: KEVIN TILLMAN

When three MLB teams eagerly recruit you, it's a pretty good sign that you're a big league prospect. Born in San Jose, California, in 1978, Kevin Tillman excelled in baseball at a young age. He was drafted by the Houston Astros in 1996, the Anaheim Angels in 1999, and the Cleveland Indians in 2000. He wanted to finish his college education, which he began at Arizona State University and completed at California Polytechnic State University in San Luis Obispo. He was MVP of Cal Poly's baseball team and a Big-West Conference First Team selection. After being signed by Cleveland, he joined the Burlington Indians in the Rookie League as a second baseman in 2001 and was then promoted to the Akron Aeros in the Double-A Eastern League. By all accounts Tillman looked to be headed for a promising MLB career when terrorists struck America on September 11.

Kevin's brother Pat Tillman was also an athlete. A Pac-10 Defensive Player of the Year at Arizona State University, he starred as a safety for the NFL's Arizona Cardinals. He gave up a multimillion-dollar pro-football contract when he decided to join the U.S. military after the terrorist attacks. "At times like this," Pat reflected, "you stop and think about not only how good we have it but what kind of system we live under. My great-grandfather was at Pearl Harbor. And a lot of my family has gone and fought in wars. And I really haven't done a . . . thing as far as laying myself on the line like that."[58] Mary Tillman, Pat's mother, claimed Pat joined the army because he thought "the country was in danger, the country was in need, and football seemed trivial."

Her son believed in "shared sacrifice and felt the military should be made up of people all across society, not just those who needed a job."[59]

When Pat enlisted, there was no doubt that Kevin would join him despite having to give up baseball to do so. The Tillmans initially deployed to Iraq in 2003 as part of Operation Iraqi Freedom. Because Pat was a high-profile enlistee, the Pentagon repeatedly approached him for recruitment purposes but he resisted being exploited.

The Tillman brothers quickly became disillusioned in Iraq. Their mother claimed they "joined the military to root out al Qaeda, not to wage war on a country that had no connection to the 9-11 attacks. Pat and Kevin felt there was no plan, no threat. It was really disturbing."[60] A fellow soldier testified that the Tillmans voiced opposition to the Iraq War and the Bush administration while in Iraq, complaining that the war was "so fucking illegal."[61]

The Tillmans returned from Iraq in late 2003, retrained as Army Rangers in the 2nd Battalion of the 75th Ranger Regiment, and left for Afghanistan. During that experience, they increasingly questioned the war on terrorism, and Pat even arranged to meet with one of his favorite authors, anti-war critic Noam Chomsky. In April 2004, however, Pat died in battle in what the U.S. Army described as "a heroic firefight with enemy fighters in the mountains of Afghanistan," for which he was posthumously awarded the Silver Star.[62]

But that story was "utter fiction," as Kevin Tillman discovered. It sought to "deceive the [Tillman] family, and more importantly, the American public."[63] Instead, friendly fire killed Pat Tillman, a presumably mistaken attack by his fellow American soldiers. Although assigned to the same platoon as Pat, Kevin was deceived about his death, which he didn't witness. Soldiers who saw Pat die were ordered not to tell Kevin what happened. As Kevin learned, the military brass knew the true story from the very beginning. It covered up the death to protect an image the military and the Bush administration had created of Pat as a selfless volunteer and used the falsified story of his death to transform him into an exemplary hero to build patriotic support for the war.

"Revealing that Pat's death was a fratricide," Kevin observed, "would have been yet another political disaster in a month of political disasters," including the emerging Abu Ghraib prison torture scandal. "So the truth needed to be suppressed."[64] Tillman's funeral was nationally televised, and in that setting and on the Arizona Cardinals stadium Jumbotron during his 2004 presidential reelection campaign, President Bush declared that Pat "was an inspiration on and off the football field, as with all who made the ultimate sacrifice in the war on terror."[65] All the while the Bush White House and the army knew the story was false. As journalist Norman Solomon put it, the spectacle was right out of "central casting as far as the [U.S. defense secretary] Rumsfeld gang was concerned."[66] It was no accident that Pat Tillman became, against his wishes, a poster boy for Bush's endless wars.

When the truth of Pat's death was exposed, the U.S. military portrayed the cover-up as a series of "missteps" yet an internal Pentagon email revealed a "Tillman SS [Silver Star] Game Plan." As Kevin Tillman told a Congressional Committee on Oversight and Government Reform investigating the incident in 2007, "[The military engaged in a series of] deliberate and careful misrepresentations . . . A terrible tragedy that might have further undermined support for the war in Iraq was transformed into an inspirational message that served instead to support the . . . wars in Iraq and Afghanistan."[67]

To the Tillman family, the death was a tragedy, Kevin observed, but to people in the military and government, "it was an opportunity." Destruction of evidence violates U.S. military regulations, yet soldiers were ordered to immediately destroy Tillman's blood-stained uniform and his journal. Although the army inspector-general reported that within seventy-two hours "at least nine military officials knew or were informed that Pat Tillman's death was a fratricide, including at least three generals," and although soldiers were ordered to provide false testimony, not a single charge of criminal negligence was ever brought.[68]

While the Tillman episode was the most egregious deception, other families reported similar fabrications about their sons or daughters in the military. The U.S. Army also falsified the wounding and rescue of Jessica Lynch, turning her into a "little girl Rambo" for propaganda purposes. Peter Phillips, the director of Project Censored, noted that the Pentagon has spent more than $1 billion on public-relations firms to create stories to protect or promote the military and are quite willing to "lie for their clients."[69]

Congressman Henry Waxman, chair of the Committee on Oversight and Government Reform, said, "The Tillman family was kept in the dark for more than a month. Evidence was destroyed. Witness statements were doctored. The Tillman family wants to know how all of this could've happened." Kevin Tillman further claimed, "The least this country can do for him in return is to uncover who was responsible for his death, who lied and covered it up, and who instigated those lies and benefited from them; then ensure that justice is meted out to the culpable."[70] Instead, the military has treated the Tillman family as pests.

Lt. Colonel Ralph Kauzlarich, who directed the first inquiry into Tillman's death, claimed the family has "a hard time letting it go. It may be because of their religious beliefs." Since Kevin Tillman declined a chaplain's offer to say prayers over Pat's body, Kauzlarich callously observed, "When you die, there is supposedly a better life, right? Well, if you are an atheist and you don't believe in anything, if you die, what is there to go to? Nothing. You are worm dirt."[71]

Kevin lashed out with a passionate public statement. He recalled a conversation he had with Pat when they signed on with the military. Pat "spoke about the risks of signing the papers. How once we committed, we were at the mercy of the American leadership and the American people. How we could be thrown in a direction not of our volition. How fighting as a soldier would leave us without a voice . . . until we got out."[72]

Kevin Tillman's experience made him increasingly critical of the Bush administration's foreign policy and illegal tactics.

> Our elected leaders were subverting international law and humanity by setting up secret prisons around the world, secretly kidnapping people, secretly holding them indefinitely, secretly not charging them with anything, secretly torturing them. Somehow that overt policy of torture became the fault of a few "bad apples" in the military.[73]

Tillman noted that neither President Bush nor Vice President Cheney had served in the Vietnam War.

> Somehow those afraid to fight in an illegal invasion decades ago are allowed to send soldiers to die for an illegal invasion they started. Somehow American leadership, whose only credit is lying to its people and illegally invading a nation, has been allowed to steal the courage, virtue and honor of its soldiers on the ground. Somehow the more soldiers that die, the more legitimate the illegal invasion becomes.[74]

Lamenting the demise of reason in favor of "faith, dogma, and nonsense," Tillman claimed that for the Iraq and Afghanistan war, "narrative was more important than reality." America's leadership, he argued, had created "a more dangerous world" where the country "projects everything that it is not and condemns everything that it is . . . Somehow the most reasonable, trusted, and respected country in the world has become one of the most irrational, belligerent, feared, and distrusted countries in the world." Demanding accountability, Kevin wondered how "the same incompetent, narcissistic, virtueless, vacuous, malicious criminals are still in charge of this country."[75]

The war on terror radicalized Kevin Tillman. But although highly critical of the politicians who pushed the United States into these wars, Tillman remained hopeful. "Luckily this country is still a democracy. People still have a voice. People still can take action."[76]

While his brother's story received most of the headlines, Kevin's story, according to Eric Stubben, a columnist for the *Mustang Daily*, Cal Poly's student newspaper, is "one of a great American hero. Not only did he give up baseball—the game he loved—he gave up much of his future, too. With Kevin's talent and work ethic, he had an opportunity to make it to the big leagues."[77] According to his Cal Poly baseball coach Rich Price, if Kevin "would've grinded it through and spent four or five years in the minor leagues, I think most definitely he could have played in the big leagues. He is without question one of the finest competitors I've ever been associated with in my 35 years of baseball."[78]

For first fighting in the war and then protesting the war, Kevin Tillman paid two huge prices: the loss of his brother and the loss of his baseball career.

III

CONCLUSION

7

Rebels for All Seasons

Throughout this book we have profiled baseball rebels who have challenged organized baseball and American society to live up to its ideals. Many got involved to address a particular practice or problem they considered unjust or unfair. Some had a wider perspective, motivated by progressive, radical, or socialist political beliefs. In this chapter we profile five individuals whose radical beliefs led them to become activists on multiple issues: Bill Veeck, George Hurley, Jim Bouton, Bill Lee, and Sean Doolittle.

HUSTLER AND SOCIALIST: BILL VEECK

What most baseball fans know about Bill Veeck is what the *New York Times* wrote in the first line of his 1986 obituary, which described him as "the baseball impresario who once sent a midget to bat as a pinch-hitter for the St. Louis Browns."[1] It is true that Veeck was an innovative and controversial promoter who would do anything to get fans in the seats. But he was also, according to John Thorn, MLB's official historian, "the Thomas Paine of a revolutionary time in baseball."[2]

As owner of the Cleveland Indians (1946–1949), St. Louis Browns (1951–1953), and Chicago White Sox (1959–1961 and 1975–1981) as well as the minor league Milwaukee Brewers (1941–1945), Veeck earned a reputation as baseball's greatest showman. He looked at baseball from the fans' perspective and sought to make the game more fun. He often sat in the bleachers to mix with fans and even listed his home number in the phone book.

Many of his innovations—such as putting players' names on the back of their uniforms—are widespread today. He advocated designated hitters, interleague play, adding new teams, the playoff system, and free agency years before they were adopted by the baseball establishment. In 2004, *Business Week* included Veeck on its list of the greatest business innovators in the past seventy-five years.

Veeck's iconoclasm extended beyond promotional stunts and changes to the game's rules. Veeck was probably the only socialist owner in major league history. He translated his views into practice by promoting racial equality and by supporting players' efforts to end the dreaded reserve clause. "I am on record since 1941 as saying that the reserve clause was legally and morally indefensible. I knew its death was coming," Veeck told an interviewer in 1981.[3]

He also tried to even out the wealth disparities between major league teams in big and small cities by proposing that they share their revenue to make MLB more competitive. For these efforts and ideas he was condemned by his fellow owners, who blocked him from buying several teams and sought to push him out of baseball. To his critics, Veeck responded, "Tradition is the albatross around the neck of progress."[4]

William L. Veeck Jr.—always known as "Bill"—was born in Chicago on February 9, 1914. His father was the long-time president of the Chicago Cubs. Bill Jr. was a constant presence at Wrigley Field as a young boy. Veeck often said, "I am the only human being ever raised in a ballpark."[5] When Bill Jr. was ten years old, his father put him to work selling tickets and food at the ballpark.

Young Bill was a rebel and troublemaker. He was kicked out of several private schools and dropped out of Kenyon College. When Bill Jr.'s father died in 1933, Cubs owner Philip K. Wrigley hired the eighteen-year-old Veeck out of a sense of loyalty. Veeck started off as a glorified office boy and jack-of-all-trades but gradually assumed more responsibilities. "By the time I was 12 I decided that I was going to own a baseball team," Veeck recalled.[6]

Put in charge of the stadium's concessions, Veeck hired a crew of vendors to sell programs, hot dogs, peanuts, and scorecards. Along with White Sox executive Harry Grabiner, Veeck helped the vendors at both Chicago ballparks organize a union so that in Veeck's words, they "would be guaranteed a living wage and all the clubs would be guaranteed a professional working force."[7]

A half century later in the 1980s, Veeck observed that the players' huge salaries were in danger of "putting vendors, ushers, ticket sellers, ticket takers, car parks, all of these out of business." In a backhanded criticism of the baseball players union, Veeck observed, "To me that doesn't seem like solidarity."[8]

By 1936 Veeck was in charge of making major renovations to Wrigley Field. But when Veeck proposed installing lights at the ballpark, Wrigley said no.

By his early teens, Veeck was exposed to outstanding African American players by attending games of the Negro League's Chicago American Giants. In early 1934, while visiting Los Angeles for the Cubs spring training, he watched Satchel Paige beat Dizzy Dean 1-0 in an exhibition game. Veeck said it was "the greatest pitchers' battle I have ever seen."[9]

Veeck was also aware that in 1934 the Negro League's annual All-Star game, the East-West Game—held in Chicago's Comiskey Park, home of the White Sox—attracted 20,000 fans while only 12,000 people watched the Cubs play a double-header at Wrigley Field. Veeck admired Abe Saperstein, the owner of the all-Black basketball team, the Harlem Globetrotters. He saw that white fans would pay to see outstanding Black athletes play exhibition games in big cities and small towns across the country.

In 1941, while taking law school courses at night at Northwestern University, Veeck wrote a letter to Commissioner Landis, calling the reserve clause "morally and legally indefensible." He suggested that major league teams sign players to seven-year contracts, similar to the practice among Hollywood film studios. It would be more than thirty years before the players' union and Curt Flood—with Veeck's support—helped break the owners' legal hold on players' professional lives.

Filled with big ideas, Veeck was eager to go out on his own but he had little money. Drawing instead on his network of friends and financiers, he purchased the Milwaukee Brewers of the American Association, the highest minor league level, in 1941. He was only twenty-seven.

He did whatever he could to make the game more fun for the fans, which often put him in the crosshairs of other owners who were threatened by Veeck's success and his irreverent approach.

During World War II, Veeck scheduled Brewers games in the morning so workers on the late shift at defense plants could attend. He also served a breakfast of cornflakes at the game. Veeck gave away promotional prizes—caps, a keg of nails, bottles of soda, pizza, and even animals (turkeys, geese, pigs, lobsters, and rabbits)—to attract fans to the park. He rarely announced the prizes in advance in order to get fans into the ballpark expecting to be surprised.

During one Brewers spring training season in Ocala, Florida, Veeck decided to sit in the "Colored" section of the stands. The local police showed up, told him he couldn't sit there, and ordered him to move, threatening to arrest him for violating Florida's Jim Crow laws.

"I'm not bothering them," Veeck said. "I'm enjoying our talk and they don't seem to resent me too much. They won't mind if I stay here." Soon the town's mayor arrived to insist that Veeck leave.

Veeck threatened, "If you bother me any more we'll move our club out of Ocala tonight. And we'll tell everybody in the country why." The local officials left him alone after that. "I sat there every day, just to annoy them, without ever being bothered again," Veeck recalled in his autobiography.[10]

If Veeck had his way, MLB would have integrated four years before Jackie Robinson signed with the Dodgers. In 1942, Veeck learned that the Philadelphia Phillies were bankrupt and for sale, and he quietly found investors, including the progressive union federation, the Congress of Industrial Organizations (CIO), then he made a deal with Phillies owner Gerry Nugent to buy the team. He believed that stocking the team with Negro League stars could turn the lowly Phillies into a winning club.

But hours before he departed by train for Philadelphia to seal the deal, Veeck made the mistake of informing baseball Commissioner Landis, a foe of integration, of his intentions. Veeck later recounted, "I got on the train feeling I had not only a Major League ball club but I was almost a virtual cinch to win the pennant next year." As Veeck told the story in his 1962 autobiography *Veeck as in Wreck*, before he reached Nugent's office the next day, Landis and NL president Ford Frick had thwarted his plans by orchestrating a quick sale of the Phillies to another buyer.[11]

After the 1943 season, the twenty-nine-year old Veeck enlisted in the Marine Corps. The next spring, while he was stationed on the Pacific island of Bougainville, the recoil of an anti-aircraft gun shattered his right leg, which was eventually amputated, requiring him to wear an artificial leg. That injury led to thirty-six more amputations over the years as infection spread up his leg.

For the rest of his life Veeck walked with a limp and was in constant pain but he never publicly complained. In fact, he used his wooden leg as a prop for his irreverent sense of humor. When he took a fall outside the Baltimore airport during a rainstorm, an attendant asked him, "Can I call you a doctor?" "No," Veeck said, "it's the wooden leg—get me a carpenter."[12] His occasional tumbles led him to quip, "There's only two things I live in mortal fear of: rain and termites."[13]

After the war he bought the Cleveland Indians in 1946 and was finally in a position to integrate the majors. In anticipation of hiring Black players, Veeck moved the team's spring training season from segregated Florida to Arizona and persuaded Giants owner Horace Stoneham to do the same. Although Arizona was hardly a bastion of racial tolerance, it was not officially a Jim Crow state. Decades later most other MLB teams would transplant their spring training facilities to Arizona.

In July 1947, three months after Robinson joined the Dodgers, Veeck signed Larry Doby as the first Black player in the AL. Veeck got twenty thousand hate letters but things were worse for Doby, who confronted bigotry from fans and fellow players alike.[14] When the Indians played the Philadelphia Athletics, players from the rival team shouted "nigger," "shoe-shine boy," and other racist epithets at the rookie.[15] But Doby became a star player. He played thirteen years in the big leagues, finishing with a .283 batting average. He twice led the league in homers and hit 253 home runs before he retired and was inducted into the Hall of Fame in 1998.[16]

Veeck also signed forty-one-year-old Satchel Paige, the greatest Negro League pitcher, to the Indians 1948 roster in early July. Paige pitched in 21 games, had a 6-1 record, and a 2.48 ERA.[17]

With Doby and Paige's help, the Indians won the AL pennant and attracted 2.6 million fans, a record that lasted fourteen years. The upsurge in attendance was enhanced by Veeck's promotional stunts, such as giving away nylon stockings and orchids to female fans on Mother's Day.

In previous World Series, owners had only sold tickets in packages for all the home games, but Veeck sold tickets for individual games, allowing many more fans to attend a specific game. The Indians beat the Boston Braves in six games.

By the start of the 1949 season, Veeck had fourteen Black players under contract, four of them—Doby, Paige, Luke Easter, and Orestes "Minnie" Minoso—on the Indians roster, the most on any major league team. [18]

Most other major league teams simply signed Negro League players to contracts without offering any compensation to the Negro League team owners, but Veeck *purchased* their contracts from their teams. Veeck also hired Louis Jones, MLB's first Black front-office executive, as the Indians' assistant director of public relations.

Veeck's commitment to racial integration extended beyond baseball. Shortly after moving to Cleveland, Veeck joined the National Association for the Advancement of Colored People (NAACP), which in 1948 was considered a radical organization. He even appeared, along with Paige and Doby, on a poster designed to recruit new members.

In February 1949 a writer for the *Cleveland Call and Post*, a Black newspaper, wrote that Veeck "did more for the Negro than any other man last year," adding that he had given Black players "a chance to show their real ability as major leaguers helped spearhead the attack on racial discrimination and segregation in this country."[19] The *Sporting News* called Veeck "the real Abe Lincoln of the game."[20] In 1949 Veeck sold the Indians and used the money to pay for a divorce settlement and to set up trust funds for his three children. In 1950 he married again. The next year Veeck purchased the St. Louis Browns, the worst team in the majors. Veeck added Satchel Paige to the Browns pitching roster for three years, a controversial move in a segregated Southern city like St. Louis.

On August 19 Veeck perpetrated his most famous stunt. He put three-foot-seven-inch Eddie Gaedel in a Browns uniform and sent him up to hit against the Detroit Tigers wearing 1/8 as his uniform number. Detroit pitcher Bob Cain walked Gaedel on four pitches. The Browns brought in a pinch runner and Gaedel waved his cap as he ran back to the dugout.

After Gaedel's at bat, Will Harridge, president of the AL, ruled that "midgets" were not eligible to play. But Gaedel's one at-bat made him a minor celebrity. He was invited to appear on several TV shows, for which he earned about $17,000.[21]

Five days later the Browns held Grandstand Manager's Day. Veeck handed out placards to fans printed with Yes and No, and at key points during the game he asked them to call the play. Steal? Bunt? Hit-and-run? The Browns manager was instructed to do what the fans instructed.

No matter what Veeck tried, attendance at Browns games was dreadful. The team could not compete with the popular St. Louis Cardinals for fan loyalty. So Veeck struck a deal to move the Browns to Baltimore. It would be the first team to change cities in the twentieth century. But Veeck's fellow owners blocked the move. He had outraged them by proposing the socialistic idea of sharing television revenue. Thwarted, he sold the Browns to a Baltimore syndicate. His fellow owners immediately approved the transfer of the franchise, which then became the Baltimore Orioles.

Eventually baseball adopted Veeck's ideas. After the Browns moved to Baltimore, the Boston Braves headed to Milwaukee, the Philadelphia Athletics relocated to Kansas City, and the Brooklyn Dodgers and New York Giants moved to California. By the 1960s the number of major league teams changing cities accelerated. In 1996 MLB instituted a revenue-sharing policy designed to help teams in smaller cities stay competitive with those in larger cities with greater attendance and more-lucrative television contracts.

After selling the Browns, Veeck worked as a scout for the Indians, spent a year running the minor league Miami Marlins, and did color commentary for NBC TV's *Game of the Week*, but he wanted to own another major league team.

In 1959 Veeck was back in Chicago as owner of the White Sox along with former Detroit Tigers slugger Hank Greenberg and financial backers. Veeck owned the team from 1959 through 1961 and then again between 1975 and 1981.

On August 25, 1959, Veeck got upset when White Sox fans booed Al Smith, the team's African American left fielder. The next day, Veeck staged Al Smith Night at Comiskey Park. He let everyone named Smith (or Smithe, Smythe or Schmidt) into Comiskey Park for free and distributed buttons that read, "I'm a Smith and I'm for Al."

The team hadn't won a pennant since 1919, but in 1959 the White Sox ended the Yankees' domination of the AL. They won the pennant but lost the World Series to the Los Angeles Dodgers in six games. They also set a club record by drawing 1.6 million customers.

In 1960 Veeck put the White Sox players' names on the backs of their uniforms—the first team to do so. That year he also introduced the exploding scoreboard to celebrate White Sox players' home runs. He staged free days for cab drivers and bartenders, whose contacts with fans made them valuable public relations boosters for the team. He gave away orchids on Mother's Day. At one game, he gave away 1,000 cans of beer, 1,000 pies, 1,000 bottles of root beer, 1,000 cupcakes, and 100 free restaurant dinners.

In 1961, seriously ill after a lifetime of smoking, Veeck sold his share of the White Sox and moved to a farm in Maryland, where (with the help of Ed Linn) he wrote his iconoclastic autobiography *Veeck, As In Wreck* and then another book, *The Hustlers' Handbook.* Despite being a wounded military veteran (or perhaps because of it), he began marching in protest against the Vietnam War. In 1968 he traveled to Atlanta to march, with this artificial leg, in Martin Luther King Jr.'s funeral procession.[22]

In 1970 he defied the baseball establishment again after Curt Flood filed a lawsuit against MLB to challenge the reserve clause. Only four prominent baseball figures testified on Flood's behalf—Hank Greenberg, Jackie Robinson, former pitcher turned writer Jim Brosnan, and Veeck. He described the ballplayers' condition as "human bondage."

Veeck tried and failed to buy several major league teams until he finally was able to put together another group of financial backers (including John Johnson, the African American publisher of *Ebony* magazine) and purchased the White Sox again in 1975.

On opening day in 1976, Veeck commemorated America's 200th birthday by re-enacting Archibald McNeal Willard's famous painting, *The Spirit of '76.* Wearing a Revolutionary army uniform and draped with bandages, Veeck exposed his peg leg and played a fife while his friend Rudie Schaffer beat a drum and manager Paul Richards carried the American flag as they marched across Comiskey Park field. In 1977 he allowed Sox fans to throw out the ceremonial first pitch with whiffle balls on Opening Day. He introduced Bat Day, Cap Day, and Jacket Day as give-aways to attract fans.

In 1979 Veeck held Disco Demolition Night, with Chicago disk jockey Steve Dahl encouraging listeners and White Sox fans to bring a disco record to the game, buy a 98-cent ticket, and watch as Dahl blew the records up between games of the doubleheader. Over 50,000 fans attended the game. After the records were blown up, fans rioted in celebration. The White Sox had to forfeit the second game.

In June 1978 Veeck fired manager Bob Lemon and hired Larry Doby, the team's batting coach, to replace him. Doby became the second Black manager in the majors, following Frank Robinson, whom the Indians hired to lead the club in 1975.

In 1981 Veeck sold the White Sox to a syndicate led by real estate investor Jerry Reinsdorf. The new owners had no room for Veeck in their operation. The sale ended Veeck's baseball career.

In the early 1980s, Veeck became active in the movement for stronger gun control, giving speeches in support of anti-handgun legislation. In October 1981 he even participated in a walk against handgun violence, limping on his artificial leg the entire ten kilometers.[23]

Veeck's widow, Mary Frances Veeck, observed, "One of the most disappointing moments of his life" was when "he learned he was not on President Nixon's famous enemies list." She explained that Veeck was "born on the right side of the tracks, and dragged himself to the other side—and then lived comfortably on both."[24]

In a 1985 interview, Veeck was asked to name his heroes. The first person he named was Norman Thomas, the leader of America's Socialist Party from the 1930s through the 1960s who ran for president six times. Veeck voted for Thomas every time and even wrote in his name in several elections after the socialist had died. "[Thomas] was abused, scorned and laughed at, and yet he persevered. He was a hero of mine." Veeck then named as his second hero Paul Robeson, the African American actor, singer, and activist who was blacklisted for his political views during the McCarthy era. "He was probably the most cultured man in the history of the United States," Veeck said. "He did more things better than probably anyone in our history." But, Veeck said, Robeson was "born too early."[25]

Veeck died of lung cancer on January 2, 1986, at seventy-one years old. As biographer Paul Dickson observed, "at the heart of Veeck's story is the conflict between a stubborn, iconoclastic individual and the entrenched status quo."[26] Sportswriter Bill Littlefield claimed Veeck's "brightest ideas bettered the game, and he brought a pure joy to his work in baseball that most men and women who own ball clubs today will never know."[27]

Given Veeck's views, it isn't surprising his enemies on the Veterans Committee kept him out of the Hall of Fame until 1991, five years after his death. His plaque at Cooperstown reads, "A Champion of the Little Guy."

POLITICO: GEORGE HURLEY

To date, more than one hundred former MLB players have been elected to public office in the United States after they retired from baseball. They won elections to Congress or to become a governor, state legislator, or county commissioner. In big cities and small towns, they've been elected mayors, city council and school board members, and sheriffs. Numerous minor league players have followed the same path. Many ballplayers have also waged unsuccessful campaigns for office.

Most American ballplayer politicians, whether Democrat or Republican, have embodied mainstream political views, generally ranging from liberal to centrist to conservative. But some, like George Hurley, embraced progressive and radical stances.

Five major leaguers have gone to Congress, including the most famous ballplayer-politician, Hall of Fame pitcher Jim Bunning. Bunning was a leader of the Major League Baseball Players Association, but as a politician he embraced conservative, even anti-union, policies. After retiring from baseball (1955–1971), he returned to his native Kentucky and was elected to the Fort Thomas city council and then the Kentucky state Senate. In 1986, he was elected to the U.S. House of Representatives, serving from 1987 to 1999. He was elected to the U.S. Senate from Kentucky in 1998, served two terms, and decided not to seek re-election in 2010.

Pius Schwert was a back-up catcher for the New York Yankees in 1914 and 1915 and continued his intermittent baseball career in the minors until 1921. He returned to his hometown of Angola, New York, where he opened a general store and worked his way up to president of a local bank. A Democrat, he was elected County Clerk of Erie County in 1933, reelected in 1936, then elected to the U.S. House of Representatives in 1938. He was reelected in 1940. In March 1941, he was about to announce his candidacy for mayor of Buffalo when he died of a heart attack.

Outfielder Fred Brown had a political career that lasted 30 years, much longer than his two years (1901–1902) in the majors. A native of New Hampshire, he served as mayor of Somersworth and as U.S. Attorney for the state before winning a race for Governor, serving from 1923 to 1925. In 1932, Brown, a Democrat, won a U.S. Senate seat by narrowly defeating the Republican incumbent, but he lost his bid for re-election in 1938. President Franklin Roosevelt then appointed Brown to a 15-year term as Comptroller General of the U.S., but he only served one year due to illness.

Like Brown, outfielder John Tener was both a governor and Congressman. He spent three years in the majors (1888–1890), then returned to Pennsylvania, where he was elected to the U.S. House of Representatives in 1908. He organized the first Congressional baseball game, pitting Republicans against Democrats, which is now an annual tradition on Capitol Hill. He served two terms as Pennsylvania governor, from 1911 until 1915.

The last of the major leaguers in Congress was pitcher Wilmer "Vinegar Bend" Mizell. He played in the majors from 1952 to 1962 and then served three terms in the House of Representatives from North Carolina from 1969 to 1975.

Local voters have elected a number of former big leaguers to serve as mayors, including Jesse Winters (Abilene, Texas), Johnny Wyrostek (Fairmont City, Illinois), Les Willis (Jasper, Texas), Wiman Andrus (Miles City, Montana), Tommy Byrne (Wake Forest, N.C.), Dave Edler (Yakima, Washington), Fred Herbert (Beloit, Wisconsin), Charlie Hickman (Morgantown, West Virginia), Ron Kline (Callery, Pennsylvania), Em Lindbeck (Kewanee, Illinois), Bill McAfee (Albany, Georgia), Bob Prichard (Stamford, Texas), C.V. Matteson (Seville, Ohio), Jake Propst (Columbus, Mississippi), Art Jones (Kershaw, S.C.), Harry Atkinson (Fulton, Missouri), and Fred Snodgrass (Oxnard, California).

Hall of Famer "Cap" Anson (who played from 1871 to 1897 and led the effort to exclude African Americans from big league baseball) won a race for Chicago City Clerk in 1905, but lost his campaign for sheriff the following year. Hall of Famer Walter Johnson (who pitched for the Washington Senators from 1907 to 1927) retired to his farm in Germantown, Maryland, in 1936, was elected Montgomery County Commissioner in 1938, and, as a Republican candidate, lost a close election for the U.S. Congress in 1940, promising voters that he'd "study up on them issues" if he won the election. But other Hall of Famers have struck out as politicians. Honus Wagner, the Pittsburgh Pirates shortstop (1897–1917), lost his race for Pennsylvania's Allegheny County Sheriff in 1928. Nap Lajoie, a star infielder from 1896 to 1916, lost his campaign for sheriff of Cuyahoga County, Ohio. Roger Bresnahan, one of baseball's best catchers in the early 1900s, failed in his bid for county commissioner in Ohio in 1944. Second baseman Bill Mazeroski (1956–1992), the Pirates' hero in the 1960 World Series, failed in his 1986 bid for the Democratic nomination for county commissioner in Westmoreland County, Pennsylvania.

Several minor league players who never made it to the big time in baseball found success as big time politicians. Frank Lausche, who played in the minor leagues in 1916 and 1917, served as the Mayor of Cleveland from 1942 to 1945, Governor of Ohio from 1945 to 1947 and from 1949 to 1957, and U.S. Senator from 1957 to 1969. Scott Lucas spent three years in the minors, went to law school, and was elected Illinois Attorney General and then spent 16 years in Congress, serving as Senate Majority Leader in 1949. Pete Domenici went 0-1 in three relief appearances for the Albuquerque Dukes of the West Texas-New Mexico League in 1954, but later became Mayor of Albuquerque (1967–1970) and U.S. Senator from New Mexico (1973–2009). After a brief minor league career that never got beyond single-A, Roger Williams returned to his family's business in Texas before being voted into Congress in 2012 and re-elected every two years, including 2020.

But George Hurley was unique among these other ballplayer politicians. Born in Seattle in 1907, Hurley was a hard-hitting shortstop for Broadway High School. The New York Giants signed him to a contract. He made their major league roster but injured his ankle sliding into second base before he got into a game. Dropped by the Giants, he was signed by the Yankees but suffered another injury when he was hit in the eye by a baseball. Suffering some permanent vision loss, he had to abandon his baseball career.

In the 1940s Hurley turned to politics, winning election to the Washington State Legislature from Seattle. He became immediately notorious for his radical views and his raucous speeches. Hurley "was a strong advocate for the things he believed in" according to long-serving Washington House speaker John O'Brien.[28] He was a strong supporter of increased unemployment benefits, a shorter work week, and Social Security.[29]

Hurley served two terms in the Washington legislature but was defeated in 1946. He repeatedly ran for reelection between 1950 and 1963, losing each time because he was considered too radical for the repressive Cold War climate. In 1948 he broke away from the Democrats by supporting the Progressive Party's candidate for president, former vice president Henry Wallace. Hurley and several other former Democrats issued a statement explaining their switch: "We can no longer follow President Truman, who by his Wall Street program is attempting to lead us into World War III."[30] Hurley's opposition to the Cold War and support for nuclear disarmament got him labeled as a communist sympathizer.

When not serving in office, Hurley got heavily involved in the Washington labor movement, including the Building Service Employees Union.

A report appearing in the 1949 *Congressional Record*, "In the Case of George Hurley," indicated,

> Another person with communistic affiliations who was appointed by Mr. [Monrad] Wallgren while he was governor was George Hurley, inspector in the Department of Transportation, appointed April 17, 1946 at $300 to $350 a month. George Hurley has also been identified under oath as a member of the Communist Party by a number of witnesses before the UnAmerican Activities Committee of the State of Washington.[31]

Hurley wouldn't be deterred. He kept seeking reelection and finally succeeded in 1974, representing a Seattle district in the state House of Representatives. Serving two terms, he fought against higher property and sales taxes, instead advocating a tax system based on ability to pay as well as new corporate excise taxes. He opposed nuclear power plants, prison system expansion, and U.S. aid for foreign dictatorships. He was an early opponent of the Vietnam War. In 1972 he supported the antiwar presidential campaign of Senator Eugene McCarthy, a Minnesota Democrat.[32] Hurley died in 1999 at the age of ninety-two. His wife, Lenore Hurley, recalled that he had "a great desire to help people. His life was all baseball and all politics."[33]

OUTCAST: JIM BOUTON

Jim Bouton's involvement in the anti–Vietnam War movement (see chapter 4) was only one part of his wide-ranging challenges to the status quo inside and outside baseball. Bouton was an All-Star pitcher but he is best known as the author of *Ball Four*, his 1970 memoir of his baseball playing days, which revolutionized how journalists cover baseball and how fans think about their favorite teams and players.

Born in 1939, Bouton attracted attention as a high school pitcher in Chicago's suburbs. He briefly studied painting at the Art Institute of Chicago, attended Western Michigan University for a year, and then signed with the New York Yankees in 1958. Bouton made the Yankees roster in 1962. In 36 appearances, including 16 starts, he went 7-7 with a 3.99 ERA and got a World Series ring when the Yankees beat the Giants. While earning the MLB minimum as a rookie, Bouton asked for a raise. Yankee executive Dan Topping reminded Bouton that he'd be making more money in October since the Yankees always made the World Series. Bouton said, "Fine, I'll sign a contract that guarantees me $10,000 more at the end of the season."[34] They eventually settled on a bigger but still meager raise, but it was clear that Bouton wasn't going to be your typically compliant ballplayer.

Although a six-month hitch in the Army kept Bouton out of the rotation until mid-June, he nevertheless had a sensational 1963 season, going 21-7 with a 2.53 ERA plus 10 relief appearances, played in the All-Star game, and helped the Yankees win the pennant. After the season, Bouton claimed he deserved a much bigger raise but again the Yankees stonewalled, with new Yankees general manager Ralph Houk reducing Bouton's salary by $100 each day he didn't sign and report to spring training camp. With few alternatives, Bouton ended his holdout, settling for an $8,000 raise instead of the $15,000 he thought he deserved.

In a discussion one day in the Yankees clubhouse, Bouton's teammates claimed that a fair minimum salary should range between $7,000 and $12,000. Bouton proposed $25,000, explaining, "Everyone in this room has a PhD in hitting or pitching. We're in the top 600 in the world at what we do. In an industry that makes millions of dollars, and we have to sign whatever contract they give us? That's insane."[35]

Bouton repeated his success in 1964, finishing 18-13 with a 3.02 ERA. He led the league in starts and won two World Series games. As he began speaking out on social issues, Yankee management and some teammates saw him as a "flake"—too intelligent and outspoken for his own good. He even sat at the back of the team bus, reading! As sportswriter Ron Kaplan observed, "though he tried to be one of the boys, he was constantly 'accused' of being a free-thinker, which in those days was one step away from being a Communist, to conservative sports minds."[36]

The Yankees tolerated this until Bouton suddenly became a marginal performer in 1965. Handicapped by arm problems, he slipped to 4-15 with a 4.85 ERA. In 1966, his ERA bounced back to 2.69 but poor run support held his win-loss record to 3-8. In 1967 the Yankees demoted him to their Syracuse farm team. He made the Yankees roster again the next year but team executives disapproved of his iconoclastic views and they sold him mid-season to the expansion Seattle Pilots, a team that wouldn't begin play until 1969. Bouton finished out the 1968 season with the Triple-A Seattle Angels.

In early 1968 the South African Non-Racial Olympic Committee (SAN-ROC) approached Bouton to sign a petition protesting the ban on non-white athletes on that nation's Olympic team even though 80 percent of South Africans were Black. Jim became friendly with anti-apartheid activist Dennis Brutus, SAN-ROC's executive secretary, whom Bouton called "the greatest man I ever met." He noted that "we need fellow athletes to stand up for us and change this injustice."[37]

Bouton and teammate Ruben Amaro traveled to Mexico City to protest South Africa's sports apartheid during the Olympics but they were rebuffed by the Olympic Committee: "They knew all about the discrimination against the Black South African athletes," Bouton observed, "and they simply didn't care. They were a bunch of pompous racists. It was sickening."[38] He wrote about the issue and his ordeal for *Sport* magazine later that year.

Sportswriter Leonard Shecter wrote an appreciative profile of Bouton for *Sport* magazine, observing that "all this is enough to have earned Bouton a reputation as a bit of an oddball. Of course he is not. He stands out because he is a decent young man in a game which does not recognize decency as valuable."[39]

Bouton and Shecter became friends. Before leaving the Yankees, Bouton had taken notes on his experiences, and Shecter suggested that he keep a diary. He continued writing in his journal while playing for the Seattle Pilots and after he was traded to the Houston Astros. Bouton's diary, as edited by Shecter, was published as *Ball Four* in 1970.

In *Ball Four*, Bouton portrayed laudable characters and accomplishments but also aspects of players' lives rarely revealed before: their drunken hang-overs, crass language and behavior, pep pills and drug use, political views, questionable baseball smarts, anti-intellectualism, womanizing, voyeurism, and extramarital affairs. He described ballplayers as normal young men with special athletic skills but otherwise not necessarily idealistic heroes as they had been portrayed. The book generated a firestorm of protest from players, management, and sportswriters.

A few ballplayers, such as Cy Young Award winner Mike Marshall, defended Bouton's book, saying, "I thought it was funny, and made us look far better than we were. It made us look human, and vulnerable, and strug-gling, all the things we were." Most players didn't see it that way, however. When Bouton faced Pete Rose, the Cincinnati Reds superstar shouted, "Fuck you, Shakespeare." *New York Daily News* sportswriter Dick Young portrayed Bouton as a "social leper" and a "commie in baseball stirrups."[40] As far as Young and others were concerned, Bouton had committed the cardinal sin: he'd tarnished baseball icon, Mickey Mantle, by suggesting that maybe it wasn't Mantle's injuries that shortened his career but rather his drinking problem and skirt-chasing until all hours of the morning. After Young's attacks, fans greeted Bouton with boos, curses, and obscene gestures when he returned to New York to play the Mets.

The Yankees barred Bouton from their annual Old Timers' games for nearly thirty years. Commissioner Bowie Kuhn launched a campaign to discredit Bouton and demanded a meeting with the pitcher. Several fans appeared outside Kuhn's office, protesting with placards reading, "Jim Bouton Is a Real Hero," "No Punishment for Exposing the Truth," and "Kuhn: Stop Repression and Harassment."

Players union head Marvin Miller, union attorney Richard Moss, and Shecter joined Bouton at the meeting with Kuhn, who claimed that Bouton was undermining baseball. Bouton responded, "You're wrong . . . People will be more interested in baseball, not less . . . People are turned off by the phony goody-goody image." Kuhn told Bouton that baseball "gave you what you have," but Bouton protested, "I always gave baseball everything I had. Besides, baseball didn't give me anything. I earned it."[41]

Kuhn ordered Bouton to release a statement saying he falsified or exaggerated his stories, but Bouton refused. When Kuhn told him to regard the meeting as a warning, Miller shot back, "A warning against what . . . against writing about baseball? . . . You can't subject someone to future penalties on such vague criteria." Kuhn's intimidation tactics ignited a debate and turned the book into a best seller.

Most sportswriters attacked Bouton but there were exceptions. "Bouton should be given baseball's most valuable salesman of the year award," Robert Lipsyte wrote in the *New York Times*. "His anecdotes and insights are enlightening, hilarious, and most important, unavailable elsewhere. They breathe new life into a game choked by pontificating statisticians, image-conscious officials, and scared ballplayers."[42] George Foster of the *Boston Globe* called *Ball Four* a "revolutionary manifesto." *New York Times* writer David Halberstam observed that Bouton "has written . . . a book deep in the American vein, so deep in fact that it is by no means a sports book . . . A comparable insider's book about, say, the Congress of the United States, the Ford Motor Company, or the Joint Chiefs of Staff would be equally welcome."[43]

According to sportswriter Nathan Rabin, "the times were changing outside the ballpark, but the major league mindset seemed stuck somewhere in the mid-'50s. The old guard still ruled with crew cuts, knee-jerk patriotism, reactionary politics, and a near-religious belief in . . . maintaining the status quo." MLB officials pressured, if not required, players to wear their hair short to counter the hippies and anti-war protesters.[44]

Bouton was repulsed by the segregation he saw especially in spring training and in games in other Southern cities. He was angered by his white teammates' casual racism and their ridiculing Emmett Ashford, the lone Black AL umpire. More than a decade after Robinson broke baseball's color line, Bouton witnessed his fellow Yankees catcher Elston Howard, the team's first Black player, subjected to endless humiliation.

Much of the protest against *Ball Four* focused on how it assaulted the sanctity of the clubhouse. But for MLB owners, Bouton's real threat was challenging their economic power and, more broadly, America's unequal economic system and the undue influence of big corporations.

In *Ball Four* Bouton revealed that major leaguers led lives with little financial or professional security. The owners cared about nothing except their profits, kept salaries indecently low, traded or demoted loyal players, and treated their workers as poorly paid slaves. Salary negotiations were a farce, and many players couldn't make a living on their baseball pay despite generating millions in profits for owners. Except for the superstars, ballplayers led a vagabond existence.

By disclosing these conditions, Bouton thought fellow ballplayers would appreciate him blowing the whistle. Instead they complained about him violating their privacy and tarnishing their reputations. But Bouton's book touched a nerve. Marvin Miller claimed that *Ball Four* contributed significantly to bringing on free agency and escalating player salaries.

With his baseball career apparently ended in 1970, Bouton became a sportscaster for two New York television stations. In 1971 he published a second book, *I'm Glad You Didn't Take It Personally*, mostly describing the reaction to *Ball Four*. While many people did take it personally, Bouton made no apologies. He believed that

> athletes and entertainers have a special obligation to take a stand on issues of the day. In our profession, we tend to be tranquilizers for a whole nation. We contribute to a false feeling of well-being [when instead] we have a responsibility to let people know that, even though we are playing games, we are also aware of problems outside the ball fields.[45]

Following his own advice, Bouton was an early supporter of Senator Eugene McCarthy's anti-war presidential campaign in 1968 and served as a Democratic Party Convention delegate for anti-war presidential candidate Senator George McGovern in 1972.

Bouton kept pitching in various adult leagues in New Jersey in the early 1970s, and in 1975 he joined the Portland Mavericks in the independent Northwest League. He went 4-1 with a 2.20 ERA. He staked his success on learning to throw a knuckleball. He remained in the minors until the Atlanta Braves called him up late in the 1978 season, and at age thirty-eight he pitched five games and had a 1-3 win-loss record. He decided not to return to the Braves in 1979, but he continued pitching competitively in semipro leagues into his fifties.

When Bouton pitched for Portland in 1977, players were chewing tobacco and getting sick. One of his teammates, Rob Nelson, observed, "Too bad there isn't something that looks like tobacco but tastes good like gum." Bouton responded, "Hey, that's a great idea. Shredded gum in a pouch, call it Big League Chew and sell it to every ballplayer in America." Bouton put in the start-up money, contacted an attorney, and sold the idea to the Wrigley Chewing Gum Company. A big hit, the company won a health and safety award from *Collegiate Baseball Magazine* for creating the first healthy alternative to chewing tobacco—no doubt sparing many ballplayers from getting mouth cancer.

In 1998 the Yankees ended their boycott and finally invited Bouton back for its Old Timers' Game. Bouton pitched one inning, enjoying an emotional reunion with fans and some old teammates.

In 2001 Bouton learned that an old ballpark in Pittsfield near his home in western Massachusetts would be abandoned in favor of a new field to be built in the city's downtown. He launched a campaign to renovate and save Wahconah Park, the oldest minor league ballpark in the United States (built in 1919) and among the few remaining wooden grandstand fields. Local political and business leaders in Pittsfield opposed Bouton's idea of having local fans buy shares in the park to guarantee that it would be locally owned and be a community resource.

Pursuing his campaign, Bouton discovered that in the previous fifteen years, $16 billion in taxpayers' money had been spent on new stadiums, replacing more than one hundred older, beloved ballparks "because baseball's powers-that-be can get away with it. They have a monopoly, granted by the federal government, and they use it to bludgeon local governments to bid against each other for the right to teams. . . . These owners are capitalists who don't want capitalism." He called it "massive corporate welfare."[46] As freelance writer Karl Seigfried observed,

> What began as a small-time crusade . . . became an exposé of a shocking conspiracy between banks, business owners, government officials, and multinational corporate conglomerates to manipulate the stadium as a massive cash grab, consolidation of power, and cover-up of serious environmental pollution.[47]

Bouton wrote another book about the campaign: *Foul Ball: My Life and Hard Times Trying to Save an Old Ballpark* (2003).

After suffering a stroke in 2012, Bouton died in 2019 at age eighty. As baseball historian Mark Armour noted, "Bouton's detractors had called him a communist during his playing days, but in many ways he was actually a traditionalist, a man who fought on the side of baseball for five decades."[48] *Ball Four* was the only sports book named to the New York Public Library's list of the Books of the Century. Bouton ended the book observing that "you spend a good piece of your life gripping a baseball and in the end it turns out that it was the other way around the whole time."

SPACEMAN: BILL LEE

Pitcher Bill Lee was often described as a "flake," but he disagreed: "Flake is an egotistical, right-handed, exploitative, carnivorous, non-recycling, Republican word." He preferred the label "eccentric."[49]

In his successful career playing for the Boston Red Sox (1969–1978) and Montreal Expos (1979–1982), Lee was a rebel on and off the field. His eccentricities were mostly political (of the left-wing variety) rather than merely idiosyncratic. Lee refused to give pat answers or conform to conventional behavior. For these traits, Lee was nicknamed "Spaceman." He was able to get away with his eccentric behavior and radical viewpoints because he performed well on the mound, with a 119-90 win-loss record and a 3.62 ERA in fourteen seasons.

Born in Burbank, California, in 1946, Lee had an impressive baseball pedigree. His grandfather was a stand-out infielder for the PCL's Hollywood Stars and his father was a well-known semipro ballplayer. His aunt Annabelle Lee was a star pitcher in the Women's Semi-Pro Hardball League in Chicago and with three teams in the All-American Girls Professional Baseball League. She pitched a perfect game for the Fort Wayne Daisies in 1944. According to Bill, she was "the best athlete in the family." A southpaw like Bill, "she taught me how to pitch," Lee explained.[50]

After moving to northern California, Lee graduated from Terra Linda High School in Marin County. At the time, he recalled, "I was the button-down three-piece suit guy with a crewcut." "I was basically *Leave It to Beaver*"—not the shaggy-haired, free spirit baseball fans would come to know.[51]

At the University of Southern California, Lee helped the Trojans win the 1968 College World Series. After the Boston Red Sox selected him in the twenty-second round of the free-agent draft that summer, Lee made a quick leap to the majors.

Lee quickly became an effective reliever for the Red Sox but in June of 1970, his second year with the team, he began serving six months in the U.S. Army Reserve. While he had passed his physical and gotten a low lottery number (making him very eligible for the draft), the Red Sox kept him out of Vietnam. Feeling guilty about those who had to go to war, Lee observed, "The moral of the story is that if you are left-handed and can throw strikes, you don't go to 'Nam." One of his tasks while stationed at the Boston Army Base was calling the families of dead soldiers from New England, to say, "You can come get what's left of your son."[52]

Lee described white Bostonians' opposition to busing Black students to predominantly white schools as racist. Such statements could have alienated white fans but his solid work ethic and stellar pitching won them over.

In his first four years with the Red Sox, Lee appeared in 125 games, all but nine in relief, compiling a 19-11 record. He became a starter in 1973. That year, as well as in 1974 and 1975, he won seventeen games and became an

All-Star. In 1975, Lee helped the Red Sox win the American League pennant. In the World Series, Lee started two games, both times leaving with the lead, which Red Sox relievers couldn't hold. Lee injured his pitching arm during a brawl between the Red Sox and Yankees in May 1976. Although he had some good seasons after the injury, he was never the same dazzling hurler.

Lee's teammates respected him, viewing his antics and high spirits as a safety valve for the team and knowing his attitude on the field was all business. Despite his youth, they elected Lee a Red Sox representative to the players' union, serving as a backup to Carlton Fisk.

Lee acknowledges that he and teammate Bernie Carbo "would get high together, but only during rainouts. We were the flower children of baseball." When the Red Sox traded Carbo to the Indians in 1978. Lee was so upset he stormed out of the clubhouse shouting, "Today just cost us the pennant," and claimed he was retiring from baseball.[53] Lee returned a day later, however, wearing a T-shirt reading "Friendship First, Competition Second." Manager Don Zimmer fined him $500 for the one-day walkout, and Lee asked if it could be $1,500 since "I'd like to have the whole weekend."[54]

Lee struggled on the mound through mid-August, and Zimmer relegated him to the bullpen. In a four-game showdown against the Yankees in September, Zimmer refused to start Lee even though he had a lifetime 12-5 record against the team.

Despite playing in Fenway Park, a graveyard for southpaws, Lee was one of the best pitchers in Red Sox history. He held the Red Sox record for the most games pitched (321) and the third-highest win total (94) by a left-handed pitcher. But after the 1978 season, the Red Sox traded Lee to the Montreal Expos for Stan Papi. Lee started 33 games, pitching 222 innings, with 16 wins and a 3.04 ERA. The *Sporting News* named him 1979 National League Left-Hander of the Year. Lee's next three seasons were subpar, however, when he missed time due to injuries. During the strike-truncated 1981 season, he helped pitch the Expos to their only post-season appearance but with diminishing effectiveness.

Lee's career ended with another run-in with baseball management. In May 1982, Montreal released Lee's teammate Rodney Scott. As he had done with Carbo, Lee walked out on the team in protest. Thinking better of it, Lee came back to the Expos the next morning. The team president told him that he'd been released.

Lee was convinced he had been blackballed by MLB teams. "I had three or four more years, easy," he said, insisting that he was banished

> because I stuck up for Bernie Carbo and then Rodney Scott. But I did it for the right reasons. I believed at that moment those people needed my help and I was the player rep. But that wasn't the main reason . . . The player reps were the ones that were punished [because we took money] from the billionaire owners and redistributed it to the players.[55]

More specifically, Lee noted that "Joe Torre, Bill Lee, Marvin Miller, and Dick Moss, the four of us . . . came up with the idea for arbitration and free agency in the early '70s. That's why I'm the most hated person in organized baseball—I'm the Bernie Sanders of baseball."[56] It didn't help when Lee also observed, "Each [MLB] baseball represents some Haitian slave's eight-hour work day," referring to the sweatshop factory where Rawlings manufactured the balls used in all MLB games.[57] Asked whether he minded being out of baseball for good, Lee responded, "Oh, I'll never be out of baseball for good. It's my life. The game gave up on me but I never gave up the game."[58]

Lee never stopped playing. "For me, baseball is passion," he said. "If I can still walk, if I can still move, if I can still see, I will play baseball."[59] He's pitched for dozens of independent, semipro, and other teams in over forty leagues, both inside and outside the United States, continuing to throw two hundred innings a year into his late sixties. In 1975, even before leaving MLB, Lee visited China for two weeks and pitched there. In 1982, after the Expos released him, Lee pitched in the Senior League in Florida primarily against retired major leaguers. He pitched in the Venezuelan League and then played first base and pitched for four seasons with the Moncton Mets in New Brunswick, Canada.

In 1999 Lee initiated the first of four goodwill baseball tours to Cuba, bringing American ballplayers to the island and hosting Cuba players in the United States. The trips led to a 2006 documentary *Spaceman: A Baseball Odyssey*. The film follows Lee and a senior men's team from San Diego as they barnstorm across the island.

Lee was impressed by Cuba's accomplishments under challenging circumstances. "They have education, they have health services. They've developed a conscience whereby they take care of one another," Lee said. He expressed hope that Cuba would become "the jewel of the Caribbean again," noting that "contrary to what's said, they love America."[60]

Filmmaker Ken Burns observed that *Spaceman* evokes "the hope and spirit of baseball, and of the great heart of Bill Lee, who in every joyful breath shames us into remembering why we really love this game so much."[61]

Lee continued to play with barnstorming teams of former major leaguers and teams in independent pro leagues. In 2008 Lee pitched for the Alaska Goldpanners in the annual Midnight Sun Game at night during the summer solstice. In 2010 Lee pitched 5 2/3 innings for the Brockton Rox, a Massachusetts team in the Canadian-American League, allowing only two runs, winning the game, and setting the record for being the oldest pitcher, at age sixty-three, to appear in or win a professional game. In 2012, at sixty-five, he broke his own oldest-pro-player record, throwing a complete game victory for the San Rafael Pacifics in the North American League while also getting a hit and an RBI with one of his homemade bats. The Cooperstown Hall of Fame now houses his uniform and bat from that game.

Lee lives in Vermont, where he's a farmer and plays semipro baseball in New England for the Grey Sox, comprised of former Red Sox players. His team has won three Senior League championships and he's personally won at least 130 games with them over the years. With his 119 major league victories and the hundreds of other games he's pitched and won, Lee believes that, next to Satchel Paige, he might be the winningest pitcher in baseball history.

Lee has always enjoyed tweaking the powers that be. He opposed nuclear weapons and nuclear power. He supported Greenpeace's environmental activism, the Equal Rights Amendment, and the busing of Black students to white schools in Boston. Soon after the Apollo moon landing, Lee showed up in an astronaut suit for a game in Milwaukee to protest air pollution.

Lee claims that Ron Shelton—the former minor league player who wrote and directed the hit 1988 baseball film *Bull Durham*—stole one of his lines. When Crash Davis (played by Kevin Costner) goes to the mound to convince his pitcher Nuke LaLoosh (played by Tim Robbins) that he's throwing too hard, he says, "Quit trying to strike everybody out. It's fascist. Throw some ground balls. It's more democratic."[62]

Channeling the Tom Joad character in the Depression-era film *The Grapes of Wrath*, Lee proclaimed, "Whenever there's a fat kid who doesn't get picked on a team, I'll be there. Whenever there's a girl the boys won't let play, I'll be there. Whenever there's a guy who screws up and kicks away a game and needs a friend, I'll be there."[63] Spiritually, Lee is a former Catholic who once observed, "You should enter a ballpark the way you enter a church."[64]

Lee believes in sharing the wealth. "The fans are the ones who support the franchises and they're paying the players' salaries," Lee explained. "As a socialist, I see only one solution. They have to storm the commissioner's office as the peasants stormed the Bastille during the French Revolution. They have to take control. I will lead the mob."[65]

During his playing days, Lee admitted he sprinkled marijuana each morning on his organic buckwheat pancakes, claiming it made him impervious to bus fumes while jogging to work at Fenway Park. This got him hauled into Commissioner Bowie Kuhn's office and fined. It also landed Lee on the cover of *High Times*, a counterculture, pro-marijuana magazine that printed a lengthy article about the pitcher. "If Nolan is the 'Ryan Express,'" he observed, "then I guess I'm the Marrakesh Express." The magazine featured him again in 2007, and in 2013 he reiterated his claim that he smoked weed with future president George W. Bush in 1972. Lee believed his openness about marijuana hurt his career. "It definitely affected me as far as getting along with upper management and everything else, but 'To thine own self be true, right?'"[66] He's surely the only ballplayer to earn feature articles in both *Sports Illustrated* and *High Times* magazines. When the steroids issue arose in MLB, Lee was asked what he thought about mandatory drug testing. He claimed, "Well, I've tried just about all of them, but I wouldn't want to make it mandatory."[67]

Lee has coauthored four books: *The Wrong Stuff*; *Have Glove, Will Travel*; *The Little Red (Sox) Book*; and *Baseball Eccentrics*. In his fictional story "Fuhrer Furor at Fenway!" (in *The Little Red (Sox) Book*), Lee imagines a visit to the United States by Adolf Hitler in August 1939 during which ballplayers Moe Berg and Ted Williams collaborate to assassinate the German dictator, which spares the world a terrible war.

Lee started the Old Bat Company, which specializes in maple, ash, and yellow birch bats made from wood taken from old growth forests. He has released his own wine label, Spaceman Red, which he distributes throughout New England. He has also released a beer, Spaceman Ale, in partnership with Vermont's Magic Hat Brewing Company. Rocker Warren Zevon wrote "The Ballad of Bill Lee" using Lee's quotes as lyrics.[68] Lee was also the subject of the 1996 song "What Bothers the Spaceman" by the rock group They Might Be Giants. In 2016 Josh Duhamel starred in a feature film, *Spaceman*, about Lee's baseball life.

Lee has made two unconventional forays into formal politics. In 1988, after years endorsing progressive candidates, Lee made a whimsical run for U.S. president. Still living in Canada, he ran as a candidate for the Rhinoceros Party, headquartered in Montreal. His slogan was "No guns, no butter. Both can kill." He called for a ban on Astroturf and the law of gravity, the bulldozing of the Rocky Mountains to give Alberta extra sunlight, and the conversion of the White House into a Mexican restaurant. As part of his platform, he also called for the elimination of baseball's designated hitter rule, calling it "one of America's greatest evils."[69]

Asked to describe his political views, Lee once explained, "I'm more of a socialist than a libertarian. I believe in the underdog." Paraphrasing Eugene Debs, the Socialist Party's iconic leader in the early 1900s, Lee said, "'If there's a man in a class lesser than me, I'm with him. If there's a man incarcerated, I'm not free.' I'm more that type of guy."[70]

Hoping to benefit from Lee's celebrity, in 2016 the tiny Liberty Union Party asked Lee to run for governor of Vermont. Bernie Sanders ran for governor on the Liberty Union Party ticket in 1976, earning 11,317 votes, 6.1 percent of the total. Lee agreed to run "in the best interests of mankind," campaigning on the slogan "So far left, we're right."[71]

His platform included support for a paid family-leave policy and for a Canadian-style, single-payer universal health care system, Lee recalled that when he injured his shoulder he went to a Canadian hospital for the surgery and paid only a few thousand dollars for a procedure that would have cost at least $70,000 in the United States.

"If you want to see money come down from the 1 percent, then we're going to need umbrellas when I'm elected, because it's going to be raining dollars," Lee said.[72] "When I'm elected, we're going to keep our youth in Vermont because we're going to legalize marijuana . . . tax it, and make hemp clothing, [including] Little League uniforms so the kids don't get epilepsy," Lee said. Lee generated considerable publicity for his campaign but in the end he received only 2.8 percent of the vote.

ACTIVIST: SEAN DOOLITTLE

Major league ballplayers were part of a wave of athletes' activism that emerged in the wake of Donald Trump's election in 2016 and continued throughout his presidency.

During the 2016 presidential election, Dodgers first baseman Adrian Gonzalez refused to stay at a Trump hotel. He told reporters, "You can draw your own conclusions. They're probably right."[73] On election night Dodgers pitcher Brandon McCarthy tweeted, "Tonight's result affects me none because I'm rich, white and male. Yet, it'll be a long time until I'm able to sleep peacefully."[74] Two months after Trump's inauguration, McCarthy was back on Twitter poking fun at Trump's campaign pledge to "drain the swamp" of corporate and Wall Street influence-peddlers. "Was the 'swamp' Goldman Sachs itself?" McCarthy tweeted, referring to the powerful investment bank that provided top officials in Trump's administration. St. Louis Cardinals outfielder Dexter Fowler, whose wife emigrated from Iran, told ESPN that he opposed Trump's anti-Muslim executive order. In response to angry comments from fans, Fowler tweeted, "For the record. I know this is going to sound absolutely crazy, but athletes are humans, and not properties of the team they work for."[75] He was echoing Curt Flood's comments a half-century before.

In September 2017, after Trump attacked NFL quarterback Colin Kaepernick for kneeling during the national anthem to protest racism, Bruce Maxwell, the Oakland Athletics African American rookie catcher, bashed Trump on Instagram: "Our president speaks of inequality of man because players are protesting the anthem! F- this man!"[76] Later that day Maxwell, the son of an Army veteran, became the first major league player to kneel for the national anthem before a game against the visiting Texas Rangers. Outfielder Mark Canha, who is white, stood behind Maxwell and placed his right hand on his teammate's shoulder in solidarity. "My decision had been coming for a long time," Maxwell told the media, citing his own experiences with racism growing up in Huntsville, Alabama.

In May 2018 Houston Astros players Carlos Beltrán and Carlos Correa, both natives of Puerto Rico, skipped the team's visit to the White House in honor of their 2017 World Series victory to express their dismay with Trump's bungled recovery efforts after Hurricane Maria devastated the island. In 2019 nine African American and Latino members of the 2018 World Series winners Boston Red Sox—Mookie Betts, Jackie Bradley Jr.,

Rafael Devers, Hector Velazquez, Xander Bogaerts, Sandy Leon, Christian Vazquez, Eduardo Nunez, David Price, and manager Alex Cora—refused to join Trump at a White House celebration for the same reason.[77]

During his first three years in office, Trump declined to toss the first pitch on opening day, a tradition that began with President William Howard Taft in 1910. He feared that he would be met with a chorus of boos from the fans since over three-quarters of Washington, DC, area voters (and 91 percent in the capital city) supported Hillary Clinton in 2016. In 2019, however, he promised to attend the fifth game of the World Series between the Washington Nationals and Houston Astros at Nationals Park. Nationals owner Mark Lerner told the *Washington Post*, "He's the president of the United States whether you like him or not. It's a special event. He should be at it."[78]

Lerner had already invited José Andrés, a chef whose World Central Kitchen serves meals to victims of natural disasters, to throw out the first ball. Trump arrived at the stadium during the third inning, but did not venture onto the field. He sat in a luxury suite with several loyal Republican members of Congress. After his arrival was announced over the public address system, fans greeted him with loud and sustained boos, a large "Impeach Trump" banner, and chants of "Lock Him Up!"

One of the Nationals players that day was pitcher Sean Doolittle, who had become the most outspoken professional baseball player of the twenty-first century even before Trump began running for president. He epitomizes the baseball maverick. He explained to the *New York Times*, "When I was a kid, I remember my parents would say, 'Baseball is what you do, but that's not who you are'—like that might be my job, but that's not the end-all, be-all. I feel like I might even be able to use it to help other people or open some doors or explore more opportunities."[79]

Doolittle is clear about his priorities. "Sports are like the reward of a functioning society," he said when the COVID-19 pandemic hit in early 2020. He was upset that the owners and players' union were negotiating about salaries, not health and safety, and that the billionaire owners were ignoring the needs of stadium workers and other low-wage employees who would be laid off.[80]

Doolittle comes from a military family. His father—who served in the Air Force for twenty-six years, including deployment to the Middle East after 9/11—teaches aerospace science to high school ROTC students in New Jersey.

His stepmother is an active-duty member of the Air National Guard. A distant cousin, Jimmy Doolittle, was an aviation pioneer who led the first attack against Japan after it bombed Pearl Harbor in December 1941.

Born in 1986, Doolittle led Shawnee High School to a New Jersey state championship as an outstanding pitcher and was named the state's high school player of the year by *Baseball America* in 2004. In his freshman year he hit .313 and went 3-2 with a 1.64 ERA, and *Baseball America* named him a freshman All-American at first base. The next year he made the All-Atlantic Coast Conference team as a starting pitcher and as the Conference Player of the Year with a 11-2 win-loss record and a 2.38 ERA while batting .324. In his junior year he hit .301 at the plate, went 8-3 with a 2.40 ERA on the mound, and was again First-Team All-Conference. After three years he was the University of Virginia's all-time leader in both wins (22) and RBIs (167).

Drafted in 2007 by the Oakland Athletics in the first round as a first baseman, Doolittle left college after his junior year. He spent three years in the minors but in 2009, playing for the Athletics Triple-A team in Sacramento, his season ended after twenty-eight games due to tendinitis in both knees. Following surgery on his left knee, he missed all of the next two seasons except for one game as a pitcher in the Arizona League in 2011.

Doolittle began his comeback in 2012 as a full-time relief pitcher. The A's called him up to Oakland in June. He played for Oakland until July 2017, when he was traded to the Nationals. He pitched spectacularly for both teams but his career has been riddled with injuries and surgeries, forcing him to miss many games. In 2012 he pitched 47 innings in 41 games, struck out 60 batters, walked only 11 hitters, and was 2-1 with a 3.04 ERA. In 2014 he made the All-Star team. After missing most of the 2015 season on the disabled list, he returned in 2016 and pitched in 44 games, recording 45 strikeouts and only 8 walks in 39 innings but missed part of the season with injuries. In 2017 with the Nationals, he again made the All-Star team but injuries limited him to pitching in only 43 games, going 3-3 with 25 saves and a 1.60 ERA. In 2019 Doolittle got off to a spectacular start with 23 saves by the end of July, adding 5 more in August, but then went back on the disabled list with right-knee tendinitis. He returned in time to help the National win the AL pennant, finishing the regular season with 29 saves, and 66 strike outs and only 15 walks in 60 innings. Doolittle allowed just two runs in 10 1/3 innings in the postseason and didn't allow a run in three World Series appearances against the Houston Astros. His 2020 season was a disaster not only because of the COVID–shortened season but also because injuries limited him to 11 games and 7 innings.

In both Oakland and Washington, Doolittle was one of the most popular players. He and his girlfriend Eireann Dolan, whom he met while she was a reporter covering the A's for Comcast SportsNet and married in October 2017, approach life with a sense of humor, often poking fun at each other in their constant tweets. A huge *Star Wars* fan, Doolittle calls himself "Obi-Sean Kenobi Doolittle." His Twitter handle is @whatwouldDOOdo.

In addition to participating in a variety of community activities, both Doolittle and Dolan (who earned her master's degree in theology and religious studies from Fordham University) have been consistently outspoken about their progressive political views.

In 2015 Doolittle and Dolan organized a Thanksgiving dinner for seventeen Syrian refugee families in Chicago, Dolan's hometown, recruiting Mayor Rahm Emmanuel and several city council members to serve as greeters and waiters to get publicity for the refugee cause. "We just felt it was a way we could welcome them to America, to let them know there are people who are glad they're here," Doolittle recalled.[81]

In January 2017, a week after Trump's inauguration, the president signed his first travel ban, sparking nationwide protests. Doolittle tweeted, "These refugees are fleeing civil wars, terrorism, religious persecution, and are thoroughly vetted for 2 yrs. A refugee ban is a bad idea . . . It feels un-American. And also immoral."[82]

Doolittle further observed,

> I think America is the best country in the world because we've been able to attract the best and brightest people from all over the world. We have the smartest doctors and scientists, the most creative and innovative thinkers. A travel ban like this puts that in serious jeopardy. I've always thought that all boats rise with the tide. Refugees aren't stealing a slice of the pie from Americans. But if we include them, we can make the pie that much bigger, thus ensuring more opportunities for everyone.[83]

In an interview with *Time* magazine, Doolittle said that the Trump administration "is relying on stereotypes and Islamophobia, using false information to support its immigration reforms. The facts tell a different story: Crime rates are lower for refugees and immigrants than for American citizens, and net illegal immigration from Mexico is thought to be at or less than zero."[84]

In 2016, after Trump, then a presidential candidate, dismissed his vulgar "grab their pussy" comment as just "locker room talk," a dozen pro athletes—from football, basketball and soccer—denounced Trump, mostly on Twitter. Doolittle was the only baseball player to record his disgust, writing, "As an athlete, I've been in locker rooms my entire adult life and uh, that's not locker room talk."[85]

In July 2017, neo-Nazis and white supremacists descended on Charlottesville, Virginia, triggering violent protests that resulted in the death of one anti-Nazi protester. In a series of tweets, Doolittle, who attended college there, condemned them. "The C'Ville I knew from my time at @UVA is a diverse and accepting community. It's no place for Nazis," he wrote. "People say 'if we don't give them attention they'll go away.' Maybe. But if we don't condemn this evil, it might continue to spread. This kind of hatred was never gone, but now it's been normalized. They didn't even wear hoods. It's on us to condemn it and drive it out. It's just white fear,"[86] Doolittle told the *Washington Post*. "It's the worst kind of hatred. It's disgusting."[87]

Doolittle has also been an advocate for workers, especially those with ties to organized baseball. In early 2019, New Era Cap Company, which makes caps for all major league teams, announced it was closing its union factory in Derby, New York, to move its production to nonunion facilities in Florida. In a *Washington Post* op-ed, Doolittle expressed his concern that he and other players "will be wearing caps made by people who don't enjoy the same labor protections and safeguards that we do."[88] He told *ThinkProgress*, "It's basically union-busting, plain and simple. The only people wearing (the New Era caps made in Derby) are the players, and these are the players in the union, so we want to make sure they're wearing caps that are made by people earning a union wage."[89]

When the COVID pandemic hit in early 2020, no player was more eager than Doolittle to return to play but he was the first ballplayer to publicly oppose MLB's plans to restore play without adequate guarantees that the players and support staff would be safe and that stadium workers would be compensated for the long lay-off. In a series of tweets, Doolittle expressed concern about an omission from MLB's restart plan: "the health protections for players, families, staff, stadium workers and the workforce it would require to resume a season."[90]

When MLB proposed to save money during the pandemic by shaving $100 off every minor leaguer's $400 weekly paycheck, Doolittle and several Nationals teammates pledged to cover the lost income of players on the Nationals farm teams. Doolittle tweeted, "Minor leaguers are an essential part of our organization and they are bearing the heaviest burden of this situation as their season is likely to be cancelled. We recognize that and want to stand with them in support."[91] Players on other teams did the same. Embarrassed, the owners withdrew the plan.

Doolittle has been a consistent supporter of LGBTQ rights. He raised money to provide tickets and buses for nine hundred LGBT youth to attend the A's Pride Night. "There should be no discrimination or hate in the game or at the stadium," Doolittle told a local newspaper."[92]

In 2018 when the media exposed anti-gay slurs tweeted by several major ballplayers, Doolittle tweeted, "It takes courage to be your true self when your identity has been used as an insult or a pejorative."[93] With the Nationals he celebrated Pride Day by having a trans flag on his right baseball shoe and the rainbow flag on his left shoe. He tweeted, "Everyone deserves to feel safe and free to be who they are and to love who they love. Love is love."[94] According to *OutSports*, "There may not be a bigger advocate for LGBTQ rights among Major League Baseball players" than Doolittle.[95]

After the Nationals won the 2019 World Series, Doolittle announced that he would not join his teammates at the White House celebration with President Trump. He had a problem with Trump's "divisive rhetoric and the enabling of conspiracy theories and widening the divide in this country," he told the *Washington Post*. "I don't want to hang out with somebody who talks like that."[96] All-Star third baseman Anthony Rendon, outfielders Victor Robles and Michael A. Taylor, and pitchers Javy Guerra, Joe Ross, and Wander Suero also boycotted the event.[97]

The *Washington Post* reported that "in a sport with a conservative culture defined by tradition and a near-dogmatic acceptance of the social status quo, they (Doolittle and Dolan) have been unafraid to be different, while determined not to be different for difference sake."[98]

In May 2020, following the murder of George Floyd by a Minneapolis police officer that provoked nationwide protests, Doolittle spoke out, tweeting,

> Race is America's original sin . . . passed down from generation to generation. And we struggle to acknowledge that it even exists, much less to atone for it. . . . Racism and violence are killing Black men and women before our eyes. We are told it is done in the name of "law and order," but there is nothing lawful nor orderly about these murders. We must take action and call it for what it is. We must recognize our shared humanity and atone for our Original Sin or else we will continue to curse future generations with it. RIP George Floyd.[99]

Doolittle—who, along with Dolan, is a member of Democratic Socialists of America—was thrilled to meet civil rights activist and Congressman John Lewis at a Nationals game in 2018. "I've been trying to raise some good trouble around here," Doolittle told him, using the phrase that Lewis frequently used to describe his activism.[100]

Doolittle is an avid reader. During the baseball season, he reads for an hour or two after each game—at home or in his hotel room. "Reading is just a way for my brain to focus on something else," Doolittle explained to *Sports Illustrated*.[101]

He visits locally owned independent bookstores on every road trip during the baseball season and documents his visits on Twitter. "I want to support local businesses. I want to support these places that are active in their communities," Doolittle explained. The big online chains like Amazon, he said, "might be a little bit cheaper, but they're not furthering anything as far as author's careers or supporting their workers."[102]

Doolittle discussed the problem of illiteracy during a *CBS This Morning* interview. "Over half of kids who are in fourth grade read below basic level—that's a really crucial time for them because there's so many indicators about where they're at in fourth grade that can determine where they go in their education level down the road."[103]

Doolittle participated in a reading program for the children of soldiers from military bases in the Washington, DC, area. He explained, "I hope they came and saw . . . a major league baseball player that reads books. It shows that maybe reading is not something that's just a part of their homework. It can be something that you enjoy as much as being outside and playing sports."[104]

Doolittle considers his left-wing views consistent with his support for American soldiers. His baseball career, he said,

> gives you [the perspective] on how fortunate I am to be able to do what I do when there's teenagers leaving the country with M-16s and they're going to the Middle East. And I get to play baseball every day. You start to look at things a little bit differently and you really appreciate the opportunities you have and some of these things other people do for you getting little or no recognition for it.[105]

Doolittle and Dolan have long been strong advocates for military veterans. They support Operation Finally Home, which builds houses for wounded veterans and their families. They started a registry to help furnish two such houses in Northern California and offered signed A's gear to those who donated. The couple worked with Human Rights Watch and wrote an op-ed column in *Sports Illustrated* urging the Veterans Administration to provide adequate mental health services to military vets with less than honorable discharges, or "bad paper."[106] They've also supported Swords to Ploughshares, a Bay Area organization that helps veterans with housing and employment. In 2018 Doolittle received the Bob Feller Act of Valor Award in recognition of his work with military veterans and their families.

Doolittle has criticized ostentatious displays of patriotism at ballparks. He claims it isn't enough to "just capitalize on people's patriotism, and sell hats and shirts with your team's logo and camouflage on it." Instead it's important to "use your platform as a sports league to shine a light on some of the issues facing veterans and military families."[107] He once tweeted that "as long as we have an all-volunteer military, it's on us—the civilians at home—to advocate for our military families. To make sure they are deployed responsibly and that they get the care they were promised when they signed up."[108]

When Doolittle's former A's teammate Bruce Maxwell, who also comes from a military family, was criticized for refusing to stand for the national anthem in solidarity with Colin Kaepernick and other athletes, Doolittle came to his defense: "I came from a military family, so there are a lot of things I think about when the anthem is playing," he told ESPN.

> One thing that bothers me is the way people use veterans and troops almost as a shield. They say that's the reason they stand and that veterans deserve to be

honored and respected during the anthem. But where is that outrage in taking better care of veterans? The most recent statistics say that we still lose 20 veterans to suicide every day.[109]

Doolittle elaborated,

I worry sometimes in this country that we conflate patriotism exclusively with love of the military and militarism and the strength of our armed forces. That's not the only way that you can be patriotic. People draw a direct line between the national anthem and the military, or patriotism and the military. But there are a lot of things that we're not doing for veterans.[110]

In February 2021, as a free agent, he signed a contract to pitch for the Cincinnati Reds. Many baseball fans probably believe that even before the trade, Doolittle—who has used his celebrity to fight for social justice—was already a "Red." A more apt description for Doolittle is patriotic progressive—and major league rebel.

8

Baseball Justice: An Unfinished Agenda

As we enter the third decade of the twenty-first century, the agenda for social justice in general, and baseball justice in particular, remains unfinished. In this chapter we offer an agenda for the next wave of baseball rebels on issues of corporate power, workers' rights, and baseball colonialism and militarism.

CURT FLOOD BELONGS IN THE HALL OF FAME

In a 2016 *Sporting News* article "Has Curt Flood Been Overlooked for the Hall of Fame?" Graham Womack observed, "If and when [Marvin] Miller is posthumously inducted, Flood might be a logical next choice. While he's merely a symbol, it wouldn't be the first time the Hall of Fame's inducted one."[1] The Hall of Fame ended its blacklist of Marvin Miller in December 2019. It's time for Curt Flood to join Miller in the Cooperstown shrine.

Flood, who played from 1956 to 1971, was one of the greatest defensive outfielders in history, with seven straight Gold Gloves. He hit above .300 in six seasons. He was a key reason for the Cardinals' 1964 and 1967 World Series victories. But, the *Sporting News* argued, "statistically, Flood doesn't have much to impress a Hall of Fame committee, hitting .293 with 1,861 hits and just 12 full seasons. No position player who's retired since 1959 has gotten in with less than 2,000 hits."

That criticism is unfair. Flood would no doubt have accomplished 2,000 hits and posted other Hall of Fame eligible numbers had he not been banished from baseball at age thirty-two at the height of his career because he challenged the baseball establishment by suing MLB to end the reserve clause.

In 1996, a year before his death, Flood received only 15.1 percent of the votes from the Baseball Writers Association of America. Posthumously, the Hall of Fame Veterans Committee has considered his candidacy three times (2003, 2005, 2007) but failed to vote him into Cooperstown. Flood has been a victim of the same corporate and anti-union baseball establishment that kept Marvin Miller out for decades.

As sportswriter William Rhoden observed, "Many members of the Veterans Committee who refuse to vote for Flood were direct beneficiaries of his protest," referring to former ballplayers on the committee.[2] Rhoden also noted, "Every time a free—note free—agent signs a lucrative contract, or a star refuses a trade or forces his way out of an undesirable situation, Flood's presence is felt."[3] In February 2020 and again in June 2021 more than one hundred members of Congress—Democrats and Republicans alike—held a news conference and signed a letter to Jane Forbes Clark, Hall of Fame chairwoman, urging the hall's Golden Age Committee to elect Flood at its next meeting.

"Curt Flood changed the game of baseball when he courageously spoke truth to power in the name of what was right," said Rep. David Trone, a Maryland Democrat. "Flood sacrificed his own career so players after him could have free agency, leaving one of the biggest impacts on the game to this day." Added Senator Roy Blunt, a Missouri Republican, "I have always admired the talent he brought to the game and his bravery off the field. He deserves to be honored with his rightful place alongside America's greatest baseball players."

Representatives from players' unions from the MLB, NFL, NBA, and MHL joined the 2020 press conference and signed a joint statement: "Curt Flood's historic challenge of the reserve clause a half century ago transcended baseball. He courageously sacrificed his career to take a stand for the rights of all players in professional sports, bringing the issue of free agency to the forefront of national discussion."[4] Tony Clark, the MLBPA's president, said, "If the Hall of Fame is a museum that is reflective of our game's history and historic performances, [Flood's] enshrinement would be an affirmation of Curt's contribution to our game and our history."[5]

Flood didn't win his Supreme Court case to outlaw the reserve clause but he laid the groundwork for that breakthrough. As Miller often explained, Flood's case educated players on the unfairness of the reserve clause. Flood's legal battle also educated skeptical reporters, some of whom criticized the Supreme Court's decision. Flood lost his battle and paid an enormous price—the end of his baseball career—but the players eventually won the war. Every ballplayer—indeed, every professional athlete who has played since Flood's groundbreaking effort—owes him a debt of gratitude.

The combination of Flood's on-field performance and path-breaking challenge to the baseball establishment (so future players might have it better than he did) should be more than enough to get him into the Hall of Fame. In baseball labor history, Flood was as significant in the twentieth century as John Montgomery Ward. Ward, the player and manager who organized baseball's first players' union and the Players' League was inducted into the Hall of Fame in 1964.

Ironically, Flood is already in the Hall of Fame. A copy of the letter he wrote to Commissioner Bowie Kuhn on Christmas Eve in 1969 in which he refused to accept being traded from the Cardinals to the Phillies because "I do not feel that I am a piece of property to be bought and sold irrespective of my wishes" is on display in the Cooperstown shrine. Some observers have described that letter as baseball's declaration of independence.[6]

END BASEBALL'S SWEATSHOPS

MLB owns a sweatshop. That needs to change. Thanks to the players' union, wages and working conditions for major league players have dramatically improved since the 1960s. But a large part of baseball's workforce still labors under sweatshop conditions, including workers in the factory where all baseballs are made.

Every year MLB uses almost 2 million baseballs. They're made in a factory in the remote town of Turrialba, Costa Rica. Reports in both 2004 and 2014 exposed the factory's terrible working conditions, which is now owned jointly by MLB and Rawlings.[7]

MLB's sole supplier of baseballs since 1977, Rawlings moved its baseball factory from Haiti to Costa Rica in 1986 after Haitian dictator Jean-Claude "Baby Doc" Duvalier—with whom the company had a friendly business relationship—was forced out.[8] Costa Rica offered Rawlings a 5,000 square meter free-trade zone in Turrialba for its factory. The company pays no import taxes on the raw materials—cowhide, cork, rubber, and sheep-wool thread—it imports to make the baseballs. Newell Brands, based in Hoboken, New Jersey, owned Rawlings until 2018, when it was purchased for $395 million by a private investment firm, Seidler Equity Partners (SEP), cofounded and led by San Diego Padres general partner Peter Seidler, with MLB owning a 25 percent equity share of the company.[9] SEP also owns LA Fitness.

A 2004 *New York Times* story based on a National Labor Committee report, "Foul Ball," revealed that the Costa Rican workers who stitch major league baseballs were paid 30 cents a ball for balls that were then sold for $15 in U.S. sporting goods stores. According to a local doctor, about 90 percent of the Rawlings workers experienced work pain from minor cuts to disabling injuries, and about one-third of the workers developed carpal tunnel syndrome, an often-debilitating pain and numbness of the hands and wrists. Most workers at the time lasted less than three years on the job. The report called conditions "like being in jail."

The workers who sewed the baseballs had to complete one ball every fifteen minutes. The factory lacked air conditioning and temperatures reached upwards of 97 degrees. Workers were required to ask permission to use bathrooms. The company prohibited workers from speaking to each other on the factory floor. Employees worked an average of eleven to twelve hours per day and had to be available to work on Saturdays or risk being fired.

The *New York Times* story didn't stir MLB to demand that the Rawlings company improve conditions. A 2014 report indicated, a decade later, that things were basically the same. Workers earned $1.88 per hour—about $100 a week—although wages varied based on their productivity. Most Rawlings workers could not make ends meet.

The workers were required to sew 108 stiches per ball by hand. Each stitch had to be perfect. At the time, about three hundred of the factory's employees were sewers while others were assemblers or winders who constructed the ball's core. The terrible pain in workers' arms and wrists, depicted in the 2004 report, continued a decade later due to the "poor ergonomics of hunching over a ball for nine or more hours a day, and performing difficult and meticulous movements repeatedly over the course of years."

According to the 2014 story, workers with injuries were afraid to see a doctor or report their pain for fear of losing their job, with few other jobs available in the area. "We are like machines," said one worker. "It's easier to replace us than to repair us," added another worker. Rawlings often fired workers with injuries rather than provide them with medical care or transferring them to a less strenuous position. "If you miss a quota once, they bother you about it. Twice, they suspend you. The third time they fire you," explained one employee. "The bosses have air-conditioned offices and we're suffocating in there," said a worker interviewed in 2014.

During the 2020 season, shortened by the COVID pandemic, MLB needed fewer baseballs and the Rawlings plant laid off many employees, but the Costa Rican factory was back at full capacity to start the 2021 season, producing baseballs with different specifications to reduce the record number of home runs in 2019.[10] But MLB and Rawlings didn't hire back all the laid-off workers, opting instead to replace them with younger workers.

MLB and the players' union (including major league players) should cosponsor a fact-finding inspection tour of the Costa Rican factory to shine a spotlight on the sweatshop working conditions. Reporters should be permitted to inspect the factory and interview workers with the promise workers will not be punished for talking with the media. MLB and the union should ask the Workers Rights Consortium, a U.S.–based human rights group that monitors working conditions in apparel factories around the world, to conduct a study of the factory's wages and working conditions and make recommendations. As a part-owner of Rawlings, MLB should also agree to a long-term contract to continue the Costa Rican factory operation, pay decent wages, guarantee humane working conditions, and cease any threats to move to a cheaper location. MLB should allow workers at the Costa Rican factory to hold an election to vote for or against a union without interference or intimidation. The union effort should be monitored by a neutral human rights organization.

All uniforms worn by major league players have been made in Palmer Township, near Easton, Pennsylvania, for many years. The five hundred workers are represented by Workers United (a Service Employees International Union affiliate) and have decent pay, working conditions, vacation pay, health care benefits and job security. Ownership of the factory has changed hands several times.[11] Since 2019, the Fanatics company has produced all MLB uniforms at the Pennsylvania factory in partnership with Nike, which owns the licensing rights. The workers make the uniforms, base layers, gameday outerwear, and training apparel as well as MLB–approved "authentic" uniforms sold to the public in stadiums and retail stores. (A Nike-branded jersey at MLBShop.com sells for $359.99.) Nike also sells cheaper "replica" uniforms, made elsewhere, in retail outlets. The ten-year deal was valued at more than $1 billion and brought each MLB team about $3 million in licensing fees. From the deal, Nike now gets to put its swoosh on MLB uniforms.

The employees take pride in their work making the uniforms. Union leader David Melman compares it to making costumes for plays and films rather than standard apparel because each uniform is tailored specifically for each player and is on display before big crowds in stadiums and on television. When players are traded from one team to another, the workers must quickly produce home and away uniforms in time for that player's next game.[12]

For years, all MLB caps were made by the New Era company in its Derby, New York, factory outside Buffalo. In 2019 New Era closed the factory and moved production to non-union facilities in Florida. More than two hundred workers, represented by the Communications Workers of America, lost their jobs. Under its contract with MLB, the hats New Era makes for MLB must be produced in the United States but not necessarily in a union shop.

New Era's move should stir the players' union to insist that MLB purchase all players' uniforms, shoes, bats, caps, and other equipment from union companies that provide decent pay, working conditions, and benefits. These provisions should be incorporated into the next collective bargaining agreement along with a requirement for annual inspections that include major league players.

Players are on their own in choosing their footwear. Companies sign licensing agreements with players for the privilege of associating with big-name athletes. In 2018 Nike made 41 percent of the baseball shoes worn by starting players followed by Adidas (21 percent), New Balance (18 percent), and Under Armour (14 percent).[13] But neither the players nor their union have weighed in on the conditions under which their shoes are produced. Each of these companies is notorious for producing footwear in sweatshops, primarily in Asia.

END PUBLIC SUBSIDIES OF BILLIONAIRE BASEBALL OWNERS

Politicians provide huge taxpayer-funded handouts to professional teams owned by some of the country's richest men, who then make additional millions by selling naming rights to corporations that affix their brand on ballparks such as Citi Field in New York, Target Field in Minnesota, Coors

Field in Denver, Minute Maid Park in Houston, T-Mobile Park in Seattle, and Citizens Bank Park in Philadelphia. Demonstrating no loyalty to local fans and only to the thirst for higher profits, these owners pit cities against each other in search of the most lucrative deals.

At least twenty of the thirty owners of major league teams are billionaires. The poorest owner, Cincinnati Reds owner Bob Castellini, has a net worth of $400 million. Castellini purchased the team in 2016 for $270 million. In 2019, *Forbes* estimated that the Reds were worth $1.05 billion. The richest owner, the Mets' Steve Cohen, is worth $15.9 billion. Most owners inherited their wealth from their families, primarily through real estate, banking, media, and telecommunications.[14]

Owning an MLB team is highly lucrative. In 2019 the average baseball team was worth $1.8 billion, ranging from the Miami Marlins ($1 billion) to the New York Yankees ($4.6 billion), according to *Forbes*. Between 1997 and 2019, team values increased an average of 11 percent per year. In 2018, MLB received $2.7 billion from national television money that it shared equally with the thirty teams. Each team also raises local revenue, primarily from sales of tickets, food, clothing, and parking as well as naming rights and local TV revenues. These local revenues totaled $7.29 billion in 2018—an average of $243 million per team.[15]

How then do politicians justify handing over large sums of taxpayer dollars to these wealthy tycoons? Team owners and local politicians argue that besides providing a big boost of civic pride, local sports teams offer economic benefits to cities and metropolitan regions not only in jobs at the sports facilities but also in "spillover" effects for local businesses.[16] But decades of research have demonstrated that this is a myth. Instead there's been "no discernible positive relationship between sports facility construction and local economic development, income growth, or job creation."[17] The money consumers spend attending professional baseball, football, basketball, or hockey games would otherwise be spent on another entertainment activity and food in the area so it contributes no net gain to the local economy. Sports teams don't employ many people. Most of the stadium jobs—parking lot attendants, food clerks, ushers, and others—are low-wage and part-time.

Some local politicians are no doubt persuaded by campaign contributions from team owners. Others are moved by a sense of civic pride, the belief that a MLB team brings a city prestige and is thus worth subsidizing even if the city lacks sufficient funds to provide adequate schools, infrastructure, housing, and other basic services. Some elected officials and fans have resisted this trend, arguing that the costs of subsidizing a professional sports franchise outweigh the benefits.

How did it start? And when will it end? The first sports stadium built exclusively with public money was Cleveland Stadium, a municipal project that opened in 1931, partly to create jobs for unemployed workers during the Depression. Until the 1950s every other MLB ballpark was built by team owners, who sometimes named the stadiums after themselves such as the Philadelphia Athletics' Shibe Park (1909), the Chicago White Sox' Comiskey Park (1910), the Washington Senators' Griffith Stadium (1911), the Brooklyn Dodgers' Ebbets Field (1913), the Detroit Tigers' Navin Field (1912), and Briggs Stadium (1938).

In 1951 Baseball Commissioner Ford Frick encouraged owners to persuade local governments to provide public subsidies to build and maintain ballparks.[18] The next publicly funded stadium was built in 1953, and Milwaukee used it to lure the Braves away from Boston. The city and county paid for the project.

From 1901 through 1960, MLB had sixteen teams that, with a few exceptions, stayed in the same city. By the 1950s air travel had made it easier for MLB to expand beyond its narrow geographic confines. Besides the Boston Braves moving to Milwaukee in 1953, the St. Louis Browns became the Baltimore Orioles in 1954, the Philadelphia Athletics moved to Kansas City in 1955, and the Brooklyn Dodgers and New York Giants moved to Los Angeles and San Francisco, respectively, in 1958. The Dodgers forged a deal with Los Angeles to trade a minor league stadium for much more valuable real estate close to downtown, Chavez Ravine, where Mexican-American families had been evicted by the city's development agency for public housing, which was never built. The city also paid over $4 million to prepare the site and improve roads for Dodger Stadium. San Francisco built a new stadium, Candlestick Park, for the Giants at a cost of $32 million to taxpayers.

In 1961 the AL expanded from eight to ten teams. The NL followed suit a year later. By 1969, MLB had expanded to twenty-four teams and by 1998 to thirty teams.[19] The collaboration or collusion between pro baseball teams and local governments (which politicians call "public-private partnerships") became well-established. That trend accelerated in subsequent decades as teams pushed cities into bidding wars to attract franchises. Teams routinely move—or threaten to move—to different cities and states.

This is similar to how other major corporations—such as Amazon and Boeing—pit cities against each other to lure them to provide a variety of public subsidies, a form of corporate welfare. In fact, government subsidies to entice corporations to remain or relocate are a boondoggle as demonstrated by numerous studies. These rarely generate the jobs and other economic benefits that politicians and corporate leaders claim.

After persuading the city and county to build a new stadium in 1953, the Braves stayed in Milwaukee for only thirteen years, moving to Atlanta in 1966. To lure the team, Fulton County built Atlanta–Fulton County Stadium for $18 million (equal to $146 million in 2020). The Braves signed a twenty-five-year agreement to play there. The Braves played at County Stadium until 1997, when they moved to Turner Field, the new name for the converted Centennial Olympic Stadium, which had been built with private donations for the 1996 Summer Olympic games in Atlanta. Turner Field was renamed for Ted Turner, CEO of Atlanta-based CNN and Turner Broadcasting, who also owned the Braves. In 2017 the Braves moved to a new stadium, SunTrust Park, built in Cumberland, a suburb ten miles from downtown Atlanta, although the team kept the name Atlanta Braves. In 2020 the stadium was renamed Truist Park as a result of a corporate merger. The stadium, which cost $622 million, was built with $397 million in bonds issued by the Cobb-Marietta Coliseum and Exhibit Hall Authority, a public agency; an additional $14 million from county transportation taxes; and $10 million from local businesses. The public funded almost two-thirds of the facility's cost. The Braves contributed the remaining funds.

Between 2000 and 2015, about $13 billion in public money was spent on thirty-six privately owned sports stadiums (out of the forty-five stadiums built or renovated during that period).[20] The federal government contributed through the use of municipal bonds that exempt federal taxes, while city, county, and state governments absorbed the remaining tab, including long-term exemptions or reductions in property taxes, infrastructure improvements, operating cost subsidies, and cash payments. A Brookings Institution report described the federal subsidy process this way:

> When a stadium is being built, a city can sell municipal bonds to help pay for its construction, like cities often do with public works projects. But if those bonds are issued as tax-exempt bonds (meaning that the interest payments to the bond holders are not counted as taxable income), the federal government loses a large chunk of revenue that it would have collected had the interest payments been taxable. And because this is lost federal revenue, the cost is footed by all taxpayers. On top of that, wealthy citizens who hold the bonds receive an implicit tax benefit due to their relatively high marginal tax rates, costing the federal government even more revenue.[21]

Since 1990, MLB teams have opened twenty-five new parks, most of which replaced existing stadiums, many of which have subsequently been renovated at great cost, and one of which (Globe Life Park in Arlington, Texas) has already been abandoned for a newer stadium in the same city. Most of them received a variety of federal, state, and local government subsidies.

In the 1990s, teams began selling naming rights to their stadiums. At the start of the 2020 season, MLB teams were playing in nineteen ballparks named for banks, insurance companies, a high-tech company, beer makers and other beverage companies, media and telecommunications firms, a pet supplies chain, and a large retailer.

Miller Park in Milwaukee was completed in 2001 to replace County Stadium at a cost of $290 million. Wisconsin's Republican governor Tommy Thompson and Milwaukee Brewers owner (and later baseball commissioner) Bud Selig pushed for a 0.1 percent five-county sales tax to finance the government-owned facility. At the time, many voters objected to using public funds for a privately owned sports team. The Brewers owners threatened to leave Wisconsin if a new stadium wasn't built.[22] The sales tax was initially supposed to sunset as early as 2010 but it was still in place in 2020. Mark Attanasio bought the team from Selig's family in 2004 for $223 million, and by 2019 it was worth $1.17 billion, according to *Forbes*—a five-fold growth in value in fifteen years.[23] Attanasio is now worth $700 million.[24] The Miller Brewing Company purchased the naming rights for $40 million for twenty years. In 2021 the stadium was renamed American Family Field after American Family Insurance Company, which bought the naming rights.

In the 1980s, at the initiative of local businesspeople, city officials in St. Petersburg, Florida, decided to lure a major league team and agreed to build a permanent fixed-dome stadium (to deal with the hot summer weather and thunderstorm threat). Construction began in 1986, at a cost of $130 million before any team had agreed to move to the area. To make room for the new ballpark, the city razed many homes in the Gas Plant Neighborhood, occupied primarily by African American families, reneging on promises to create new affordable housing and an industrial park that would bring jobs to the district. Originally St. Petersburg officials had hoped to entice the Chicago White Sox to relocate to the new ballpark. White Sox owner Jerry Reinsdorf used that offer to persuade the Chicago and Illinois governments to build his team a new stadium. Owned by the State of Illinois through the Illinois Sports Facilities Authority, the new stadium, named Comiskey Park after the team's former owner, was opened for the 1991 season. It was renamed U.S. Cellular Field in 2003 after that corporation purchased the naming rights for $68 million. In 2016 it was renamed Guaranteed Rate Field for a mortgage company that purchased the naming rights for the next thirteen years.

In 1995 MLB agreed to expand to the Tampa Bay area. The new team was called the Tampa Bay Devil Rays and later renamed the Tampa Bay Rays even though the stadium wasn't located in Tampa. Tropicana purchased the naming rights and changed the stadium name to Tropicana Field. The city upgraded the stadium at a cost of $70 million. The Devil Rays played their first game there in 1998.

The city of St. Petersburg has a contract with the Rays to lease the stadium until 2027. But that hasn't stopped Rays owner Stuart Sternberg—who has a net worth of $800 million[25]—from proposing that the team move to another nearby city or that it split home games between the Tampa area and Montreal if the Canadian city will build a new stadium.

Team owners often threaten to pull up stakes and move their franchises to another city if local governments do not help pay for the construction or remodeling of local ballparks. City officials typically don't know if the owners are bluffing and they worry that they will look bad if they allow a team to get away—a blow to civic pride. As a result, cities often compete for the privilege of hosting—and paying for—professional sports franchises despite research showing that government subsidies don't improve the local economy. Professional sports teams have been able to play cities against each other to get them to pony up for stadiums and arenas.

It is time to end this taxpayer charity to baseball's billionaires. Congress should stop the use of tax-exempt municipal bonds for stadium construction. Without tax-exempt bonds, cities and states will think twice about borrowing money to build stadiums because they'd have to borrow at higher interest rates.

But if politicians insist on providing baseball and other professional sports franchises with public subsidies then they should at least insist on including the public in the profits. As *New York Times* columnist Michael Powell wrote about New York City's outrageous subsidy for the construction of the new Yankee Stadium, "a clever city official might have sought an ownership stake" for the city.[26]

In 2013, Orlando was about to seal another deal to build a new $85 million soccer stadium for a new professional franchise—with the team paying just $30 million and the rest coming from the city and county. After seeing the local government help pay for two arenas for the Orlando Magic basketball team without getting a slice of the profits as the team's revenues and value skyrocketed, Orange County commissioner Pete Clark proposed legislation to require sports teams with government subsidies to share the team profits with the public by making the government part owners. Clark said, "I do not want another example of the county expending millions of dollars watching from the sidelines, as our investment climbs in value without the prospects of our taxpayers benefiting."[27] Sportswriter Barry Petchesky called it "the best idea for stadium financing we've ever heard." Under Clarke's plan, the government subsidies would be what stadium finance watchdog Neil DeMause called "an investment, not a gift."[28]

It turned out that Florida's constitution bars local governments from owning businesses except in rare cases involving utilities—a law designed on behalf of private corporations to prohibit competition from the public sector. But that doesn't mean that Florida politicians couldn't have negotiated to get a slice of the revenues from the new team. Their reluctance to do so was not a matter of law but of political cowardice.

In 2011, after owner Frank McCourt mismanaged the Dodgers and steered it close to bankruptcy, MLB insisted that he sell the team. That led Los Angeles City Council member Janice Hahn to propose that the city purchase the team. After being elected to Congress later that year, she cosponsored a bill (with Congressman Earl Blumenauer of Oregon) to allow public ownership of professional sports teams. She called it the Give Fans a Chance Act, explaining, "Fans across this country have really been upset with many of the owners who really are all about corporate greed and profits, and not so much about the team or the fans." The bill would have given public entities 180 days to make an offer on a team when an owner announces plans to move the team to another city but it never came to a vote.[29]

As Neil deMause, coauthor of *Field of Schemes*, has observed, "if the goal of fronting cash for new sports venues is to keep team owners from using their monopoly-given right to skip town and leave fans with no one to root for, then one workaround is obvious: cut out the middleman, and buy the team."[30] Under such an arrangement, according to one analysis, the team's "revenue would stay with the team, and not vanish into a greedy owner's pocket."[31]

This idea isn't as radical as some might think. Many state governments own profitable football teams and stadiums. They are called state universities, and their football and basketball operations are typically profit centers for large universities. Perhaps more relevant, several professional sports franchises have been owned by either community-based nonprofit organizations or local governments. The NFL's Green Bay Packers were incorporated in 1923 as a private, nonprofit, tax-exempt organization. The bylaws state that "this association shall be a community project, intended to promote community welfare . . . Its purposes shall be exclusively charitable." A board of directors, elected by the stockholders, manages the team. The team can move out of Green Bay if the franchise is dissolved.

The Appleton Wisconsin Timber Rattlers, a Class-A affiliate of the Milwaukee Brewers, are structured as a nonprofit like the Packers. Appleton has had a minor league team since the 1890s but in 1994 city officials worried that the team, then called the Appleton Foxes, would leave because Goodland Field ballpark, built in 1940, required expensive repairs to meet minor league standards. The city agreed to build a modern facility, 5,500-seat Fox Cities Stadium, owned by a public agency, the Fox Cities Sports Authority. The ballpark is leased to the Appleton Baseball Club, a non-stock, community-owned, nonprofit organization. It has 240 members, each of whom bought from one to fifty shares in the team at $25 per share. They elect a twenty-one-member board of directors who in turn elect an eight-member executive committee. Because the team is a nonprofit organization, its revenues are pumped back into the team and the stadium.

The Toledo Mud Hens, a Detroit Tigers farm team, are owned and operated by the nonprofit Toledo Mud Hens Baseball Club. This ownership arrangement began in 1965 when Lucas County formed a nonprofit corporation to buy and manage the team. The county board of commissioners appoints a volunteer board of directors that operates the team with the county as the ultimate financial benefactor. In 2016 *Forbes* ranked the Mud Hens as the twelfth most-valuable minor league franchise, worth $35.5 million, with an operating income of $2.7 million on $12.5 million in revenue.

One of the biggest obstacles to public or community ownership of major league teams is the unwillingness of MLB's owners—who must approve the sale of any franchise—to support that approach. After her husband and McDonald's founder Roy Kroc died in 1984, his widow Joan wanted to donate the Padres to the City of San Diego as a charitable donation plus $100 million for operating expenses. But the MLB owners vetoed the plan. Instead she sold the team in 1990 for $75 million to Tom Werner and a group of fifteen Southern California businessmen. In 1994 John Moores purchased the Padres from the Werner group for $80 million. In 2012 Moores sold the team for $800 million to a group led by Ron Fowler (CEO of Liquid Investments, a San Diego beer distributorship); professional golfer Phil Mickelson; and four heirs of the O'Malley family, former owners of the Brooklyn and Los Angeles Dodgers. Between 2012 and 2019 the franchise's value grew from $458 million to $1.3 billion with $49 million in profits. The taxpayers and residents of San Diego received none of that bonanza.

Public ownership—or at least some form of revenue-sharing between teams and cities—could give fans and the local community a stronger stake and voice in major league teams. That doesn't mean that city council members or local baseball enthusiasts would decide who is pitching on a specific day or whether to trade a poorly performing player. All teams hire professional management to run teams.

But while MLB owners block communities from buying local teams, the owners changed the rules in 2019 to allow more Wall Street investors to purchase shares of teams.[32] Even more than local owners, Wall Street investors have a bigger focus on short-term profit than long-term success and even less loyalty to particular communities. At some point baseball fans might have to start their own version of Occupy Wall Street.

MLBPA SHOULD BUILD TIES BETWEEN PLAYERS, THE LABOR MOVEMENT, AND BASEBALL FANS

Soon after the New York Yankees arrived in Boston to play the Red Sox in the 2019 AL division series, the Yankee players crossed union picket lines at the Ritz-Carlton hotel where housekeepers, cooks, doormen, and other hotel workers were in the second day of a strike. About 1,500 members of Unite Here, the hotel workers' union, had walked out October 3 at seven Boston Marriott-owned hotels, including the Ritz-Carlton. They wanted Marriott to provide steadier hours, health insurance, higher pay, more job security, and pension protection for employees approaching retirement. Two weeks later, when the Dodgers came to Boston to play the Red Sox in the World Series, they also crossed the picket line at the same hotel. The players acted like the Ritz-Carlton's striking workers were invisible.

"As a lifelong Yankee fan and a proud New Yorker, I am disgusted the management of a team representing the strongest union town in America would choose a hotel where workers are on strike," said Mario Cilento, president of the New York State AFL–CIO. Brian Lang, president of the Boston branch of Unite Here (Local 26), also criticized the players for crossing his members' picket line.

Donald "D." Taylor, the international president of Unite Here, pointed out that despite their millions, many of the players come from backgrounds like the striking workers. "We wanted the Yankees to at least talk to our strikers and express their support," Taylor said. "Whether they are from the Dominican Republic or the United States, these are people who could be the players' mothers and fathers. It's time for them to speak out."[33]

The players' union issued a statement of support for the strikers but not a single Yankee or Dodger player bothered to join the picket line or walk out of the hotel and demand that the team find another union hotel, where workers aren't on strike, for the players, coaches, and other personnel to stay in. A photo-op of a player on the picket line would have gone a long way to put the players in the good graces of baseball fans who, like most Americans, have seen their wages and family incomes stagnate or even decline over the past few decades.

To avoid putting major league players in such an embarrassing situation again, the MLBPA should insert language in their union contract that requires teams to stay in union hotels and prohibits teams from staying in hotels where workers are in the middle of a labor dispute with management so players don't have to cross picket lines. (Only three of the twenty-six cities with major league teams—Cincinnati, Tampa, and Arlington, Texas—don't have union hotels.)

MLB owners have tried to take advantage of the public's perception that baseball players and other professional athletes are excessively paid. Ordinary fans may find it difficult to sympathize with ballplayers whose starting salary is $555,000 even if they know that the typical player spends only four years in the majors.

The MLBPA needs to improve its public image to gain the support and sympathy of baseball fans. These athletes and their union need to demonstrate their solidarity with the sports industry's working class and with the struggles and everyday lives of their fans.

Both MLB and the MLBPA failed that test during the coronavirus pandemic. Over the course of an eighty-one-game home season, at least two thousand different people work at each stadium serving the food and drinks, selling and taking tickets, selling concessions like caps and shirts, providing security, helping park cars, picking up the trash, and cleaning the bathrooms. Most of them piece together a very modest income by working at home games during the baseball season and working at other venues in the same city—the baseball and soccer stadiums, the hockey rinks, the basketball arenas, and the convention centers. While the owners and players were negotiating whether, how, and when to re-open the baseball season, these stadium workers were the shutdown's real victims. While highly paid athletes could weather the storm of an economic shutdown, the stadium workers lost their jobs, income, health insurance, and even their homes. They were among the millions of workers nationwide who were laid off or had their work hours dramatically cut. The double whammy of a major economic downtown and a public health crisis was unprecedented in American history.

The shutdown of professional sports cost the teams substantial revenue. But most of the owners of pro basketball, football, hockey, soccer, and baseball franchises are billionaires or at least multimillionaires. Two months into the shutdown, *USA Today* surveyed ninety-one professional sports teams and discovered that only about twenty-nine had a compensation plan that included employees of the teams' contractors—who represent the vast majority of workers at baseball and soccer stadiums, and hockey and basketball arenas.[34]

The first response came from some NBA players, but soon a handful of MLB players—the Astros' George Springer, Justin Verlander, Carlos Correa, and Alex Bregman; the Indians' Trevor Bauer; the Cubs' Jason Hayward; and the Braves' Freddie Freeman—announced they were making cash donations to stadium workers, to local food banks and other charities, and for medical equipment to help working families during the pandemic. In response, MLB and the MLBPA supplemented this effort with a joint $1 million donation to two nonprofit groups—Feeding America and Meals on Wheels America—to help fight hunger caused by school closures and quarantines caused by the coronavirus pandemic. After dragging its feet, MLB finally announced that each team would also donate $1 million—$30 million in total—to provide relief for ballpark employees laid off during the coronavirus outbreak.[35] A few teams kicked in more.

Each team's contribution didn't stretch very far: between $300 and $700 for each employee, depending on how long they had worked. And in some cities the money only went to workers employed directly by the team even though the vast majority were employed by third-party contractors like Aramark, Compass, and Delaware North.[36] In response to protests by Unite Here, the union that represents many of these workers, most teams sent checks to these workers but the checks barely covered half a month's rent.

The fate of professional sports' blue-collar workers shouldn't depend on the whims and compassion of a handful of owners and players to help them cover basic necessities during hard times. The federal government needs to address the health and economic plight of workers hurt by crises not of their own making—including earthquakes, tornadoes, pandemics, and economic recession. But wealthy employers, like major league teams and their owners, also have a responsibility to pay their full-time and part-time stadium employees a living wage with decent benefits and to provide sick leave, health insurance, and pension benefits.

If MLBPA members vote for another strike, they should establish a fund to help stadium employees make ends meet during the players' work stoppage but also negotiate with owners to ensure stadium workers don't suffer as a result of the strike. The MLBPA should also follow the NFL Players Association's example and join the AFL–CIO, the organization that promotes solidarity among all unions.

More broadly, the MLBPA should encourage its members to express solidarity with other workers facing tough times. Baseball needs fans who make enough money to afford the increasing cost of tickets, parking, and hot dogs at the stadiums. Walking picket lines with striking workers is only one such gesture. When schoolteachers, nurses, factory workers, hotel employees, utility company employees, and others are negotiating contracts with their employers, a statement of support from major league players would help draw public attention to their struggle. When unions, faith groups, and community organizations are pushing local and state governments, and Congress, to raise the minimum wage to a living wage, ballplayers could express their backing for the plan. When Congress is debating a bill like the Protect the Right to Organize Act to reform the nation's labor laws to level the playing field and give workers a fair chance to form a union, an endorsement from major league players would help promote the campaign.

But athletes can do much more to challenge the political status quo. Tennis superstar Billie Jean King testified before Congress and spoke out frequently for Title IX, the federal anti-discrimination provision in the education amendments of 1972. Thanks to that law, the number of high school girls who participate in sports has increased from 294,015 in 1972 to 3.3 million in 2015.

When was the last time you saw a major league baseball player standing in front of a post office or grocery store, holding voter-registration forms, or walking precincts and door-knocking in low-income and working neighborhoods urging people to vote? If athletes ventured onto the streets to participate in rallies, protests, and pickets about police abuses, voter suppression, workers' rights, or deportation of immigrants, their gestures would generate considerable media attention for these causes. Billboards that say "Mookie Betts Wants You to Vote" or "Sean Doolittle Says: Tell Your Congressperson to Raise the Minimum Wage" could be powerful rallying forces and demonstrate that athletes are concerned about their country and its working families.

UNIONIZE MINOR LEAGUE PLAYERS

In 1922 the U.S. Supreme Court absurdly ruled that professional baseball was not engaged in interstate commerce and was thus exempt from federal anti-trust laws. Since then MLB has used its political clout to preserve this status, which allows baseball's corporate titans to conspire in ways that would otherwise violate the anti-trust laws such as MLB's amateur draft, its control over the sale of rival teams, its licensing of intellectual property rights, and its ability to block the movement of teams to cities where they would compete with another MLB franchise.

The MLBPA fought hard to overturn the reserve clause and dismantle the semi-feudal system that had ruled professional baseball for most of its history. But minor league players still live under that system. Under the collective bargaining agreement between MLBPA and MLB, minor league players—who had no voice in that deal—are still subject to their team's absolute control. As a result they endure pay and working conditions far different from how the general public perceives the lives of professional athletes.

After leading Trinity University to the NCAA Division III Baseball Championship and graduating with a degree in communications in 2016, outfielder Jeremy Wolf was drafted by the New York Mets in the thirty-first round of the baseball draft. The Mets sent him to play with the team's rookie franchise in Kingsport, Tennessee. [37]

He batted .290 and was promoted the next season to the Class-A Brooklyn Cyclones. The season lasted seven months, March through September. As Wolf explained,

> March was unpaid. April—unpaid. May—unpaid. Sixteen days in June—unpaid. For 8–10 hours a day, six days a week, for sixteen weeks, I made $0. For my short season (72 games), I was paid $45 per game, or $3 an hour for 70 hours a week. I was guaranteed two meals in my contract and rarely got food to eat. I had to purchase my own equipment (bats, cleats, batting gloves, first base mitt, etc.), rent, travel, and $80 a month for a group of rich high schoolers to clean my jersey. I played in front of 8,000 people a night and went to bed hungry. I made less money that summer than the batboy and after seven months of work, I left with less money than when I started, and $2,000 in credit card debt.[38]

He was released after that season after a back injury that ended his professional baseball career.

Wolf's experience isn't unusual. Minor league players can't make ends meet. In 2019 the starting salary was $1,100 a month—a poverty-level wage. Players only get paid during the baseball season.[39] Salaries range from as little as $2,750 to $14,500 per year.[40] The average player salary is about $7,500 a year. During the season, minor league players work between 60 and 70 hours a week including travel to and from both home and away games, practice, and the games themselves.[41]

Players work and live in terrible conditions. They often lack the money to eat three square meals a day. Many rely on their parents, or wife, to help pay their rent, food, and cell phone bills. Some teams don't provide players with bats and gloves.[42] It is hard to find landlords willing to rent apartments for a four-, five-, or six-month period especially in small towns and small cities. Rent is high so players wind up living in overcrowded apartments with teammates. When minor league players are released, traded, or promoted, they often don't get their first month rent deposit back. Some minor leaguers can fall back on the money they received from one-time signing bonuses, but most players sign for as little as $1,000 and 40 percent sign for $10,000 or less.[43]

Pitcher Dirk Hayhurst was signed by the San Diego Padres in 2003 after starring for Kent State University for four years. In his first season in the minors, playing for the Padres' affiliate in Eugene, Oregon, he was paid $800 a month. After paying for housing, taxes, clubhouse dues, and insurance, he had little left to make ends meet. He and his teammates would "look at our checks and have sad, satirical chuckles, punctuated with the now tongue-in-cheek phrase, 'Living the dream!' Over time, however, it became much less funny." While playing in the low minors, he lived without a refrigerator. "I had a Styrofoam cooler in which I put milk and bread with ice I took from hotels. I didn't have any means by which to cook raw food—no range, not even a microwave. I lived entirely off of peanut butter and jelly simply because it wouldn't spoil, and it's what I could afford." During spring training, the team gave players $120 per week in meal money—$17 a day. "I bought a glass bowl with a lid and used it to make pasta in the hotel microwave or reheat the food I snuck from the complex."[44]

The wife of one of Hayhurst's teammates on his Double-A team gave birth to their second daughter in the Dominican Republic. "We all put money in a hat to help him get home to see her because neither he nor his wife could afford to visit the other on the wages we were paid," he wrote. Playing for the Triple-A Portland Beavers in 2006, his sixth year in the minors, Hayhurst shared a two-bedroom apartment with two other players and their wives and kids. He had the least seniority so he slept on an air mattress in the living room. During the off season Hayhurst worked two or three jobs, sleeping on the floor of a friend's home, and working out at a nearby school gym, too poor to afford a gym membership.

Even players on Triple-A teams—just a step below the majors—live precarious lives. In the middle of the 2018 season, twenty-five-year-old Jonathan Perrin, a pitcher for the Colorado Springs Sky Sox, the Milwaukee Brewers Triple-A affiliate, gave an NPR reporter a tour of the spare apartment he shared with three teammates. "So this is kind of it. This is the living room with the only furniture being a twin mattress." He said his situation made him feel "like you're camping out. Except as a professional baseball player."

During his off seasons, Perrin worked in restaurants and as a substitute teacher. "One off-season," he explained. "I would wake up at 6 a.m., go throw at 7, do all my arm care stuff, shower, go to work, from 8 to 2, then work out from 2:30 to 4, then go home and eat. Then I'd give pitching lessons from 5 or 6 to 8 p.m. And that was the routine for three, four months."

"I'm not sitting here saying everybody [in the minors] should get 50 grand or whatever," Perrin said. "I mean, we know what we signed up for. Just help give us a chance to continue to develop and not have to be drawn in so many different directions trying to pay our bills during the times when we're not actually playing." Just getting paid the minimum wage for the entire year would be an improvement, he said.

Perrin thinks that major league teams should pay their minor leaguer players year-round. "Just keep the salary structure the same," he said "but make it a 12-month thing where we can help cover our costs in the off-season, which is the toughest part of it." He also thinks that the big-league teams should cover the minor league players' housing expenses year-round. That, he says, is "the biggest cause of stress and that's what eats away at most of your paycheck."[45] For players, year-long pay would not only improve their working and housing conditions during the season but also allow them to concentrate on staying in shape and training during the off-season.

The Professional Baseball Agreement spells out the relationship between the major league teams and their minor league affiliates. Typically major league teams pay for the players and coaching staff and minor league teams pay for the fields, equipment, uniforms, and travel.[46] Just as Walmart and Nike squeeze their overseas contractors by demanding they produce toys and clothing at lower and lower prices, major league teams have been squeezing their minor league affiliates to pay for upgraded facilities without compensating them for the cost. The Minnesota Twins demanded that its affiliate in Elizabethton, Tennessee, a small town of fourteen thousand, spend $1 million modernizing the clubhouse at the city-owned ballpark. The town coughed up the money by delaying its police station renovation. Likewise the Kansas City Royals—whose owner and CEO David Glass was the former CEO of Walmart—forced its Lexington, Kentucky, affiliate to spend $140,000 to improve the Whitaker Bank Park infield.[47] The public also subsidizes much of MLB's job-training costs by funding baseball programs at state universities.

Minor league teams provide families with inexpensive entertainment but having a minor league team in a small city or town adds little overall economic value to municipal coffers. According to one study, minor league franchises only increase a community's per capita income by between $67 and $250 because fans who spend their money on tickets and food would otherwise spend the same amount elsewhere in the area. Despite this, minor league owners often persuade local governments to subsidize their teams. Local officials view the presence of a minor league franchise as a source of community pride and prestige even if it isn't an economic engine.[48]

Attendance at minor league games has been steadily increasing. In 2019, 41.5 million fans went to minor league games, a 2.6 percent increase over the previous year.[49] Some minor league franchises are highly profitable. An analysis by *Forbes* discovered that in 2016 the twenty most-valuable minor league teams were worth an average of $37.5 million, an increase of 35 percent in the previous three years.[50]

The minor league clubs—often called "farm teams"—are essentially job-training programs for major league baseball. The major league teams expect the athletes to make sacrifices for the privilege of competing to climb into the better-paying major leagues. It is, owners claim, and many players agree, the price they pay for pursuing their baseball dream. So they endure the misery of life in the minors because if they complain, they fear they will be blacklisted by their parent club. But 80 percent of draft picks will never wear a major league uniform.[51]

In 2014 attorney Garrett Broshuis, who pitched in the minor leagues from 2004 to 2009, sued MLB on behalf of forty-five former minor league players. "The organization traces its roots to the nineteenth century," according to the suit, filed in a California district court. "Unfortunately for many of its employees, its wage and labor practices remain stuck there."[52]

The suit, *Senne v. Office of the Commissioner of Baseball*, was the first legal challenge to MLB's minor league labor practices. It claimed that MLB and its thirty teams violated the federal Fair Labor Standards Act by failing to follow federal minimum wage and overtime rules for minor league players during the season and by paying players nothing at all for spring training, fall instructional leagues, and mandatory off-season workout programs.[53]

The lead plaintiff, Aaron Senne, played first base and outfield for the Miami Marlins' low minor league teams from 2010 to 2013. He was drafted by the Marlins in the tenth round of the 2009 MLB draft after an outstanding four years playing for the University of Missouri, hitting .400 with 16 homers in his senior year. Plagued by injuries, he never got higher than Single-A and retired in June 2013. In the lawsuit, Senne says that he was paid about $3,000 for the entire 2010 season, $3,000 in 2011, about $7,000 in 2012, and $3,000 in 2013.[54]

Not surprisingly, MLB opposed the lawsuit. "We've said from the beginning that Minor League Baseball was never meant to be covered by those [federal] minimum wage laws," said Baseball Commissioner Rob Manfred.[55] "Well it's pretty rare that people get paid when they don't work. It's sort of the way it works: you go to work, you get paid for the part of the year," Manfred said. (Manfred didn't mention that *he* gets paid all year.)

Most business leaders warn that higher wages, unions, and government regulations are "job killers."[56] Owners of both major and minor league teams are no different. If the *Senne* lawsuit succeeded, claimed Gary Ulmer, president of the Louisville Bats club, "Teams like the Louisville Bats, Bowling Green Hot Rods, and Lexington Legends may well disappear, along with a source of wholesome entertainment for Kentucky families, and an economic generator for those cities."[57]

Paying minor leaguers a minimum wage, and compensating them for spring training, would cost MLB teams a total of $5.5 million a year.[58] But MLB refused to do this. Instead, in response to the lawsuit, MLB spent at least $2.6 million in 2016 and 2017 to quietly lobby Congress to insulate itself from this and future legal challenges to its minor league labor practices.[59] It persuaded Congress to insert a one-page provision, the Save America's Pastime Act, into a 2,232-page omnibus federal spending bill. That bill, signed by President Trump in March 2018, requires teams to pay players the minimum wage for forty hours a week during the regular season but not during the off season or even spring training. It was drafted to shut down the lawsuit by defining minor league players as seasonal employees not subject to federal wage and overtime rules.[60]

MLB was obviously worried by minor leaguers displaying the kind of solidarity needed to win improvements in pay and working conditions. Minor league baseball president Pat O'Conner warned that increased labor costs could cause minor league teams to shut down. In 2019 Manfred proposed eliminating 42 minor league teams, more than one-quarter of the 160 minor league affiliates, mostly teams in small towns and cities like the Bluefield (West Virginia) Blue Jays, the Lancaster (California) JetHawks, and the Lexington (Kentucky) Legends. The plan wiped out entire leagues like the eighty-year-old Pioneer League with eight teams in Montana, Idaho, Utah, and Colorado.[61]

Under Manfred's plan, which he implemented before the 2021 season, 22 states lost their minor league teams and 14 million people are now at least 50 miles away from a minor league team, which are both more affordable and more accessible than major league teams.[62] The plan cut the baseball draft from forty to twenty rounds. Each team is limited to four full-season affiliates. It eliminated the short-season rookie league and sends prospects—whose numbers would be cut in half—to each team's training complex.[63]

Slashing the number of players in the draft eliminates the likelihood of long-odds players finding a way to sign a contract and climb their way into the majors—players like Freddie Patek, a 5-foot-5-inch shortstop who was a twenty-second-round pick but who wound up playing the majors from 1968 to 1981 and became a three-time All-Star; and Hall of Fame catcher Mike Piazza, who was drafted in the sixty-second round, the 1,390th player picked in 1988.

In March 2019 the Toronto Blue Jays announced that it would unilaterally give every player in its minor league system a roughly 50 percent salary increase. "It puts us right now up at the top of the scale in the industry," said Ben Cherington, the Jays vice president of baseball operations. "My hope is it doesn't stay that way. My hope is other teams eventually do the same."[64] The Jays owners didn't explain why they made that move but it may have had something to do with Canada's political culture, which has a stronger labor movement than the United States, considerably less poverty, and more income equality.[65]

A few months later in August 2019, the U.S. Court of Appeals for the Ninth Circuit handed the baseball players a legal victory, allowing them to proceed as a class action lawsuit and challenge the new law railroaded through Congress by MLB and signed by Trump.[66] Six months later, MLB—no doubt concerned that it would not only lose the lawsuit but also damage its already troubled reputation—capitulated and decided to follow the Blue Jays' lead. In February 2020 MLB announced that starting in 2021 teams would give minor league players a pay increase of between 38 percent and 72 percent. Players at rookie and short-season levels would get a minimum weekly pay raise from $290 to $400—meaning they could earn $4,800 during the three-month season. Players in Class A would get an increase from $290 to $500 a week, Double-A players would see a jump from $350 to $600, and Triple-A would go from $502 to $700 a week, or a maximum of $14,000 for the five month season.[67] (The major league minimum was $563,500 in 2020.)

"It's a start, but there's a long way to go before these young players are being compensated and treated fairly," said MLBPA president Tony Clark.[68] "Even with this increase, the majority of players are still going to be paid at a level that's below the poverty line," said Broshuis. "And this increase doesn't do anything about the players who are required to report to spring training and extended spring training, and who aren't paid at all during those work periods," he said. "This is an encouraging step, but more work needs to be done, without a doubt."[69]

But the battle to improve minor league conditions isn't likely to end with MLB's voluntarily action. What MLB can give, MLB can take away. Although players are glad for the pay raise, the larger structural issues—MLB's almost unilateral power over minor leaguers' playing and working conditions—remains intact.

In 2018, the year after his playing career ended, Jeremy Wolf launched a website—morethanbaseball.org—as a first step toward creating a nonprofit organization where fans could donate money to support minor league players—especially those without an agent—with equipment, food, housing, and student loans. "A lot of guys are struggling," he said.[70] The website's mission statement includes this sentence: "We believe that all ballplayers deserve proper housing, food, and equipment." He hoped that the website would generate discussion among minor league players and catalyze a union movement. He explained, "Even minor league umpires have a union and Major League

Baseball has its own union. But minor league players are kind of on their own island. I want this [website] to be a kind of backbone. That support."[71]

"The situation facing minor leaguers will not be resolved through litigation and it won't be resolved through legislation," said Bill Fletcher, former assistant to the president for the national AFL–CIO. "It's going to be solved through organization."[72] In March 2020 Broshuis and several other former minor league players launched a new organization, Advocates for Minor Leaguers, dedicated to fighting to improve minor league pay and working conditions, including a demand to double players' salaries to $15,000 a year.

"Even though they work in an industry with over $10 billion in annual revenue that is enjoying record profits, minor league baseball players are among the most poorly paid workers in America. Advocates for Minor Leaguers seeks to change that," Broshuis said. The other cofounders included Bill Fletcher; Ty Kelly (a retired MLB player); Matt Paré (a former minor league player who made the YouTube channel "Homeless Minor Leaguer" as a player);[73] Raul Jacobson (a former minor league player who attended law school after his playing career was over); Lisa Raphael (producer of an Emmy Award–winning documentary about minor league life for the Brooklyn Cyclones); and a current longtime MLB player who wished to remain anonymous.

"Minor leaguers have been systematically silenced for decades," said Kelly. "They enter this time of great uncertainty equipped only with the hope that their basic needs will finally not go forgotten. They need a voice more than ever."[74] Some minor leaguers had hoped that the MLPBA would help fund a union organizing drive among minor league players but that hasn't happened. Several other unions—including the Professional Hockey Players Association, which represents minor league hockey players—expressed an interest. The biggest obstacle was overcoming the players' fear that they would be blacklisted if they participated in a union campaign or that MLB would carry out its threat to shut down minor league teams.[75]

Commissioner Manfred's elimination of forty-two minor league teams saves MLB about $20 million. That's chump-change for the billionaires who own major league teams. Moreover, the combined annual pay for all minor league players is currently less than $10 million a year.[76] MLB—which earned $10.7 billion in revenue in 2019—can afford to pay minor league players decent wages and provide decent working conditions. Each of the thirty major league teams has about two hundred players in its minor league system. If MLB raised each player's salary to $2,000 a month year-round ($24,000 per player), that would translate to an additional $4.8 million per team. That's roughly the average salary of *one* major league player.[77]

Following Manfred's contraction announcement, Sean Doolittle posted a link to an article about the proposal, observing, "This is really sad and I hope it doesn't happen." Doolittle tweeted that

> it would eliminate an MLB opportunity for over a thousand players. It would also remove thousands of jobs from local economies in small towns where minor league baseball is (a) convenient and affordable way for fans to watch our sport in person. It also doesn't feel like a good way to grow our sport? Especially when MLB attendance is on the decline . . . I wish the conversation was about finding ways to improve the existing structure of minor league baseball (paying players more, improving facilities, etc.) rather than tearing it down to try and save money.[78]

Two days later, Senator Bernie Sanders of Vermont said "Sean is absolutely right. Closing Minor League teams, like the Vermont Lake Monsters, would be a disaster for baseball fans, workers, and communities across the country. We must protect these teams from corporate greed."[79] The Lake Monsters are an affiliate of the Oakland Athletics whose owner, John Fisher also owns GAP, which he inherited from his parents. Fisher is worth $2.8 billion and is a major donor to political causes and charter schools.[80] As Sanders knows, Fisher can afford to keep a minor league team in Burlington.

MLB, Sanders said,

> is a business that uniquely receives an antitrust exemption from the United States Congress and over the years has received many hundreds of millions of dollars in corporate welfare from communities all over this country where taxpayers build stadiums for their owners. So this is a business that must respond to the needs of the American people, and you cannot do that—they should not do that—by shutting down baseball in 42 communities around this country.[81]

Although Sanders led the charge, his support was bipartisan. More than one hundred members of Congress—Democrats and Republicans, including

House Minority Leader Kevin McCarthy, a California Republican whose district includes the Lancaster JetHawks—sent a letter to Manfred expressing outrage about his "radical proposal" to eliminate teams that provide "affordable, family-friendly entertainment to members of our communities, support scores of allied businesses, employ thousands of individuals, donate millions of dollars in charitable funds, and connect our communities to Major League Baseball."[82]

The unequal power relationship between MLB and its minor league teams and players gives MLB a huge advantage. As major league players learned after Marvin Miller became head of the MLBPA, only a labor union will give minor leagues the voice they need to improve their pay and working conditions. And only public pressure by fans and politicians will thwart the efforts of MLB to increase team profits on the backs of minor league players and the cities and towns that host their teams.

DEMILITARIZE BASEBALL

President Dwight D. Eisenhower once reportedly proclaimed, "The true mission of American sports is to prepare young people for war."[83] But according to Boston College professor Michael Serazio, author of *The Power of Sports: Media and Spectacle in American Culture*, "the true mission of American sports is to remind the nation that it remains ever at war. Since the 9/11 attacks, professional leagues have pursued that mission single-mindedly."[84]

Few Americans objected when ballplayers helped raise money for war bonds during World War II. Nobody cries foul when ballplayers visit wounded veterans at military hospitals or when fans cheer a returning soldier who is honored at a ball game. These are examples of ballplayers and fans being patriotic citizens. But baseball, like other professional sports, often crosses the line to become an instrument of U.S. imperialism and militarism. In this book we've discussed the use of baseball to promote corporate America's overseas investments and to impose American culture on nations the United States is seeking to influence.

After 9/11, MLB ramped up its displays of patriotism, including weekend-long Armed Forces Day celebrations that included players wearing camouflage-speckled special uniforms as well as uniforms with a patch inscription, "Lest we forget." Commissioner Bud Selig postponed the full schedule of games for six days—the longest stoppage (other than for strikes) since World War I forced the cancellation of the final month of the 1918 season. When play resumed on September 17, Selig ordered every team to play "God Bless America" during the seventh-inning stretch in addition to or instead of "Take Me Out to the Ball Game." Players on every team wore the Stars and Stripes on their uniform.[85]

During the first game of the 2001 World Series between the Arizona Diamondbacks and the Yankees, soldiers unfurled a giant American flag on the field at Bank One Ballpark. When the series moved to Yankee Stadium for the third game, 56,000 people sang "God Bless America" as a tattered flag—recovered at the World Trade Center site—fluttered on a pole over the center-field scoreboard.

The question of why professional sports requires the playing of the national anthem at games is rarely asked. After all it isn't part of the ritual at plays, concerts, movie theaters, and even public schools. Some fans who refused to participate in the ritual faced verbal harassment from other spectators. As noted earlier, during the 2004 season Toronto Blue Jays slugger Carlos Delgado remained in the dugout to protest the U.S. invasion of Iraq. Delgado took a great deal of flak for his stance while nobody attacked Blue Jays president Paul Godfrey when he criticized the Canadian government for not sending troops to Iraq.

Similar protests reached a crescendo in 2016 when NFL quarterback Colin Kaepernick refused to stand for the national anthem to protest U.S. racism. President Trump sought to redefine Kaepernick's gesture as an anti-American statement of disloyalty. Kaepernick's protest had significant ripple effects across the country. Many other NFL players, some NBA players, and athletes in high school and college sports followed his example. Bruce Maxwell, an African American catcher for the Oakland A's, was the first MLB player to take a knee during the national anthem but others eventually followed his example.

The late Senator John McCain, a decorated war hero, criticized what he called "paid-for patriotism" when the U.S. military signed contracts with MLB (and other sports) to help market the armed services with garish and expensive displays of military might. Ironically, baseball and other major sports have become part of what Eisenhower warned the nation about back in 1961: the military-industrial complex.

In 2015 McCain issued a 150-page report investigating the $53 billion that the U.S. military had spent during the previous four years on advertising with professional and even university sports teams. At least $6.8 million was spent on "paid-for patriotism" tributes. Team-by-team it listed the events paid for by the Department of Defense at sports events. According to the report,

> DOD paid for patriotic tributes at professional football, baseball, basketball, hockey, and soccer games. These paid tributes included on-field color guard, enlistment and reenlistment ceremonies, performances of the national anthem, full-field flag details, ceremonial first pitches and puck drops. The National Guard paid teams for the "opportunity" to sponsor military appreciation nights and to recognize its birthday. It paid the Buffalo Bills to sponsor its Salute to the Service game. DOD even paid teams for the "opportunity" to perform surprise welcome home promotions for troops returning from deployments and to recognize wounded warriors.[86]

The McCain report didn't clarify how much MLB teams were paid for their military marketing efforts, but it did include several examples, including $49,000 the Wisconsin Army National Guard paid the Milwaukee Brewers in 2014 to sponsor the playing of "God Bless America" at Sunday home games along with displaying the National Guard's logo on the ballpark's video board. The Brewers were also paid $10,000 for a promotion to recognize soldiers and their families and provide twelve passes to each of four Brewers home games and another $7,500 for twelve field-access passes for National Guard members to perform an on-field award presentation and throw out the ceremonial first pitch before three Brewers home games as well as a private suite rental for two of those games. The DOD paid the Philadelphia Phillies over $46,000 for tickets and food to home games. It paid the Mets $10,000 for a swearing-in ceremony at Citi Field.[87]

When fighter jets fly over baseball stadiums at the start of games, the taxpayers foot the bill and the major league teams pocket the profits. When team announcers introduce military women and men waving to the fans at home plate, what appear to be displays of support turn out to be parts of a propaganda campaign paid by the military as a fee-for-service to major league owners. "If the most compelling message about military service we can deliver to prospective recruits and influencers is the promise of game tickets, gifts and player appearances, we need to rethink our approach to how we are inspiring qualified men and women to military service," explained McCain's report. McCain cosponsored an amendment to the next year's defense spending bill to prohibit the use of taxpayer money to pay for military tributes at sporting events.

In 2018 the Mets fired Nick Francona, a former scout sniper platoon commander in Afghanistan who had been the team's assistant director of player development, for his criticism of MLB profiting from these paid-for celebrations, including proceeds from military-theme apparel worn by players on Memorial Day. He found the displays of faux patriotism at ballparks "offensive." Meanwhile, he pointed out, only ten of MLB's roughly five thousand employees were military veterans.[88]

Every year, MLB celebrates Armed Forces Day as a tribute to the American military. In 2021, for example, players on every team were required to wear caps in military camouflage colors on that day. Players wore shoes that said "Home of the brave" on the back of one shoe and "Land of the free" on the other.

"I'm like all the other fans: a big plane goes overhead—'Wow!' That's kind of awe inspiring," observed Bill Astore, a retired Air Force lieutenant colonel. "But at the same time, to me, it's not something that I see should be flying over a sports stadium before a baseball game or a football game. You know, these are weapons of death. They may be required, but they certainly shouldn't be celebrated and applauded." He said he was "disgusted" that "corporate teams, teams owned by billionaires, basically, were collecting money from the military. Paid for, obviously, by you and me, by the American taxpayer."

"Under the Bush-Cheney administration, we weren't even able to see the caskets of dead soldiers. The cost of war—that very ugly face of war—was being kept from us," Astore observed.

> And the only time we see it, sometimes, is when they bring out a wounded soldier, for example. And maybe he or she has lost two or three limbs, but they're brought out into an NFL stadium or an MLB baseball game. And the impression that you get is, "Everything's OK, see?" But we don't see this person struggling to get around at home. And maybe being depressed because they've suffered this horrible wound in war.[89]

Retired Army Colonel Andrew Bacevich, a West Point graduate and Vietnam War veteran, calls tributes to current soldiers and veterans at ball games "contrived spontaneity." In *Breach of Trust: How Americans Failed Their Soldiers and Their Country*, Bacevich—a Boston University professor whose son was killed in Iraq—writes that events "leave spectators feeling good about their baseball team, about their military, and not least of all about themselves—precisely as it was meant to do" but does little for the troops or our understanding of war.[90]

It is not enough to simply tell our soldiers "thank you for your service" while we ignore their basic needs while they are in the military and after they return home to civilian life. "Instead of billionaires profiting off veterans, the best way to honor returning soldiers is to hire them," observed sportswriter Howard Bryant.[91] As pitcher Sean Doolittle pointed out, "I worry sometimes in this country that we conflate patriotism exclusively with love of the military and militarism and the strength of our armed forces. That's not the only way that you can be patriotic."

Doolittle's efforts to rally support for providing military troops and veterans with better housing, job training, mental health counseling, and other services is a better way for MLB to honor soldiers and a much better way for the DOD to spend its tax dollars.

END THE EXPLOITATION OF LATIN AMERICAN PLAYERS

MLB recruits and signs large numbers of young, impressionable ballplayers from South America, Central America, and the Caribbean with promises of professional stardom, diverting them from education and other opportunities for their future. Major league teams that sign Latin American players send them to their baseball academies. But most of these players never get to the minor leagues much less to the major leagues. For example, no more than 3 to 5 percent of Dominican Republic players ever reach the majors.[92]

Earlier we recounted the story of Venezuelan Alexis Quiroz, who was signed by an unscrupulous representative of the Chicago Cubs at age seventeen and sent to a team in the Dominican Republic to live under miserable conditions until an injury and poor medical treatment ended his career. Over the years, many newspapers, magazines, and watchdog groups have described MLB's exploitation of athletes like this as "neocolonialism," "racist," a "race to the bottom," "abusive of human rights," and "reminiscent of West African slaving trading techniques." *Sports Illustrated* reporter Jon Wertheim described "tales of bribes, kickbacks, side deals with smugglers, dubious immigration documents and middlemen skilled at working around immigration laws."[93] In 2017, in a trial that led to convictions of the predators three years later, Chicago White Sox first baseman Jose Abreu testified how he and other Cuban ballplayers were illegally smuggled into the United States.[94]

Dominican native Jose Bautista observed, "This is the proposition presented to Dominican families: Have your child give up school at age 12 for a 3 percent chance to play in the majors."[95] Latino minor leaguers have no labor union. Japan and Korea have forced MLB to sign contracts and follow certain rules that protect its players from exploitation, but this is not the case in Latin America.

Only players from the United States, Puerto Rico, and Canada are eligible for the annual player draft. Because Latino players aren't covered by the draft, few of them have agents and none of them have the legal protections of the draft system. These include bans on signing players in youth leagues and on trying to induce players to leave school. Latino players also lack regulations for tryouts, written notices of major and minor league contract rules, contracts in Spanish, service toward minor league free agency, and minimum training and medical facilities with quality standards. U.S. ballplayers can't be drafted until they finish high school but this doesn't apply to Latin American youth although MLB has raised the minimum age to seventeen.

For years, major league teams have signed Latin American players for much less money than they would have had to pay U.S. players in the draft, saving teams millions of dollars.[96] Most of these players never make it onto an American minor league roster, and those who do earn less than the minimum wage. Even Latinos who make it to the major leagues are paid at least 30 percent less than other players unless they become superstars.[97]

Many players with extraordinary skills are controlled by local headhunters, called *buscones*, who are often unscrupulous. They persuade young men to leave school, then they house and feed them and provide them with training in baseball skills. When the young athletes reach seventeen, the *buscones* take them to tryouts hoping to trigger a bidding war by major league teams. Sometimes they secure lucrative salaries for their players but in exchange for a hefty percentage (30 percent or more) of the signing bonus. To avoid having to pay these bonuses to budding Latino superstars, MLB has imposed limits on how much each major league team can spend on international signings. While free agency aids a few Latino players, the vast majority would be better off participating in the draft. MLB has promised to reform these practices but the mistreatment continues.

MLB needs to stop exploiting Latino minors with false expectations about their prospects. It should establish an international draft that includes Latino players so they have the same access to recruitment, agents, bonuses, and high signing salaries as other players. It should also financially support the Caribbean leagues that develop the Latino players that MLB recruits.

In 2010, after years of criticism, MLB set up a Latin American Administrative Office in the Dominican Republic, purportedly to investigate and fix abuses. The effort was led by MLB executive Sandy Alderson, who "came into the Dominican Republic with an air of imperiousness and a swagger that can only be likened to the U.S. Marines invading a Caribbean nation," according to anthropologist Alan Klein.[98]

Even so, some improvements have been made including investments in new, modern facilities by several MLB teams. Salaries have improved. Yet the problems remain. Trainers have injected players with steroids, which are far less regulated in Latin American countries.[99] Media investigations still refer to the baseball academies' sweatshop conditions: overcrowding, substandard food, and poor medical support. An analysis of minor league salaries in 2018 found that players in the Dominican Summer League got $300 a month, or $900 a year for the three-month season. They weren't even subject to the United States' minimum wage law.[100]

In 2018 the U.S. Justice Department began an investigation into abuses of Latin American players and focused on possible violations of the Foreign Corrupt Practices Act, including allegations of smuggling and human trafficking operations in the recruitment of athletes.[101] Congress should hold hearings exposing the problem of U.S. companies exploiting foreign athletes, particularly those from poor countries. The MLBPA and Latino stars could help by insisting that MLB put its own house in order.[102]

Notes

CHAPTER 1

1. *American Worker*, "The War between Capital and Labor," November 6, 2018, http://sageamericanhistory.net/gildedage/topics/capital_labor_immigration.html.

2. *American Worker*, "The War between Capital and Labor."

3. David Voigt, "Fie on Figure Filberts: Some Crimes against Clio," *Baseball Research Journal* (1983), https://sabr.org/journal/article/fie-on-figure-filberts-some-crimes-against-clio/.

4. Christopher W. Schmidt, "John Montgomery Ward: The Lawyer Who Took On Baseball," *Chicago Kent Law School 125th Anniversary Materials* (2013): 45, https://scholarship.kentlaw.iit.edu/docs_125/8.

5. John Montgomery Ward, "Is the Base-Ball Player a Chattel?" *Lippincott's Monthly Magazine* (August 1887).

6. Ward, "Is the Base-Ball Player a Chattel?"

7. Ward, "Is the Base-Ball Player a Chattel?"

8. John Montgomery Ward, *Base-Ball: How to Become a Player, with the Origin, History and Explanation of the Game* (Cleveland: Society of American Baseball Research, 1993), 4.

9. "Big Strike Imminent," *Sporting News*, June 22, 1889, 1.

10. Robert B. Ross, *The Great Baseball Revolt: The Rise and Fall of the 1890 Players League* (Lincoln: University of Nebraska Press, 2019), http://explorepahistory.com/odocument.php?docId=1-4-4E.

11. Ross, *The Great Baseball Revolt*, 87.

12. Stuart Banner, *The Baseball Trust: A History of Baseball's Antitrust Exemption* (New York: Oxford University Press, 2013), 16.
13. Ted Vincent, *The Rise and Fall of American Sport: Mudville's Revenge* (Lincoln: University of Nebraska Press, 1994), 203.
14. Robert F. Burk, *Never Just a Game: Players, Owners and American Baseball to 1920* (Chapel Hill: University of North Carolina Press, 2000), 116.
15. Mike Roer, *Orator O'Rourke: The Life of a Baseball Radical* (Jefferson, NC: McFarland, 2006), 33.
16. Roer, Orator *O'Rourke*, 33.
17. Roer, Orator *O'Rourke*, 33.
18. Roer, Orator *O'Rourke*, 71.
19. Roer, Orator *O'Rourke*, 99.
20. Bob Tedeschi, "Touching All the Bases for a Legend," *New York Times*, February 20, 2009, www.nytimes.com/2009/02/22/nyregion/connecticut/22colct.html.
21. Roer, Orator *O'Rourke*, 158.
22. Roer, Orator *O'Rourke*, 174.
23. Tedeschi, "Touching All the Bases."
24. Charlie Bevis, *Tim Keefe: A Biography of A Hall of Fame Pitcher and Players-Rights Advocate* (Jefferson, NC: McFarland, 2015), 8.
25. Warren Goldstein, *Playing for Keeps: A History of Early Baseball* (Ithaca, NY: Cornell University Press, 1989), 99.
26. Bevis, *Tim Keefe*, 33.
27. Bevis, *Tim Keefe*, 45.
28. Bevis, *Tim Keefe*, 89.
29. Bevis, *Tim Keefe*, 69.
30. Kevin Moran, "The Trojan Horses: Five for the Ages," *Troy Record*, November 10, 2010, www.troyrecord.com/news/the-trojan-horses-five-for-the-ages/article_eefd487e-2553-505f-ba24-c1cb6b3babe0.html.
31. Bevis, *Tim Keefe*, 254.
32. Bevis, *Tim Keefe*, 96.
33. Bevis, *Tim Keefe*, 125.
34. Bevis, *Tim Keefe*, 111.
35. Bevis, *Tim Keefe*, 141.
36. Bevis, *Tim Keefe*, 167.
37. Bevis, *Tim Keefe*, 173.
38. Bevis, *Tim Keefe*, 170.

39. Daniel Merle Pearson, *Baseball in 1889: Players vs. Owners* (Bowling Green, OH: Bowling Green State University Popular Press, 1993), 92.
40. Bevis, *Tim Keefe*, 185.
41. Bevis, *Tim Keefe*, 181.
42. Bevis, *Tim Keefe*, 201.
43. Brian McKenna, "Mark Baldwin," *Society for American Baseball Research*, https://sabr.org/bioproj/person/mark-baldwin/#:~:text=He%20threw%20hard%2C%20as%20the,a%20terror%20to%20opposing%20batsmen.
44. McKenna, "Mark Baldwin."
45. "Anson and the Released Men," *Daily Inter Ocean*, April 25, 1889, 2.
46. McKenna, "Mark Baldwin."
47. Thomas J. Hetrick, *Chris Von der Ahe and the St. Louis Browns* (Lanham, MD: Scarecrow Press, 1999), 182.
48. Zachary L. Brodt, "Strike Out: A Pirates Pitcher at the Battle of Homestead," *Western Pennsylvania History* (Summer 2015): 53.
49. McKenna, "Mark Baldwin."
50. David Nemec, *The Beer & Whiskey League* (Chicago: Lyons Press, 1994), 223.
51. Hetrick, *Chris Von der Ahe*, 213.
52. Brodt, "Strike Out," 52.
53. Brodt, "Strike Out," 58.
54. Brodt, "Strike Out," 56.
55. Brodt, "Strike Out," 58.
56. Brodt, "Strike Out," 60.
57. McKenna, "Mark Baldwin."
58. Jeff Kittel, "The Baldwin Affair: Glad Tidings," *This Game of Games: St. Louis Baseball in the 19th Century*, http://thisgameofgames.com/home/category/the-baldwin-affair/.
59. Kittel, "The Baldwin Affair."

CHAPTER 2

1. Harry Truman, "Veto of the Taft-Hartley Labor Bill," *American Presidency Project*, www.presidency.ucsb.edu/documents/veto-the-taft-hartley-labor-bill.
2. Cesar Gonzalez, "The Secret History of How Mexico Pushed Baseball toward Racial Integration," *Remezcla*, July 28, 2015, https://newstaco.com/2015/07/30/the-secret-history-of-how-mexico-pushed-baseball-toward-racial-integration/.
3. Gonzalez, "The Secret History."
4. Conor Nicholl, "Pasquel Was a Force for Integration," MLB.com, November 14, 2007.

5. Gonzalez, "The Secret History."
6. John Virtue, *South of the Color Barrier: How Jorge Pasquel and the Mexican League Pushed Baseball toward Racial Integration* (Jefferson, NC: McFarland, 2007), 202.
7. Roberto Gonzalez Echevarria, "Just How American Was It?" *New York Times*, April 7, 1996, 14.
8. Ron Briley, "Danny Gardella and Baseball's Reserve Clause: A Working-Class Stiff Blacklisted in Cold War America," *Nine* 19, no. 1 (Fall 2010): 56.
9. Colin D. Howell, "'A Tale of Two Outlaws': Jorge Pasquel, Jean Pierre Roy and the Postwar Challenge to Organized Baseball's Authority from the Borderlands." Paper Presented at the Thirty-Fourth Annual Conference of the North American Society for Sport History, Glenwood Springs, Colorado, May 2006.
10. William Marshall, *Baseball's Pivotal Era, 1945–1953* (Lexington: University Press of Kentucky, 2014), 53.
11. Briley, "Danny Gardella and Baseball's Reserve Clause," 62.
12. Richard G. McKelvey, *Mexican Raiders in the Major Leagues: The Pasquel Brothers against Organized Baseball, 1946* (Jefferson, NC: McFarland, 2006), 67.
13. Marshall, *Baseball's Pivotal Era*, 55.
14. McKelvey, *Mexican Raiders in the Major Leagues*, 4.
15. John Phillips, *The Mexican Jumping Beans: The Story of the Baseball War of 1946* (Perry, GA: Capital Publishers, 1997), 64.
16. Milton Bracker, "Mexico's Baseball Raiders Ride Again," *Saturday Evening Post*, March 8, 1947, 27.
17. John Phillips, "The Mexican Jumping Beans of 1946," in Joseph Wayman, ed., *Grandstand Baseball Annual, 1997* (Downey: CA: Grandstand Baseball Annual, 1997), 60.
18. Phillips, *The Mexican Jumping Beans*, 53.
19. Alan M. Klein, "The Baseball Wars: The Mexican Baseball League and Nationalism in 1946," *Studies in Latin American Popular Culture* 13 (1994): 33.
20. Klein, "The Baseball Wars," 33.
21. Virtue, *South of the Color Barrier*, 187.
22. Phillips, *The Mexican Jumping Beans*, 67.
23. Robert McG. Thomas, "Sports World Specials; Sweetening the Pot," *New York Times*, May 2, 1983, C2.
24. Virtue, *South of the Color Barrier*, 232.
25. Charlie Bevis, "Tony Lupien," *Society forAmerican Baseball Research*, https://sabr.org/bioproj/person/40a1236a.

26. Frederick Day, *Clubhouse Lawyer: Law in the World of Sports* (Bloomington, IN: iUniverse Star, 2004), 205.
27. Day, *Clubhouse Lawyer*, 205.
28. Dave Egan, "Swings on Baseball for Lupien Brushoff," *Boston Record*, February 25, 1946, 28.
29. Bevis, "Tony Lupien."
30. Lee Lowenfish, *The Imperfect Diamond: A History of Baseball's Labor Wars* (Lincoln: University of Nebraska Press, 2010), 132.
31. Jeff Obermeyer, "Disposable Heroes: Returning World War II Veteran Al Niemiec Takes on Organized Baseball," *Baseball Research Journal* (Summer 2010), https://sabr.org/research/disposable-heroes-returning-world-war-ii-veteran-al-niemiec-takes-organized-baseball.
32. Obermeyer, "Disposable Heroes."
33. Jeff Obermeyer, *Baseball and the Bottom Line in World War II: Gunning for Profits on the Home Front* (Jefferson, NC: McFarland, 2013), 168.
34. Obermeyer, "Disposable Heroes."
35. Obermeyer, "Disposable Heroes."
36. Lowenfish, *The Imperfect Diamond*, 135.
37. Obermeyer, *Baseball and the Bottom Line*, 177.
38. Obermeyer, "Disposable Heroes."
39. Charlie Weatherby, "Danny Gardella," *Society forAmerican Baseball Research*, https://sabr.org/bioproj/person/c141e904.
40. Frederick Turner, *When the Boys Came Back: Baseball and 1946* (New York: Henry Holt, 1996), 16.
41. Oscar Ruhl, "From the Ruhl Book," *Sporting News*, July 13, 1944, 14.
42. John Drebinger, "Ott Shifts Line-Up to Bolster Giants," *New York Times*, July 15, 1945, 1, 3.
43. McKelvey, *Mexican Raiders in the Major Leagues*, 136.
44. "A Jolly Good Fellow," *Baseball Magazine*, February 1946, 29.
45. David Mandell, "Danny Gardella and the Reserve Clause," *National Pastime* 26 (2006): 41.
46. Marshall, *Baseball's Pivotal Era*, 233.
47. Briley, "Danny Gardella and Baseball's Reserve Clause," 58.
48. Marshall, *Baseball's Pivotal Era*, 243.
49. Marshall, *Baseball's Pivotal Era*, 241.
50. Marshall, *Baseball's Pivotal Era*, 247.

51. Ron Briley, *Class at Bat: Gender on Deck and Race in the Hole, A Line-Up of Essays on Twentieth-Century Culture and America's Game* (Jefferson, NC: McFarland, 2003), 58.
52. Warren Corbett, "Voices for the Voiceless: Ross Horning, Cy Block, and the Unwelcome Truth," *Baseball Research Journal*, Fall 2018, https://sabr.org/journal/article/voices-for-the-voiceless-ross-horning-cy-block-and-the-unwelcome-truth/.
53. McKelvey, *Mexican Raiders in the Major Leagues*, 92.
54. Briley, "Danny Gardella and Baseball's Reserve Clause," 54.
55. Briley, "Danny Gardella and Baseball's Reserve Clause," 61.
56. Marshall, *Baseball's Pivotal Era*, 239.
57. Thomas Mulligan, "He Helped Blaze Free Agents' Trail: Baseball, Gardella Challenged the Major Leagues' Antitrust Exemption in 1947," *Los Angeles Times*, October 22, 1994, www.latimes.com/archives/la-xpm-1994-10-22-sp-53439-story.html.
58. Marshall, *Baseball's Pivotal Era*, 243.
59. Lowenfish, *The Imperfect Diamond*, 162.
60. Lowenfish, *The Imperfect Diamond*, 164.
61. Brad Snyder, *A Well-Paid Slave: Curt Flood's Fight for Free Agency in Professional Sports* (New York: Penguin, 2007), 105.
62. Briley, "Danny Gardella and Baseball's Reserve Clause," 60.
63. Marshall, *Baseball's Pivotal Era*, 242.
64. Jim Callaghan, "Baseball Rebel: Ex-Giant Took On Owners in '40s," *New York Daily News*, September 18, 1994, 45.
65. Callaghan, "Baseball Rebel," 45.
66. Mandell, "Danny Gardella and the Reserve Clause," 44.
67. Phillips, *The Mexican Jumping Beans*, 58.
68. Briley, "Danny Gardella and Baseball's Reserve Clause," 65.
69. "Danny Gardella Trades and Transactions," *Baseball Almanac*, www.baseball-almanac.com/players/trades.php?p=gardeda01.

CHAPTER 3

1. Gunnar Myrdal, *An American Dilemma: The Negro Problem and Modern Democracy* (New York: Harper & Brothers, 1944), 21.
2. Jules Tygiel, *Baseball's Great Experiment* (New York: Random House, 1983), 69; Wendell Smith, "Plan to Boycott Yankees," *Pittsburgh Courier*, April 14, 1945; "Baseball Ban Draws Pickets at 1st Game," *New York Amsterdam News*, April 21, 1945; "Pickets Protest Baseball Bigotry," *Afro-American*, April 28, 1945; "Picket Yankee Stadium Game," *Chicago Defender*, April 28, 1945.

3. Ric Roberts, "Chandler's Views on Player Ban Sought: New Czar Must Face Bias Issue," *Pittsburgh Courier*, May 5, 1945, 12.
4. Krister Swanson, *Baseball's Power Shift* (Lincoln: University of Nebraska Press, 2016).
5. Jerome M. Mileur, *The Stars Are Back: The St. Louis Cardinals, the Boston Red Sox, and Player Unrest in 1946* (Carbondale: Southern Illinois University Press, 2013), 90.
6. John Helyar, *Lords of the Realm: The Real History of Baseball* (New York: Ballantine Books, 1994), 13.
7. Helyar, *Lords of the Realm.*
8. Bob Broeg, "Sandy Started Slowly … But Oh What a Finish," *Sporting News*, August 14, 1971.
9. Jane Levy, *Sandy Koufax: A Lefty's Legacy* (New York, Harper, 2010), 204.
10. Bill Shaikin, "Fifty Years Ago, Dodgers' Sandy Koufax and Don Drysdale Engaged in a Salary Holdout That Would Help Change Baseball Forever," *Los Angeles Times*, March 28, 2016, www.latimes.com/sports/dodgers/la-sp-koufax-drysdale-holdout-20160329-story.html.
11. Levy, *Sandy Koufax*, 205.
12. Shaikin, "Fifty Years Ago."
13. Levy, *Sandy Koufax*, 207.
14. Levy, *Sandy Koufax*, 209.
15. Joe Falls, "Was Player Rep Bunning Too Busy?" *Detroit Free Press*, December 8, 1963.
16. Charles P. Korr, *The End of Baseball As We Knew It: The Players Union, 1960–81* (Urbana: University of Illinois Press, 2002), 31.
17. Helyar, *Lords of the Realm.*
18. In at least one instance, Bunning was an advocate for racial justice. Before the 1968 season began, even though he led the NL in strikeouts and innings pitched, the Phillies traded Bunning to the Pittsburgh Pirates—obviously in retaliation for his union activities. Bunning's new teammates wanted to elect him as their player representative, but according to Korr, Bunning was upset by the lack of Black and Latino involvement in the union leadership and convinced his fellow players to elect superstar outfielder Roberto Clemente.
19. Marvin Miller, *A Whole Different Ball Game: The Sport and Business of Baseball* (New York: Birch Lane Press, 1991), 31.
20. Robert F. Burk, *Marvin Miller: Baseball Revolutionary* (Urbana: University of Illinois Press, 2015), 104.
21. Burk, *Marvin Miller*, 106.

22. Levy, *Sandy Koufax*, 207.
23. Peter Dreier and Kelly Candaele, "Hall of Fame Shut Out," *Nation*, July 22, 2008, www.thenation.com/article/archive/hall-fame-shut-out/.
24. Dreier and Candaele, "Hall of Fame Shut Out."
25. Korr, *The End of Baseball As We Knew It*, 78.
26. Roger Abrams, "Arbitrator Seitz Sets the Players Free," *Baseball Research Journal* (Fall 2009), https://sabr.org/research/arbitrator-seitz-sets-players-free.
27. Curt Flood with Richard Carter, *The Way It Is* (New York: Pocket Books, 1971), 24.
28. Flood, *The Way It Is*, 25.
29. Brad Snyder, *A Well-Paid Slave: Curt Flood's Fight for Free Agency in Professional Sports* (New York: Plume, 2007), 62.
30. Snyder, *A Well-Paid Slave*, 65.
31. Judy Pace Flood, interview with Peter Dreier, June 15, 2021.
32. Flood, *The Way It Is*, 114.
33. Allen Barra, "How Curt Flood Changed Baseball and Killed His Career in the Process," *Atlantic*, July 12, 2011, www.theatlantic.com/entertainment/archive/2011/07/how-curt-flood-changed-baseball-and-killed-his-career-in-the-process/241783/.
34. Kevin Blackistone, "Baseball's Hall of Fame Cannot Be Complete Without Curt Flood," *Washington Post*, December 25, 2019, www.washingtonpost.com/sports/mlb/baseballs-hall-of-fame-cannot-be-complete-without-curt-flood/2019/12/23/68e9a526-25b7-11ea-ad73-2fd294520e97_story.html.
35. Gabe Lacques, "50 Years After His Letter Changed Baseball Forever, Curt Flood's Sacrifice Still Resonates," *USA Today*, December 24, 2019, www.usatoday.com/story/sports/mlb/2019/12/24/curt-flood-letter-mlb-free-agency-bowie-kuhn/2722291001/.
36. Snyder, *A Well-Paid Slave*, 162.
37. Snyder, *A Well-Paid Slave*, 67.
38. Mitchell Nathanson, "Who Exempted Baseball, Anyway? The Curious Development of the Antitrust Exemption that Never Was," *Harvard Journal of Sports and Entertainment Law* 4, no. 1 (2013); Mitchell Nathanson, interview with author, April 8, 2021.
39. Ross Newhan, "Player Champion Flood Dead at 59," *Los Angeles Times*, January 21, 1997, www.latimes.com/archives/la-xpm-1997-01-21-sp-20694-story.html.
40. Major League Baseball Players Association, "History," www.mlbplayers.com/history.
41. Miller, *A Whole Different Ball Game*.

42. Roger Abrams, *Legal Bases: Baseball and the Law* (Philadelphia: Temple University Press, 1998), 132.
43. Miller, *A Whole Different Ball Game*, 302.
44. Murray Chass, "Baseball Players Said to Hit Collusion Jackpot," *New York Times*, November 4, 1990, www.nytimes.com/1990/11/04/sports/baseball-players-said-to-hit-collusion-jackpot.html.
45. Cliff Corcoran, "The Strike: Who Was Right, Who Was Wrong and How it Helped Baseball," *Sports Illustrated*, August 12, 2014, www.si.com/mlb/2014/08/12/1994-strike-bud-selig-orel-hershiser.
46. Barry Petchesky, "20 Years Ago Today, Sparky Anderson Said No to Scab Players," *Deadspin*, February 17, 2015, https://deadspin.com/20-years-ago-today-sparky-anderson-said-no-to-scab-pla-1686368183.
47. Miller, *A Whole Different Ball Game*, 109.
48. Ronald Blum, "Curt Flood Set Off the Free-Agent Revolution 50 Years Ago," *Minneapolis Star Tribune*, December 24, 2019, www.startribune.com/curt-flood-set-off-the-free-agent-revolution-50-years-ago/566439402/.
49. Emma Baccellieri, "Marvin Miller Didn't Want to Be a Hall of Famer: Now What?" *Sports Illustrated*, December 10, 2019, www.si.com/mlb/2019/12/10/marvin-miller-hall-of-fame.
50. William C. Rhoden, "Lion Who Made Players Roar Faces the Quiet," *New York Times*, May 22, 2008, www.nytimes.com/2008/05/22/sports/baseball/22rhoden.html.
51. Dennis Eckersley, interview with Peter Dreier, June 5, 2021.
52. Tony Clark, interview with Peter Dreier, July 29, 2021.

CHAPTER 4

1. Congressional Research Service, *Instances of Use of United States Armed Forces Abroad, 1798–2020* (Washington, DC: Congressional Research Service, 2020), https://fas.org/sgp/crs/natsec/R42738.pdf.
2. Albert G. Spalding, *America's National Game: Base Ball* (New York: American Sports Publishing, 1911), 14.
3. Michael Mott, "Making the World Safe for Baseball: World War I, the National Pastime, and *Baseball Magazine*," April 2, 2006, www.sfsu.edu/~mpmott.
4. Mott, "Making the World Safe."
5. Wanda Ellen Wakefield, *Playing to Win: Sports and the American Military, 1898–1945* (Albany: State University of New York Press, 1997).
6. Jim Leeke, *From the Dugouts to the Trenches: Baseball during the Great War* (Lincoln: University of Nebraska Press, 2017), 72.
7. Leeke, *From the Dugouts*, 85.

8. Mike Lynch, "Fred Toney," *Society for American Baseball Research*, https://sabr.org/bioproj/person/fred-toney/#sdendnote27anc.
9. Leeke, *From the Dugouts*, 107.
10. Lynch, "Fred Toney."
11. William E. Mead, *Even the Browns: Baseball during World War II* (New York: Dover, 2010), 1.
12. James Gould, "The President Says Play Ball," *Baseball Magazine* 68, no. 3 (January 1, 1942): 435.
13. Mead, *Even the Browns*, 16.
14. Steve Bullock, *Playing for Their Nation: The American Military and Baseball during World War II* (Lincoln: University of Nebraska Press, 2004).
15. Robert F. Burk, *Much More Than a Game: Players, Owners and American Baseball Since 1920* (Chapel Hill: University of North Carolina Press, 2001).
16. *Sporting News*, "Uncle Sam, We Are at Your Command!" December 11, 1941.
17. Robert Van Gelder, "The Men Who Refuse to Fight." *New York Times*, May 10, 1942.
18. John Henshell, "Bill Zuber," *Society for American Baseball Research*, https://sabr.org/bioproj/person/bill-zuber/
19. Samuel Regalado, *Nikkei Baseball: From Immigration and Internment to Major League Baseball* (Urbana: University of Illinois Press, 2013), 163.
20. Alex Coffey, "A Field of Dreams in the Arizona Desert," *National Baseball Hall of Fame*, https://baseballhall.org/discover/a-field-of-dreams-in-the-arizona-desert.
21. Bill Staples, *Kenichi Zenimura: Japanese-American Baseball Pioneer* (Jefferson, NC: McFarland, 2011), 114.
22. Charlie Vascellaro, "Kenichi Zenimura: America's Pastime Helped Interned Japanese-Americans Pass the Time," *Global Matters*, February 20, 2019, https://globalsportmatters.com/culture/2019/02/20/americas-pastime-helped-interned-japanese-americans-pass-the-time/.
23. Coffey, "A Field of Dreams."
24. "Dr. King Leads Chicago Peace Rally," *New York Times*, March 26, 1967, 44, https://timesmachine.nytimes.com/timesmachine/1967/03/26/83583234.html?pageNumber=44.
25. Ron Briley, "Baseball and Dissent: The Vietnam Experience," *Nine* 17, no. 1 (2008): 55.
26. Max Frankel, "Why the Gap between L.B.J. and the Nation?" *New York Times*, January 7, 1968, www.nytimes.com/1968/01/07/archives/why-the-gap-between-lbj-and-the-nation-lbj-and-the-nation-if-i.html.

27. Ron Briley, "Ambiguous Patriotism: Baseball and the Vietnam War," in *The Cooperstown Symposium on Baseball and American Culture 2005–2006*, ed., William Simons (Jefferson, NC: McFarland, 2007), 168.
28. Ron Briley, *Class at Bat, Gender on Deck and Race in the Hole: A Line-Up of Essays on Twentieth Century Culture and America's Game* (Jefferson, NC: McFarland, 2003), 204.
29. Briley, "Ambiguous Patriotism," 171.
30. Peter Golenbock, *Amazin': The Miraculous History of New York's Most Beloved Baseball Team* (New York: St. Martin's, 2002), 205–206.
31. Brett Walton, "Baseball and the Vietnam War," *Elysian Fields Quarterly* 24, no. 2 (2007): 83.
32. David Voigt, *America through Baseball* (Chicago: Nelson Hall, 1976), 86.
33. Briley, "Ambiguous Patriotism," 172.
34. Bill Haney, "Ernie Harwell's Role in a Notorious Anthem," *Detroit Free Press*, September 20, 2014, www.freep.com/story/opinion/contributors/2014/09/20/michigan-book-jose-feliciano-ernie-harwell-detroit-tigers-world-series/15913001/.
35. Russell E. Crawford, "Consensus All-American: Sport and the Promotion of the American Way of Life during the Cold War, 1946–1965," https://digitalcommons.unl.edu/dissertations/AAI3131539.
36. Crawford, "Consensus All-American."
37. Robert Creamer, "Sacrilege," *Sports Illustrated*, June 19, 1972, 10.
38. Peter Dreier, "Half a Century before Colin Kaepernick, Jackie Robinson Said 'I Cannot Stand and Sing the Anthem,'" *Nation*, July 18, 2019, www.thenation.com/article/archive/huac-jackie-robinson-paul-robeson/.
39. Ron Swoboda, *Here's the Catch* (New York: St. Martin's Press, 2019).
40. Swoboda, *Here's the Catch*, 30.
41. Swoboda, *Here's the Catch*, 31.
42. Swoboda, *Here's the Catch*, 32.
43. Swoboda, *Here's the Catch*, 69.
44. Swoboda, *Here's the Catch*, 70.
45. Golenbock, *Amazin'*, 206.
46. Steven Travers, *The Last Icon: Tom Seaver and His Times* (Lanham, MD: Taylor Trade Publishing, 2011), 62.
47. Travers, *The Last Icon*, 62.
48. "Tom Seaver Says U.S. Should Leave Vietnam," *New York Times*, October 11, 1969, 4, https://timesmachine.nytimes.com/timesmachine/1969/10/11/83781878.html?pageNumber=4.
49. Travers, *The Last Icon*, 105.

50. Travers, *The Last Icon*, 106.
51. Ron Fimrite, "He's Some Piece of Work," *Sports Illustrated*, June, 5, 1978, www.si.com/vault/1978/06/05/822710/hes-some-piece-of-work-cardinals-catcher-ted-simmons-is-a-collector-of-antiques-and-an-art-museum-trustee-but-none-of-his-old-treasures-is-as-masterfully-wrought-as-his-game.
52. Jay Jaffe, "Ted Simmons' Election to the Hall of Fame Is Overdue," *Fangraphs*, November 12, 2019, https://blogs.fangraphs.com/ted-simmons-election-to-the-hall-of-fame-is-overdue/.
53. Fimrite, "He's Some Piece of Work."
54. Donald Hall, *Dock Ellis in the Country of Baseball* (New York: Touchstone Press, 1989), 24.
55. Mark Aldrich, "A Letter from Jackie Robinson," *The Gad about Town*, December 22, 2015, https://thegadabouttown.com/2015/12/22/a-letter-from-jackie-robinson/.
56. Hall, *Dock Ellis*, 25.
57. Hall, *Dock Ellis*, 194.
58. Hall, *Dock Ellis*, 199.
59. Hall, *Dock Ellis*, 199.
60. Hall, *Dock Ellis*, 200.
61. "Athletes in Protest: Joe Willie Black Shoes, Bouton, and the Vietnam War," *Florence Times–Tri-Cities Daily*, February 9, 1969, https://news.google.com/newspapers?nid=1842&dat=19691109&id=RBksAAAAIBAJ&sjid=hsYEAAAAIBAJ&pg=894,1067831.
62. "Athletes in Protest," *Florence Times–Tri-Cities Daily*.
63. Jim Bouton with Leonard Shecter, *Ball Four* (New York: John Wiley, 1990), 84.
64. Briley, "Ambiguous Patriotism," 173.
65. Bouton, *Ball Four*, 59.
66. Dave Zirin, "A Q&A with the Late, Great Jim Bouton," *Nation*, July 12, 2019, www.thenation.com/article/jim-bouton/.

CHAPTER 5

1. William Phelon, "August 1914 *Baseball Magazine*," *Baseball Fever*, www.baseball-fever.com/forum/general-baseball/history-of-the-game/33715-the-federal-league?q=mysteries.
2. Lew H. Freedman, *Latino Baseball Legends* (Santa Barbara, CA: Greenwood, 2010), 48.
3. Freedman, *Latino Baseball Legends*, 49.
4. Freedman, *Latino Baseball Legends*, 49.

5. Joe Black, *Ain't Nobody Better Than You* (Scottsdale, AZ: Ironwood Lithographers, 1983), 75–76.
6. "Fidel Castro's Human Rights Legacy: A Tale of Two Worlds," Amnesty International, www.amnesty.org/en/latest/news/2016/11/fidel-castro-s-human-rights-legacy-a-tale-of-two-worlds/.
7. Stew Thornley, "Minneapolis Millers: 1959 Junior World Series vs. Havana," https://stewthornley.net/millers_havana.html.
8. Cesar Brioso, *Last Seasons in Havana: The Castro Revolution and the End of Professional Baseball in Cuba* (Lincoln: University of Nebraska Press, 2019), 190.
9. Robert Cassidy, "Connie Marrero: A Cuban Treasure," *Newsday*, April 6, 2008, 34.
10. Peter Orsi, "Oldest Living Ex–MLB Player Dies in Cuba at 102," *Associated Press*, April 23, 2014, https://apnews.com/article/a95a2287e38441d395fd9453395c5373.
11. Gerald Peary, "Conrado Marrero," in *Cult Baseball Players—The Greats, the Flakes, the Weird, and the Wonderful*, ed., Danny Peary (New York: Simon & Schuster, 1990), 234.
12. Peter Bjarkman, "Cuba's and the World's Oldest Ballplayer Celebrates 100 Years," *CubaDebate*, April 14, 2011, http://en.cubadebate.cu/news/2011/04/14/cubas-and-worlds-oldest-ballplayer-celebrates-100-years/.
13. Nick Miroff, "At 100, Cuban All-Star to Get a Pension at Last," *NPR*, March 23, 2012, https://wamu.org/story/12/03/23/at_100_cuban_all_star_to_get_a_pension_at_last/.
14. Mark Onigman, "Cuba vs. the Major Leagues: Game Is No Longer the Same," *New York Times*, March 19, 1978, S2.
15. Paula J. Pettavino and Geraldine Pye, "Sport in Cuba: The Diamond in the Rough," *PBS*, www.pbs.org/stealinghome/sport/diamond.html.
16. David Waldstein, "When M.L.B. Broke the Ice with a Game in Havana," *New York Times*, March 21, 2016, D8.
17. Waldstein, "When M.L.B. Broke the Ice," D8.
18. Peter Schmuck, "Orioles' Goodwill Trip to Cuba Was Educational But Not Transformational," *Baltimore Sun*, November 26, 2016, www.baltimoresun.com/sports/orioles/bal-orioles-goodwill-trip-to-cuba-was-educational-but-not-really-transformational-20161126-story.html.
19. Waldstein, "When M.L.B. Broke the Ice," D8.
20. Waldstein, "When M.L.B. Broke the Ice," D8.
21. Philip Brenner, "Washington Loosens the Knot (Just a Little)," *North American Congress on Latin America*, September 25, 2007, https://nacla.org/article/washington-loosens-knot-just-little.

22. Peter C. Bjarkman, "Connie Marrero," *Society for American Baseball Research*, https://sabr.org/bioproj/person/connie-marrero/.
23. Jeff Stein, "Foul Ball," *Salon*, April 30, 1999, www.salon.com/news/feature/1999/04/30/baseball/print.html.
24. Stein, "Foul Ball."
25. Timothy P. Carney, "Flashback: When Orioles Owner Peter Angelos Refused to Hire Cuban Players Out of 'Respect' for Communist Dictator Fidel Castro," *Washington Examiner*, December 14, 2017, www.washingtonexaminer.com/flashback-when-orioles-owner-peter-angelos-refused-to-hire-cuban-players-out-of-respect-for-communist-dictator-fidel-castro.
26. Dave Zirin, "Major League Baseball in Havana, 17 Years Ago," *Nation*, March 23, 2106, www.thenation.com/article/major-league-baseball-in-havana-seventeen-years-ago/.
27. Dave Zirin, "A Whole New Ball Game," *Nation*, March 15, 2006, www.thenation.com/article/archive/whole-new-ball-game/.
28. Jack Curry, "Baseball Set to Continue Fighting Cuba," *New York Times*, December 16, 2005, D1.
29. Zirin, "Major League Baseball in Havana."
30. Clemente Family with Mike Freeman, *Clemente: The True Legacy of an Undying Hero* (New York: Celebra, 2013), 34.
31. Stew Thornley, *Roberto Clemente* (Minneapolis, MN: Twenty-First Century Books, 2006), 56.
32. David Maraniss, "The Last Hero: Roberto Clemente, Baseball's Latin Legend," *Washington Post*, April 2, 2006, www.washingtonpost.com/archive/opinions/2006/04/02/the-last-hero-span-classbankheadroberto-clemente-baseballs-latino-legendspan/7c38584c-a70d-4ff1-9eea-1febd1c05402/.
33. Joe Posnanski, "A Legacy Cherished: Remembering Roberto, Hall of Famer Synonymous with Heroism Thanks to Charitable Spirit, Baseball Feats," *MLB.com*, December 28, 2017, www.mlb.com/news/roberto-clemente-s-legacy-still-resonates-c264059654.
34. Posnanski, "A Legacy Cherished."
35. Mashkur Hussain, "The Great One," *The Ball Point*, August 26, 2017, https://theballpoint.org/the-great-one-11985eb949c4.
36. Clemente Family, *Clemente*, 58.
37. Matt Snyder, "Remembering Roberto Clemente, 40 Years After His Death," *CBS Sports*, December 31, 2012, www.cbssports.com/mlb/news/remembering-roberto-clemente-40-years-after-his-death/.

38. C. B. Ways, "'Nobody Does Anything Better Than Me in Baseball,' Says Roberto Clemente," *New York Times*, April 9, 1972, SM38.
39. Peter Dreier, "Athletes' Racial Justice Protest Last Week Made History, But It Wasn't the First Wildcat Strike in Pro Sports," *TalkingPointsMemo.com*, September 3, 2020, https://talkingpointsmemo.com/cafe/athletes-racial-justice-protest-history-wasnt-first-wildcat-strike-pro-sports.
40. Clemente Family, *Clemente*, 35.
41. "Beyond Baseball: The Life of Roberto Clemente," Smithsonian Institution, www.robertoclemente.si.edu/english/virtual_legacy.htm.
42. Roger Bruns, *Finding Baseball's Next Clemente: Combating Scandal in Latino Recruiting* (Santa Barbara, CA: ABC-CLIO, 2015), 79.
43. David Maraniss, *Clemente: The Passion and Grace of Baseball's Last Hero* (New York: Simon & Schuster, 2006), 220.
44. Kevin Blackistone, "'More Than a Ballplayer': After MLK Shooting, Roberto Clemente Halted MLB Opening Day 1968," *Washington Post*, March 28, 2018, www.washingtonpost.com/sports/more-than-a-ballplayer-after-mlk-shooting-roberto-clemente-halted-mlb-opening-day-1968/2018/03/28/658f94b2-3289-11e8-8abc-22a366b72f2d_story.html.
45. John Florio and Ouisie Shapiro, "When King Died, Major League Baseball Struck Out," *The Undefeated*, April 4, 2018, https://theundefeated.com/features/when-martin-luther-king-died-major-league-baseball-struck-out/.
46. Blackistone, "'More Than a Ballplayer.'"
47. "Roberto Clemente Quotes," *Baseball-Almanac.com*, www.baseball-almanac.com/quotes/roberto_clemente_quotes.shtml.
48. Clemente Family, *Clemente*, 78.
49. Richard Nixon, "Remarks at a Ceremony Honoring Roberto Clemente," *American Presidency Project*, May 14, 1973, www.presidency.ucsb.edu/documents/remarks-ceremony-honoring-roberto-clemente.
50. David Maraniss, "No Gentle Saint: Roberto Clemente Was a Fierce Critic of Both Baseball and American Society," *The Undefeated*, May 31, 2016, https://theundefeated.com/features/roberto-clemente-was-a-fierce-critic-of-both-baseball-and-american-society/.
51. Maraniss, "No Gentle Saint."
52. Maraniss, "No Gentle Saint."
53. Roger Burbach, "Et Tu, Daniel? The Sandinista Revolution Betrayed," *North American Congress on Latin America*, February 25, 2009, https://nacla.org/article/et-tu-daniel-sandinista-revolution-betrayed.

54. Bruce Newman, "Return of the Native," *Sports Illustrated*, December 30, 1991, https://vault.si.com/vault/1991/12/30/return-of-the-native-dennis-martinez-labors-with-few-laurels-as-the-ace-of-the-montreal-expos-but-in-nicaragua-hes-a-beloved-and-benevolent-hero.
55. Ira Berkow, "Players: Pitcher for Twins Has Intriguing Past," *New York Times*, April 3, 1984, www.nytimes.com/1984/04/03/sports/players-pitcher-for-twins-has-intriguing-past.html.
56. Patrick Reusse, "Tamer Times for Williams," *Sporting News*, August 2, 1980, 39.
57. Berkow, "Players."
58. Berkow, "Players."
59. Berkow, "Players."
60. Berkow, "Players."
61. Eric Wagner, "Sport and Revolution in Nicaragua," in *Nicaragua in Revolution*, ed., Thomas Walker (New York: Praeger, 1982), 295.
62. Burbach, "Et Tu, Daniel?"
63. Burbach, "Et Tu, Daniel?"
64. Robert Dvorchak, "Clemente All-Star Tribute Another Touching Moment," *Pittsburgh Post–Gazette*, July 12, 2006, www.post-gazette.com/sports/pirates-all-star-game/2006/07/13/Clemente-All-Star-tribute-another-touching-moment/stories/200607130453.
65. Mark Kiszla, "All-Powerful Oz Does More Than Talk the Talk," *Denver Post*, October 23, 2005, www.denverpost.com/2005/10/23/all-powerful-oz-does-more-than-talk-the-talk/.
66. Brett Ballantini, *Wit and Wisdom of Ozzie Guillen* (Chicago: Triumph Books, 2006), 71.
67. S. L. Price, "War of the Words," *Sports Illustrated*, February 20, 2006, https://vault.si.com/vault/2006/02/20/war-of-the-words.
68. Joe Lapointe, "Guillen Echoes Union, Criticizing Arizona Law," *New York Times*, April 30, 2010, www.nytimes.com/2010/05/01/sports/baseball/01pins.html.
69. Ballantini, *Wit and Wisdom*, 26.
70. Adam Kress, "MLB Players Association Slams Immigration Bill," *Phoenix Business Journal*, April 30, 2010, www.bizjournals.com/phoenix/blog/business/2010/04/mlb_players_accoc_slams_immigration_bill.html.
71. Lapointe, "Guillen Echoes Union."
72. Dexter Rogers, "Ozzie Guillen Blasts Major League Baseball for Treating Latino Players Unfairly," *HuffPost*, May 25, 2011, www.huffpost.com/entry/ozzie-guillen-blasts-majo_b_674424?guccounter=1.
73. Lapointe, "Guillen Echoes Union."

74. "Realities Behind America's Favorite Pastime: The Dominican Republic's Cheap Labor Bazaar for the Major Leagues," *Council for Hemispheric Affairs*, April 20, 2010, www.coha.org/realities-behind-america%E2%80%99s-favorite-pastime-the-dominican-republic%E2%80%99s-cheap-labor-bazaar-for-the-major-leagues/.
75. Arturo Guevara and David Fidler, *Stealing Lives: The Globalization of Baseball and the Tragic Story of Alexis Quiroz* (Bloomington: Indiana University Press, 2002).
76. Rogers, "Ozzie Guillen."
77. Nick Carbone, "Ozzie Guillen Suspended by Marlins Following Castro Comments," *Time*, April 10, 2012, https://keepingscore.blogs.time.com/2012/04/10/ozzie-guillen-marlins-suspended-fidel-castro/.
78. "Tolerating Ozzie Guillen's Intolerance," *Washington Post*, April 11, 2012, www.washingtonpost.com/opinions/tolerating-ozzie-guillens-intolerance/2012/04/11/gIQA94pUBT_story.html.
79. "Ozzie Guillen Suspended Five Games," *ESPN*, April 10, 2012, www.espn.com/mlb/story/_/id/7795152/ozzie-guillen-miami-marlins-suspended-five-games.
80. Mark Memmott, "Miami Marlins Manager Ozzie Guillen Suspended for 'I Love Fidel' Comment," *NPR*, April 10, 2012, www.npr.org/sections/thetwo-way/2012/04/10/150348493/marlins-manager-ozzie-guillen-suspended-following-i-love-fidel-comment#:~:text=According%20to%20the%20Miami%20Herald,with%20victims%20of%20the%20dictatorship.%22&text=He%20was%20trying%20to%20say,in%20power%20for%20so%20long.
81. David Trifunov, "Hugo Chavez Baseball Career Gave Way to Politics," *Global Post*, March 6, 2013, www.pri.org/stories/2013-03-06/hugo-chavez-baseball-career-gave-way-politics#:~:text=%E2%80%9CIt%20was%20my%20dream%2C%E2%80%9D,play%20in%20the%20Yankee%20Stadium.%E2%80%9D.
82. Steve Ellner, "Chavez Hits a Home Run," *In These Times*, August 23, 2004, https://inthesetimes.com/article/chez-hits-a-home-run.
83. Jim Caple, "Guillen Never at a Loss for Words," *ESPN*, October 21, 2005, https://africa.espn.com/mlb/playoffs2005/columns/story?columnist=caple_jim&id=2200205.
84. "AL Championship Series: Angels *v* White Sox: Ozzie Guillen," *ASAPSports.com*, October 12, 2005, www.asapsports.com/show_interview.php?id=27227.
85. "Venezuelan President Calls Guillen 'A True Leader,'" *Associated Press*, October 30, 2005, www.espn.com/mlb/news/story?id=2208756.
86. David Zirin, "Over the Edge: The Year in Sports 2005," *Edge of Sports*, December 28, 2005, www.edgeofsports.com.

87. Danna Harman, "In Chavez Country, US Ambassador Tries Baseball Diplomacy," *Christian Science Monitor*, June 7, 2006, www.csmonitor.com/2006/0607/p01s04-woam.html.
88. Clark Spencer, "Venezuelan Manager Luis Sojo Calls Late President Hugo Chavez 'A Man of Baseball,'" *Miami Herald*, March 5, 2013, https://miamiherald.typepad.com/fish_bytes/2013/03/venezuelan-manager-luis-sojo-calls-late-president-hugo-chavez-a-man-of-baseball.html.
89. Maria Burns Ortiz, "Politics Makes Toxic Mix with MLB's Investment in Venezuela," *ESPN*, November 18, 2007, www.espn.com/mlb/news/story?id=3077371.
90. Danny Wild, "Venezuelan Summer League Closes Its Doors," *Minor League Baseball*, January 21, 2016, www.milb.com/news/gcs-162470356.
91. Paul Kix, "The Morning According to Us: Magglio and Hugo Chavez," *ESPN*, March 16, 2009, www.espn.in/espnmag/story?id=3984227.
92. Jon Heyman, "Ordonez Roundly Booed at WBC," *Sports Illustrated*, March 14, 2009, www.si.com/more-sports/2009/03/15/magglio-boobirds.
93. Richard Zuniga, "Cheers Amid the Boos for Ordonez," *Morning Call*, March 16, 2009, www.mcall.com/sdut-bbi-wbc-venezuela-ordonez-politics-031609-2009mar16-story.html.
94. "Chavez Defends Ordonez," *Associated Press*, March 15, 2009, www.espn.com/mlb/worldclassic2009/news/story?id=3982112.
95. Bennett Baumer, "Viva Magglio! Baseball and Politics Collide," *The Indypendent*, March 16, 2009, https://indypendent.org/2009/03/viva-magglio-baseball-and-politics-collide/.

CHAPTER 6

1. Aaron Talent, "When Terror Stopped Baseball: 9/11, 20 Years Later," *Athlon Sports*, March 11, 2021, https://athlonsports.com/mlb/when-terror-stopped-baseball-9-11-20-years-later.
2. Talent, "When Terror Stopped Baseball."
3. Francis D. Cogliano, "Baseball and American Exceptionalism," in *Sport and Identity in the Post-War World*, ed. Dilwyn Porter and Adrian Smith (New York: Routledge, 2004), 155.
4. Rebecca S. Kraus, "A Shelter in the Storm: Baseball Responds to September 11," *Nine* 12, no. 1 (2003): 88.
5. Mark Sappenfield, "Baseball in Wartime? It's Been the American Way Since 1861," *Christian Science Monitor*, March 31, 2003, 2.
6. Kevin Cook, "Schilling's War Games: World War II Ace," *Sports Illustrated*, May 24, 1999, 34.

7. Lara Nielsen, "Exertions: Acts of Citizenship in the Globalization of Major League Beisbol" (PhD dissertation, New York University, 2002).
8. Bill Littlefield, "Of Baseball and Country," *Only a Game*, April 13, 2006, www.onlyagame.org/features/2006/04/country.asp.
9. Nielsen, "Exertions."
10. Robert J. Hughes, "Futures & Options: Play Ball!" *Wall Street Journal*, March 29, 2002, W2.
11. Dan Wachtell, "Make Baseball, Not War: Returning to a Pastime," *Daily Princetonian*, April 8, 2002.
12. Bob Herbert, "Stepping Up to the Plate," *New York Times*, July 8, 2002, A19.
13. Cogliano, "Baseball and American Exceptionalism," 155.
14. George Vecsey, "When Clemens Touched a Family Touched by 9/11," *New York Times*, March 16, 2008, C3.
15. William C. Rhoden, "Sports of the Times: Delgado Makes a Stand by Taking a Seat," *New York Times*, July 21, 2004, D1.
16. Sheryl Kaskowitz, *God Bless America: The Surprising History of an Iconic Song* (New York: Oxford University Press, 2013), 48.
17. Dave Zirin, "The Silencing of Carlos Delgado," *Nation*, December 19, 2005, www.thenation.com/article/silencing-carlos-delgado/.
18. Steve Treder, "THT Interview: Jim Bouton," *Hardball Times*, January 10, 2006, www.fangraphs.com/tht/the-tht-interview-jim-bouton/.
19. Ben Walker, "Blue Jays Star Delgado Protests War in Iraq," *Pittsburgh Post-Gazette*, July 21, 2004, www.post-gazette.com/sports/pirates/2004/07/22/Blue-Jays-star-Delgado-protests-U-S-war-in-Iraq/stories/200407220163.
20. Rhoden, "Sports of the Times."
21. Walker, "Blue Jays Star Delgado."
22. D. Torres, "Baseball Player Sits Down for God Bless America," *Narkive News Group*, https://alt.politics.greens.narkive.com/IWe9IC30/baseball-player-sits-down-for-god-bless-america.
23. Steve Wilstein, "Patriotism, Protest at Stadium," *Los Angeles Times*, July 25, 2004, http://articles.latimes.com/2004/jul/25/sports/sp-dogwilstein25.
24. Rhoden, "Sports of the Times."
25. Wachtell, "Make Baseball, Not War."
26. Steven Wine, "Delgado Cleanly Fields Questions Regarding War Protest," *Associated Press*, January 28, 2005.
27. Will Leitch, "Better Than You Remember: Carlos Delgado," *MLB.com*, www.mlb.com/news/carlos-delgado-had-great-career-on-and-off-field#:~:text=

%E2%80%9CI%20think%20it%20is%20important,I%20say%20God%20bless%20America.
28. Rhoden, "Sports of the Times."
29. Tyler Shipley, "Carlos Delgado and the Less-Comfortable Legacy," *Left Hook*, September 2, 2013, https://lefthookjournal.wordpress.com/2013/09/02/carlos-delgado-and-the-less-comfortable-legacy/.
30. Geoff Baker, "Citizen Carlos," *Puerto Rico Herald*, July 3, 2004, www.puertorico-herald.org/issues/2004/vol8n28/CitizenCarlos.html.
31. Baker, "Citizen Carlos."
32. Dave Zirin, "Blue Jays Slugger Stands Up Against War," *Counterpunch*, July 9, 2004, www.counterpunch.org/2004/07/09/blue-jays-slugger-stands-up-against-war/.
33. Baker, "Citizen Carlos."
34. Baker, "Citizen Carlos."
35. Zirin, "The Silencing of Carlos Delgado."
36. Zirin, "The Silencing of Carlos Delgado."
37. Zirin, "The Silencing of Carlos Delgado."
38. Zirin, "The Silencing of Carlos Delgado."
39. Ron Briley, "'God Bless America': An Anthem for American Exceptionalism and Empire," in *Sport and Militarism: Contemporary Global Perspectives*, ed. Michael Butterworth (New York: Routledge, 2017), 123.
40. Brendan Kennedy, "Carlos Delgado Calls MLB's Lack of Latin American Managers 'Really Sad,'" *Star*, www.thestar.com/sports/bluejays/2016/05/23/carlos-delgado-calls-mlbs-lack-of-latin-american-managers-really-sad.html.
41. "Carlos Delgado: Colin Kaepernick's Actions Rooted in American Ideals," *ESPN News*, September 26, 2016, https://tv5.espn.com/mlb/story/_/id/17648761/carlos-delgado-12-years-later-colin-kaepernick-protest-ideals.
42. "Carlos Delgado," *ESPN News*.
43. Adrian Burgos, "Carlos Delgado on Facing His Biggest Adversary: Hurricane Maria," *La Vida Baseball*, www.lavidabaseball.com/carlos-delgado-puerto-rico-relief/.
44. Tatiana Morales, "Sarandon to Bush: Get Real on War," *CBS News*, February 14, 2003, www.cbsnews.com/news/sarandon-to-bush-get-real-on-war/.
45. Stephen M. Silverman and Carly Bashkin, "Sarandan Leads D.C. Anti-War Protest," *People*, October 28, 2002, https://people.com/celebrity/sarandon-leads-d-c-anti-war-protest/.
46. Amy Goodman, "Silence Is No Longer An Option: Jane Fonda, Sean Penn, Susan Sarandon, and Tim Robbins Speak Out," *Democracy Now*, www.democracynow.org/2007/1/29/silence_is_no_longer_an_option.

47. Maureen Dowd, "'Hollywood Is Changing,' Says Its Veteran Activist, Tim Robbins," *New York Times*, February 3, 2018, www.nytimes.com/2018/02/03/style/tim-robbins.html.
48. ESPN, "Petroskey's Regret: Not Calling Before Nixing 'Bull' Gala," *Associated Press*, April 18, 2003, www.espn.com/mlb/news/2003/0418/1541133.html.
49. Eric Enders, "Petroskey Shames Hall," *Elysian Fields Quarterly* 20, no. 3 (Summer 2003), www.efqreview.com/NewFiles/v20n3/noisefromthedugout.html.
50. Enders, "Petroskey Shames Hall."
51. Tim Robbins, "Tim Robbins vs. the Hall of Fame," *Nation*, April 11, 2003, www.thenation.com/article/tim-robbins-vs-baseball-hall-fame/.
52. Robbins, "Tim Robbins vs. the Hall of Fame."
53. "Author Kahn Snubs Hall of Fame in Protest," *Detroit Free Press*, April 12, 2003, 8B.
54. Mitch Albom, "The Lunacy of Misguided Patriotism," *Detroit Free Press*, April 13, 2003, 1E.
55. Albom, "The Lunacy of Misguided Patriotism."
56. Gwen Knapp, "Bullheaded Decision by Hall President," *San Francisco Chronicle*, April 13, 2003, B2.
57. "Tim Robbins: Hall of Fame Violates Freedom," *The Age*, www.theage.com.au/entertainment/celebrity/tim-robbins-hall-of-fame-violates-freedom-20030413-gdvj96.html.
58. "Pat Tillman's Brother Blasts Iraq War, Bush," *Washington Post*, October 22, 2006, www.washingtonpost.com/wp-dyn/content/article/2006/10/22/AR2006102200937.html.
59. "The Exploitation of Pat Tillman," *Bohemian*, www.bohemian.com/northbay/the-exploitation-of-pat-tillman/Content?oid=2171356.
60. "The Exploitation of Pat Tillman," *Bohemian*.
61. Steven Wells, "The Inconvenient Truth about Patrick Tillman," *Guardian*, June 2, 2008, www.theguardian.com/sport/2008/jun/02/ussport.
62. Aamer Madhani, "Brother of Pat Tillman Accuses Military of Deception," *Seattle Times*, April 25, 2007, www.seattletimes.com/nation-world/brother-of-pat-tillman-accuses-military-of-deception/.
63. "Soldier: 'Ordered Not to Tell' of Tillman's Death," *NBC News*, April 24, 2007, www.nbcnews.com/id/wbna18287244.
64. "Soldier: 'Ordered Not To Tell,'" *NBC News*.
65. Robert Scheer, "A Cover-up as Shameful as Tillman's Death," *Los Angeles Times*, May 31, 2005, www.latimes.com/archives/la-xpm-2005-may-31-oe-scheer31-story.html.

66. "The Exploitation of Pat Tillman," *Bohemian*.
67. "U.S. Military Accused of Lying to Create War Heroes," *Dawn*, www.dawn.com/news/244041.
68. "The Exploitation of Pat Tillman," *Bohemian*.
69. "The Exploitation of Pat Tillman," *Bohemian*.
70. Madhani, "Brother of Pat Tillman."
71. "The Exploitation of Pat Tillman," *Bohemian*.
72. Kevin Tillman, "After Pat's Birthday," *Truthdig*, May 27, 2019, www.truthdig.com/articles/after-pats-birthday-2/.
73. Tillman, "After Pat's Birthday."
74. Tillman, "After Pat's Birthday."
75. Tillman, "After Pat's Birthday."
76. Tillman, "After Pat's Birthday."
77. Eric Stubben, "Kevin Tillman Leaves a Legacy of Service," *Mustang News*, May 27, 2014.
78. Stubben, "Kevin Tillman Leaves a Legacy."

CHAPTER 7

1. Joseph Durso, "Bill Veeck, Baseball Innovator, Dies," *New York Times*, January 3, 1986, www.nytimes.com/1986/01/03/obituaries/bill-veeck-baseball-innovator-dies.html?pagewanted=all.
2. "Bill Veeck," *Bloomsbury*, www.bloomsbury.com/au/bill-veeck-9780802778314/.
3. Michael McCambridge, "Director's Cut: 'Always Leave 'em Laughing,' by Thomas Boswell: Revisiting the 1981 Inside Sports Profile of One of Baseball's Most Legendary Characters," *Grantland*, June 11, 2013, http://grantland.com/features/director-cut-thomas-boswell-bill-veeck.
4. Durso, "Bill Veeck."
5. Gerald Eskenazi, *Bill Veeck: A Baseball Legend* (New York: McGraw-Hill Book Company, 1988), 5.
6. Paul Dickson, *Bill Veeck: Baseball's Greatest Maverick* (New York: Walker & Company, 2012), 26.
7. Bill Veeck with Ed Linn, *Veeck—As in Wreck* (New York: G. E. Putnam's Sons, 1962); Dickson, *Bill Veeck*, 42.
8. Media Burn, "[Studs Terkel with Bill Veeck at Billy Goat Tavern]," http://mediaburn.org/video/studs-terkel-with-bill-veeck-at-billy-goat-tavern/.
9. Dickson, *Bill Veeck*, 45.
10. Veeck, *Veeck*, 177–178.

11. Veeck, *Veeck*, 171–172; Dickson, *Bill Veeck*, 79. Baseball historians disagree on whether Veeck's story of trying to purchase the Phillies is true. His biographer Paul Dickson believes it is true but the debate can be found in Larry Gerlach, David Jordan, and John Rossi, "A Baseball Myth Exploded: Bill Veeck and the 1943 Sale of the Phillies," *National Pastime* 18 (1998); Jules Tygiel, "Revisiting Bill Veeck and the 1943 Phillies," *Baseball Research Journal* 35 (2007); and Robert D. Warrington and Norman Macht, "The Veracity of Veeck," *Baseball Research Journal* (Fall 2013).
12. Dickson, *Bill Veeck*, 2.
13. Dickson, *Bill Veeck*, 332.
14. Peggy Beck, "Working in the Shadows of Rickey and Robinson: Bill Veeck, Larry Doby, and the Advancement of Black Players in Baseball," in *The Cooperstown Symposium on Baseball and American Culture, 1997*, ed. Peter M. Rutkoff (Jefferson, NC: McFarland, 2000), 109.
15. Dickson, *Bill Veeck*, 130.
16. "Larry Doby," *Baseball Reference*, www.baseball-reference.com/players/d/dobyla01.shtml.
17. "Satchel Paige," *Baseball Reference*, www.baseball-reference.com/players/p/paigesa01.shtml.
18. Dickson, *Bill Veeck*, 3; Edgar Munzel, "14 Negro Players Give Tribe Corner on Colored Talent," *Sporting News*, April 13, 1949, www.baseball-reference.com/teams/CLE/1949.shtml.
19. Dickson, *Bill Veeck*, 173.
20. Munzel, "14 Negro Players."
21. Durso, "Bill Veeck."
22. Dickson, *Bill Veeck*, 265.
23. Dickson, *Bill Veeck*, 327.
24. Dickson, *Bill Veeck*, 5.
25. "A Man for Any Season Raw #3," *Media Burn*, http://mediaburn.org/video/veeck-a-man-for-any-season-raw-3/.
26. Dickson, *Bill Veeck*, 6.
27. Dickson, *Bill Veeck*, 339.
28. Robert T. Nelson, "George Hurley, Ex-Lawmaker Championed Liberal Message," *Seattle Times*, November 9, 1999, https://archive.seattletimes.com/archive/?date=19991109&slug=2994052.
29. "Former State Rep. George S. Hurley Dead at 92," *Longview Daily News*, November 9, 1999.
30. "Demo Leader on Coast Switches to Wallace," *Spokane Spokesman–Review*, March 7, 1948.

31. United States Congress, *Congressional Record: Proceedings and Debates of the 81st Congress*, V. 95, Part 2 (March 1949).
32. "Former State Rep," *Longview Daily News*.
33. Nelson, "George Hurley."
34. John Florio and Quisie Shapiro, *One Nation Under Baseball* (Lincoln: University of Nebraska Press, 2017), 39.
35. Joan Mellen, "Jim Bouton," in *Cult Baseball Players—The Greats, the Flakes, the Weird, and the Wonderful*, ed. Danny Peary (New York: Simon & Schuster, 1990), 158.
36. Ron Kaplan, "Jim Bouton: Still Crazy After All These Years?" *Bleacher Report*, https://bleacherreport.com/articles/240033-jim-bouton-still-crazy-after-all-these-years.
37. Dave Zirin, "A Q&A with the Late, Great Jim Bouton," *Nation*, July 12, 2019, www.thenation.com/article/jim-bouton/.
38. Steve Treder, "THT Interview: Jim Bouton," *The Hardball Times*, January 10, 2006, www.fangraphs.com/tht/the-tht-interview-jim-bouton/.
39. Mark Armour, "Jim Bouton," *Society for American Baseball Research*, https://sabr.org/bioproj/person/jim-bouton/.
40. Dick Young, "Young Ideas," *Daily News*, May 28, 1970, C26; William Ryczek, *Baseball on the Brink: The Crisis of 1968* (Jefferson, NC: McFarland, 2017), 181.
41. Florio and Shapiro, *One Nation Under Baseball*, 188.
42. Robert Lipsyte, "Sports of the Times," *New York Times*, June 22, 1970, 67.
43. Mark Armour, "Ball Four," *Society for American Baseball Research*, https://sabr.org/bioproj/topic/ball-four.
44. Zirin, "A Q&A."
45. Jim Bouton with Leonard Shecter, *I'm Glad You Didn't Take It Personally* (New York: William Morrow, 1971), 84.
46. Ted Miller, "Jim Bouton Still Brings It with Gusto from the Inside," *Seattle Post-Intelligencer*, June 30, 2006, www.seattlepi.com/sports/baseball/article/Jim-Bouton-still-brings-it-with-gusto-from-the-1207789.php.
47. Karl E. H. Seigfried, "Jim Bouton, Pray for Us," *Wild Hunt*, https://wildhunt.org/2019/08/column-jim-bouton-pray-for-us.html/.
48. Armor, "Jim Bouton."
49. Bill Lee with Jim Prime, *Baseball Eccentrics* (Chicago: Triumph Books, 2007), xiii.
50. Jim Prime, "Bill Lee ('Spaceman')," *Society for American Baseball Research*, https://sabr.org/bioproj/person/bill-lee-spaceman/.
51. Sam Laird, "Catching Up with Bill Lee, Baseball's Legendary 'Spaceman,'" *Mashable*, https://mashable.com/2016/08/24/bill-lee-spaceman-baseball/.

52. Mike Abadi, "State of the State: Bill Lee," *YouTube*, www.youtube.com/watch?v=f9ac5PqxrjA#action=share.
53. George Kimball, "Bill Lee," in *Cult Baseball Players—The Greats, the Flakes, the Weird, and the Wonderful*, ed. Danny Peary (New York: Simon & Schuster, 1990), 166.
54. Prime, "Bill Lee ('Spaceman')."
55. Matt Juul, "Bill 'Spaceman' Lee on Running for Governor and Why the MLB Really Blackballed Him," *Boston Magazine*, August 22, 2016, www.bostonmagazine.com/arts-entertainment/2016/08/22/bill-spaceman-lee-interview/.
56. "Legendary Pitcher Bill Lee's Unorthodox Life Put on Screen in 'Spaceman,'" *WBUR*, August 19, 2016, www.wbur.org/hereandnow/2016/08/19/bill-lee-spaceman.
57. Curry Kirkpatrick, "In An Orbit All His Own," *Vault*, https://vault.si.com/vault/1987/11/09/in-an-orbit-all-his-own-whether-hes-pouring-in-points-or-putting-together-business-deals-high-flying-michael-jordan-of-the-chicago-bulls-is-out-of-this-world.
58. "Bill Lee," *Baseball Reference*, www.baseball-reference.com/bullpen/Bill_Lee#Biographical_Information.
59. Callum Hughson, "Spaceman: A Cuban Baseball Odyssey," *MopUpDuty*, https://mopupduty.com/spaceman-a-cuban-baseball-odyssey/.
60. Prime, "Bill Lee ('Spaceman')."
61. Hughson, "Spaceman."
62. Ryan Fagan, "'Bull Durham': Ranking the 37 Best Quotes from the Classic Baseball Movie," *Sporting News*, April 18, 2019, www.sportingnews.com/us/mlb/news/bull-durham-ranking-the-37-best-quotes-from-the-classic-baseball-movie/nb6vi55np0h71fs7yx6dzwh70.
63. Karl Lindhorn, "Lefty and the Vet," *Middlebury Magazine* (Spring 1993), 21.
64. David Jenemann, "'The Way You Enter a Church': The Dialectics of Ken Burns's *Baseball*," *Journal of Sport and Social Issues* (February 2020), https://doi.org/10.1177/0193723520903353.
65. Bill Lee with Jim Prime, *The Little Red (Sox) Book* (Chicago: Triumph Books, 2003), xix.
66. "Bill Lee: 5 Fast Facts You Need to Know," *Heavy.com*, https://heavy.com/sports/2016/05/bill-lee-vermont-third-party-red-sox-governor-pitcher-pot/.
67. Laird, "Catching Up with Bill Lee."
68. "Bloop Hits: Warren Zevon and Bill Lee," *Fox Sports*, March 19, 2015, www.foxsports.com/stories/other/bloop-hits-warren-zevon-and-bill-lee.
69. "Bill Lee," *Heavy.com*.

70. James Sullivan, "Baseball's Spaceman Talks Weed, Politics, & New Biopic," *Men's Journal*, www.mensjournal.com/entertainment/spaceman-bill-lee-talks-weed-running-for-governor-and-josh-duhamel-w434699/.
71. Juul, "Bill 'Spaceman' Lee."
72. Nik DeCosta-Klipa, "Former Red Sox Pitcher Bill 'Spaceman' Lee Is Running for Governor of Vermont," *Boston Magazine*, May 24, 2016, www.boston.com/news/politics/2016/05/24/former-red-sox-pitcher-bill-spaceman-lee-running-governor-vermont.
73. Dylan Hernandez, "Dodgers' Adrian Gonzalez Chose Not to Stay in a Trump Hotel, But He Didn't Want It to Be News," *Los Angeles Times*, October 17, 2016, www.latimes.com/sports/la-sp-gonzalez-trump-hernandez-20161017-snap-story.html.
74. Brandon McCarthy, Twitter, https://twitter.com/bmccarthy32/status/796278973072216064.
75. Mark Saxon, "Dexter Fowler Unapologetic for Criticism of Trump's Travel Ban," *ESPN*, February 20, 2017, https://abc7news.com/sports/dexter-fowler-unapologetic-for-criticism-of-trumps-travel-ban/1763719/.
76. Joe Rodgers, "A's Rookie Bruce Maxwell First MLB Player to Take a Knee for the Anthem," *Sporting News*, September 25, 2017, www.sportingnews.com/us/mlb/news/as-rookie-first-mlb-player-to-take-a-knee-for-the-anthem-bruce-maxwell-comments/mvlcoq8js3q11g06myqp4mhok.
77. Peter Dreier and Kelly Candaele, "The Red Sox Should Not Visit the White House," *Nation*, October 30, 2018, www.thenation.com/article/red-sox-world-series-donald-trump/; Michael Tackett, "Trump Welcomes the Red Sox to the White House, But Not All of Them Are There," *New York Times*, May 9, 2019, www.nytimes.com/2019/05/09/us/politics/boston-red-sox-white-house-visit.html.
78. Adam Gilgore, "Nationals Owner Mark Lerner Says Trump 'Has Every Right to Come' to World Series," *Washington Post*, October 25, 2019, www.washingtonpost.com/sports/2019/10/25/nationals-owner-mark-lerner-says-trump-has-every-right-come-world-series.
79. Tyler Kepner, "Off the Mound, Sean Doolittle Brings Relief to the Ostracized," *New York Times*, March 12, 2016, www.nytimes.com/2016/03/13/sports/baseball/off-the-mound-sean-doolittle-brings-relief-to-the-ostracized.html.
80. Alex Reimer, "Sean Doolittle Challenged U.S. to Become Functioning Society for Sports to Return, and We're Failing," *Forbes*, July 9, 2020, www.forbes.com/sites/alexreimer/2020/07/09/sean-doolittle-challenged-us-to-become-functioning-society-for-sports-to-return-and-were-failing/?sh=1ecc78ff5a64.

81. Mike Digiovanna, "Whether on the Mound or for Refugees in Need, Relief Is a Calling for the A's' Sean Doolittle," *Los Angeles Times*, February 20, 2017, www.latimes.com/sports/nba/la-sp-mlb-sean-doolittle-refugees-20170217-story.html.
82. Obi-Sean Kenobi Doolittle, Twitter, https://twitter.com/whatwouldDOOdo/status/825565333805162497.
83. Digiovanna, "Whether on the Mound."
84. Jack Dickey, "All-Star Athlete Speaks Out on Immigration," *Time*, June 5, 2017, https://time.com/collection/american-voices-2017/4714382/sean-dolittle-american-voices/.
85. Max Blau, "Not 'Locker Room' Talk: Athletes Push Back Against Trump's Remark," *CNN*, October 10, 2016, www.cnn.com/2016/10/10/politics/locker-room-talk-athletes-respond-trnd/index.html.
86. Sean Doolittle, Twitter, https://twitter.com/whatwouldDOOdo/status/896612968129073152.
87. Jorge Castillo, "U–Va. Product Sean Doolittle on Charlottesville Rally: 'It's the Worst Kind of Hatred. It's Disgusting,'" *Washington Post*, August 12, 2017, www.washingtonpost.com/news/nationals-journal/wp/2017/08/12/u-va-alum-sean-doolittle-on-charlottesville-rally-its-the-worst-kind-of-hatred-its-disgusting/.
88. Sean Doolittle, "MLB Players Love Our Caps: The People Who Make Them for Us Deserve Fair Wages," *Washington Post*, February 28, 2019, www.washingtonpost.com/outlook/mlb-players-love-our-caps-the-people-who-make-them-for-us-deserve-fair-wages/2019/02/28/73568324-3acd-11e9-aaae-69364b2ed137_story.html.
89. Lindsay Gibbs, "This MLB Power Couple Is Fighting to Save 200 Union Jobs," *ThinkProgress*, February 20, 2019, https://thinkprogress.org/baseball-couple-union-campaign-003ec8963027/.
90. "Nationals Players to Cover Minor Leaguers' Lost Weekly Stipend Wages, Sean Doolittle Says," *ESPN*, June 1, 2020, www.espn.com/mlb/story/_/id/29251556/nationals-players-cover-minor-leaguers-lost-wages-sean-doolittle-says?platform=amp.
91. Nick Selbe, "Nationals Players Pledge to Compensate for Minor Leaguers Facing Pay Cuts," *Sports Illustrated*, June 1, 2020, www.si.com/mlb/2020/06/01/washington-nationals-sean-doolittle-compensate-minor-league-pay-cuts.
92. Ted Berg, "A's Closer and Girlfriend Buying Up Tickets to Team's LGBT Pride Night to Donate to LGBTQ Youth," *USA Today*, April 1, 2015, https://ftw.usatoday.com/2015/04/oakland-athletics-sean-doolittle-girlfriend-eireann-dolan-lgbt-pride-night-mlb; Ron Leuty, "Pride, Prejudice and an A's Player's Big LGBT Pitch," *San Francisco Business Times*, June 13, 2016, www.bizjournals.com/sanfrancisco/blog/2016/06/lgbt-pride-night-oakland-athletics-sean-doolittle.html.

93. Dan Steinberg, “Sean Doolittle: ‘There’s No Place for Racism, Insensitive Language or Even Casual Homophobia,’” *Washington Post*, July 30, 2018, www.washingtonpost.com/news/dc-sports-bog/wp/2018/07/30/sean-doolittle-theres-no-place-for-racism-insensitive-language-or-even-casual-homophobia.

94. “Ally and Baseball Pro Sean Doolittle Wears Pride on His Cleats,” *Washington Blade*, June 20, 2019.

95. Jim Buzinski, “Nationals Pitcher Sean Doolittle: ‘Homophobic Slurs Are Still Used to Make People Feel Soft or Weak,’” *OutSports*, July 30, 2018, www.outsports.com/2018/7/30/17632762/washigton-nationals-pitcher-sean-doolittle-rebuts-homophobic-racist-slurs.

96. Jesse Dougherty, “Sean Doolittle on Declining White House Invite: ‘I Don’t Want to Hang Out with Somebody Who Talks Like That,’” *Washington Post*, November 2, 2019, www.washingtonpost.com/sports/2019/11/01/sean-doolittle-declining-white-house-invite-i-dont-want-hang-out-with-somebody-who-talks-like-that/; Peter Dreier, “The World Series Winners Should Not Visit the White House,” *Nation*, November 1, 2019, www.thenation.com/article/world-series-washington-nationals-trump/.

97. David Nakamura and Jesse Dougherty, “Nationals Embraced by Trump at White House, Where They Can’t Escape Politics,” *Washington Post*, November 4, 2019, www.washingtonpost.com/sports/2019/11/04/washington-nationals-white-house-visit/.

98. Chelsea Janes, “Sean Doolittle and Eireann Dolan May Be Baseball’s Most ‘Woke’ Couple,” *Washington Post*, March 27, 2018, www.washingtonpost.com/sports/nationals/sean-doolittle-and-eireann-dolan-may-be-baseballs-most-woke-couple/2018/03/27/646b32ca-2dda-11e8-8688-e053ba58f1e4_story.html.

99. “Nationals Sean Doolittle Makes Statement on the Death of George Floyd,” *NBC Sports*, June 29, 2020, www.nbcsports.com/washington/nationals/nationals-sean-doolittle-makes-statement-death-george-floyd.

100. Jesse Dougherty, “Sean Doolittle Wants to Be a Better Ally,” *Washington Post*, July 22, 2020.

101. Emma Baccellieri, “An Activist and a Bookworm, Sean Doolittle Is the Conscience of Baseball,” *Sports Illustrated*, April 2, 2020, www.si.com/mlb/2020/04/02/sean-doolittle-washington-nationals.

102. Baccellieri, “An Activist.”

103. “MLB Player Sean Doolittle Pitches for Independent Bookstores,” *CBS News*, www.cbsnews.com/news/washington-nationals-star-sean-doolittle-pitches-for-independent-bookstores-mlb-2019-09-21/.

104. Kristine Froeba, "Washington Nationals Major League Baseball Player Sean Doolittle Reads to Military Children," *Military Times*, June 24, 2019, www.militarytimes.com/2019/06/24/baseballs-washington-nationals-sean-doolittle-hosts-military-children/.
105. Janie McCauley, "Sean Doolittle Gets Lesson on Gen. James Doolittle," *ESPN*, August 22, 2013, www.espn.com/espn/wire/_/section/mlb/id/9592565.
106. Sean Doolittle and Eireann Dolan, "Stand Up: A's Pitcher Sean Doolittle's Quest to Properly Help Veterans with 'Bad Paper,'" *Sports Illustrated*, May 25, 2017, www.si.com/mlb/2017/05/25/sean-doolittle-veteran-affairs-bad-paper-memorial-day.
107. Noah Frank, "Honored with Act of Valor Award, Doolittle Presses Sports Leagues to Do More for Veterans," *WTOP*, December 5, 2018, https://wtop.com/washington-nationals/2018/12/honored-with-act-of-valor-award-doolittle-presses-sports-leagues-to-do-more-for-veterans/.
108. Sean Doolittle, Twitter, https://twitter.com/whatwouldDOOdo/status/1221596484765921281.
109. Jerry Crasnick, "Sean Doolittle on Bruce Maxwell, Respecting Veterans and Defining Patriotism in a Polarized America," *ESPN*, September 30, 2017, www.espn.com/mlb/story/_/id/20851364/sean-doolittle-bruce-maxwell-respecting-veterans-defining-patriotism-polarized-america.
110. Crasnick, "Sean Doolittle."

CHAPTER 8

1. Graham Womack, "Has Curt Flood Been Overlooked for the Hall of Fame?" *Sporting News*, July 6, 2016, www.sportingnews.com/us/mlb/news/mlb-hall-of-fame-cooperstown-curt-flood-marvin-miller-free-agency/en1xoelbpxmt13tdwbvb3mt5h.
2. William Rhoden, "A Vote for the Boss Is a Vote for Flood," *New York Times*, July 21, 2010, www.nytimes.com/2010/07/22/sports/baseball/22rhoden.html.
3. William Rhoden, "'I Want My Father in the Hall of Fame': Curt Flood's Heroic Legacy," *The Undefeated*, https://theundefeated.com/features/curt-flood-and-the-legacy-of-his-children/.
4. Bradford William Davis, "Congress Calls for Curt Flood's Induction to the Hall of Fame," *New York Daily News*, February 28, 2020, www.nydailynews.com/sports/baseball/ny-20200228-w2dammmixnblzkfntovu4qy76q-story.html.
5. William Rhoden, "The Push for Curt Flood's Enshrinement in the Baseball Hall of Fame Intensifies," *The Undefeated*, https://theundefeated.com/features/cause-for-curt-flood-enshrinement-into-baseball-hall-of-fame-continues-fifty-years-since-letter/.

6. Derrick Goold, "Fifty Years Ago on Christmas Eve, Curt Flood Mailed a Letter That Changed Baseball History," *St. Louis Post-Dispatch*, December 24, 2019, www.stltoday.com/sports/baseball/professional/fifty-years-ago-on-christmas-eve-curt-flood-mailed-a/article_fe33784a-553c-52ba-87bb-ac981b077b37.html.

7. Tim Weiner, "Low-Wage Costa Ricans Make Baseballs for Millionaires," *New York Times*, January 25, 2004, www.nytimes.com/2004/01/25/world/low-wage-costa-ricans-make-baseballs-for-millionaires.html; Leslie Josephs, "Made in Costa Rica: U.S. Major League Baseballs," *Reuters*, March 9, 2010, www.reuters.com/article/us-costarica-baseballs/made-in-costa-rica-u-s-major-league-baseballs-idUSTRE62831Z20100309; Sarah Blaskey, "Costa Rica's Major League Concern," *Tico Times*, November 12, 2014, https://ticotimes.net/2014/11/12/costa-ricas-major-league-concern.

8. Richard Sandomir, "A Manufacturer's Debt to Haiti," *New York Times*, February 3, 2010, www.nytimes.com/2010/02/04/sports/baseball/04sandomir.html?_r=0.

9. Kevin Reichard, "MLB, Seidler Equity Partners Buying Rawlings Sporting Goods," *Ballpark Digest*, June 5, 2018, https://ballparkdigest.com/2018/06/05/mlb-seidler-equity-partners-buying-rawlings-sporting-goods/.

10. James Wagner, "M.L.B. Will Change Its Baseballs after Record Home Run Rates," *New York Times*, February 9, 2021, www.nytimes.com/2021/02/08/sports/baseball/mlb-change-baseball-rawlings.html.

11. Jon Harris, "Could Deal Lead to Great Un-American Pastime?" *Morning Call*, October 23, 2016.

12. Interview with David Melman, head of the Pennsylvania Joint Board of Workers United/SEIU, February 6, 2020.

13. "WPW Report: MLB Cleats 2018 (Brand Usage, Cleat Types)," *What Pros Wear*, www.whatproswear.com/baseball/news/wpw-report-mlb-cleats-2018-brand-usage-cleat-types/.

14. Paul Ladewski, "All 30 MLB Owners, Ranked," *Stadium Talk*, October 11, 2019, www.stadiumtalk.com/s/mlb-owners-ranked-9c52d648971e42b7; *Forbes*, "Steve Cohen," www.forbes.com/profile/steve-cohen/?sh=1de2ee1a63f8. The best overview of the sport's financial condition in the twentieth century is Andrew Zimbalist, *Baseball and Billions: A Probing Look Inside the Big Business of Our National Pastime*, New York: Basic Books, 1994. See also Andrew Zimbalist, *In the Best Interests of Baseball? Governing the National Pastime*, Lincoln: University of Nebraska Press, 2013.

15. Michael Ozanian and Kurt Badenhausen, "Baseball Team Values 2019," *Forbes*, April 10, 2019, www.forbes.com/sites/mikeozanian/2019/04/10/baseball-team-values-2019-yankees-lead-league-at-46-billion/#995b66a69b2e.

16. Kevin Delaney and Rick Eckstein, "Local Growth Coalitions, Publicly Subsidized Sports Stadiums, and Social Inequality," *Humanity & Society* 30, no. 1 (February 2006): 84–108.
17. Ted Gayer, Austin J. Drukker, and Alexander K. Gold, "Tax-Exempt Municipal Bonds and the Financing of Professional Sports Stadiums," *Brookings Institution*, www.brookings.edu/wp-content/uploads/2016/09/gayerdrukkergold_stadiumsubsidies_090816.pdf.
18. Rodney Fort, *Sports Economics* (Boston: Prentice-Hall, 2011).
19. Brian Lokker, "History of MLB Expansion and Franchise Moves," *How They Play*, https://howtheyplay.com/team-sports/major-league-baseball-expansion-and-franchise-relocation.
20. Gayer, Drukker, and Gold, "Tax-Exempt Municipal Bonds."
21. Eric Bull, "The Top 10 Federal Subsidies for Pro Stadiums," *Brookings Institution*, www.brookings.edu/blog/brookings-now/2016/09/09/top-10-biggest-federal-subsidies-for-pro-stadiums-hint-the-yankees-are-1/; *PBS*, "Why Should Public Money Be Used to Build Sports Stadiums?" July 13, 2016, www.pbs.org/newshour/nation/public-money-used-build-sports-stadiums; Neil deMause and Joanna Cagan, *Field of Schemes: How the Great Stadium Swindle Turns Public Money Into Private Profit* (Monroe, ME: Common Courage Press, 2002).
22. Richard Sandomir, "Stadiums Are Proposed, But Public Isn't Always Disposed to Pay Price," *New York Times*, May 7, 1998, www.nytimes.com/1998/05/07/nyregion/stadiums-are-proposed-but-public-isn-t-always-disposed-to-pay-price.html.
23. "The Business of Minor League Baseball," *Minor League Baseball*, www.milb.com/about/faqs-business#13.
24. Nat Berman, "The 20 Richest MLB Owners in the World," *Money Inc*, https://moneyinc.com/the-20-richest-mlb-owners-in-the-world/.
25. Berman, "The 20 Richest."
26. Michael Powell, "Grumbling About Socialism, the Yankees Profit From It," *New York Times*, April 16, 2016, www.nytimes.com/2016/04/17/sports/baseball/grumbling-about-socialism-the-yankees-profit-from-it.html?ref=business.
27. David Damron, "Clarke Seeks Slice of Soccer Team for Orange Taxpayers," *Orlando Sentinel*, August 20, 2013, www.orlandosentinel.com/business/os-xpm-2013-08-20-os-orange-county-soccer-stadium-20130820-story.html.
28. Barry Petchesky, "This Is The Best Idea for Stadium Financing We've Ever Heard," *Deadspin*, https://deadspin.com/this-is-the-best-idea-for-stadium-financing-weve-ever-1179741278.
29. Adam Fusfeld, "Could the Los Angeles Dodgers Become a Publicly Owned Franchise?" *Business Insider*, October 13, 2010, www.businessinsider.com/could

-the-dodgers-become-a-publicly-owned-franchise-2010-10; David Zirin, "Taking Back the Los Angeles Dodgers," *Nation*, April 25, 2011, www.thenation.com/article/archive/taking-back-los-angeles-dodgers/; Jonathan Lloyd, "LA Council Cheers on Fan Ownership Plan for Dodgers," *NBC Los Angeles*, June 15, 2011, www.nbclosangeles.com/news/local/council-cheers-on-fan-ownership/1900580/.

30. Neil deMause, "The Radical Case for Cities Buying Sports Teams, Not Sports Stadiums," *Vice*, www.vice.com/en_us/article/vvakva/the-radical-case-for-cities-buying-sports-teams-not-sports-stadiums; Chris Rabb, "Professional Sports Teams Need a Better Ownership Model," *Talking Points Memo*, https://talkingpointsmemo.com/cafe/professional-sports-teams-need-a-better-ownership-model.

31. Henry Druschel, "Imagining a Fan-Owned Team," *Beyond the Box Score*, www.beyondtheboxscore.com/2017/9/27/16367428/public-ownership-baseball-teams-socialism-universal-basic-income.

32. Scott Soshnick, "Investors Get Path to Buy Into Major League Baseball Teams," *Bloomberg*, October 16, 2019, www.bloomberg.com/news/articles/2019-10-16/investors-get-path-to-buy-stakes-in-major-league-baseball-teams?utm_source=newsletter&utm_medium=email&utm_campaign=newsletter_axiossports&stream=top.

33. Peter Dreier and Kelly Candaele, "The Yankees Cross the Picket Line in Boston," *Nation*, October 10, 2018, www.thenation.com/article/archive/yankees-players-cross-the-picket-line-in-boston/.

34. Nancy Armour, Rachel Axon, Steve Berkowitz, and Tom Schad, "Owners Pledged to Pay Workers When Sports Shut Down, But Many Are Being Overlooked," *USA Today*, April 26, 2020, www.usatoday.com/story/sports/2020/04/26/coronavirus-owners-pledged-pay-workers-but-many-being-overlooked/3012573001/.

35. Matt Weyrich, "Each MLB Team to Donate $1 Million to Cover Wages for Ballpark Employees during Coronavirus Outbreak," *NBC Sports*, www.nbcsports.com/washington/nationals/each-mlb-team-donate-1-million-cover-wages-ballpark-employees-during-coronavirus-outbreak.

36. Ken Coleman, "Detroit Arena, Stadium Workers Go Unpaid during COVID-19 Crisis," *Michigan Advance*, May 19, 2020, www.michiganadvance.com/2020/05/19/detroit-arena-stadium-workers-go-unpaid-during-covid-19-crisis/; Tony Paul, "Ilitches' $1M employee Fund Might Not Cover LCA's Food, Beverage Workers," *Detroit News*, March 14, 2020, www.detroitnews.com/story/sports/2020/03/14/ilitchs-employee-fund-may-not-cover-lcas-food-beverage-workers/5051606002/; Armour, Axon, Berkowitz, and Schad, "Owners Pledged."

37. Tom Goldman, "Fight Against Low, Low Pay in Minor League Baseball Continues Despite New Obstacles," *NPR*, August 3, 2018, www.npr.org/2018/08/03/

635373608/fight-against-low-low-pay-in-minor-league-baseball-continues-despite-new-obstacl.

38. Jeremy Wolf, "I've Lived My Dream," *Baseball & Business*, June 6, 2018.

39. "The Business of Minor League Baseball," *Minor League Baseball.*

40. Nathanial Grow, "The Save America's Pastime Act: Special-Interest Legislation Epitomized," *University of Colorado Law Review* 90 (2019), https://papers.ssrn.com/sol3/papers.cfm?abstract_id=3169957.

41. Kent Babb and Jorge Castillo, "Baseball's Minor Leaguers Pursue Their Dreams Below the Poverty Line," *Washington Post*, August 26, 2016, www.washingtonpost.com/sports/nationals/the-minor-leagues-life-in-pro-baseballs-shadowy-corner/2016/08/26/96ab542e-6a07-11e6-ba32-5a4bf5aad4fa_story.html.

42. Dirk Hayhurst, "An Inside Look Into the Harsh Conditions of Minor League Baseball," *Bleacher Report*, https://bleacherreport.com/articles/2062307-an-inside-look-into-the-harsh-conditions-of-minor-league-baseball; Brandon Sneed, "This is What It's Like to Chase Your Pro Baseball Dreams . . . for 12 Bucks an Hour," *Bleacher Report*, https://bleacherreport.com/articles/2700299-this-is-what-its-like-to-chase-your-pro-baseball-dreamsfor-12-bucks-an-hour; Goldman, "Fight Against Low, Low Pay."

43. Grow, "The Save America's Pastime Act"; Ben Walker and Jake Seiner, "Minor Leaguers to Get Pay Raise Next Year," *Austin Statesman*, February 15, 2020, www.statesman.com/sports/20200215/minor-leaguers-to-get-pay-raise-next-year.

44. Hayhurst, "An Inside Look."

45. Goldman, "Fight Against Low, Low Pay."

46. Tyler Kepner, "In Fighting Over the Minors, What Might Baseball Lose?" *New York Times*, December 23, 2019, www.nytimes.com/2019/12/23/sports/baseball/minor-league-baseball-proposal.html.

47. Dan Barry, "Across the Country, Minor League Towns Face Major League Threat," *New York Times*, November 16, 2019, www.nytimes.com/2019/11/16/sports/minor-league-baseball.html.

48. Zach Bergson, "Sports and Money: The Economics of Minor League Baseball," *Business Journalism*, August 11, 2015.

49. Sheryl Ring, "Let's Talk About the Minor Leagues," *Beyond the Box Score*, www.beyondtheboxscore.com/platform/amp/2019/12/19/21026413/lets-talk-about-minor-leagues-mlb-milb-rob-manfred.

50. Sergei Klebnikov, "Minor League Baseball's Most Valuable Teams," *Forbes*, July 8, 2016, www.forbes.com/sites/sergeiklebnikov/2016/07/08/minor-league-baseballs-most-valuable-teams/#24d3353643b2.

51. Babb and Castillo, "Baseball's Minor Leaguers."

52. Henry Shulman, "A Former Giants Prospect's Biggest Win Could Help Thousands in Minor Leagues," *San Francisco Chronicle*, January 8, 2020, www.sfchronicle.com/sports/article/A-former-Giants-prospect-s-biggest-win-could-14957389.php; www.baseball-reference.com/register/player.fcgi?id=broshu001gar.
53. Grow, "The Save America's Pastime Act"; Michael Arria, "Organize the Minor Leagues," *Jacobin*, September 29, 2017, www.jacobinmag.com/2017/09/minor-league-baseball-union; Ian Gordon, "Minor League Baseball Players Make Poverty-Level Wages," *Mother Jones*, July/August 2014, www.motherjones.com/politics/2014/06/baseball-broshuis-minor-league-wage-income/.
54. Susanna Kim, "Pro Sports Glamour? Minor Leaguers Say They Barely Get Paid," *ABC News*, February 12, 2014, https://abcnews.go.com/Business/minor-league-baseball-players-minimum-wage/story?id=22467458; Jesse Spector, "Guy Who Never Even Got a Cup of Coffee Could Cost MLB Owners Much, Much More," *Jacobin*, March 10, 2017, https://dealbreaker.com/2017/03/guy-never-got-cup-coffee-could-cost-mlb.
55. Levi Weaver, "On Minor-League Pay, MLB's Stance Doesn't Line Up with the Facts," *The Athletic*, https://theathletic.com/293189/2018/04/04/on-minor-league-pay-mlbs-stance-doesnt-line-up-with-the-facts/?redirected=1.
56. Peter Dreier and Christopher Martin, "'Job Killers' in the News: Allegations without Verification," Occidental College, Urban and Environmental Policy Institute, June 2012, https://sites.uni.edu/martinc/JobKillerStudy_June2012.pdf; Christopher Martin, *No Longer Newsworthy: How the Mainstream Media Abandoned the Working Class* (Ithaca, NY: Cornell University Press, 2019).
57. Kent Hoover, "Overtime Pay for Extra Innings?" *Louisville Business First*, June 29, 2016, www.bizjournals.com/louisville/news/news-wire/2016/06/29/overtime-pay-for-extra-innings.html.
58. Tom Goldman, "Minor League Players Push Forward Pay Lawsuit Against MLB," *NPR*, May 2, 2017, www.npr.org/2017/05/02/526607440/minor-league-players-push-forward-pay-lawsuit-against-mlb.
59. Weaver, "On Minor-League Pay."
60. J. J. Cooper, "MLB, MiLB Lobbying Pays Off," *Baseball America*, March 21, 2018, www.baseballamerica.com/stories/mlb-milb-lobbying-pays-off-in-save-america-s-pastime-act/; Mike Axisa, "Congress' 'Save America's Pastime Act' Would Allow Teams to Pay Minor-Leaguers Less Than Minimum Wage," *CBS Sports*, March 22, 2018, www.cbssports.com/mlb/news/congress-save-americas-pastime-act-would-allow-teams-to-pay-minor-leaguers-less-than-minimum-wage/.

61. "The Minor League Teams That Could Lose M.L.B. Ties," *New York Times*, November 16, 2019, www.nytimes.com/2019/11/16/sports/baseball/mlb-minor-league-proposal.html; Ron Blum, "Minor Leagues Get a Reset with 120-Team Regional Alignment," *Associated Press*, February 12, 2021, https://apnews.com/article/sports-mlb-baseball-rob-manfred-coronavirus-pandemic-f8a0f1c09161e83db87bca8e78219725; Chris Creamer, "A Breakdown of Minor League Baseball's Total Realignment for 2021," *SportsLogos.net*, February 15, 2021, https://news.sportslogos.net/2021/02/15/a-breakdown-of-minor-league-baseballs-total-realignment-for-2021/baseball/; Dennis Young, "Bernie Sanders Rips Rob Manfred's Greedy Gutting of Minor League Baseball Again," *New York Daily News*, March 13, 2021, https://www.nydailynews.com/sports/baseball/ny-bernie-sanders-minor-league-baseball-20210313-w7hnf2lgpfe55gucz6awjzxnhy-story.html.

62. Matt Johnson, "Why MLB's Record Revenue Shows Absurdity of Fight with MiLB," *Sportsnaut.com*, https://sportsnaut.com/2019/12/why-mlbs-record-revenue-shows-absurdity-of-fight-with-milb/amp/; Ben Clemens and Meg Rowley, "Take Me Out to the Ballgame? Mapping the New MiLB Landscape," *Fangraphs*, https://blogs.fangraphs.com/take-me-out-to-the-ballgame-mapping-the-new-milb-landscape/.

63. Kepner, "In Fighting Over the Minors."

64. Emily Waldron and Ken Rosenthal, "Blue Jays Ready to Embrace Change, Finalizing Minor-League Pay Increase of More Than 50 Percent," *The Athletic*, https://theathletic.com/872732/2019/03/17/blue-jays-ready-to-embrace-change-finalizing-minor-league-pay-increase-of-more-than-50-percent/.

65. Dan Zuberi, *Differences That Matter: Social Policy and the Working Poor in the United States and Canada* (Ithaca, NY: Cornell University Press, 2006).

66. Maury Brown, "Court Ruling Allows Minor League Baseball Players to Seek Wage Increase as Class Action," *Forbes*, August 16, 2019, www.forbes.com/sites/maurybrown/2019/08/16/court-ruling-allows-minor-league-baseball-players-to-seek-wage-increase-as-class-action/#3edc4ee7fed3.

67. Walker and Seiner, "Minor Leaguers."

68. Walker and Seiner, "Minor Leaguers."

69. Walker and Seiner, "Minor Leaguers."

70. "More Than Baseball," *More Than Baseball*, www.morethanbaseball.org.

71. Goldman, "Fight Against Low, Low Pay."

72. Goldman, "Fight Against Low, Low Pay."

73. Matt Paré, "Homeless Minor Leaguer," *YouTube*, https://www.youtube.com/playlist?list=PLT1tsbBeztJSTguACtgPG5tiZb5vGaUj-.

74. James Wagner, "Minor Leaguers Lack a Safety Net: A New Group Wants to Create One," *New York Times*, March 20, 2020, www.nytimes.com/2020/03/20/

sports/baseball/minor-league-advocates.html; Bill Shaiken, "Minor League Players' Advocacy Group Launches, Calls for Livable Wages," *Los Angeles Times*, March 20, 2020, www.latimes.com/sports/story/2020-03-20/advocates-for-minor-leaguers-players-advocacy-group-launches (the group launched.advocatesforminorleaguers.com/).

75. Donald Wollett, *Getting On Base: Unionism in Baseball* (Bloomington, IN: IUniverse, 2008).

76. Brian Cohn, "Pay Inequality in the Minors—A Deeper Dive," *SB Nation*, www.crawfishboxes.com/2019/1/11/18178200/pay-inequality-in-the-minors-a-deeper-dive.

77. Goldman, "Fight against Low, Low Pay."

78. Obi-Sean Kenobi Doolittle, Twitter, https://twitter.com/whatwouldDOOdo/status/1196248523118927874.https://twitter.com/whatwouldDOOdo/status/1196248523118927874.

79. Matthew Paras, "Bernie Sanders Joins Sean Doolittle Against Minor League Contraction," *Washington Times*, November 19, 2019, https://amp.washingtontimes.com/news/2019/nov/19/bernie-sanders-backs-sean-doolittle-over-mlb-minor/; Bill Shaikin, "Bernie Sanders Is On a Crusade to Save 42 Minor League Baseball Teams," *Los Angeles Times*, December 6, 2019, www.latimes.com/sports/story/2019-12-06/bernie-sanders-major-league-minor-league-baseball-rob-manfred.

80. "#342, John Fisher," *Forbes*, www.forbes.com/profile/john-fisher/#66b0a7cc21ba; Ladewski, "All 30 MLB Owners"; Michela Tindera, "At Least 20 Billionaires Behind 'Dark Money' Group That Opposed Obama," *Forbes*, October 26, 2019, www.forbes.com/sites/michelatindera/2019/10/26/at-least-20-billionaires-behind-dark-money-group-that-opposed-obama/#7ddda45a6c66.

81. Shaikin, "Bernie Sanders."

82. Shaikin, "Bernie Sanders"; Michael Arria, "Bernie Sanders Is Trying to Save Minor League Baseball—and Get Its Players a Raise," *Jacobin*, January 28, 2020, https://jacobinmag.com/2020/01/bernie-sanders-major-minor-league-baseball-mlb-mlbpa; Michael McCann, "MLB Faces Tough Legal Road to Restructure Minor League Baseball," *Sports Illustrated*, November 19, 2019, www.si.com/mlb/2019/11/19/minor-league-baseball-lawsuit.

83. Varda Burstyn, *The Rites of Men: Manhood, Politics, and the Culture of Sport* (Toronto: University of Toronto Press, 1999), 187.

84. Michael Serazio, "How Empty Displays of Sports Patriotism Allow Americans to Forget the Troops," *Washington Post*, May 24, 2019, www.washingtonpost.com/outlook/2019/05/24/how-empty-displays-sports-patriotism-allow-americans-forget-troops/.

85. Howie Rumberg, "'God Bless America' and Baseball, Ten Years Later," *Washington Times*, August 11, 2011, www.washingtontimes.com/news/2011/aug/11/god-bless-america-and-baseball-10-years-later/.
86. Eric Ortiz, "Follow the DOD's Money: The 'Tackling Paid Patriotism' Report," *Truthdig*, www.truthdig.com/articles/read-the-full-tackling-paid-patriotism-report/.
87. Emmarie Huetteman, "Senate Report Says Pentagon Paid Sports Leagues for Patriotic Events," *New York Times*, November 4, 2015, www.nytimes.com/politics/first-draft/2015/11/04/senate-report-says-pentagon-paid-sports-leagues-for-patriotic-events/.
88. Bob Collins, "At the Baseball Stadiums, Patriotism Is Always On Sale," *MPR News*, https://blogs.mprnews.org/newscut/2019/05/at-the-baseball-stadiums-patriotism-is-always-on-sale/.
89. Howard Bryant, "Veterans Speak Out Against the Militarization of Sports," *WBUR*, June 20, 2018, www.wbur.org/onlyagame/2018/07/20/military-sports-astore-francona; William J. Astore, "How Pro Sports Became Part of the U.S. Military's War Machine," *In These Times*, 2018, http://inthesetimes.com/article/21393/sports-military-patriotism-corporate-war-baseball-football-hockey.
90. Andrew Bacevich, *Breach of Trust: How Americans Failed Their Soldiers and Their Country* (New York: Metropolitan Books, 2013).
91. Howard Bryant, "When Leagues Pay for Patriotic Acts, Sports Fans Cover the Cost," *ESPN*, November 27, 2015, www.espn.com/mlb/story/_/id/14173360/mlbs-nfl-paid-showings-patriotism-cost-fans-more-ways-one.
92. Rob Ruck, "The Promise and Peril of the Dominican Baseball Pipeline," *The Conversation*, https://theconversation.com/the-promise-and-peril-of-the-dominican-baseball-pipeline-113242.
93. Jon Wertheim, "Exclusive: The Evidence That Persuaded U.S. Department of Justice to Investigate MLB Recruitment of Foreign Players," *Sports Illustrated*, October 2, 2018, www.si.com/mlb/2018/10/02/fbi-investigation-mlb-atlanta-braves-los-angeles-dodgers.
94. Paula McMahon, "White Sox Star Jose Abreu to Testify in Cuban Smuggling Trial in Miami," *Sun-Sentinel*, February 28, 2017, www.sun-sentinel.com/local/miami-dade/fl-reg-jose-abreu-white-sox-testify-20170228-story.html; Aimee Sachs, "11th Circuit Upholds Convictions of Men Who Smuggled Cuban Baseball Players Into US," *Courthouse News Service*, August 13, 2020, www.courthousenews.com/11th-circuit-upholds-convictions-of-men-who-smuggled-cuban-baseball-players-into-us/.

95. Maya Miller, "Behind America's Pastime Are Some Murky Labor Practices," *Century Foundation*, https://tcf.org/content/commentary/behind-americas-pastime-murky-labor-practices/?agreed=1.

96. Ian Gordon, "Inside Major League Baseball's Dominican Sweatshop System," *Mother Jones*, March/April 2013, www.motherjones.com/politics/2013/03/baseball-dominican-system-yewri-guillen/.

97. Matt Swartz, "Searching for Racial Earnings Differentials in Major League Baseball," *Hardball Times*, https://tht.fangraphs.com/searching-for-racial-earnings-differentials-in-major-league-baseball/; Thomas Kraemer, "Wage Penalties in Major League Baseball," thesis, 2017, http://scholarworks.umb.edu/honors_theses/32.

98. Rob Ruck, "Baseball's Recruitment Abuses," *Americas Quarterly* (Summer 2011) www.americasquarterly.org/node/2745.

99. Jackeline Pou, "Dominican Teens Keep Baseball Hopes Alive, But Not Without Risks," *NBC News*, October 3, 2019, www.nbcnews.com/news/latino/dominican-teens-keep-baseball-hopes-alive-not-without-risks-n1062061.

100. Weaver, "On Minor-League Pay."

101. Wertheim, "Exclusive."

102. Ruck, "Baseball's Recruitment Abuses."

Index

About the Authors

Robert Elias is a professor of politics, Dean's Scholar, and founding director of the Legal Studies Program at the University of San Francisco. He's taught previously at McGill University, the University of California—Berkeley, Tufts University, the University of Maryland, and Pennsylvania State University. He received his BA in history and political science from the University of Pennsylvania and his MA and PhD in political science from Pennsylvania State University. His articles have appeared in *Nine*, *Jacobin*, *Pacific Historical Review*, *Peace Review*, *Diplomatic History*, *International Journal of History of Sport*, *The Progressive*, *Transatlantica*, *Buffalo Law Review*, the *Washington Post*, *Minneapolis Review of Baseball*, *Sports History Review*, and other publications. His baseball books include *Baseball Rebels: The Players, People, and Social Movements That Shook Up the Game and Changed America*, *The Empire Strikes Out*, *The Deadly Tools of Ignorance*, and *Baseball and the American Dream.* His publications include *The Politics of Victimization*, *Victims Still*, *Rethinking Peace*, *Victims of the System*, and *The Peace Resource Book.*

Peter Dreier is E. P. Clapp Distinguished Professor of Politics and founding chair of the Urban & Environmental Policy Department at Occidental College. He's also worked as a community organizer, journalist, and deputy to Boston mayor Ray Flynn. He earned his BA in journalism at Syracuse

University and his PhD in sociology at the University of Chicago. His articles have appeared in the *New York Times*, the *Washington Post*, the *Los Angeles Times*, *The Nation*, *The New Republic*, *Dissent*, *American Prospect*, and *Talking Points Memo* as well as many scholarly journals. His books include *Baseball Rebels: The Players, People, and Social Movements That Shook Up the Game and Changed America*, *We Own the Future: Democratic Socialism—American Style*, *The 100 Greatest Americans of the 20th Century: A Social Justice Hall of Fame*, *Place Matters: Metropolitics for the Twenty-First Century*, *The Next Los Angeles: The Struggle for a Livable City*, and *Up Against the Sprawl: Public Policy and the Making of Southern California*.

CPSIA information can be obtained
at www.ICGtesting.com
Printed in the USA
BVHW061047110222
628403BV00001B/1